# Addressing
# Cultural Issues
# in Organizations

D1566323

# Robert T. Carter

Editor

# Addressing Cultural Issues in Organizations

Beyond the

Corporate

Context

Sage Publications, Inc.
*International Educational and Professional Publisher*
Thousand Oaks ▪ London ▪ New Delhi

HF
5549.5
.M5
A337
2000

#42643456

*For information:*

Sage Publications, Inc.
2455 Teller Road
Thousand Oaks, California 91320
E-mail: order@sagepub.com

Sage Publications Ltd.
6 Bonhill Street
London EC2A 4PU
United Kingdom

Sage Publications India Pvt. Ltd.
M-32 Market
Greater Kailash I
New Delhi 110 048 India

Printed in the United States of America

*Library of Congress Cataloging-in-Publication Data*

Addressing cultural issues in organizations: Beyond the corporate
context / edited by Robert T. Carter.
    p. cm. — (Winter roundtable series ; 1)
Includes bibliographical references and index.
ISBN 0-7619-0548-0 (cloth: alk. paper)
ISBN 0-7619-0549-9 (pbk.: alk. paper)
    1. United States—Race relations. 2. United States—Ethnic relations.
3. Race awareness—United States. 4. Pluralism (Social
sciences)—United States. 5. Minorities—United States—Social
conditions. 6. Diversity in the workplace—United States. 7.
Organizational behavior—United States. I. Carter, Robert T., 1948- II.
Series.
 E184.A1 A337 1999
 302.3'5'08900973—dc21                                    99-050447

This book is printed on acid-free paper.

00  01  02  03  04  05  06  7  6  5  4  3  2  1

*Acquisition Editor:*    Jim Nageotte
*Editorial Assistant:*   Heidi Van Middlesworth
*Editorial Assistant:*   Nevair Kabakian
*Indexer:*               David Fischer
*Cover Designer:*        Michelle Lee

*To my wife, Adrienne Millican Carter*

# Contents

# Preface

*Our deepest fear is not that we are inadequate. Our deepest fear is that we are powerful beyond measure. It is our light, not our darkness, that most frightens us. We ask ourselves, who am I to be brilliant, gorgeous, talented and fabulous? Actually, who are you not to be? . . . as we let our own light shine, we unconsciously give other people permission to do the same. As we are liberated from our own fear, our presence automatically liberates others.*
—Nelson Mandela (1994)

Organizations, like individuals, have enormous power and potential to facilitate change. They can release their potential only by letting go of their fear of it. One means by which organizations may harness their potential to facilitate change in the 21st century and beyond is by coming face to face with the changing demographics in North America and directly addressing cultural issues.

It is well known that North American demographics are shifting rapidly. In *Workforce 2000*, Johnston & Packer (1987) predict a sizable increase in the population and work force participation of women and people of color. These changing demographics signify changing dominant American cultural patterns. They also signify the need for developing new organizational and institutional practices.

*Addressing Cultural Issues in Organizations: Beyond the Corporate Context* is a collection of articles about organizational issues that intersect with dominant American cultural patterns. It is these cultural patterns, after all, that interact to form the environment in which organizations in the United States operate and function. Typically, organizational literature has dealt with how diversity, rather than cultural patterns, may influence corporate culture. In this context, the term "diversity" may refer to differences in race, culture, social class, gender or age, as well as differences in work function (e.g., one's level and professional or technical expertise). Diversity also may refer to differences in physical or mental disability, nationality and language. Although organizational scholars have paid attention to issues concerning diversity, less attention has been paid to examining the influence of dominant American cultural patterns upon organizations. Even less attention has been paid to analyzing how these cultural patterns may shape the functioning of organizations other than corporations, such as families, schools, the courts or probation officers, hospitals or community agencies, and non-profit institutions.

A core focus of this volume is an analysis of how unexamined cultural patterns·can and do influence the cultures of numerous organizations. The term "culture," in this instance, is not as broadly as defined as diversity; rather, culture is defined in terms of group memberships. These group memberships include gender, race, social class and ethnicity. It is these group memberships that have had and continue to have significant roles in the country's economic, occupational, political, health and educational institutional structures.

In North American society, racial-ethnic groups, women, and people from lower socioeconomic backgrounds are arranged in a hierarchical order wherein the dominant (white, male, and upper class) groups receive more of the social rewards due to greater political and economic power. It is recognized that organizations, like society, have distinct cultures, also known as "organizational" cultures. The culture of an organization derives from the people who create, lead and manage it. If the people who make up the work force of an organization share the same cultural values as the organization, there is a good fit between the organization and the individuals that comprise it. Where differences exist between the cultures, or group memberships, of the work force and the organization, the potential for conflict and poor performance exists.

The growth of scholarship on managing cultural differences or diversity began with Johnston & Packer's (1987) *Workforce 2000* report that predicted an increase in the population and work force participation of women and People of Color. Carnevale and Stone's (1995) subsequently found further support for Johnston and Packer's report in their forecast for beyond the year 2000. They pointed out that when one analyzes the total population and work force, one finds that between 1990-2005 whites (men and women) will comprise only 73% of the work force. Although non-Hispanic white males will remain the single largest work force group, this work force participation represents a decline from 80%. People of color, in contrast, will increase their participation in the labor force: the combined increase for black, Asian, and Hispanic Americans is projected to be 21%. Contributing to this higher rate are increased participation rates for women of color and immigrants. The largest group of people of color is projected to be black/African Americans, followed by Hispanic Americans and Asian Americans. Moreover, it is anticipated that both white women as well as women of color will increase their level of participation in the labor force relative to men. According to Carnevale and Stone "by the year 2005 more than 6 of every 10 working-age women will participate in the labor force—close to the rate of men" (p. 42).

In addition to these changing demographics, other imperatives drive the necessity for organizations in the United States to address cultural issues. According to Cox (1993), these imperatives concern moral, legal, and economic issues. For example, a significant moral imperative involves abandoning the legacy of domination, oppression, and exclusion that has characterized North American organizations. Legal imperatives include reducing the vulnerability of organizations to litigation for violations of numerous federal, state, and local laws that are designed to protect underrepresented and disenfranchised groups. Finally, with regard to economic imperatives, scholars have found that heterogeneous work units can be more productive then homogenous ones (Cox, 1993).

Overall, it is agreed that lack of attention to cultural issues in organizations can result in great expense, poor performance and untenable conflict among organizational participants. Therefore, it is essential that cultural issues be addressed by organizational leadership as well as those on the vanguard of change in institutions.

## Intentions and Observations

This book is intended to broaden the base of work on organizations as cultural institutions. It is intended to provide intervention strategies that disrupt the integration of multiple cultural perspectives in schools, social service agencies, hospitals, correctional facilities, and other types of organizations. No one approach to the content of this work is universally appropriate. It is our intention to provide an overview of approaches to organizational analysis and interventions that, if considered and applied, have the potential to increase organizational effectiveness.

I believe that this book represents some of the best available thinking on the critical issues associated with culture affecting organizations today and in the next century. In addition to the groundbreaking conceptual models that are included in the book, ideas about how to build practical approaches to organizational interventions are provided. Just as visitors to other cultures must learn new customs and a new language, so too must organizational members and leaders learn systematically the culture and language used to deal with difference in the organizations in which they operate. A central theme for the text is the illustration of the complex array of interpersonal, organizational, and psychological factors that operate in modern organizations.

## Origins

The book's contents draw, in part, from presentations given at the 1992 Teachers College Winter Roundtable on Cross-Cultural Psychology and Education. The conference theme that year was cross-cultural issues in institutions and organizations. The contributors have extensive research and publication histories in psychology, education, and organizational consulting. The contributors and editor are scholars on the cutting edge of scholarship in their respective areas of expertise and knowledge of particular types of organizations.

## Outline of the Book

The book is organized into three sections. *Part I: Perspectives*, consists of five chapters that focus on broad issues, such as how organizational leaders shape and influence the agenda surrounding culture and how culture matters in the country's organizational life. *Part II: Organizational and Institutional Settings*, consists of six chapters that discuss a wide range of institutional and organizational issues in corporate, educational, mental health, and service organizations. Finally, *Part III: Interventions and Applications for Training*, consists of five chapters that focus on various organizational intervention strategies and approaches.

I believe that this book makes a unique contribution to the existing and growing literature in racial-cultural education and psychology. The contribution is unique in that it addresses multiple settings and types of organizations while highlighting common themes, issues, and concerns. As a consequence, the book provides guidance to numerous policymakers, administrators, staff people, and consultants to various organizations. To my knowledge, most organizational texts focus on a specific type of organization. Few texts attempt to connect commonalties across organizations and institutions, whereas this book provides a conceptual framework for understanding cultural issues in organizations and institutions. Such a framework will assist in the development of more effective policies, practices and management strategies.

# Acknowledgments

I wish to acknowledge my contributors for their work, time and commitment. I also wish to thank Leah DeSole who worked tirelessly as my editorial assistant in the latter phase of production. In addition, I wish to thank Evangeline Sicalides for serving in a similar role during the early phase of editing first drafts of chapters. Both Leah and Evangeline (affectionately known as Renee) were invaluable in assisting me with this project. Finally, my thanks go to Sonja Hubbert, Betty Engel, and Robert J. Schwarz for their work on preparing the manuscript and to Heather Shangold for proofreading the final copy.

# PART I

# Perspectives

# 1

# Perspectives on Addressing Cultural Issues in Organizations

## Robert T. Carter

During the past three decades, organizational psychologists and other social scientists have given more recognition to the influence of race and culture in organizational systems than was previously given (Block & Carter, in press; Carnevale & Stone, 1995; Chemers, Oskamp, & Costanzo, 1995; Cox, 1994; Morrison, Ruderman, & Hughes-James, 1993; Sackman, 1997; Thompson & Carter, 1997). Carnevale and Stone (1995) point out that societal culture is embedded in our organizations. They observe that "people naturally bring their culture to the workplace. The dominant culture of most American organizations reflects the values of the American born white (Anglo) males [and females] who established them" (p. 93). How societal culture influences organizations is a central issue in this chapter and also in subsequent chapters.

Several factors have contributed to the increased attention to cultural difference, or what many call diversity, in organizations. This chapter describes these factors and how organizational literature has conceptualized diversity issues. Subsequently, a model of racial identity and a framework for understanding cultural patterns in organizations are presented. Finally, I contend that organizations may approach diversity from one of four perspectives: universal, ubiquitous, traditional and race-based. In conclusion, I discuss the ramifications of each of these perspectives on organizational diversity in terms of policies, practices, and outcomes.

## Cultural Issues in Organizations: The Changing Workforce

Organizations and institutions have been motivated by numerous forces to consider and incorporate cultural issues into their organizational "cultures." As Cox (1994) noted, these forces include effectiveness and work performance as well as legal and moral considerations. More important, many laws have been enacted during the past three decades to ensure that people from various groups

3

that historically have been treated unfairly in the workplace are given nondiscriminatory access and opportunity in North American organizations.

In addition, the concern about diversity has been driven by reports such as *Workforce 2000* by Johnston and Packer (1987). These reports project changes in the North American population and implications for the workplace, the most significant being the growth in the number of people of color and women. Carnevale and Stone (1995) note that in the 1960s 1 in 10 working Americans were People of Color. By the 1980s, the proportion had risen to 2 in 10; by the 1990s, 3 in 10 working Americans were people of color. "The growth in the diversity of the nation's population is projected to continue well in to the next century" (Carnevale & Stone, p. 33). By the middle of the new century (2050), people of color will comprise approximately half (47%) of the nation's population. Whites will account for the other half (53%), representing a decline from two thirds (73%) of the population. It is expected that Hispanics will show the largest increase, followed by blacks and Asians.

Although workforce participation of people of color has increased considerably during the past few decades and will continue to increase, whites will still comprise the majority of the population and perhaps hold on to their positions of leadership, power, and control in organizations. For example, Cox (1994) notes that although women comprise 46% of the workforce, they hold less than one half of a percent (0.5%) of top executive positions, and white males hold 99.5% of the top-level positions in the country.

## Diversity Issues in Organizational Literature

The growth of scholarship on managing diversity began when it was predicted that the proportion of women and people of color entering the workforce would increase. It is these demographic shifts in the workforce that have raised interest in and commitment to diversity-oriented organizational interventions. However, in the literature in organizational psychology or management, little is said about how cultural issues will influence organizations in the future. When diversity is discussed, it is done so in terms of how to manage the people of color who are entering the workforce.

Organizational literature typically focuses on general concepts, models, and issues, such as communication, interpersonal, group, and leadership skills that enhance managerial competence. Managers, administrators, and organizational employees are expected to acquire a range of skills and competencies that will increase organizational effectiveness, performance, and productivity. For managers and executives, organizational specialists would argue that these skills and competencies include self-awareness, dealing with personal stress, developing creative problem-solving strategies, being able to create supportive and effective communication systems, and enhancing job performance through effective motivation. Managers and executives also must be able to understand and use power and influence while learning to create processes that improve effective group decision making. Moreover, they must be able to foster leadership capability while managing conflicts and delegating authority.

As the workforce becomes more diverse, it is essential that the aforementioned factors be understood from a more complex cultural perspective. There is considerable evidence to support the proposition that people from varying cultural groups perceive the world and attribute meaning to events and experiences differently. Thus, self-awareness, communication patterns, decision making, support systems, interaction styles, and motivation are simply different for people from different cultural or racial groups. Kochman (1989) demonstrated this process in the cultural styles of blacks and whites. For example, other researchers have shown that cultural identity variables influence how people interpret their experiences.

Knowledge of these skills sets is enhanced by an understanding of individual personality and human developmental processes. Comprehension of the bias of people's attitudes, perceptions, problem-solving techniques, and behaviors is critical because the individual is the core unit of organizational systems. Moreover, knowledge of individual processes and functioning needs to be enhanced with information about interpersonal and group processes, particularly because an organization requires work to be done in groups by individuals who interact with one another. It is in group interactions that issues about communication, such as how group members within and between groups interact and then form attitudes and perceptions, become salient.

The individual is the core unit of the group and therefore the organization. The individual is also, in part, defined in terms of group memberships, and many of these groups are social and cultural in nature. In fact, for some people their pride and self-esteem are grounded in some of their cultural group identities. Also, group or cultural identities have salience, even when unimportant for the individual's self-concept, because they will influence how others interact with the person.

Cultural identity may manifest itself for a person in two ways. It may derive from one's subjective worldview and represent membership in a range of salient groups, such as the Boy Scouts, one's region of birth, a school, an ethnic group (one's nationality or religion), one's social class, a political group, relationships, and hobbies. Cox (1994) refers to these types of groups as sociocultural identity structures. This notion is taken from Trandis's (1976) notion of subjective culture, which refers to sharing with others a particular worldview and perceptions of the environment. Culture in this context is defined as a group that shares norms, values, and goals, and these patterns distinguish the group from others. Cultural identity strengths or sociocultural group memberships reflect groups that have personal significance for the individual, and the strength with which one identifies each group may vary.

In addition to the subjective personally significant or sociocultural elements of cultural identity, there is racial or cultural identity. Some groups are visible because of physical characteristics, such as race, gender, and physical appearance. Associated with these are attributions about skin color, physical features, hair texture, attractiveness, and so on. Visible aspects of identity form "our initial impressions of, and predisposition toward, people . . . [who] are greatly influenced by them. Reactions such as stereotyping and prejudice are typically activated" (Cox, 1994, p. 45) by such characteristics. According to Cox (1994),

> We use visible signals as a basis of categorizing people, men, women, blacks, Asians, [whites], physically disabled, and so on. Once the visual identification has been made, our minds automatically call forth any stored data about other members of that group. A set of expectations and assumptions is therefore often attached to these . . . identifications and predispose us to interact with a person in a particular way. (p. 45)

## Racial Identity

Racial or cultural identity is associated with psychological variation. A member of a cultural or racial group may or may not identify with membership in that group. Culture has meaning only on a group level, but it is expressed and enacted by individuals. Scholars have presented models of cultural and racial identity to explain how individuals' psychological orientation to their various racial or cultural group memberships may vary.

Racial identity theories were first introduced in the 1970s. The first models of racial identity were proposed to explain the black American metamorphoses from a people referred to as colored to a people who insisted on being called black Americans. Thomas (1971), for instance, proposed a stage model that was the precursor for later models. In the typical stage model of racial identity, a person would move in a linear progression from the least developed stage to the most advanced stage (Cross, 1980) in which less group identification was expressed at the lower stages and it was more personally significantly expressed at the advanced stages. Each stage had associated emotional, psychological, and behavioral elements.

Scholars began to apply black racial identity theories to other groups in the late 1970s and 1980s. Atkinson, Morten, and Sue (1979) introduced a minority identity development model that was supposed to be applicable to all people of color. In the mid-1980s, Helms (1984) introduced a white racial identity model and subsequently extended and expanded black racial identity theory and presented a people of color model (Helms, 1995).

Recently, racial identity theory has been expanded further (Carter, 1995, 1996; Helms, 1995; Helms & Piper, 1994; Sue, et al., 1998; Thompson & Carter, 1997). The theory now contends that racial and cultural identity development is applicable to all racial groups, even though separate models are presented for blacks, whites, and members of other racial groups. The different models reflect distinct sociopolitical histories of the groups because each group's history and sociopolitical interactions in the society have some impact on how racial or cultural issues are understood and dealt with. Second, racial identity involves two sets of worldviews and cultural and individual lenses, one about self that influences how one views self as a racial and cultural being that in turn affects how one understands members of the dominant and nondominant groups. Finally, racial and cultural identity represents ego differentiation of the personality, in which one's racial and cultural worldview is more or less mature. Less mature ego statuses derive definition from external sources (peers, media, family, institutions, etc.) and more mature and differentiated racial and cultural identity ego statuses are internally derived through a personal process of exploration, discovery, integration, and maturation.

Thus, current theory and research on racial and cultural identity refers to these processes as ego statuses or levels. The manner in which one's own racial and cultural identity is integrated into his or her personality depends on one's family composition and experience, the composition and attitudes of one's neighborhood or community, one's personal and unique interpretive style, and the way in which peers validate or ignore race as an aspect of one's identity. (For a more in-depth discussion of racial and cultural identity, see Carter [1995], Helms [1990], and Thompson and Carter [1997].)

In American society, visible characteristics have also taken on cultural meaning. As Cox (1994) notes, "the most important group identities have both physical and cultural significance. Among them are racioethnicity, gender, and, in many cases, nationality" (p. 45). The concern of this book is groups and culture. Cultural analysis by its very nature is a group phenomenon.

## Cultural Patterns in Organizations

Each organization in our society is embedded in the dominant cultural patterns of our societal culture. As noted previously, whites have been the dominant racial and cultural group in North American society. White Anglo-Saxon Protestant culture has been at the core of American cultural patterns (Marger, 1997). Some would argue that there is no distinct dominant white American cultural pattern. Katz (1985) and Stewart and Bennent (1991), however, believe that white Americans, regardless of social class, share a common set of racial and cultural values and beliefs. These scholars suggest that white culture is the integration of ideas, values, and beliefs merged from descendants of white European ethnic groups in the United States. Thus, Katz argues that white cultural patterns are superordinate to ethnic background. Some of the dimensions that characterize white American culture are rugged individualism, an action orientation measured by external accomplishments, a majority-rule decision-making system when whites are in power—otherwise, a hierarchical structure is used, a communication system that relies on written and "standard" English forms, a view of time as a commodity and future oriented, a religious system primarily based on Christian ideals, social customs (e.g., holidays) founded on and celebrations of the Christian religion, white Euro-American history and male leaders, a patriarchal family system centered on the nuclear family structure as the ideal social unit, and aesthetic qualities that emphasize the value of music and art based on European cultures.

The cultural values that form the foundation for many organizations and institutions in our society are grounded in the values described by Katz (1985) and Stewart and Bennent (1991). It is possible to compare and contrast cultural systems and values by using the Kluckhohn and Strodtbeck (1961) model of value orientations that suggests that each cultural or racial group must solve five common problems and that each problem has three possible solutions. The following are the problems: (a) What is the innate character of human nature? (Good, Evil, or Mixed); (b) What is the relationship between people and nature? (Subjugation, Harmony, or Mastery); (c) What is the temporal focus of the culture? (Past, Present, or Future); (d) What is the appropriate form of self-expression? (Being, Being-in-Becoming, or Doing); and (e) What are the proper social relations? (Lineal, Collateral, or Individual). Researchers (Carter, 1990; Kluckhohn & Strodtbeck, 1961; Papajohn & Spiegel, 1975) have found that dominant white American cultural values can be characterized by preferences for Person/Nature, Mastery-Over-Nature, Doing activity orientation, a Future time sense, and Individual social relations.

According to Carter (1995), People seldom question their racial-cultural learning. Only when they encounter others who are different and the conflict of diverging worldviews is experienced do they begin to question their worldview or racial and cultural underpinnings. Consequently, it is only those whites who experienced themselves in racially-culturally different relationships that have had the opportunity to develop knowledge and awareness of themselves as racial-cultural beings. Their worldview influences the way white Americans live and develop. For example, the future temporal preference is expressed in the manner in which white Americans plan their families, educations, and occupations. The Doing preference for self-expression is seen in how they compete for upward mobility and their emphasis on controlling feelings in most human interactions. White American children are taught from childhood to be independent, and to express their own needs and desires. As Spiegel (1982) notes,

> The dominant American choices in each dimension fit together nicely. Thus, if the personal achievement implied by Doing is to be facilitated, then it is good to be able to plan for the Future, as an Individual not too constrained by family or group ties, with optimism supplied by the Mastery-Over-Nature orientation, and the pragmatic morality, with which such self-interest is justified, afforded by the Neutral view of the Basic Nature of [people]. (p. 42)

Each organization within the context of the dominant culture also develops its own culture that refers to the values, beliefs, norms, and principles that ground its management systems and that in turn direct its policies and practices. Each organization has socialization practices, performance expectations, and other elements that characterize its organizational culture. Hellriegel, Slocum, and Woodman (1998) defined organizational culture as "a pattern of beliefs and expectations shared by organizational members" (p. 546). Thus, the organization's meaning system is composed of routine behavior reflected in organizational rituals, ceremonies, language, and daily interactions. Organizational norms that are shared throughout the organization are the dominant values held by the organization, such as its "traditions." The philosophy determines the organization's policies toward its employee and customers. The rules of the game for being accepted in the organizations and the climate conveyed through the layout and the manner in which employees interact reflect the organization's culture.

Organizational culture is expressed through symbols, jargon, or pictures particular to the company or through shared behavior, such as company norms, cultural values or collective beliefs, and assumptions and feelings about what should be and which things are good and which are not. Lastly, organizational culture is expressed through shared assumptions that represent members' beliefs about reality and human nature. These beliefs and assumptions are reflected in an organization's reward systems, rules, and procedures. It seems that the cultural patterns of North America are assumed and not openly explored or discussed, with the exception of cultural issues that arise for multinational companies.

According to organizational experts, an organization's culture has content and strength and is related to its performance and effectiveness. Where the content of the culture (its norms) are clear and reinforced, the content is known and the culture is strong. A strong organization culture communicates clear role definitions for its managers, has consistent messages and guidelines for expected employee behavior and performance, and sets unambiguous goals and objectives for handling human resources that in turn helps maintain the culture.

Several mechanism are used to inculcate the organization's culture. A main mechanism is socialization, the process used to teach new employees the rules and show them the ropes. Ragins (1995) connects the culture of organizations to it leadership when she notes that:

> Organizational culture is shaped and supported by the power-holders of the organization. These individuals influence the values, assumptions, and ideologies of the organization's culture. Power-holders use ethnocentric perspectives to define and develop criteria for successful performance. Because most power-holders in America are European American males (in some cases female), their experience is held to be the standard by which performance is evaluated and rewarded .. . One

result of this is that individuals who share common physical characteristics or values with the power-holders are more likely to gain access to powerful positions than those who are different, thus perpetuating a cycle of exclusionary power relationships among groups in organizations. (p. 97)

It is within the framework of an organization's culture that the aforementioned driving forces are addressed; that is, how and in what ways an organization or institution copes with or responds to the legal, moral, and performance issues associated with addressing cultural issues. The culture of the organization will also determine how and from what perspective it will address cultural issues. I later discuss the notion of varying perspectives and how each might deal with the forces that drive the need for organizations to address cultural issues. In the following discussion, I attempt to integrate issues of perspective on cultural difference and how that perspective shapes the organization's response to culture, how it influences or reflects the organizational culture, and how the forces driving cultural issues (moral, legal, and effectiveness/performance) are affected by the perspective taken. Within this framework, issues of group identity, intergroup interaction, power and influence, and leadership will be discussed.

## Approaches to Diversity in Organizations: Four Perspectives

I contend and have argued elsewhere (Carter & Qureshi, 1995) that it is possible to identify and define assumptions about difference and definitions of culture. The assumptions and perspectives about culture are important because they circumscribe the types of knowledge and methods used to frame and address cultural diversity. I extended the model that was proposed for mental health to organizational diversity (Carter, 1995). When people refer to diversity, it is unclear what meaning of cultural difference is being used. What is missing in the literature is a way to understand the various perspectives that underlie approaches to understanding cultural difference in organizations. The perspectives are designed to capture organizational life and diversity practices in North American organizations. It is essential that any attempt to understand cultural difference in the United States consider the sociocultural environment in which Americans have typically understood cultural difference. Also, I note that the perspectives are not mutually exclusive. In fact, I suspect that in many instances there is some overlap or blending.

I think each assumption or perspective about cultural difference has strengths and weaknesses. Therefore, each perspective will be discussed in terms of its advantages and disadvantages. I will describe each perspective and provide a brief discussion of training that might be associated with each type.

**Assumptions About Cultural Differences**

The four perspectives on how to define cultural differences presented here are adopted from Carter (1995) and Carter and Qureshi (1995), who presented five training approaches. These training approaches are adopted here as perspectives or alternative ways to define or frame cultural differences in organizations and institutions. The four perspectives or definitions are universal, ubiquitous, traditional, and race-based. I will point out the difference between basic assumptions and strategies used to teach about cultural difference. I believe that regardless of the strategies (i.e., approaches, content, and so forth) used by a trainer or consultant, he or she works from basic and fundamental assumptions about the nature of cultural difference. It is possible for strategies to be mistaken for one's basic assumptions of cultural difference. The descriptions of the types of perspectives that follow are intended to highlight basic assumptions, and not to identify training strategies.

*Universal*

The Universal perspective on culture places emphasis on human similarities, whereas group differences are deemphasized. The essential assumption of the universal perspective is that all people are basically human. What is paramount is our unique status as an individual human being. Thus, aspects of our identity that are derived from other group memberships (e.g., ethnicity, race, and gender) are salient only as descriptors and not as influences on one's particular development. Therefore, cultural differences are housed in personality and understood only from this vantage point. Much of traditional psychological and organizational theory and practice is characterized by the universal perspective. The universal perspective closely resembles the color-blind vision of all people living in harmony wherein group differences are of little or no relevance.

An example of this approach was provided by Hellriegel, et al. (1998); they describe an international hotel chain that recognizes its diverse workforce and client base. They observe the following:

> Prickly racial, ethnic, and gender concerns are an undercurrent in virtually every interaction at the Marriott. Some workers are quick to charge discrimination when conflicts with managers arise. Just maintaining a basic level of civility can be a daily struggle. In required diversity training classes, managers are taught that the best way to cope with diversity-related conflict is to focus narrowly on performance and never define problems in terms of gender, culture, or race. Marriott managers are instructed to bend over backwards to be fair about issues large and small. (p. 561)

As this example demonstrates, an organization that operates from the universal perspective works to minimize the actual cultural differences of employees. One might surmise that organizations with such a perspective have a culture that is reflective of the dominant culture and strives toward assimilation of its members to the norms of the organization. For organizations operating from this perspective, the moral and ethical imperatives are relatively weak, because the power holders would contend that they treat all people the same regardless of their group memberships. The organization leaders are not aware of the types of social issues that give rise to intergroup inequities. Leaders of such organizations would proclaim that they select the best people regardless of their racial or cultural and other group memberships. Universal perspective adherents seldom examine the biases that may influence their perception of the best, nor do they scrutinize the assumptions that guide the standards and criteria they set to evaluate people's abilities and performance. Therefore, the organization using the universal perspective to define cultural difference would expect all its members to abide by its established standards crafted in the image of its leaders and power holders. Thus, the organization would promote an assimilation-oriented organizational culture.

Assimilation involves complete adaptation to the dominant group and denial or rejection of one's salient identity groups (gender, race, ethnicity, etc.). When assimilation is the emphasis, "an organization's culture becomes the standard of behavior for all other cultures merging into the organization. The goal of assimilation is to eliminate cultural differences, or at least the expression of the different (nondominant) cultures at work" (Cox, 1994, p. 166).

There are many laws that govern workplace practices in the United States. The Civil Rights Act enacted in 1964 and extended in 1991 bans discrimination in education, employment, and voting practices for protected classes (gender, religion, race, nationality, etc.). In addition, the Americans with Disabilities Act of 1990 protects people with physical and other types of disabilities. These federal laws, in conjunction with state and local statutes, provide protection for people working in U.S. organizations. An organization working from the universal perspective would contend that all legal mandates for fairness and equity are adequately dealt with because the organization does not emphasize cultural differences of any sort and all employees are treated in the same way.

The failure to address cultural difference at individual identity and group levels suggest's that the organization will suffer in terms of its capacity to perform. There will likely be considerable tension and conflict accompanied by high rates of turnover and departures. The advantage of the universal perspective is that it emphasizes the fact that humans have many characteristics and attributes in common and that each person is unique. The disadvantage of this type of approach is that it avoids historically based intergroup relationships by assuming group memberships have meaning only for each individual.

*Ubiquitous*

The ubiquitous approach holds that all difference associated with group membership is salient. All forms of social or group membership are cultural. Culture can be a function of geography, income, gender, age, religion, sexual preference, and so forth. Carnevale and Stone (1995) stated, "[B]y definition, members of any identity group—be they women, gay men and lesbians, black Americans, etc.—have a common culture; that is, they share certain ideas that make them identify with that group" (p. 7). It equates social group affiliations or domains of differences within a superordinate culture as representing distinct cultures. The view of difference as common experience or identity presumes that one's commonness cuts across dominant cultural patterns. Thus, all disabled people, gay people, or women or men share a culture that results from their reference group affiliation irrespective of their dominant culture of origin (e.g., American, African, Asian, and Indian). Ferdman (1995) describes the notions of this perspective as follows: "Diversity in organizations is typically seen to be composed of variations in race, gender, ethnicity, nationality, sexual orientation, physical abilities, social class, age, and other socially meaningful categorizations, together with additional differences caused by or signified by these markers" (p. 37).

According to the ubiquitous perspective, differences in cultural groups are acknowledged, but less awareness exists regarding the influences of the dominant culture on the various groups. By its very nature, the ubiquitous perspective deemphasizes preferences and influences of the dominant cultural patterns. Thus, little consideration is given to the shared cultural patterns of whites regardless of gender, sexual preference, religion, or ethnicity. As noted by Cox (1994) and other scholars (Carter, 1997; Jones & Carter, 1996), in studies whites have been found to exhibit monocultural life histories. Moreover, this perspective denies the historical relationships between various racial or ethnic and cultural groups. It ignores the current and historical legacy of segregation and exclusion that has limited or restricted the workforce participation of people of color. Therefore, although some cultural difference are acknowledged, there are still powerful influences of the dominant white European-American cultural patterns on the culture of organizations that subscribe to this perspective.

The organizational culture of ubiquitous organizations would be expected to mimic the culture of society and its structure. Thus, separation of people from different cultures and groups would occur. There may be some inclusion of women from the same racial or cultural group as the primary form of addressing cultural differences, but other groups would participate in very limited or structured ways. That is, they may be overrepresented in lower non-power-holding roles and functions in the organization. Therefore, the workforce would in fact be diverse but separated, and all higher-level positions would be held by members of the dominant group and these would be pressured to conform to the standards of the power-holding group.

Examples of ubiquitous organizations are colleges and universities, in which the power holders are predominantly white males and many white women also participate in the organization at all levels at much greater numbers than people from other racial or cultural groups. These organizations espouse equality but seldom achieve it.

Moral issues are important to the power holders and leaders of ubiquitous organizations, and many believe that they have addressed their social responsibility by including women, gays and lesbians, and some disabled people. In many of these institutions, however, they have remained within the cultural patterns of their own group. This does not in any way suggest that there are not differences between men and women or gay and lesbian and heterosexual people. This point is made to show that for some it is easier to accept domains of difference within the same cultural group because of some degree of familiarity than it is to go beyond the boundaries of one's own group in addressing cultural differences.

Similar views hold for legal and performance-related issues. The ubiquitous perspective emphasis on various groups within the same cultural group allows for compliance with legal statues. Performance and effectiveness might be an issue, however, in that the separation of racial or cultural groups might generate the types of conflicts described in the Marriott example noted previously.

Organizations working from this perspective insist that differences be acknowledged and celebrated, and that everyone's social identity be "accepted." By defining the various social group affiliations, or what I call "domains of difference," as cultural, the domains of difference are legitimated. This results in a focus on multiple group differences, that is supported by the concept of culture. The advantage of this perspective is that social group differences of any sort will not be seen as abnormal or deviant. In addition, it recognizes a range of groups that have been denied access and opportunity in the U.S. workforce. The ubiquitous perspective, however, can lead to avoidance and denial of in-group relations and power dynamics and the relative salience of various reference group memberships in the country's history of work inclusion and its occupational structure. Also minimized is the role and influence of dominant American cultural patterns.

An organization that operates from a ubiquitous perspective would seek to heighten the awareness of its employees to multiple sources of difference and would equate diversity as encompassing many group identities. For instance, managing diversity in organizations would involve helping individual members in the organization cope better with cultural differences. The aim of this type of training is to teach people in organizations, usually through sensitivity training, the skills necessary to deal with people who are different in various ways.

## Traditional

The traditional perspective defines culture as country, which means a common language, values, beliefs, rituals, symbols, and so forth. One is a member of a cultural group by national boundaries. The assumption of the traditional perspective is that shared language, geography, and customs are the basis of culture. Ideally, variability within cultures is acknowledged; cross-cultural scholarship, however, suggests that some variation within groups is recognized. Proponents of the traditional cultural perspective assume that exposure to the culture or cultural knowledge is the primary key to effective cross-cultural learning. In part, the traditional cultural focus may stem from concern that such exposure is required as a way for people to develop comfort with the culturally different (Margolis & Rungta, 1986; Parker et al., 1986).

For organizations that adhere to this perspective, the emphasis is on cultural differences that arise from being a member of another country. This perspective might be held by an organization that works in various countries. Therefore, the concerns associated with addressing cultural issues would be less focused on within-country sources of bias and discrimination. Rather, the organization would strive for cultural representation that would reflect its consumers and places of operation. The concerns regarding addressing culture differences would be more focused on values, assumptions, customs, and language.

The culture of the superordinate society would have a considerable influence on the cultural styles of the leaders of the organization. Thus, decision making and interpersonal and communication processes would be guided by the culture in which they originate. For instance, Maznevski and Peteron (1997) assert that organizational leaders in North America approach decisions assuming their decisions should:

> . . . be clear, firm, and concise. Key events are noted. Problems are formulated. Situations are assessed. Alternatives are generated. Decisions are made. Actions are taken . . . the centrality of decision and choice is replaced in the Arab world and in much of Latin America by a language of relationships and trust. (p. 63)

The obstacles to effectiveness arise from conflicts in worldviews and perceptions about what is important in terms of relationships, thought processes, and language. Therefore, leaders need to be cognizant of the potential sources of cultural conflict in assumption and values. Thus, the moral concerns broaden in scope, and the legal issues are generally complied with given the participation of people from different countries and cultures. Performance and effectiveness will suffer only if the organization does not attend to the internal culture differences and those that are external.

The advantage of this type of approach is that it reminds us that society's institutions reinforce the meanings of behavior, thought, and feelings learned through family. The disadvantage of this approach is that it deemphasizes similar

16

processes that occur within a particular country or that e
of ethnocentrism or racism. The traditional perspectiv
address intergroup power dynamics.

*Race-Based*

This approach holds that race or ethnicity is the primar
United States. People are classified into races by skin
physical features. Race-based theorists hold that the
culture, for example, cultural values (Carter, 1991)
psychological identity (i.e., racial or cultural ident
perspective assumes that the experience of belonging to a
is the more salient cultural factor in the United States. Because race is the most
visible of all "cultural differences" and because of the current and historical
legacy of racial segregation and racism that has and continues to exist in the
United States, race has been and continues to be the ultimate measure of social
exclusion and inclusion, particularly in U.S. organizations. Visibility is of
importance because it determines the rules and bounds of social and cultural
interaction (Copeland, 1983; Kovel, 1984). The race-based perspective assumes
that intergroup power dynamics are important. Hence, proponents of the race-
based view stress the importance of understanding how racism and racial
identity development influence the operation and functioning of U.S.
organizations (Carter, 1990; Helms, 1990; Katz, 1985; Katz & Johnson, 1991). The
race-based approach makes explicit how untenable the idea is that it is possible
to become sensitive to another's culture without first dealing with the overlay of
race (Midgette & Meggert, 1991).

As noted previously, whites will continue to dominate the workforce, and the
vast majority of the growing portions of the workforce are people of color,
Hispanics, Asians, and blacks. One could argue that the cultural issues that are
at the root of addressing cultural diversity are racial. Given our history and
continuing practices of living, playing, and working in separate parts of society,
race difference has become equivalent to cultural difference. Numerous reports
document the gaps in worldviews, communication, and behavioral styles that
exist between racial groups. It is also true that members of the oppressed racial
groups have been exploited for their value as cheap labor. The struggle for civil
rights and the laws that prohibit discrimination were enacted to bring a halt to
such practices and to end the exclusion of people of color, blacks in particular,
from schools, employment beyond menial service, and political participation.
Thus, what we now refer to as diversity or cultural differences actually began as
and in large part continues to be about race relations.

Organizations that operate from this perspective would be strongly influenced
by dominant cultural patterns. The organization's culture would most likely be
guided by the patterns regarding race that permeate social practices. Moral
obligations would not be very strong, and legal compliance would be guided by

the letter of the law. Efforts would be made to find qualified people of color, but few would be found or, if found, hired. Stereotypes and casual attributions are prevalent, and there is considerable in-group bias favoring those who are from the same racial or cultural group and disfavoring those from out-groups. Attributions of ability are made about in-group members and those of luck for out-group members.

White racism and dominance is perhaps the most important barrier to effective organizational interaction and performance. Inasmuch as one's identity is defined by oneself and others, racism is not so much a function of misinformation about other peoples; rather, it is about misinformation about the self that leads to distortions about others.

The race-based perspective holds that racism and racial identity should be a basic and primary focus of organizational cultures and efforts to address cultural difference while using racial diversity to grapple with other aspects of difference. This means that diversity training programs that use this approach would focus on trainee's race awareness, and racial identity status development for members of all racial groups and social, cultural and institutional racism, particularly as it affects the organization (Carter, 1995).

The advantage of this perspective is that it considers the importance of sociopolitical and historical dynamics on current events. It also introduces psychological variability to racial groups such that membership alone does not determine cultural affiliation. The disadvantage of this approach is that it requires a deeply personal and potentially painful journey and soul-searching for each person to become comfortable with his or her racial socialization. It is difficult to address race as a social and personal issue because it tends to be treated as invisible in the social structure, particularly in organizations. Alderfer (1986) noted, "The historical evidence indicates that white people, especially those in power, tend not to reflect on their own contributions to racial dynamics except under the most unusual circumstances" (p. 124). The status quo cannot be ignored or passively accepted because racism is a contributing factor to occupational and employment structures and processes for all racial groups, including whites.

## Conclusion

Moving institutions toward the objective of increased capacity to address and cope with cultural differences is difficult. This discussion provides a systems perspective of institutions that suggests a range of strategies and several specific ways to undertake the task. The process of changing major institutions is long and arduous, and it can easily consume a career and an individual. In this situation, it is important to emphasize that there is no "one right way" and that the exploration must be critical, ongoing, and inclusive. Institutions with long histories of ignoring cultural differences will need to admit there is room for improvement. Long-standing conflicts that have kept groups at a distance will need to be set aside. All those involved will need to be more supportive and open and perhaps more aware that mistakes will be made and feelings will be hurt. The scale of institutions and the scale of the task demand that all parties commit to the process for the "long haul."

# 2

# National Cultural and the New Corporate Language for Race Relations

*Clayton P. Alderfer*

## Historical Background

From its founding to the present, the United States as a nation has struggled with its own internal conflict about the relationship between black and white Americans. More than 100 years after the first white settlers brought slaves to North America, the country had a revolution and established a constitution that sanctioned slavery and withheld citizenship from black African Americans, even though many had fought and died in that revolution.

More than 200 years after the first white settlers arrived, the country had a civil war and passed constitutional amendments eliminating slavery, granting citizenship to blacks, and prohibiting discrimination in voting based on race. Nearly a century after the Civil War, the nation spawned a civil rights movement aimed *finally* at making the legal rights of black African Americans equal to those of their white neighbors—a change that appeared to have been made by the Thirteenth, Fourteenth, and Fifteenth Amendments to the Constitution.

In the years immediately following the Civil War, there was an attempt to bring about progressive change in race relations during the Age of Reconstruction. This period lasted from the end of the war until the election of 1876, when regressive change began again. At this point in history, the era of legalized segregation became a central element of our national culture. It lasted until the beginning of the Civil Rights movement in the middle of the twentieth century.

Following the assassination of Martin Luther King, Jr. in 1968, the Civil Rights movement ended. Nevertheless, until the end of the 1970s, the United States government responded predominantly progressively to the changes in national culture wrought by the movement. Republican Presidents Nixon and Ford as well as Democrat Carter acted to effect progressive change in black-white race relations. Throughout the country, there was a conscious awareness of blatant and subtle forms of bias against black people in the United States and strong sentiments toward reducing the destructive forces of racism.

The national mood changed in 1980, however, with the election of Ronald Reagan as president. He appointed Edwin Meese as attorney general and William Bradford Reynolds as assistant attorney general for civil rights. Together, these men crafted a legal strategy aimed toward reversing the improvements in race relations that had been brought about by preceding administrations. They fashioned their program as an attack on affirmative action.

Although Reagan administration leaders were unconflicted in the regressive direction they attempted to take U.S. race relations, Bush administration leaders, who followed those of the Reagan administration into office in 1988, were more complicated in their attitudes and practices. Their directions were both backward and forward. On the one hand, Bush campaigned for and won the presidency using the Willie Horton commercial, which played directly to the racist fears of white Americans. For a time, Bush's White House staff blocked efforts by white male business leaders and black civil rights leaders to forge a civil rights bill that would reverse the regression spawned by Reagan, Meese, and Reynolds. Eventually, a civil rights bill was passed, but because of the compromises involved the content and consequences of the law remained uncertain. On the other hand, among Bush's senior leadership group were Louis Sullivan and Colin Powell, two black men of visible competence and forcefulness. There were no equivalents of Sullivan and Powell in the Nixon, Ford, or Reagan administrations. Moreover, Bush was overtly criticized by extreme right wing members of the Republican party for his progressive attitudes on racial matters. In Louisiana, for example, David Duke, a former Ku Klux Klan leader, campaigned for the U.S. Senate using white supremacist rhetoric. At the 1992 Republican convention, Patrick Buchanan spoke powerfully—and, many thought, in ways that reflected blatant white racial bias—against progressive change in race relations. Perhaps the inner conflict of the Bush administration on racial matters was most graphically demonstrated in their nomination and appointment to the Supreme Court of Clarence Thomas, a black African American with racially conservative views on judicial matters (Danforth, 1994; Mayer & Abramson, 1994).

Presidents of the United States both bring their personal commitments to the office and reflect the national culture of those who elect them. Thus, conflicted presidential leadership on racial matters did not end with the defeat of Republican George Bush in 1992 by Democrat Bill Clinton. Although Clinton's overt stance on racial matters has appeared on the surface to be more progressive than that of his predecessor, he too has behaved in ways that have communicated mixed signals about how much progressive change in black-white race relations he is willing to support. Perhaps the clearest case was the nomination and then the withdrawal of Lani Guinier as a candidate to become assistant attorney general for civil rights.

When she was nominated in 1993, Guinier brought to her candidacy a career as both government official with civil rights experience and legal scholar specializing in voting rights and race relations (Guinier, 1994a & 1994b; Carter, 1994b). She was also a friend of Bill and Hillary Clinton from law school days.

Shortly after her nomination was announced, the *Wall Street Journal* published a column labeling her "Quota Queen" and setting off a period of angry controversy about what were termed her radical views. Eventually, President Clinton withdrew her nomination without allowing her to testify before the Senate Judiciary Committee.

Guinier (1994a) and other legal scholars (Carter, 1994) argued that the view of her legal writings presented to the public by the press and political leaders was highly distorted. In an academic sense, her scholarship was innovative; neither her analyses nor her prescriptions, however, employed reasoning that was outside of well-accepted principles in other areas of legal scholarship both in the United States and in other countries. Indeed, her fundamental premise began with founding father James Madison's writings about potential tyranny of majorities over minorities.

In withdrawing Guinier's nomination, Clinton indicated that he had read her articles (and presumably therefore was not subject to the distortions of the press, his advisers, and other politicians) and stated that, "This is about *my* center not about the political center" (as quoted in Drew, 1994, p. 211). Although statements by political leaders at controversial moments usually have multiple determinants, there is reason to believe that Clinton was affirming his own beliefs. One of Guinier's (1994b) key articles included material about racially biased election law manipulations in Arkansas, Clinton's home state. By withdrawing Guinier's nomination and by refusing to allow her to testify, Clinton prevented further conversations at that time about race relations in the United States. Although his overt position on racial matters has been more progressive than that of President Bush, his actual behavior shows similar patterns of sometimes moving forward and sometimes backward. Like Bush's, Clinton's leadership reflects the deep conflict about race in the national psyche. Myrdal (1944) and Jaynes and Williams (1989) provide systematic empirical accounts of this conflict at different times during the twentieth century.

## National Culture and the New Corporate Language

A linguistic creation of the most recent historical period is called "the new corporate language of race relations." In a narrow sense, the language is not brand new; it has been used for more than a decade after being elevated to national discourse by Reagan, Meese, and Reynolds. Within the broader historical context of more than 350 years, however, the language is novel in one important manner: It takes words that previously meant one thing and uses them in ways that often mean virtually the opposite of their original use. For some, such as Meese, Reynolds, and Buchanan, the new meaning of the words probably involved little more than inventing a new code for speaking regressively about race relations. Others, however, may pick up the usage more unconsciously and with fewer conscious intentions to employ the language to reverse progressive changes in black-white race relations.

I use the word "corporate" in this context not only to refer to private enterprise, in which the new language can certainly be found, but also to refer to other organizations—public and private—in which talk about racial matters occurs. This new corporate language is a form of racial double talk. On the surface, it appears to be saying one thing, whereas at a deeper, sometimes unconscious level, it is saying something else. As a form of intergroup communication about racial groups, it reflects the problematic state of relations between these groups (Alderfer, 1987).

The following analysis may be called deconstruction, hermeneutics, or etymological inquiry. I prefer a different intellectual tradition, however—one more athletic in nature. It was founded by Yogi Berra. As manager of the New York Yankees, Berra was fired after winning an American League pennant. He thereby learned the meaning of meritocracy in practice. Yogi articulated such methodological principles as "You can hear a lot by listening" and "You can see a lot by looking." Until recently, Berra's work remained largely outside the mainstream of conventional social science scholarship, but in May 1996 he was awarded an honorary doctorate by Montclair State University. There is a new movement (to which I belong) toward greater acceptance of Yogi in scholarly methodological circles (cf. Berra, 1998). In the following section, I examine many of the most prominent specimens of the new corporate language and apply Yogi's method to their analysis.

## Specimens and Their Meanings

In this section, I explain the origins, describe the effects, and reveal the consequences of the new corporate language for black-white race relations. Because language is a part of culture, this examination also helps one to better understand one aspect of our national culture on matters of race. The new language is the latest way in which Americans express their deeply conflicted views about fairness on matters of black-white relations. The new corporate language both reflects and expresses this aspect of American culture.

### Opposing Reverse Discrimination

"Reverse discrimination" was one of the earliest forms of the new language for race relations promoted by Edwin Meese and associates. What is reverse discrimination? When employed as part of the legal assault on affirmative action, it means that a white man believes he did not get a job, a raise, or a promotion because a person of a different race or gender, who usually is assumed to be less qualified, received the opportunity.

How is reverse discrimination different than plain discrimination? If a white man is treated unfairly because of his race and gender, why is that *reverse* discrimination? Do we white men need a special language to protest when we believe unfairness has been directed at us because of our race and gender? Maybe there is more to it than just a choice of words.

"Reverse discrimination!" can also be a command. Such an order might be given by an authorized leader or a legitimized group, for example, the president or the Supreme Court of the United States and the chief executive or the board of directors of a corporation. If given as an order by an appropriate authority, the command means to reverse the discrimination that has characterized our society and its organizations. What does it mean when someone says "I am against reverse discrimination" in this sense? It means the speaker prefers not to reverse the discrimination that has characterized our society and its organizations. How is the meaning of reverse discrimination in the second sense different from its intent in the first sense? I doubt that it is different.

### Saying "Race Had Nothing to Do With It"

When George Bush announced his nomination of Clarence Thomas to replace Thurgood Marshall on the Supreme Court, he said Thomas' race had nothing to do with the selection. The next day on a national television news program, when former Attorney General Edwin Meese was asked whether he thought Thomas' race had influenced the nomination, he answered affirmatively. The reporter then asked Meese whether he was calling the president of the United States a liar. Meese replied that he would not say that.

In nominating Clarence Thomas for the Supreme Court, the Bush administration was replacing a racially progressive and highly qualified black African American judge with a conservative judge of more questionable qualifications. Within both the black African American and the white judicial communities, questions were raised about Thomas' qualifications for the high court (Higginbotham, 1991, p. 382). The dialogue among Bush, Meese, and the press on these matters reflected the new corporate language for race relations.

Had Bush spoken more fully, he might have said, "I know that race had a lot to do with the nomination, but I wish it did not." Had Meese spoken more completely, he might have said, "I know race mattered in just the way I hoped it would; now there will be an underqualified black conservative Supreme Court Justice. We have made quite a statement to those who favor affirmative action for blacks." Had the reporter been more interested in inquiry rather than putting Meese on the spot, he might have asked Meese, "How do you as a former attorney general assess the nomination of Clarence Thomas to the Supreme Court?" None of the parties spoke as they might have if the aim had been to engage in a more complete conversation about race. I doubt whether any of the parties spoke honestly.

Given the racial history of the United States and the role of Thurgood Marshall in this history, why would it not be appropriate to discuss the role of race in choosing his successor? Both Bush and Meese avoided being asked about the full set of reasons for supporting Thomas' candidacy by keeping a thoughtful conversation about race out of their public assessment of the man. The reporter avoided direct talk about race by attempting to provoke a controversy between Meese and Bush rather than by addressing the question of race directly. Perhaps that was one of the deeper motives for adding a new order of double talk to conversations about race. It becomes even more difficult—especially for those not participating in the decisions—to learn what is occurring among those who exercise power about racial matters.

## Being Against Quotas

To begin a discussion of "quotas," one must acknowledge that virtually everyone who speaks about the matter is against quotas. George Bush was against quotas. Democrat legislators are against quotas. Members of minority groups are against quotas. As a matter of personal reflection, you might consider whether you have ever heard someone speak who is in favor of quotas. I never have, and I have been working professionally on race relations for approximately 25 years. If virtually no one speaks on behalf of quotas, why do so many individuals representing so many groups speak so often and so forcefully against that which virtually no one speaks for? What is going on here?

Historically, the idea of quotas meant limiting the numbers of certain racial, ethnic, cultural, and religious groups to a fixed proportion of memberships in predominantly white or Anglo organizations. An Ivy League university (e.g., Yale) might have a policy of admitting no more than 10% of Jews to its freshman class, regardless of applicants' grades and test scores. In this sense, the idea of quotas ran directly counter to what today is called meritocracy. Certain group memberships were the basis for keeping people out rather than taking them in based on their written records of academic accomplishment.

In the new corporate language for race relations, the meaning of being against quotas is different. As the words are used today, the meaning of being against quotas is similar to observing and counting how many people who are different from white men occupy positions in various places in organizational hierarchies. Usually, the jobs receiving special attention are the more desirable ones (i.e., line rather than staff, higher ranking rather than lower ranking, etc.). Sometimes, the observing and counting includes comparisons between the population at large or the field of interest and current job profiles. For certain of the highest ranking jobs, the quota with the word used in the older sense is either zero or very small. Do people who speak against quotas mean they are against quotas of very small numbers? I do not think so.

If observing and counting leads to results showing notably low numbers of black men and black women in certain jobs, for example, then specific kinds of conversations might follow. An attempt might be made to understand why the organization seems to populate such jobs only, or almost only, with white people. Then an effort might be made to change these patterns—that is, try to fill these positions with individuals other than whites. In the new corporate language for race relations, this is what critics mean by being in favor of quotas. In the context of black-white race relations, the old meaning of quotas was to limit the numbers who were other than whites. The new meaning of quotas is to expand the numbers who are other than whites. How does one explain why the word quotas has changed to virtually the opposite of the meaning it once had?

One explanation is that the new meaning is still about not having limits, but now it is about not having limits for whites. This logic does not change the old meaning of the word quota. It does change the group toward whom the lack of limits refers. Another explanation is more complex. This logic pertains to how organizations act to change patterns that historically have resulted in certain desirable jobs being restricted mainly to white people, especially white men. In this context, resistance to promoting blacks can take on a particularly perverse form.

Faced with a request to consider blacks for upward mobility opportunities, some white managers respond with a complicated defense. First, they convert the request into a demand: "We have to promote a black!" Second, they inform subordinates with words such as, "Send me a black, any black." Third, wishing to be cooperative, the subordinates talk it over among themselves and say, "Let's send them the dumbest turkey we can find." Then, if such a promotion actually occurs, the white men who effected the promotion can say with a justification that their behavior helped to create that "So-and-so is not qualified for the position; he or she was an affirmative action promotion. He or she was promoted just to fill a quota." In consulting about race relations in organizations, white men have told me under conditions of confidentiality that exactly these processes occur (Alderfer, 1992).

Similar phenomena have also been observed in the military. Information collected about U.S. Army promotions showed that for white enlisted people, promotion rates were positively associated with aptitude test scores (i.e., the higher the test score, the faster the promotion rate), whereas for black enlisted people promotion rates were negatively associated with aptitude test scores (i.e., the higher the test score, the slower the promotion rate) (Nordlie, 1972). These statistics suggest that the verbal reports I received were not just isolated incidents in one organization. Rather, they were part of a willful effort to sabotage efforts to change the balance of power between blacks and whites in organizations based on merit. Speaking against quotas is thus part of a larger pattern of resisting change in race relations.

Indeed, this process of whites' sabotaging the promotions of blacks by supporting weak candidates consists of whites behaving against the widely espoused values of meritocracy. The complementary process, of course, is failing to promote blacks who are highly qualified. In situations such as these, more powerful whites rather than less powerful blacks are responsible for lowering the overall competence level of individuals in organizational roles. Regarding the appointment processes of both Republican and Democrat presidents, Bush promoted Thomas, a man whose qualifications were in doubt, to the Supreme

Court, and Clinton withdrew his support for Guinier, a woman whose qualifications were unquestioned by appropriate observers, to be deputy attorney general for civil rights.

## Speaking About "Women and Minorities"

The phrase "women and minorities" is used so frequently that only rarely does anyone wonder about the meaning or implications of thinking in these terms. The words are used by the press and they are used in management discussions, scholarship by investigators of diverse backgrounds, and by government officials. The one thing that women and minorities have in common is that they are not white men. In other ways, use of the phrase in any setting covers up important differences and limits conversations about these issues: What is the relationship between black men and white women? What is the relationship between white women and black men? What is the relationship between black men and black women? What is the relationship between white women and black women? What is the relationship between black men and white men? What is the relationship between white men and white women?

Thus, in taking explicit account of race and gender on matters of race relations, one asks six questions rather than one. How likely is it that the answers to all six of these questions would be substantially the same? I think it is extremely unlikely (cf. Morrison, 1992). The use of one question, as implied by the phrase "women and minorities," implies that the answers would be substantially the same, and only one question would be necessary: What is the relationship between white men, on the one hand, and women and minorities, on the other hand? Faced with a choice between one question or six questions, which would a person who prefers not to understand be more likely to ask?

Using the phrase "women and minorities," therefore, can serve a defensive function for those who speak in this manner. It can eliminate the need to inquire about which groups are in minority positions in particular contexts. It can reduce the potential intellectual complexity of discussing both race and gender in combination. Consequences of the defense are that race relations appear easier to understand; observers reach less complex conclusions about the meaning of events; and, the status quo is easier to maintain.

## Comparing Blacks and Whites Inappropriately

The August 5, 1991 issue of *Sports Illustrated* was devoted to the black athlete. In one article, E. M. Swift analyzed how "some black superstars cash in big on ability to shed their racial identity." This article included a quotation from Marvin Bressler, then chairman of sociology at Princeton University, who said,

> I *do* think there's been a kind of abstract improvement in race relations
> in this country, more of a willingness to recognize merit. A white guy

sitting in a bar in Detroit acknowledges that [Michael] Jordan should make more money than John Paxson, and commercial endorsements are seen as part of the rewards for athletic merit. Some sense of fairness exists that now includes black people and formerly didn't. But does the white guy on the stool necessarily regard the black man on the street as any less threatening? I don't think so. (p. 55)

To understand fully what is contained in the Bressler quotation, it is helpful if one knows professional basketball and followed the 1991 National Basketball Association (NBA) playoffs. Michael Jordan, a black man, and John Paxson, a white man, were teammates in the starting five lineup of the championship-winning Chicago Bulls. The relatively easy victory of the Bulls over the Los Angeles Lakers was achieved in part because Jordan and Paxson played extraordinarily well together. Jordan, known throughout his career as an outstanding scorer, frequently assisted Paxon's scoring during the playoff series. In the post-victory celebration during a nationally televised interview, Jordan, who had been named most valuable player, made a special point of praising Paxson, who had played very well in the championship series. I doubt if anyone who knows basketball would find the Jordan-Paxson comparison made by Bressler to be meaningful. Arguably, Michael Jordan is the best basketball player in the history of the game. John Paxson was a good (white) professional player.

There are additional features of the Bressler quotation that deserve attention. Given that Paxson and Jordan played for Chicago, why did the sociology chairman choose to locate his white guy in a Detroit bar? Did he think for some reason he did not disclose that a white guy in Detroit would have a special interest in the Jordan-Paxson comparison? Detroit also had a fine NBA team, led by, among others, Isaiah Thomas, a black man who, like Jordan, was an all-star guard. Detroit, a former NBA champion, is a major rival of Chicago.

In terms of the politics of race relations, Chicago and Detroit are different cities. In terms of basketball, it would seem that people in Chicago would be more interested in their players than would the people of Detroit. For some time, however, Detroit has had a black mayor, Coleman Young. In 1991, Chicago had recently elected a white mayor, Richard Daley, Jr., who succeeded a black mayor who died in office. Might these political differences in the cities (i.e., who is in charge?) have had something to do with Bressler's placing his hypothetical white guy on a stool in Detroit rather than in Chicago?

There is also a question about why Bressler placed his hypothetical white guy in a Detroit bar rather than at the Princeton Faculty Club. Is it likely that Bressler knows Detroit bars better than the Princeton establishment? Depending on Bressler's history and habits, it is possible. One effect of placing the white guy in Detroit rather than in Princeton, however, is that it puts greater social distance between Bressler, who is also a white guy, and his hypothetical white guy on a stool, whose racial perceptions and attitudes he purports to understand.

Perhaps the most important question is why, when the Jordon-Paxson relationship offered so much to symbolize black-white cooperation, did Bressler present this relationship from a perspective that was fundamentally divisive. The hypothetical white guy in the Detroit bar agrees that Jordan deserves more money than Paxson. In terms of achievements in professional basketball, the Jordan-Paxson comparison is not meaningful. Paxson was not comparable to Jordan in accomplishments or skills. A more meaningful black-white comparison would involve finding a white player who might match Jordan. In times past, Larry Bird of the Boston Celtics might be such a person. A Jordan-Bird comparison corrected for age and position (Jordan is a guard; Bird was a forward) at least would be sensible in terms of lifetime achievements.

Moreover, framing the Jordan-Paxson relationship as competitive after it had been publicly shown to be cooperative suggests a desire on Bressler's part to view race relations competitively, even when the visible behavior is cooperative in deeds (how the two played together) and in words (Jordan's praise for Paxson). An element in this cooperation, which may have influenced Bressler's portrayal, was that the black member of the pair was in the dominant position. Jordan was clearly the better player, and he assisted Paxson on the court and praised him publicly off the court. Disturbance about the relevant dominance of blacks over whites might also account for Bressler's choosing Detroit (with a black mayor) over Chicago (with a white mayor) when locating his hypothetical white guy on a barstool.

The observations offered by the *Sports Illustrated* writer were cloaked with the authority of Bressler's university and academic profession. Bressler, the author of the quotation, was a Princeton sociology chairman who said race relations in the United States had improved in the abstract. Careful listening, however, shows that Bressler's message was clearly more complex. The unanswered questions are what did Bressler really believe about race relations in the United States and what did the *Sports Illustrated* writer really wish to convey by means of Bressler's words? The answer to both questions is probably more than their words literally say.

### Criticizing Explicit Discussion of Race Relations

Contemporary culture includes a variety of subtle and forceful messages that discourage explicit talk about race relations. Specific forms are familiar to most people: They say they want to get beyond black and white; corporations say their aim is to be color-blind in hiring and promotion decisions; the legal system says it wants to be color-blind in the administration of justice; and, corporations and management consultants increasingly say they want to support all forms of diversity, not just racial differences. These phrases—to get beyond black and white, to be color-blind, and to support all forms of diversity—represent goals that are admirable and acceptable to many people. What do these phrases mean in theory and practice? Why are they readily accepted?

To get beyond black and white means to eliminate conflicts between blacks and whites. This condition may be achieved by bringing about racial justice. There are other means as well. If people stop noticing and pointing out economic, educational, health care, and occupational injustices based on race, we get beyond black and white. If black and white people completely separate themselves from one another, we get beyond black and white. If people stop responding to each other based on race, we get beyond black and white. If history were rewritten to eliminate any discussion of slavery based on race, we get beyond black and white. In short, there are a variety of ways to get beyond black and white, but only some of them are based on fair, respectful and productive relationships between black and white people.

To be color-blind means not to see color. Within the context of race relations, to be color-blind is not to notice one's own and other people's races. Outside the context of race relations, being color-blind is a disability. On racial matters, when people are asked to be color-blind, they are asked to deny what they see. The natural condition of human beings is to see color. Generally, when we do not see color, we function less well than when we do. Why should being color-blind be a desirable state in race relations when it is undesirable for other purposes?

Those with good intentions advocate being color-blind in race relations for many reasons. They know people are often treated unfairly based on skin color. If those who treat them unfairly did not see color, they could not treat people unfairly based on color.

Can people be taught not to see color in relation to others? Is it conceivable that people could be taught not to see color in relation to human beings and yet to retain their capacity to see color in other matters? When examined, this line of reasoning seems seriously flawed. Therefore, why do we retain the injunction to be color-blind?

What color of light does one see if one does not see color? From the point of view of physical optics, the answer to this seemingly paradoxical question is white light. The unconscious message to be color-blind is to see race relations from a white perspective.

There are other less benevolent consequences to being color-blind. If one does not see color, then one cannot associate happenings in one's life to the effects of color. When a black man is senselessly beaten by a group of white police, for example, one cannot see the association between race and the abuse of power by whites. When the secretary of health and human services, a black man, told cigarette companies to stop misleading advertisements in urban ghettos, one could not see the association between race and the use of government power to improve public health among inner-city people. In general, becoming color-blind on matters of race results in the loss of the capacity to perceive racial dynamics.

Finally, there is the personal psychology of being color-blind. In this sense, to be color-blind is to deny one's own racial identity. Such messages include the following: Do not think of yourself as a white person, do not think of yourself as a black person, do not think of yourself as a brown person, just think of yourself as a human being. The problem with these messages, and others like them, is that we all have racial identities that influence our life experiences. The message to be color-blind removes both the pride and the pain associated with racial group membership. In denying our racial identities, we diminish ourselves as human beings, and we diminish others.

## [De-]Valuing Diversity

The newest addition to the corporate language of race relations is the word "diversity." When the word was introduced several years ago, the objective was to find new language that was respectful of the many dimensions of human difference that increasingly characterize the United States. These dimensions appear as group memberships by race, gender, generation, ethnicity, physical ability, sexual orientation, religion, and veteran status. The new preference was for diversity to be positively valued. Positively valuing diversity was to replace the old negative slant of not discriminating based on race, gender, age, and so on. At inception, the concept of diversity was rooted in affirmation, and not denial.

As time has passed, however, the practical meaning of diversity has become increasingly diffuse. It no longer stands just for a variety of meaningful group memberships. It has been transformed to include virtually any dimension of human difference that someone might choose to notice. I observed the following dialog during a brief management training program about valuing diversity:

> **White male (age approximately 40):** Now take Harry over there. I used to think of Harry as an obnoxious S. O. B., but now that I have learned about diversity, I just think of Harry as diverse, and I value diversity. Right, Harry? (Laughter)

> **Harry (also white male, age approximately 40):** Right. Now take this company. We used to be required to wear only red neckties. Now that we have a corporate policy to value diversity, we can wear blue ties as well. This corporation values diversity. (Laughter again)

Unless one is attentive—and the incentives for managers and consultants are against observing and listening carefully regarding these matters—the movement to value diversity will become the kind of joke depicted here. The conversation about diversity will be transformed from authentic talk about real group differences to trivial conversation about shallow substance. The new corporate language for race relations will have been so captured by the infinite number of potential diversity dimensions that conversation about the group memberships that shape people's lives will be nearly impossible.

## Conclusion

Left unexamined, the new corporate language for race relations serves to limit direct conversations about racial issues and thereby either intentionally or unintentionally operates as a regressive force affecting black-white relations in the United States. To aid the reader's self-reflective processes, Table 2.1 provides a list of seven examples of this language. This list is not exhaustive. Other elements of the language also might be identified.

Each example of the language in Table 2.1 has a overt message that seems to favor fundamental fairness in human relations and a covert message that communicates just the opposite. Although there are certainly political motives for suppressing examination of racial issues, there are also psychological reasons. Race relations is a complex subject, both emotionally and intellectually. Strong emotions are part of the phenomena for people of all races. Therefore, capacities to address strong emotions and to think complexly are necessary to develop sophisticated understanding. Because the real work of sound racial dialogue is demanding, there are short-term psychological benefits for evasion, denial, duplicity, and double talk. This is why individuals who do not consciously intend to promote regressive race relations nevertheless engage in behaviors that serve these ends.

The new corporate language for race relations allows speakers to express their conflicts about black-white race relations with all the difficult emotions and complex issues, on the one hand, and to appear to say the right thing on the other hand. This form of racial talk is a means to express more of the speakers' messages about race relations than would be possible, if saying the right thing were all that occurred. Whether consciously intended or not, because of the strong emotions associated with racial issues it is extremely difficult for speakers to say only the right thing. Careful listening combined with psychologically informed reflection reveal that double-talk speakers in fact communicate complex messages. Their words therefore can be used to enhance rather than to diminish conversations about race if people can learn to understand that despite their intentions to say only the right thing, they actually say more. Listen to Yogi!

**Table 2.1**     Specimens of the New Corporate Language for Race Relations

| |
|---|
| Opposing reverse discrimination |
| Saying, "Race had nothing to do with it." |
| Being against quotas |
| Speaking about 'women and minorities' |
| Comparing blacks and whites inappropriately |
| Criticizing explicit discussion of race relations |
| [De-]Valuing Diversity |

There are also potential hazards. The debate about being "politically correct" arises in part because, by and large, we cannot conduct the kind of examination proposed here. Speakers on the Left believe that they need to call certain phenomena "racism" and certain people "racists" (both overtly and covertly) to stop destructive practices. Respondents from the Right say that such talk inhibits free speech. As speakers from the Left engage in explicit and tacit name calling, defensiveness on the part of speakers from the Right increases. As speakers from the Right object to the pressures they feel to speak in ways that are politically correct, they limit what others with different views feel free to say. Thus, in the name of promoting free speech, they limit acceptable talk.

This pattern of mutual accusation combined with inhibited conversation is thus maintained by both speakers from the Left and speakers from the Right. To develop more sophisticated forms of conversations, both parties in these mutually reinforcing cycles of behavior must change. Both parties must reduce their racial double talk.

Any form of double talk has two dysfunctional consequences. First, it communicates multiple messages that seem to contradict one another. Second, it contains secondary messages that prohibit commenting on the multiple messages (Bateson, 1972). The crucial step in breaking the mutually reinforcing pattern is being able to comment on both the mixed messages and the inhibition about discussing the contradictions. By making explicit mention of the mixed messages in racial double talk, I hope to reduce some of the inhibitions about discussing the contradictions.

I believe that, regarding racial matters, we need realistic, direct, and mutually respectful talk—not denials, evasions, duplicities, and condemnations. Everyone has a race, and all racial groups have their difficulties, their contributions, and their pride. To the degree that each of us and all of us (i.e., the process is both individual and collective) can face and address our racial experiences, there will be less need to project our problems onto others in order to avoid facing them in ourselves. Corporate groups—both private and public—and corporate leaders need to recognize and to appreciate the many identity group differences that increasingly are present within organizations. Unless we can deal directly and respectfully with our racial differences and difficulties, we shall live increasingly in organizations in which no one feels welcome, and everyone is alien.

# 3

## "Whiting Out" Social Justice

### Michelle Fine

*The problem of the 20th century is the problem of the color line.*
—W. E. B. DuBois (*The Souls of Black Folk*, 1990)

We all remember W. E. B. DuBois worrying that the color line was the defining feature of the twentieth century. We may all too easily predict that DuBois was a two-century prophet. These are, indeed, troubling times for racial equity, affirmative action, institutional "diversity," and social justice, especially in schools. The Right has declared a broad-based assault while the once solid "middle" has shifted—been bumped and acquiesced—dramatically toward conservatism. Prime indicators include the perverse maldistribution of social resources, violent cuts in public sector programs, attacks on affirmative action, and educational retreats from policies and practices of racial, economic, and gendered justice.

It is this last arena of social (im)morality, at the end of the twentieth century, in which I seek to explore strategies of *leadership for (and against) social justice* in institutions presumably designed for democratic education. Within the matrix of public/private school and racial/gendered discrimination, we must ask what educational leaders are doing to create, inspire, and/or inhibit social justice within the institutional walls for which they are accountable.

For the purposes of this chapter, when I talk about social justice inside school I am concerned with the ways in which students who carry their genders, their racial/ethnic identities, and their social class biographies into school "become"— that is, are seen as and see themselves as—bright or not; talented or deficient; filled with potential or filled with needs. I seek to understand the social psychological processes by which institutional hierarchies, patterned by race and ethnicity, gender and class, come to be embodied by students so that faculty and students can be so sure about who is promising and who is not. I choose to deploy this analysis with the learnings of Michael Foucault (1977), Howie Winant (1996), Joan Scott (1992), and Stuart Hall (1991), all of whom have helped

AUTHOR'S NOTE: This chapter is adapted from *Off-White: Essays on Race, Culture, and Society,* edited by Michelle Fine, Linda C. Powell, Lois Weis, and L. Mun Wong. Copyright © 1996. Reproduced by permission of Routledge, Inc.

me understand that the very categories used to define people, and used by individuals to define ourselves, derive often unwittingly from structures and discourses of power.

I extend their analyses to try to dissect how structural inequities migrate into our personal identities, and I call institutional leaders to consciously interrupt those processes. In the midst of enormous backlash against affirmative action, frivolous debates about "quotas," and incredibly sheepish behavior by once-progressive educational leaders about advocating for social justice, I want to return the gaze of responsibility from individual students of color or individual female students who appear "not to be making it" back onto institutional leaders who have been made aware of these structural constructions of deficit and have chosen not to act. In this chapter, the focus is on race and gender justice in schooling.

I speak to questions of leadership not simply to lay massive structural problems at the feet of individual principals, deans, and administrators, but to suggest that if educational leaders choose not to interrupt social injustice, choose not to defend racial and economic justice, choose not to notice differential opportunities and outcomes, and choose not to transform the conditions of teaching and learning so that outcomes are no longer maldistributed by race, class, and gender, then we need to question for what and to whom are educational leaders accountable? Public institutions and private educational institutions certainly do not need leadership to reproduce social inequity. That can happen without intervention. They do need leadership to interrupt it, however.

Perhaps no one needs to be reminded of the "obvious" contemporary cases in which educational leaders have committed verbal and/or procedural egregious acts of racial offense—when Fran Lawrence, then president of Rutgers University, alluded to "genetic disadvantages" of students of color or when Hulond Humphries, then principal of a public high school in Wedowee, Alabama, canceled the high school prom because of biracial dating and told a biracial student that she was a "mistake" and that the school did not want to encourage more such mistakes. Humphries, at the time, was removed as principal and has since been elected as superintendent. In these circumstances it is easy to hear the racism. Most "listeners" were appalled. Many (whites?) acted as if these statements were anomalous, unusual, outrageous, atypical slips. People of color knew better.

I want to argue, instead, that these statements were simply public pronouncements, albeit "slips" in "bad taste," of the kinds of thoughts and beliefs that many hold, beliefs fundamentally embodied, if unspoken, within institutional policies and practices that cement and ensure racially stratified policies, practices, and outcomes. These statements of "bad taste" are not clumsy blots on an otherwise race-fair system of education in the United States; they are only poorly camouflaged, public "oops" revealing a system of education that relies on stratification, ensures differential opportunities, and guarantees inequitable outcomes by race, class, and often gender.

In this chapter, I present two case studies. One involves a public school in which such an "oops" comment was released from the lips of a principal. The other involves a private school in which administrators and educators are, in admissions and curriculum, quite committed to race/gender equity. Yet, for this second case, we have data suggesting that the design of the institution—course structure, pedagogy, curriculum, climate, bell-shaped grading curves—systematically and differentially "handicap" the academic and political progress of men and women of color, and of white women, compared to white male students.

These case studies are presented in the hope that we can begin to examine not only when "oops" comments escape—which is a worry in and of itself insofar as such comments legitimate a flood of otherwise, perhaps better-kept-to-yourself, barrages of racism/sexism. These cases are presented further to bring to vivid and contested consciousness how it is that schools, both public and private, are organized in ways that, by design or not, students of color, poor students, and sometimes girls are systematically disadvantaged and, as importantly, white students, middle- and upper-class students, and boys are systematically advantaged, as though they were merely smart.

We turn first to the theoretical task of *witnessing whiteness* so that we can develop an "eye" for seeing the ways in which educational architecture privileges privilege and camouflages whiteness, as though it were merely merit. By witnessing whiteness, I seek to make visible the structures that produce whiteness (and maleness) as smart and reduce other "races" (and girls/women) as deficient. In both cases, educators have an opportunity to reflect on the deliberate policies, but also the subtle practices, that create racial and gendered stratification as if these "differences" were entirely inside students.

For those of us concerned with racial (in)justice in schooling, I have a recommendation for what might be considered an odd turn in political and research strategy. What if we took the position that racial inequities were not solely attributable to policies/acts of discrimination targeted against persons of color but also to institutional traditions which privilege students already privileged by race/ethnicity, class, and gender? What if, by keeping our eyes on those who gather and inherit disadvantage, we have failed to notice that white students, males and elites, are nevertheless stuffing their academic and social pickup trucks with goodies otherwise not as readily available to people of color, white females, poor and working-class students? And, what if we held educational leadership accountable for this privileging and debilitation through seemingly "neutral" policies and practices?

Using whiteness as a dominant metaphor of privilege, it is to this task of "witnessing whiteness" that I choose to turn in this essay. With the raw nerve of reflection and the desperate need for better racial thinking and social change strategies, I ask us to avert our gaze from the "inequities" produced through "colors" and genders and classes (where my work has lingered for so long) and turn, instead, to the "merit" that accumulates within the hue of whiteness. While Toni Morrison (1992), Ruth Frankenberg (1993), Christine Sleeter (1993), Michael Novick (1995), and many others have argued that whiteness and "other colors" must be recognized in their rainbowed interdependence, if not in their parasitic webbing, I find myself trying to understand how whiteness accrues privilege and status; gets itself surrounded by protective pillows of resources and/or benefits of the doubt; how whiteness repels gossip and voyeurism and instead demands dignity.[1]

This chapter focuses on two sites of research in which I have had the opportunity to witness not only the ways in which people of color and white women accumulate deficits, but the ways in which white adolescents and adults (in contrast to African-Americans, and males in contrast to females) accumulate merits. My work has moved toward institutional analyses because I worry that those of us interested in critical theory and practice have focused fetishistically on those who endure discrimination, and that by so doing we have been unable/unwilling to analyze how those who inherit privilege invisibly do so. As such, we have camouflaged the intricate institutional webbing which produces and ensures the embodiment of stratification by race, ethnicity, gender, and class.

This chapter tries to chart a theoretical argument about the institutional processes by which privilege is today produced as merit and advantage through schooling and the economy. Historically, in both psychology and education, whiteness has remained both unmarked and unstudied. More recently, by some scholars, it has been elevated to the status of independent variable, one that scientists use to predict other outcomes. Here, I want to reverse conceptually this notion by asserting that institutions recruit diverse colors/genders/classes and then produce dependent variables—whiteness, maleness, and elites—as if they were walking embodiments of merit/advantage.

Four theoretical assumptions arrange my thinking. First, as I have said, whiteness, like all "colors," is being manufactured, in part, through institutional arrangements. This is particularly the case in institutions designed "as if" hierarchy, stratification, and scarcity were inevitable. Schools and work, for example, do not merely manage race; they create and enforce racial meanings. Second, in such institutions, whiteness is actually coproduced with other colors, usually alongside blackness, for instance, in symbiotic relation. Where whiteness grows as a seemingly "natural" proxy for quality, merit, and advantage, color disintegrates to embody deficit. Third, whiteness and color are therefore not merely created in parallel, but are fundamentally relational and need to be studied as a system; they might, in statistical terms, be considered "nested" rather than coherent or independent variables. Fourth, the institutional design of whiteness, like the production of all colors, creates an organizational discourse of race and a personal embodiment of race, affecting perceptions of self and "others," producing individuals' sense of racial "identities" and collective experiences of racial "tensions," even coalitions.

Once this process is sufficiently institutionalized and embodied, the observer, that is, the scholar, can easily miss the institutional choreography which has produced a stratified rainbow of colors. What remains visible are the miraculous ways in which quality seems to rise to the glistening white top. To understand this production, I import the writings of Pierre Bourdieu (1991) who invokes the word *institution* as a verb:

> The act of institution is an act of magic (p. 119).... An act of communication, but of a particular kind: It signifies to someone what his identity is, but in a way that both expresses it to him and imposes it on him by expressing it in front of everyone and thus informing him in an authoritative manner of what he is and what he must be (p. 121). This is also one of the functions of the act of institution: to discourage permanently any attempt to cross the line, to transgress, desert, or quit. (p. 336)

For Bourdieu, and the present analysis, institutions are reviewed as productive, not passive; as creating the very categories they claim to be receiving; as responsible, largely, not entirely, for inequities produced. This essay is a plea to research institutions: to notice, to remove the glaucoma that has ruined scholarly vision, as we lift up the school and work-related dynamics that make whiteness and other racial groups seem so separable, and so relentlessly rank ordered.

## Scene One: "White Lies"

The scene is Wedowee, Alabama, the site where the principal, Hulond Humphries, was charged in 1994 with racial harassment. My involvement emerged because I was representing the United States Justice Department in the lawsuit meeting. In preparation of my expert testimony, I was able to interview a group of students at Randolph County High School (RCHS). The Justice Department was arguing that Mr. Humphries should be removed as principal.

Enter the group: Callie is a young white woman. She's a junior at RCHS:

> My mother asked for someone, you know, the principal, to watch me and find out if I'm dating a black boy. So, Mr. Humphries called me in and he told me if I kept on dating John I wouldn't be able to get any white boys. No one else would go out with me. We could have a child who's not very smart. And if I go to a family reunion, I may be the only white woman there and no one's going to even talk to me. Then I'd be an outcast.

Trina, an African American eleventh grader jumps in:

He called us all into the auditorium after their talk and asked how many of us are going to the prom with someone of the other race. Lots of us raised our hands. Then he asked Rovanda [a biracial student at the school], "Rovanda, who you taking to the prom?" And Rovanda said, "I'm taking Chris," her white boyfriend. And he just looked up in the bleachers, and he said, "I won't have it. No inter-racial dating in my school." And Rovanda said, "Who would you *like* me to take to the prom?" He said, "You were a mistake, and we don't want other mistakes like you."

Tasha, an African American female, joined in, "He said he was canceling the prom." King, an African American male junior from Los Angeles, said, "When he called Rovanda a mistake, it was like he took an ax and cut through the heart of a tree. The heart of our school."

Tommy (a white student) said, "I had just transferred here from Germany, and within four days I was told by a white teacher that I shouldn't hang out with the black students, or I'd get a bad name." Natalie, an African American woman, who attended one of the Freedom schools the black community created in protest to Humphries' comment, explained, "I boycotted the high school . . . went to the Freedom schools." But Natalie came back because she was a senior and wanted to graduate. Upon returning, "I felt like I was in trouble . . . they [staff who supported Humphries] were retaliating. . . . He just stared at me in the hall, and so did all of the teachers." Recognizing the prom incident as Humphries' most vivid and public performance of racializing, I pressed on about school policies and practices that may appear race-neutral but nonetheless produce further stratification.

I opened with questions about tracking at the high school. Like many, this high school has an "advanced" and a "standard" track. Knowing something about the (unfortunately predictable) racial splitting by track, I asked the students in the group—white students and African American students—what track are you in? The white kids raised their hand when I said "advanced"; then the African American kids raised their hands when I said "standard." I later learned how profoundly the aggregate numbers, over time, bore out that simple hand-raising exercise.

It's important to know that at this school, as in many schools, students have what is considered a "choice" about which track they opt into. And they choose by race. White racism here—and elsewhere—is so thoroughly institutionalized and embodied that young people, when given an opportunity, choose their "place," seemingly with little protest (see Wells & Serna, 1996). I asked African American students in the group, "Why did you choose the standard track? The standard track doesn't allow you to attend four-year college like University of Alabama. You don't take enough math or science to make it into a four-year college." These students offered a litany of painful, if predictable, responses. "Because I was scared." "Because I thought it [advanced] was too hard."

"Because my friends were in the standard track." When Tigray mumbled, "Because maybe they are smarter than we are," Callie, the young white woman who opened the scene, responded, "That's the scam they pull on you. There are plenty of dumb white kids in my classes, but they would never go to the standard track." I pressed Callie, "What would happen if you told your guidance counselor you wanted to be in a standard track?" She laughed, "She'd say, 'Callie, what are you talking about? You're not going into the standard track, you're going to go to college.'"

Indeed in this "integrated" school the advanced track is almost all white; no varsity cheerleader had ever been black; an African American boy who ran for president of the student council talks of harassment from the principal; almost all the faculty were white. Every strata of school life—academics, social relations, postsecondary opportunities and dating—layered by race. Visually apparent and vigilantly enforced (see Oakes, 1988; Rosenbaum, 1976).

Wanting to understand the principal's motive for his public performance of racializing, I went to see Hulond Humphries. We met in the basement of the school district building. Clear that I represented the team for the Justice Department, I probed with pen in hand, "Why did you say what you said about the prom? You must have known it would cause the kind of hysteria that it did." To which he said, "It's not that I have anything against interracial dating. . . . It's just that those little black boys really want our white girls." He continued, "Now with that feminism, black girls are wanting our white boys." Clear lines. Blacks as sexual predators. Whites as prey.

The night before I went to the school, I had the privilege of visiting a small church, the African Zion Church just outside of town. I thought I was to meet with 10 elders from the church. Driving down on a winding dirt road, looking for a little church, we came upon a small building where there were about 150 cars and two buses. Thinking we were lost, we entered a building filled with song, hope, and prayer. "Praise Jesus. Here's Dr. Fine."

I sat, stood, sang for hours, ecstatic and anxious to be part of chanting, singing, praying, preaching, and testifying about what it was like to be a student, a parent, a community member, black, within reach of those schools. Then the most elder reverend, a man just five foot, over 80 years old, adjusts the microphone so all could hear him. He booms, "Every 10 years or so God tests the racial waters of the United States. We are privileged that this year He chose Wedowee for His test. And what is our job? To *love* those people to death." He gazes out at a group of teenage boys standing in the back and, in low tenor alto, he warns, "And your job is to be cool." The black church worked to bring solidarity and sanity, community and possibility, inside a thin slice of well-protected racial sediment.

That was the racial tapestry of schooling in Wedowee, Alabama; the fabric in which young whites and African American children's lives were intimately interwoven. What is striking is how much the students, white and black, knew their place, and rarely dared to protest aloud. White students' place was just "north" of black students'. Black students' place was just below white students'. In this small working-class town, Southern affect and congeniality allowed little anger to seep explicitly into cross-racial interactions. The black church was the "safe space," the emotional safety valve, the place to put and contain anger, the "sanity check" on Sunday evening which would allow all to return to the perverse, hostile, if sometimes congenial stratification that many explained constitutes community life Monday through Friday.

Discursively and materially, whiteness is here produced and maintained through the withholding of opportunity from, and the derogation of that which is, black. The prom now rises as a floating metaphor for all of the institutional filters that separate and sanitize "white" from "black." To ensure privilege. But being white, in and of itself, in troubled economic times, today guarantees little in Alabama. At least for these poor and working-class families. Unemployment and poverty rates run high across racial groups. Therefore—and this is my major point—this racial formation was filled with parasitic interdependence such that *whites need blacks in order to become, and remain, privileged.*

African American students were getting less than white students. However, as true, nobody was getting a very rigorous academic education. No one was taking math courses more difficult than advanced algebra, and still none of the African American students had been enrolled even at this level. One might cynically argue that the white students were "lucky" to have the black students so they could imagine themselves enjoying any "privilege." The cleansing of whiteness—in class tracks, dating, cheerleading, and college opportunities—was the job of the institution. And its leader clearly spoke for more than himself. He has, since this time, been elected superintendent of public schools.

Two theoretical insights warrant attention. First, in this community, poor and working-class racial identities and concomitant "racial tensions," perhaps even "desires," were invented and sustained through privilege and power defined and ensured by withholding opportunities from black students. Whiteness was produced through the exclusion and denial of opportunity to people of color. In other words, giving blacks access to white opportunities would threaten and stain, indeed blacken, that which is white. Racial justice, or access to equal opportunity, is a threat to whiteness if whiteness requires the degradation of color.

Second, this case points up how fundamentally institutional leadership and seemingly "race-neutral" policies/practices work to ensure white privilege. The leader of this institution, Hulond Humphries, articulated publicly what he believed about race, capacity, sexuality, and who deserves to be educated. And he spoke for many other whites in the community. In a racially hostile environment, it's not only very hard for biracial and African Americans to participate with full hearts and minds. As troubling, in such environments, white students and parents develop and exercise a profoundly false sense of superiority premised almost entirely on opposition to sustain the racial hierarchy. Opposition and degradation became a fix, a steroid to white identity. This public school, in its leadership, policies, and daily practices, did little to interrupt—and much to produce—this steroid. All in the name of creating and maintaining merit and "quality." As the work of Gaertner, et al. (1995) reveals, we may be witnessing today a reassertion of pro-white policies and practices in addition to actively hostile discrimination against people of color. If this is the case, that whiteness is "catching" privilege, then where we look for evidence of discrimination and prejudice will have to move to the cumulative benefits of being white, rather than the (exclusive) tracking of acts of blatant racism against, in this case, blacks. Documenting racism against, as if separable from racism for, may be a diversionary strategy by which our scholarly and activist eyes have been averted.

Questions of leadership linger all over this case. Institutional leaders set policy and practice; they also set tone. Teachers know who will be supported for saying what and who will be chastised for dissenting. In this school, some white teachers, although certainly not all, subscribed to Humphries' beliefs. More important, however, regardless of their beliefs, most conformed and all refused to interrupt his institutionalized racism. The few adults of color in and around the building were virtually unable to voice, within the school, their dissent. Instead, they found a safe space within the black church. For these educators and students of color, the school was never a *public space* of safety or democracy, but instead a site of *surveillance and social control*. How tragic, as historian Robin Kelley has brilliantly demonstrated with his analyses of race relations on "public" transit. Schools can be "free spaces" for some students (often those least in need) and "occupied territories" for others (often those who need a free space most). This may be obvious to some of you. These insights come slowly to people—like me—limited by "white vision," which has allowed us to believe in and mis-see public spaces as democratic and accessible to all.

## Scene Two: Whiting Out Social Critique

In Wedowee, stratification by race among the poor and working class was publicly institutionalized and personally internalized. Explicit critique of this treatment was hard to find. For Scene Two we head north to track an institution in which race and gender critique is voiced vociferously, among the privileged, but then gets "disappeared" over time. Expanding the analysis of institutional stratification by race, to a story of race and gender, this analysis sits in the University of Pennsylvania's law school in which we (Guinier, Fine, & Balin, 1996) studied the gender and race dynamics percolating within an elite law school. Here, we witness how white and male rise to the top through seemingly neutral policies and practices.

A first-year black woman law student offers:

> I think it is still that people don't understand why African Americans
> are still struggling, or why we're struggling. To me it's incredible! It's

like a blindness! And I listen to some of the comments in class, and I
realize that I'm just coming from an entirely different world. From the
perspective of most people, I'm just more aware of my history, and law
and things as it relates to black people. And I think that part of it has to
do to the fact that white students think they're going to be a lawyer.
They don't have to think about who they're going to represent, or that
they have to represent all black people.

This is a study in which we surveyed first-, second-, and third-year law students'
attitudes, beliefs, and experiences, and then we examined three cohorts of their
academic performance in a school in which dropouts are remarkably rare. We
conducted individual and group interviews with students throughout the law
school, men and women, and students of all colors. In the condensed version of
the findings, the attitudinal data reveal vast initial differences in political
perspective, levels of alienation and visions for the future both by race and
gender. But as bold as they were, these statistically significant initial differences
disappeared over time. They were barely discernible by graduation year. By Year
3, most law students saw the school, social justice, and the world as white males
did during Year 1.

The sad tale is that social critique by race/gender does not age very well
within educational institutions. It gets snuffed out so that over time such
concerns either turn inward into self-blame or they get muffled. Through the
process of what might be called "professional socialization," the young adults
we studied grew anesthetized to things that they once—in the beginnings of
their school career—considered outrageous (e.g., generic "he," adversarial
method, differential participation by gender, inaccessible faculty, and sexist
jokes). Among first-year women, for instance, 25% were interested in public-
interest law compared to 7% of the men. Yet by Year 3 only 8% of women and 7%
of men expressed an interest in public-interest law. First-year women were
significantly more likely than men to report concerns with the issues of social
justice, social problems, and even dismay at the use of the generic "he." By Year
3 their political attitudes were akin to the men's. The men did not get more
progressive. The women had "become gentlemen," as one professor encouraged
them to do (see Guinier, et al., 1996).

This process of anesthetizing is a process by which institutions "white out"
students' raced and gendered critiques and encourage them to develop, *instead*,
"professional" identities. At Penn, where white women and students of color
participate in a system about which they initially voice much concern (but do not
drop out), our evidence suggests that over time they accommodate to the
institutional norms—growing conservative, relatively depressed, and self-
blaming. They abandon their once vibrant raced and gendered critique of social
arrangements and the law sometime after Year 1. Unlike Wedowee, where critique
was contained on Sunday and stratification embodied Monday through Friday,
here critique saw light of day for Year 1 and then it turned inward, against self,

obvious in lowered grades, worsened mental health, and conservatized politics for white women, and women and men of color.

Indeed, when we conducted statistical analyses of incoming LSATs, grades, class rank, etc., we found another troubling shift over time. While politics started out distinct by gender, and grew more homogenous and conservative over time, on measures of academic performance there were initially no differences between incoming women and men. However, by Year 3, gendered gaps in performance were evident, enormous and stable. Even when we controlled statistically for incoming characteristics, the best predictor of class rank for Year 3 was race and gender.

As we wrote in our University of Pennsylvania law review (1994) essay, "Becoming Gentlemen,"

> We investigated academic performance to determine whether a gendered relationship exists, and, if so, whether differences in the accumulated grades and credentials earned by men and women up to the point that they leave law school are explained by differences in entry-level credentials. From these analyses, detailed below, we conclude that there is indeed a gendered academic experience. But the differences we identify are not predicted by those entry-level credentials on which the law school bases admission decisions. In fact, women and men begin Penn law school with equally stellar credentials. Holding incoming statistics constant, however, women graduate from the law school with significantly less distinguished professional credentials.

> Both men and women come to the law school with very impressive, and quite comparable, records based on undergraduate GPA and rank in class, LSAT, Lonsdorf Index, and undergraduate institution. On two of the admission criteria, the women actually present incrementally stronger records. The men, on average, achieve a 3.49 undergraduate GPA, whereas women attain a 3.52. Men, on average, enter with an undergraduate class rank of 78.44, and women with 80.13. On a scale from one to forty-eight, the men's mean LSAT is 40.98, and the women's is 40.87. Finally, the men's average Lonsdorf Index is 4.73; the average for the women is 4.74. None of these differences is significant at the .05 level.

> Tracking law school GPAs for men and women across years one, two, and three reveals a solid and stable gender difference in performance. Although men and women enter with virtually equal statistics, men receive, on average, significantly better grades by the end of year one. Further, they maintain this advantage through graduation. In terms of rank and GPA, first- and second-year men are 1.6

times more likely to be in the top fiftieth percentile of the class than are women. Third-year men are 1.5 times more likely to be in the top fiftieth percentile. 53.8% of the first-year male law students are in the top fiftieth percentile of their class, compared to 42.8% of the first-year women.

If we rely upon an even more stringent measure—the top 10% of the class—we find that in the first year men are almost three times more likely than women to reach the top 10%; in the second and third years, men are two times more likely to do so.

The data document that women and men enter the law school with comparable credentials. In a pattern established firmly in the first year and maintained thereafter, however, women receive relatively lower grades, achieve lower class ranks, and earn fewer honors.

Truth be told, not all white males thrived at this law school. But those students who did thrive were disproportionately white and male. First-year black female:

I don't know, maybe I'm just paranoid or something. I get the sense that maybe people won't listen to me as much as if I were a white person saying it. And then people, when they do listen to me, they say, Well of course she's going to say that, because she's thinking of her own self-interest. White people speak for the common good, and people of color speak for self-interest.

First-year Latino male:

One of the pressures, the initial pressures of being in a very social environment, like in law school, is feeling that what you contribute is not being weighed as much as everybody else's contribution because someone is attaching something else to what you're saying. It's very disconcerting for me, and it makes me kind of zone out of the whole process.

First-year black male:

Whenever a minority issue comes up I feel like I'm expected to say something. If I don't say something I'm shunning my race, and if I do say something nobody listens. So you're battling with both sides of the coin. And then if you come forth and you say something, people think they're complimenting you and they say, "Wow! That's really a...statement!" "That was really awesome!" "That was really intelligent!" [laughter] As if I was the first person to have ever spoken in the place. And they had no idea that I had an education. I find it very disturbing, and you have to deal with it and get along with the rest of the class.

By third year a black male confesses the impact of professional socialization on him:

I think I've changed, too, because I've grown more pessimistic about people's . . . and the kind of change that's possible. I think a lot of people here are just trying to make more money, and they care nothing about changing the world. And you feel silly if you think you're about changing the world.

An upbeat third-year black male said, "It's at law school that I started to realize how important it is to hold on to what you believe in, and how people can [really] do that, but we need a lot of help."

At Penn, like in Wedowee, institution-based racial and gendered sedimentation grew into "achievement/differences" over time. What began in Year 1 as an explicit race and gender difference in critical perspective grew silenced and converted into a covert story of gendered/racial success and failure. By Year 3, these differences just looked like "merit" and "deficiency," not gender or race. Thus, when researchers study school-based "success" and "failure" as though they were inherently individualistic or even group-level differences, we lose the history and reproduce the gaze on students, and particular groups of students. By so doing we *deinstitutionalize* these divergent paths toward success and failure, denying and obscuring the racial and gendered scaffolding of academic hierarchies.

By the end of their law school experience at Penn, many Year 3 students of color and white women felt and looked relatively inadequate (see Guinier et al. [1996] for detailed analysis of the data). With their critique whited out, and their progressive politics forced underground, their mental health faltered and their achievement torpedoed. Over time, it seemed as though race and gender were simply (naturally?) the best "predictors" of performance. It was considered heretic or heresy (if obvious) to conclude, as we did, that race and gender stratifications were products, not predictors, of institutional hierarchy, alienation, and stratification.

Liberal notions of access (without transformation) to historically exclusive institutions grow suspect under the scrutiny of these data. Institutional transformation is as necessary as it is feared. Without it, institutions (and equity advocates) may be inviting white women and men and women of color into institutions that are credentialing but also damaging, while these institutions remain unchanged. The damage may affect all, but in these cases African American and Latino, as well as white women, students pay the largest price.

At the law school, questions of leadership are far more complicated than in Wedowee. At Penn, the dean was indeed committed to notions of racial and gender equity, in access and outcomes. The faculty were for the most part supporters of a diverse student body. And yet when the institution received the data on differential outcomes by gender and race, resistance ran high. Some claimed the documented differentials were due to background variables not related to gender or race, for instance age or undergraduate major. We ran those statistical analyses and found these "alternative hypotheses" to have no empirical support. A few, among faculty and alumni, concluded that perhaps the institution does need to pay attention to the evidence on who succeeds and who doesn't, not to "correct" the problem, but to streamline admissions to better ensure success.

The administration at Penn was, throughout the process, supportive and forthright in their concern. Educational institutions more typically react with enormous resistance to analyses such as these, unwilling to hear the data or to reconstitute the institution to ensure equitable opportunities and outcomes. Herein lies the question of leadership. To what extent does a dean or a principal have a responsibility to seek out information on differential opportunities and outcomes, and transform institutional arrangements so as to maximize social justice in opportunity and outcome rather than presume that "access" alone solves the problem? I would contend—as you might guess—that a dean or principal who does not seek out such information, or one who ignores such information knowing that, for instance, African American males are disproportionately sitting in special education classrooms, or white children are disproportionately in advanced placement classes or in the top ranks of a cohort, is a leader who has chosen to reproduce social inequities. This choice cannot be tolerated for long.

## Conclusions

Psychologists and educators, in our research and institutional practices, have contributed mightily to the resurrection and reification of racial and gendered stratification. I want to suggest a shift by which academics move into the role Gramsci (1971) has called public intellectuals and activists; engaged in raising up a set of questions about racial, gendered, and class-based inequities that have not been raised; demanding transformations in institutional arrangements so that inequitable outcomes are not overpredicted.

Both of the scenes reported above raise important questions about the theories, methods, and ethics by which researchers study and produce what Omi and Winant (1989) call racial formation—the ultimate hierarchical relation of whiteness and other racial/ethnic groups. If we—that is, psychologists and educators—persist in our analyses and practices "as if" races, ethnicities, or genders were entirely distinct, separable, and independent rather than produced, coupled, and ranked, then we will likely continue to "discover" that some kids (or adults) "have it" (whatever *it* is) and others don't. Such analyses lead inevitably to exclusion, remediation, or even access to inhospitable institutions. But if, as this analysis maintains, institutional life is fundamentally constituted through racial, class, and gender sedimentation and exclusion, then "special programs" to "help" are beside point, if not reinforcing hierarchy. If schools refuse to dismantle the racial-, gender-, and class-based filters which limit opportunities for and indicators of intellectual progress, such analyses and interventions may ultimately boomerang and punish victims.

Scholars and practitioners engaged in critical work on schooling have important decisions to make. Well documented are the inequities in academic outcomes, and the disparate treatment of students by race (Banks & Banks, 1989; Delpit, 1993; Schofield, 1982), class (Fine, 1991; Weis, 1990), and gender (Biklin & Pollard, 1993). Well advocated (and/or resisted) are interventions "for" those historically at the short end of the proverbial stick. Well argued is access to historically hostile institutions for students long denied such promising opportunities. But in doing so, we have neglected the suspect structures which privilege some and disadvantage others. We have left institutions and their leaders off the hook.

If institutions are organized such that being white (or male, or elite, or all of the above) buys protection and if this protection requires the denial of opportunities for persons of color (and/or white women, poor, and working-class students) in policies/practices that appear "neutral," then liberal strategies for access are limited. By that I mean that those who have been historically excluded, now included, may disproportionately "fail" to perform "to standard." Some will drop out. A few will go nuts. A handful will survive, be separated, and labeled "the good ones." The institutional mantra of deficit and merit will inevitably tie to race (and gender and class) and will be hard to resist. Leaders will never be held accountable.

Today the cultural gaze of educational surveillance—whether it be a gaze of pity, blame, or liberal hope—falls, disproportionally, on poor students of color. Whether we consider the school in Wedowee or the students at Penn, social surveillance, as Foucault (1977) foretold, falls squarely on those who are marked. In this paper I have argued that social scientists and educational leaders have colluded in this myopia, legitimizing the fetish, turning away from the privileges that attach to white, refusing, therefore, to notice the institutional practices and leadership which ensure that privilege will be misread as meritocratic, while "others" are misread as deficient. With this paper I invite colleagues to consider not only the unfair disadvantages that attach institutionally, but the institutionalized pillows and profit that surround and grow embodied as white. I invite us all to ask—what are educational leaders doing about it? To what extent are data collected by race, ethnicity, gender, and class, and then tied back to structural opportunities available/denied? To what extent are leaders willing to boldly and publicly examine institutional policies and practices which historically privilege some and disadvantage others? We do not need schools to reproduce racial, ethnic, gender, and class inequities. Unfortunately, at the moment, the economy, the state, and sometimes families do that all too efficiently. We do need schools to resist and transform these inequities. Look around—how many educational leaders are willing to be so bold?

## Note

1. We need only note who among so many prominent adult males recently accused of violence against women have drawn and fixated our (whose "our" white woman) attention—and who appear too pudgy or dull or sleepy to watch. Need I note that we have not been obsessed with Senator Packwood's (non)hearings, the Joel Rifkin serial killings of prostitutes, esteemed Judge Sol Wachtel's masquerading as a cowboy and posing death threats to his former lover and her daughter anywhere near as passionately as "we" (there she goes again) have been obsessed by the O. J. hearings (which eventually wore off, but are still being telecast), Senator Mel Reynold's telephone sex, Colin Ferguson's masquerade as a lawyer, or Clarence Thomas. This is not an invitation to "not look" at men of color who have committed, or been accused of committing, horrendous acts of violence against women, it is simply to notice that when white men do the same our cultural instinct is to resist voyeurism. Elite white men at least enjoy the dignity of "privacy." Not quite as vulnerable to gossip, they are rejected culturally as the site for social surveillance.

# 4

# Making Sense of
# Race Relations in Organizations:
## *Theories for Practice*

*David A. Thomas and Karen L. Proudford*

Cultural diversity continues to pose significant challenges for contemporary U.S. organizations. Some of the most contentious issues faced relate to racial group differences. Although there is a long tradition of studying race relations in the social sciences, very little of this research addresses the dynamics of race relations within organizations. As a result, the predominant conceptual frameworks that guide research and intervention efforts involving cross-race exchanges give inadequate attention to the complex and changing realities of organizational life. For example, most theories of race relations frame individuals as composed of a single identity. An acknowledgment of the multiple identities that jointly make up an individual, however, is particularly important when examining work organizations. Although no one joins an organization aspiring to be a Hispanic, Asian, or white, racial group membership intersects with organizational categories in important ways that influence both how the individual views his or her experiences and how he or she is viewed by others. A second related facet of the complex reality of race in contemporary organizations is the presence of people of color at managerial and executive levels in predominantly white organizations. Theories of race relations that assume minorities occupy only positions lower in the hierarchy leave unattended a significant range of behavior. Adherence to a social justice model, for example, requires that whites be viewed as the "victimizers" and people of color, as the "victims." This premise makes it difficult to decipher racial conflict in an organization led by an interracial management team because there may be ways in which top managers are both victims and victimizers.

Prevailing models of human behavior in organizations emphasize individual rationality, self-maximizing behavior, and technical skill and exclude issues of identity. They therefore do not sufficiently explain the seemingly nonrational responses that occur in the presence of diverse employee populations. Instead, these models recast racial difficulties either as issues of overt discrimination or as

51

instances of irrationality, providing little guidance for organizational members who are attempting to find constructive ways of interacting with colleagues of different racial backgrounds.

Organizational research has largely focused on the effects of race on a variety of outcomes, such as pay (Duleep & Sanders, 1992; Roediger, 1991), promotion (Powell & Butterfield, 1997), and career opportunities (Greenhaus, Parasuraman, & Wormley, 1990). Organizational research, however, typically does not examine the interpersonal and group processes that produce these outcomes. For example, although there is evidence that the career opportunities of African Americans are limited in comparison with their white counterparts, little is known about the sequence of actions and reactions and decisions and responses that take place among whites, among African Americans, and between whites and African Americans that culminate in differential career outcomes. These patterns are often revealed in the stories people tell about race relations at work (Cose, 1993; Feagin & Sikes, 1994). Such accounts highlight the uncertainty, frustration, and inhibitions that surround cross-race interactions (Thomas, 1989). They can also provide insight into the ways in which racial diversity can enhance work relations (Thomas, 1993) and work outcomes (Thomas & Ely, 1996).

We believe that the primary arena for changing and improving race relations is the workplace. Given the persistent patterns of residential and social segregation, organizations represent one of the few remaining venues within which racially diverse Americans interact daily. Unless new approaches for analysis and intervention in these institutions are developed, efforts to improve race relations will continue to be impoverished. Moreover, these new conceptual frameworks must take into account the complex and paradoxical nature of race relations that allows progression, conflict, and regression to simultaneously exist.

Our purpose in this chapter is to put forth two complementary conceptual frameworks relevant to understanding and changing race relations in organizations. The first, embedded intergroup theory, posits a way of viewing the relationship between racial group identity and organizational group membership. Intergroup theory also prescribes a method for studying and intervening in race relations. To this we add concepts grounded in psychoanalytic theory. We have found these psychoanalytic concepts to be particularly useful in examining the tendency of racially different actors to create and maintain interaction patterns that reinforce rather than reshape problematic cross-race relationships.

Intergroup theory and the selected psychoanalytic concepts are useful for diagnosing and intervening in race relations because they are not predicated on a central hypothesis about the relationship between race and any particular dependent variable, such as promotions, attitudes, satisfaction, and network structure. Instead, they provide a mechanism through which applied behavioral scientists can explore and potentially alter the processes that produce these observed relationships. Used together for diagnosis and intervention in organizations, the two theories allow us to understand and respond to racial dynamics that emerge and persist in a specific organization setting.

We begin this chapter by outlining the embedded intergroup perspective on race relations in organizations; the concepts are based on the work of Alderfer and Smith (1982), Wells (1982), Alderfer (1977, 1986), Alderfer and Thomas (1988), and Thomas and Alderfer (1989). This theory has considerable utility as a frame for understanding race in an organizational setting. We then suggest that the affect associated with diversity is more fully understood when key psychoanalytic concepts are introduced. A psychoanalytically informed intergroup perspective on race, we conclude, is useful for untangling and making sense of the intricate, emotionally laden racial dynamics that permeate U.S. organizations. We do not argue that the two theories, as discussed here, constitute a new or overreaching framework for explaining race relations in organizations. Rather, these two bodies of knowledge inform one another and suggest a set of heuristics to guide the work of applied behavioral scientists in this area.

## An Embedded Intergroup Perspective on Race

### Examining the Intersection of Race and Structure

Intergroup theory calls attention to the importance of examining the intersection of two dimensions central to an understanding of racial dynamics in racially diverse workplace settings: race and structure. According to the theory, two types of groups exist in organizations, identity groups and organization groups (Alderfer, 1977, 1986). Members of identity groups share common biological characteristics, participate in equivalent historical experiences, and, as a result, tend to develop similar worldviews. The most commonly recognized identity groups are those based on race, ethnicity, family, gender, and age. Members of organization groups are assigned similar primary tasks, participate in comparable work experiences, and, as a result, tend to develop common organizational views. Most often, organizational groupings are based on task, function, and hierarchy. Although organization group membership can change as people enter and exit organizations, identity group membership remains constant or, as in the case of age, changes as the result of natural development rather than negotiation. Intergroup theory posits that individuals and organizations are continually attempting, consciously and unconsciously, to manage potential conflicts arising from the interface between identity and organization group memberships.

Intergroup theory also suggests that the manner in which conflict becomes manifest and focal for organizational members depends on the pattern of intergroup embeddedness in the organization. Applied to race relations, embeddedness refers to the extent to which power differences between racial groups at the suprasystem level (society) are mirrored in the relations between these groups at the system (organization) and subsystem levels (work group or dyad). Intergroup theory distinguishes between two types of embeddedness: (a) congruent embeddedness, when power differences (who holds power and who does not) between racial groups are the same across the subsystem, system, and suprasystem levels, and (b) incongruent embeddedness, when power differences between racial groups vary across these three levels. One may observe embeddedness from the perspective of individuals in relation to one another, of subgroups within groups, of whole groups in relation to one another, and of intergroup relations within organizations. Behavior that is considered nonrational when taking only structure into account may be understood when examining the interaction of the two dimensions. Behavioral outcomes for racially different actors may vary, then, even while they occupy the same structural position in the organizational hierarchy.

This was the case among middle managers at Praxis, a not-for-profit research and advocacy organization studied by D. A. Thomas.[1] Praxis' U.S. headquarters exemplified several of the changing patterns of racial group embeddedness in organizations. Its composition reflects an organization whose racial demography is less congruently embedded within the larger society than is that of most predominately white organizations. Its president is a white woman, and the second most senior executive is an African American male. The 12-person executive committee is 50% women and one third people of color. Women constitute 60% of the professional staff and people of color approximately 30%. Several people of color are responsible for some of the organization's largest and most visible projects.

Compositionally, Praxis breaks with the general pattern of congruent embeddedness that characterizes many organizations of its kind. This has not spared it, however, from experiencing race-related tensions and problems. A survey revealed that one of the major tensions in the organization related to access to and influence in decision making. Sixty-seven percent of people of color believed that they were not adequately represented in decision making. There were, however, significant differences across hierarchical lines within each of the racial groupings. People of color in senior management had views that diverged markedly from those of people of color in middle management and support staff roles. Comparatively, senior managers of color viewed people of color as having more power and access in decision making than did their middle management and support staff counterparts. Their views did not differ significantly from those of white senior managers. Among the people of color, middle managers held the most pessimistic views of people of color's decision-making power and influence. In addition, survey results revealed that only 10% of all respondents believed that they had been unfairly denied jobs or treated in negatively stereotyped ways because of their race, gender, nationality, religion, sexual orientation, or education level. People of color in the support staff, however, comprised more than 80% of those who believed they had experienced discrimination. These results underscore the importance of examining the intersection of race and hierarchical level to gain insight into differing perceptions of power and access at Praxis.

This emphasis also offers alternative interpretations of behavior. Viewing cross-race relationships solely in individual terms may lead researchers to presuppose identical behavior. The addition of system-level data, however, pushes researchers to consider the behavior as rational given the *context* of racial group embeddedness that the individuals perceive. Although people of color may behave differently from whites in an organizational unit, it is the relative position of whites and people of color to one another at the system level that actually has some predictive, although not deterministic, capacity regarding the likely behavior of individuals.

### The Impact of Race and Structure on Behavior

Cross-racial mentoring illustrates the multilevel effects of embeddedness on behavior. A mentor-protégé relationship involving an African American and white American can have one of two possible race combinations: white American mentor-African American protégé or African American mentor-White American protégé. Figure 4.1A illustrates the white American and African American mentor-protégé relationship embedded in an organization that mirrors the relationship between these groups in U.S. society, or the suprasystem, in which whites also predominate in high-status positions. Figure 4.1B illustrates the African American mentor-white American protégé combination embedded in the same system and suprasystem-level power arrangements. In the first instance, the racial group embeddedness of the pair is "congruent" across levels of the system. Just as whites predominate in positions of power in the organization, the senior party in the mentoring relationship is white. Research on mentoring reveals that protégés are aware of the hierarchical differentiation in the mentoring pair, feel obliged to accommodate the mentor, and find it difficult to assert themselves. In the second instance, the presence of an African American in the senior role deviates from the general pattern of racial group embeddedness observed across levels. Therefore, the state of embeddedness is incongruent (Alderfer & Smith, 1982). Note, however, that at the organizational or system level the racial groups are congruently embedded relative to the suprasystem. This is likely to influence the dynamics of the pair. Thomas (1993), for example, found that cross-race mentoring pairs in which the mentor is a minority were more likely to talk openly about race than were parties in relationships with white mentors.

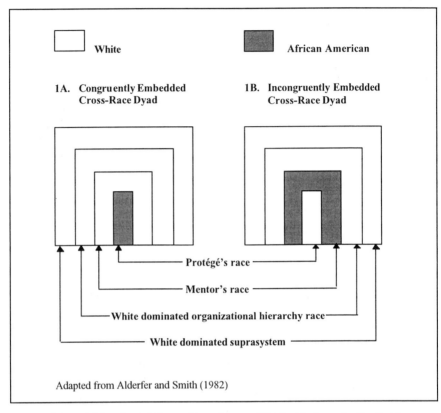

White          African American

1A. Congruently Embedded        1B. Incongruently Embedded
    Cross-Race Dyad                  Cross-Race Dyad

Protégé's race
Mentor's race
White dominated organizational hierarchy race
White dominated suprasystem

Adapted from Alderfer and Smith (1982)

**Figure 1A. and 1B.**   Racial Group Experience of Embeddedness by Parties to
Cross-Race Mentoring Dyads

Thomas (forthcoming) used an embedded intergroup perspective to examine the influence of the organization on the formation and development of cross-racial mentor-protégé relationships. He found that the presence of African Americans in the hierarchy of a department had a positive influence on the formation of cross-race relationships. Two reasons were cited. First, minority executives served as models to white peers, representing the potential of minorities to function at high levels. Observing African American managers in positions of authority diminished doubts held by whites about the competence of minorities and about the organization's willingness to accept people of color in particular jobs. Second, minority executives exerted influence on their subordinates' mentoring and hiring decisions. The whites who mentored minorities frequently reported to a minority or had at least one minority mentor or special peer in their network of relationships, suggesting that being embedded in a boss-subordinate relationship incongruent with the broader pattern shaped their choice of protégés.

The pattern of intergroup embeddedness also affects the intergroup dynamics at the system and subsystem levels (Alderfer & Smith, 1982). Organizations in which congruent embeddedness generally exists with regard to race are likely to manage the interface between racial identity group and organizational group memberships by operating from an implicit and undiscussable set of values, assumptions, and beliefs regarding race. These operating principles reflect both the more powerful group's interests and the prevailing racial perspective of the suprasystem. In the context of U.S. race relations, it is unlikely that assumptions of racial inferiority, particularly with regard to the expected performance of people of color, will be examined. An organizational culture then develops in which people of color exhibiting outstanding performance are viewed as aberrations. When an organization moves toward incongruent embeddedness in which a person of color is placed in a high-status, high-power position, this person's presence may arouse feelings of discomfort and anxiety. Wells and Jennings (1983) called this the "scandalous paradox"—the unsettling sense of curiosity whites experience when confronted with a person of color in a high-status position. Conversely, it is assumed that whites are fully qualified for and capable of performing in roles of power and authority. Powell (1969), in a study of white male executives' views on managerial succession, found that being African American or Hispanic was a hindrance to obtaining promotions because members of these groups were perceived as lacking the necessary values, social desirability, and intelligence to perform competently at the managerial level. Persons of German, Swedish, and British descent, by contrast, were highly promotable. It is likely that, few of the executives participating in the study had ever worked with a significant number of African American or Hispanic managers to accurately make such an assessment. Moreover, the managers may have overlooked or forgotten cases in which poorly qualified managers of European descent were nonetheless promoted.

Confronting values, beliefs, and assumptions such as these may prove so disturbing for organizational members that they become guarded and protective, even if doing so requires that they contradict and undermine their own interests. Consider the following case:

> An investment company asked researchers from a local university to conduct an action research project to improve the quality of work life for midlevel professionals. A particular focus of the work was to understand whether gender or race differentially impacted employees' experiences and perceptions of the organization as employee-friendly. During preliminary interviews, whites described the organization as highly political. Promotions, they said, were not based primarily on merit, which they defined as "delivering results." When the researchers later introduced data showing that people of color were the most disadvantaged in this organizational system, however, they rationalized the differential impact of race using a merit-based argument. A typical

response came from one white male who said, "the best people get the opportunities." He defined "best" as "those who deliver results by doing high-quality work." Many of his colleagues supported this merit-based view. The researchers asked the group to reconcile this view with those expressed in the preliminary interviews, which showed unambiguously that whites believed merit was *not* the primary criteria for advancement. At this point, many of the whites accused the researchers of tricking them. Some suggested they would have described the organization differently if they had known about the study's additional emphasis on race.

This account demonstrates how anxiety and emotion about inconsistencies that surface in racially diverse settings mobilized a response that contradicted earlier reports by the same individuals. Organizations often construct myths, such as the notion that promotions are based primarily on merit, as pretenses aimed at avoiding anxiety-provoking discourse or self-examination. Members, motivated by the need to protect their own material and psychological interests, then become accomplices—sometimes unwittingly—in perpetuating the myths. In this case, the response of whites to the data suppressed additional, potentially illuminating, conversations about the relationship among race, merit, and opportunities for advancement as well as other problematic aspects of the firm's practices.

Thus far, we have discussed an intergroup perspective on race relations in organizations, suggesting several key points about its use in understanding racial dynamics. The experience of race relations is one fraught with tension, anxiety, conflict, mistrust, and betrayal for which intergroup theory has no clear answer. That the presence of people of color in an organization is incongruent, or unusual, rarely accounts for the disturbing, seemingly irrational, and sometimes explosive behavior we observe in workplace settings. It is at this juncture that key concepts from psychoanalytic theory broaden the intergroup-based perspective such that knowledge about these intractable dynamics is deepened.

## Psychoanalytic Contributions to
## the Embedded Intergroup Perspective

### Origins of Race-Based Behavior

Psychoanalytic theory informs intergroup theory in ways that are significant for making sense of race relations in organizations. Organizational researchers have turned to psychoanalytic theory to aid in generating plausible explanations for behavioral patterns, including those related to race, which appear nonrational and for which extant organizational theory has no clear and consistent answer (Hirschhorn, 1988; Thomas, 1989). From its classical roots (A. Freud, 1946; S.

Freud, 1921) to the current emphasis on object-relations theory (Klein, 1959, 1975), psychoanalytic theory is influencing the way in which organizational researchers view human behavior in work settings.

Central to psychoanalytic theory is the notion that current behavior has its origin in the nature and character of the earliest relationships in an individual's life. Thus, the relationships between whites and African Americans in contemporary organizations can be expected to mirror early experiences between members of the two groups or cultural accounts of cross-race interactions during early socialization processes or both. Smith (1961), in describing the segregated South in the United States, shows how beliefs, attitudes, and expectations about the positions African Americans should occupy in relation to whites are learned at an early age:

> From the time little Southern children take their first step they learn their ritual, for Southern Tradition leads them through its intricate movements. And some, if their faces are dark, learn to bend, hat in hand; and others, if their faces are white, learn to hold their heads high. Some step off the sidewalk while other [sic] pass by in arrogance. Bending, shoving, genuflecting, ignoring, stepping off, demanding, giving in . . . . Children, moving through the labyrinth made by grownups' greed and guilt and fear.
>
> So we learned the dance that cripples the human spirit, step by step by step, we who were white and we who were colored, day by day, hour by hour, year by year until the movements were reflexes and made for the rest of our life without thinking. (p. 96)

Such memories are unarticulated and forgotten, giving the impression that current exchanges between whites and African Americans are untouched by history. Images grounded in the past, however, exert a powerful influence on present-day interactions. These symbolic representations emerge from stories evoked during the early socialization of whites and African Americans and live in U.S. culture as unresolved images of subjugation and oppression.

Thomas (1989) described the pattern of relational difficulties that besets African American-white cross-racial mentoring pairs. Chief among them is the inability to develop a deep level of personal attachment and identification. He attributes these difficulties to taboos about race and sex that have their origins in slavery, the sociohistorical root of African American-white institutional relationships in the United States. The psychodynamic underpinnings of this work give new insight into the nature of African American-white mentoring relationships in the workplace.

Goldstein, Heller, and Proudford (1995) examined race and gender relations in a large financial services corporation and discovered that metaphors articulated by organizational members closely mapped observed patterns of behavior between racial groups. African Americans in predominantly African American areas of the organization frequently referred to their departments as "plantations"—a picture that captures the dominance of a small group of whites in higher-level positions over many African Americans (see Denhardt [1987], for a discussion of slavery and organizational life). Goldstein et al. found that an associated set of cognitive and affective responses accompanied this metaphor. African Americans who believed they had limited prospects for upward mobility behaved as if they had little choice in organizational matters and were skeptical of the legitimate authority of the few African Americans in leadership roles. Goldstein et al. note that some African American women in the organization took on roles analogous to the "mammy" role on the plantation. Although some were managers, they were expected to and rewarded for providing comfort and support to whites. Some African American male supervisors were viewed as overseers in the organization; they described being responsible for ensuring the appropriate behavior of other African American males in the organization and were quite punitive toward African American males who did not behave according to convention. Young white males were frequently viewed as "sons" being groomed for leadership positions by African American and white women whom they passed on their way into the management ranks. White women were viewed as "wives" providing the image of a supportive, passive partner to white males (Kanter, 1977). These enduring images constructed boundaries that delimited the aspirations of both African Americans and whites. The costs of acting in ways that resisted familiar behavior patterns were so great that few could or would challenge them for fear of being ostracized. Articulating these common, although unsettling, images helped organizational members both become aware of the nature of cross-race interactions and begin to envision ways to alter them.

Thus, intergroup research, informed by a psychoanalytic frame of reference, considers the connection of data to past occurrences, however dim the recollection, and to current incidences. Although the intergroup researcher may be disinclined to gather data about an individual's early life, he or she may find it informative to collect data relating to the early experiences of the employee in the organization. Collecting such information from multiple individuals in an organization can provide access to the shared basic assumptions of organizational members that then aid in explaining the genesis of behavior patterns among employees.

### Anxiety as a Precursor to Racial Conflict

Psychoanalytically inclined research also focuses the organizational researcher's attention on anxiety. Although tension and conflict are acknowledged in the intergroup perspective, the psychoanalytic approach reminds intergroup researchers that survival is a constant, elemental concern for *individuals* in organizations. Events that are perceived as threats to an individual's organizational survival are likely to evoke responses more characteristic of those associated with a threat to one's life; they may indeed pose a threat to an individual's professional life. Racial identity, for many, is a part of one's core identity, and perceived or real threats to racial identity can be expected to arouse intense feeling and emotion. Thus, it is important for the researcher to regard feelings as data (Hirschhorn & Gilmore, 1992).

A key concept in psychoanalytic theory is the notion that individuals relate to the external world via projective identification (Klein, 1959, 1975). When individuals are unable to cope with the anxiety caused by complexity in their relationships, they are likely to engage in splitting, imbuing one entity with only positive attributes and another with only negative ones, even when targets of the projected attributes possess both (Klein, 1975; Wells, 1980). A common pattern in splitting is to retain the positive for one's self or own group and project the negative attributes onto the other or out-group. The other or out-group then becomes a repository for unwanted affect and aspects of the self (Jacques, 1955; Smith & Berg, 1987). Wells (1980) used this concept to explain the psychodynamics of ethnocentrism. Peck (1978) employed the concept of splitting in an examination of the My Lai massacre and its subsequent cover-up by officials in the U.S. Armed Forces. Recently, scholars have applied these concepts to analyze the dynamics in work organizations (Diamond, 1993; Hirschhorn, 1988, 1990; Kets de Vries & Miller, 1984; Smith, 1989; Smith & Berg, 1987). ·

Smith and Berg (1987) discuss the ways in which a group can avoid dealing with internal tensions by finding a repository or container for unwanted feelings. The container is viewed as having been the creator rather than the receiver of these tensions. They relate an interesting case involving race, the first of which involved a group of engineers working on a project:

> During the first few weeks, the black men remained relatively silent, doing their work and going along with the wishes of the white men. As the group got more deeply into its assigned task, there were numerous struggles as members sought to gain influence in the group, engendering anger and resentment that went unexpressed. At one point, one of the black members made an observation about how competitive everyone had become. He was immediately cut off and asked where he was coming from. He responded angrily with explicit aggressiveness that matched the implicit and angry aggression that had been directed at him. His action made public the angry feelings that had been alive in the group for some time but that had been suppressed and dealt with through intense interpersonal competitiveness among the white group members.
> Had the group as a whole understood then what was going on, they might have been angry at this black group member for stepping out of the framework of denial that they had been using for some time. Instead, one white male made the attribution that the black man had become angry not because of what was occurring in the group but because he

was black and had a chip on his shoulder about white people. In no time, the other black members joined in, arguing that this attribution was racist. The white members seemed unable to recognize this, and the blacks were put in the position of either "cooling" the event, backing down and remaining angry, thereby fueling the racist attributions of the white members, or taking on the task of attempting to reveal to the whites why their actions were seen as racist. The problem was that no matter which option the black members chose, the original difficulty that revolved around struggles for control and the attendant competitiveness would be obscured. (pp. 164–165)

Smith and Berg (1987) suggest that the African Americans acted as containers, in effect, holding the collective anger about the task on behalf of the group. It is also possible that the anger about the work was used by whites to obfuscate anger about working with African Americans. Both hypotheses are consistent with whites, in this case, making African American colleagues the container for less desirable attributes or projections while reserving positive projections for themselves. Smith and Berg suggest that there is a tendency for whites to store their unwanted feelings, doubts, and insecurities in African Americans. This makes it likely that African Americans will then be viewed by whites as unable to perform or work with others effectively, making some form of disciplinary action imminent.

Splitting can occur at multiple levels in an organization. Just as individuals may split off and project attributes onto one another, groups of employees can develop shared projections toward other groups. For example, employees may identify a unit, department, or division as "bad" and view others as "good." The "good places" become safe spaces in which to work on a daily basis. They provide a shield from the tensions and strains located in other settings in the organization. Splitting increases the scrutiny of the "bad places" such that they are seen as increasingly undesirable. At the same time, the positives of good places are amplified. Attempts to acknowledge the shortcomings of these desirable locations, or to identify their contribution to the problems of the bad places, are suppressed.

This dynamic was evident in the Praxis organization described earlier. People created for themselves "safe spaces" in which they were not affected by the tensions in the organization. The action research team, and later the liaison group, came to understand this phenomenon as central to the racially diverse work teams' abilities to manage contradictory experiences. Organization members, people of color and whites, were at a loss to reconcile the pleasure they took from working at Praxis with its failure to successfully handle troubled race relations and a widespread lack of trust in the executive committee. To manage this anxiety, members of work groups developed a shared pattern of splitting that operated at the work-unit level. They viewed the firm as bad and its leadership as the source of the problem. Their own work units, however, were viewed as good and their division leaders as exceptions to the generally disparaging views held of the executive group. For example, despite the negative aspects of race relations and feelings of mistrust in the organization, 51% of the whites and 61% of the people of color at the staff level believed that their departments were not racially polarized. Also, despite much criticism of the senior management, 39% of people of color[2] and 58% of whites did not include their division leader in their negative criticisms of senior management. Moreover, 78% of people of color and 89% of whites enjoyed working at Praxis. The organization as a whole was viewed as the source of the bad feelings, whereas positive experiences and affect were attributed to a particular department or some other subgroup. As a result, the whole organization was fragmented, making it difficult to resolve internal tensions and contradictions.

The joint dynamics of splitting and projective identification influenced racial conflict in a similar manner. Racial tensions were treated as though they resided exclusively within particular individuals or groups. The system as a whole was then absolved of responsibility and created scapegoats who were labeled "resident racists," "confrontational people," or "groups you can't satisfy." This *localization* occurred in three distinct ways. First, it was viewed as a conflict between African Americans and whites. This occurred despite evidence to the contrary. For example, 75% of Latinos believed that Latinos' expertise on Latin America was underused. They believed this produced tensions between white and Latino staff members working on Latin American projects. Moreover, people of color noted the need to engage with one another to create better cross-race and cross-cultural understanding. There were feelings among many that these groups competed for resources. Nevertheless, the predominant sentiment was that the primary, and for many the only, area of tension was between African Americans and whites. Localizing the conflict in this manner undermined race relations by overloading African Americans with the negative feelings and projections regarding race and by narrowly defining issues regarding racism in the organization.

Racial conflict was also localized at the middle-management level in Praxis. The greatest disparity in opinion about the state of race relations between people of color and whites existed at the middle-management level. The liaison group confirmed that members of these groups were most often in conflict. By contrast, the views of senior managers of color were closely aligned with those of white senior managers, as were the views of white support staff and support staff of color. Therefore, it was among middle managers that the racial conflict in the organization was most acute. This allowed others in the organization (senior managers and support staff) to disconnect from the conflict by disowning their own views. For example, when a white senior manager heard the researchers' finding that middle managers, both people of color and whites, felt the most tension regarding issues of race, he suggested that white middle managers had socialization experiences that made them more conservative than other whites. His supposition, however, was inconsistent with survey results indicating that white senior managers and white middle managers held virtually identical views. What made middle management the locus of racial tension was the disparity between the perceptions of white middle managers and middle managers of color; the latter group had the worst perception of racial tension of all surveyed groups.

Splitting and projective identification, what we term localization, is a dynamic that allows people to disassociate from the difficult and painful side of race relations until it confronts them in some unavoidable way, such as an overt and volatile conflict. When tensions are exacerbated, a *marker event*—an eruption that is precipitated by undercurrents of tensions, strains, and unresolved controversies—occurs. These critical incidents polarize members of the organization along a combination of racial and hierarchical lines and possess three common characteristics. First, they are usually punitive: often the minority person is disciplined for some action or failure of action. Second, as the organization polarizes around these events, each side views the other as behaving irrationally. Third, all sides feel victimized. At Praxis, for example, white managers frequently struggled when a person of color's performance was lacking. Whites avoided giving feedback until they were forced to act in an extraordinary (punitive) way. By contrast, people of color viewed a marker event as further evidence of their vulnerability in the organization. One African American male respondent said, "I thought my job here was pretty secure but when I saw what happened to [a minority female who was discharged], I thought, 'I could be next.' " These eruptions became symbolic of race relations at Praxis and were stored in the collective memory of Praxis employees.

**Collusive Dynamics and Stagnation**

Although much of the research focuses on individual-level dynamics, the psychoanalyst Wilfred Bion (1961) provided group-level explanations for the defenses that a group uses to cope with anxiety and to protect itself from real or imagined threats. He claimed that group members often act in concert to achieve unstated goals that allay collective anxiety. He called the pattern of behavior that emerges from the pursuit of this nonwork goal the *basic assumption group*. He contrasts it with the rational patterns of behavior designed to achieve the primary task, or legitimating work, of the group. Task groups have problems and tensions that, if driven underground and made undiscussable, give rise to "basic assumption group" dynamics that often undermine the group's ability to effectively engage in the primary task. Collusion results when group members collectively perpetuate one of the basic assumptions in a manner that may resemble our assertion under intergroup theory that organizational members act from an implicit set of unquestioned assumptions. Widespread participation by the group's members rigidifies the collusive dynamic, making the pattern resistant to change and decreasing the likelihood that group members will risk calling the problem into question.

Evidence of this form of intractable dynamic was striking at Praxis. The pattern originated from the fears of both whites and people of color. Whites feared that they would be confronted by a person of color, especially an African American. Sixty percent of whites were hesitant to criticize people of color because they "didn't want to be called racist." This had a detrimental effect on supervisor-supervisee relations because open communication about critical issues did not occur. Timely evaluative feedback was particularly important given that the majority of supervisory personnel were white middle and senior managers. These groups had the largest proportion of people who were uncomfortable critiquing the performance of people of color. People of color were also influenced by trepidation. They were wary of being labeled as confrontational if they raised issues of race in the organization. This fear was well-founded given that 75% of people of color and 69% of whites agreed that when people of color challenged whites they were labeled as confrontational. Nevertheless, when whites and people of color avoided dialogue about each other's behaviors, both parties were left with unexplored feelings and resentments. Each interaction of this type in the organization reinforced the silence and avoidance dynamic within the culture, ensuring that little meaningful change would occur.

Another form of collusion may emerge that blocks the ability of organizational members to perform effectively, as the following case illustrates:

José Citron (a pseudonym) was a young financial analyst at a large insurance company. He held a BA and a MBA from Harvard University. Immediately after graduate school, he entered the fast-track management development program at the insurance firm. José excelled in the classroom training portion of the program, graduating second in his class. Despite this promising start, his next 2 years at the firm proved very disappointing. His first request for a field training assignment to the highly regarded real estate investment group was denied. He protested, arguing that performance during the classroom training was cited as the basis for field assignments. Eventually, the organization acquiesced and José was transferred to the real estate area. There, he was given work usually performed by an analyst without graduate training. He responded by asking for more challenging tasks. Although there was some improvement, he noticed an increasing gap between the quality of assignments and level of responsibility given to him and that accorded his white peers. In addition, his managers and colleagues made comments that reflected stereotypes about Puerto Ricans and dark-skinned Hispanics. Many of them assumed he was from a poor barrio and were surprised to learn that he came from a middle-class, well-educated, fourth-generation American background.

While he did not internalize others' low expectations of him, he developed a posture toward work that complemented those prejudices. He reasoned that because his managers were incapable of recognizing and rewarding his performance fairly, he would no longer apply his full energies and talents to the job. He stopped petitioning for better work assignments and seldom gave what he described as "my best effort." In time, the quality of his work declined from outstanding to average. Although still acceptable, it supported the view of Hispanics as mediocre performers. Ironically, José was very amiable and appeared to get along well with everyone. After 2½ years on the job, however, José was deliberately underperforming and described himself as "marking time until a better opportunity came." José never mentioned his true feelings to anyone. Nor did he confront his bosses or peers about their comments and attitudes about race. Although he was angry, he took solace in knowing that he was not "busting his tail to do a great job," and his salary allowed him a comfortable lifestyle. The money and his level of personal investment seemed in balance.

In this case, José's response to what he viewed as racial discrimination ultimately justified the perceptions of those who resisted treating him as a high-potential employee. He assumed that race so constrained his opportunities that no white colleague at the insurance company could ever fairly assess his individual performance. He lost sight of his ability to excel, which was clearly demonstrated by his performance in the classroom training within the same firm. The point here, however, is not to argue whether or not he was justified in ceasing to put forth his best effort. Rather, we note that the combination of his choice to perform at a level below his ability and to remain silent colluded with the very forces of race that were already in the environment to undermine him.

## Conclusion

Our effort here has been to describe two theories we believe are crucial to making sense of complex racial dynamics in today's organizations. We suggested that key concepts from psychoanalytic theory inform the embedded intergroup perspective such that new insights are gained into race relations. Four implications follow from using these two theories conjunctively to frame action research. First, attention must be paid to the nature of racial group embeddedness and the interpretation of dynamics between levels of analysis. Second, applied behavioral scientists must determine how the tensions associated with race relations manifest themselves, are managed, and then promote or inhibit individuals from effectively assuming their task roles. Third, unproductive patterns of interaction must be viewed as purposeful, regardless of whether they seem logically and rationally self-interested. Their purpose may be connected to unconscious or overlooked routines designed to allay anxieties associated with race relations in the organization. Fourth, effective diagnosis illuminates not only the state of race relations but also the patterns of interaction and embeddedness that hold them in place.

We believe it is particularly important to uncover the microdynamics that produce disparities in outcomes and attitudes for members of different racial and hierarchical groups. Our emphasis on group-level dynamics is not intended to diminish the role of individual and institutional racism in society and organizations. The sociological data describing the relationship between race and life chances are clear in their account of its existence and continuing effects. The premise of our work is that members of both racial minority and majority groups adopt ways to cope with the anxieties that stem from their collective histories and the demands of daily interaction. These patterns of coping often inhibit progressive change. Although few would argue that integration is bad for organizations, it is clear that the transition has been and will continue to be anxiety provoking. The cases presented here suggest that diversity alone does not eliminate the tension or erase the history associated with race relations. Rather, integration may exacerbate dormant tensions, making fundamental organizational change unlikely.

Our discussion is an attempt at providing a frame for research and intervention consistent with the complex and paradoxical thinking required of those who must live in and lead contemporary organizations. Such alignment is required of applied behavioral science and will benefit organizations in the process of managing differences. The link between race, anxiety, and organizational change is a fruitful area of inquiry and one that the dual perspective called for in this chapter can inform. Intergroup theory, as discussed here, has an action-research focus. We believe that the illuminating data garnered about Praxis dynamics resulted in part from the use of a research team that reflected the composition of the organization (Alderfer & Smith, 1982; Alderfer & Tucker, 1985). A team well versed in both intergroup theory and psychoanalytic theory is equipped to unpack the tension and conflict that interlocking identity and organization group memberships and patterns of incongruent embeddedness produce in organizations. This is, from a practical standpoint, what many organizations have been attempting to do.

We presented examples of incongruent embeddedness that challenge the permeability of cherished group boundaries. When a person of color enters their organizational group, whites may ask themselves, "Am I still the same person now that you are here?" In the early phases of organizational integration, the organizational culture changes little. Relief sets in, and often it is assumed that racial differences are of little import. Once the level of integration reaches a critical mass and spreads across the hierarchy, however, the question reemerges with a new sense of urgency, in part, because whiteness is no longer the normative point of reference (Kovel, 1970). Incongruent embeddedness also raises questions for people of color, such as "How legitimate is my authority?" and "Can I bring my whole self to the enterprise or only that part that fits the expectations and prescriptions of the dominant culture?" Furthermore, as the numbers of people of color increase at all levels of the hierarchy, heterogeneity emerges among them. This creates the exciting and startling possibility of being liberated from the constraints of and losing the rewards associated with representing "the race." Such questions will continue to stimulate innovative organizational research and practice in the next century.

## Notes

1. David Thomas led a team composed of four external consultants, balanced by gender and race: two whites and two persons of color. This group worked with a Praxis liaison group composed of 12 persons representing all organizational levels and divisions and balanced with regard to race and gender. The diagnostic process followed the methodology prescribed by embedded intergroup analysis (Alderfer, 1986; Alderfer & Smith, 1982; Alderfer & Tucker, 1980). Open-ended interviews and observations were conducted in the first phase of data collection. On the basis of the information gathered in Phase 1, a survey was developed and administered. Seventy-five percent of Praxis' 149 headquarters staff members completed the survey.

2. Twenty-six percent of people of color caucus respondents were neutral on this question.

# 5

# School Contexts and Learning:
## Organizational Influences on
## the Achievement of Students of Color

## Linda Darling-Hammond

As a teacher, a researcher, and a parent, I spend a lot of time in schools. Throughout the years, I have had many occasions to look at schools with the following question in mind: "Is this a good school for *my* children?" I have learned that everyone has opinions about what makes a school good. I have also learned that what is a good school for one child may not be good for another. In particular, a school that may be "good" for most of its white students and for its most advantaged students may be damaging for many others, including African American children such as my own.

To this day, most schools in the United States do an extraordinarily poor job of educating students of color. Some, however, succeed in ways that put the lie to presumptions of racial inferiority such as those revived by Herrnstein and Murray (1994) in *The Bell Curve.* In this chapter, I discuss school policies, presumptions, and pedagogies that make a difference for children and describe what schools do when they are good for all children. I treat three major features of schools, from those that operate on a system level to those that operate within classrooms:

1. The array of educational policies that shape students' opportunities to learn

2. The structures and presumptions of schools that shape students' experiences and sense of themselves as learners and human beings

3. The more intimate interactions that occur between teachers and students in classrooms—interactions that either empower or undermine children's development and either grant or deny them the right to learn

## The Right to Learn and Access to Knowledge

In the darkening days of the early McCarthy era, W. E. B. DuBois (1949/1970) wrote these words:

> Of all the civil rights for which the world has struggled and fought for 5,000 years, the right to learn is undoubtedly the most fundamental.... The freedom to learn . . . has been bought by bitter sacrifice. And whatever we may think of the curtailment of other civil rights, we should fight to the last ditch to keep open the right to learn, the right to have examined in our schools not only what we believe, but what we do not believe; not only what our leaders say, but what the leaders of other groups and nations, and the leaders of other centuries have said. We must insist upon this to give our children the fairness of a start which will equip them with such an array of facts and such an attitude toward truth that they can have a real chance to judge what the world is and what its greater minds have thought it might be. (pp. 230–231)

DuBois knew that America's capacity to survive as a democracy relies not only on the provision of public education but also on the kind of education that arms people with an intelligence capable of free and independent thought and one that helps people to build common ground across diverse experiences and ideas. As Maxine Greene (1982) notes, if we are to create a public space for democracy, schools must consciously create community from the sharing of multiple perspectives and develop "the kinds of conditions in which people can be themselves" (1984, p. 4). This is an education that seeks competence as well as community and that enables all people to find and act on who they are, what their passions, gifts, and talents may be, what they care about, and how they want to make a contribution to each other and the world.

Providing most Americans with such an education has always been a struggle, and it remains one today. From the time southern states made it a crime to teach an enslaved person to read, through decades of separate and unequal schooling that continue to the present, the right to learn in ways that develop both competence and community has been a myth rather than a reality for many Americans. The struggle was articulated in the great debates between DuBois and Booker T. Washington about whether black children must be trained as laborers or might be educated in ways that could allow them to think for a living (DuBois, 1930/1970); it was also enacted in the ideological battles that shaped urban schools for the children of immigrants at the turn of the century (Tyack, 1974).

Factory model schools with highly developed tracking systems that stressed rote learning and unwavering compliance for the children of the poor were counterposed against small elite schools—and carefully insulated special tracks within comprehensive schools—that offered a stimulating curriculum, personalized attention, high-quality teaching, and a wealth of intellectual resources for an advantaged few. Some of these have been democratic schools that have worked to create what James Banks (1993) calls an "equity pedagogy," seeking to construct a thinking curriculum for diverse students who learn to live and work together. Most "good" schools (or "good" programs within schools), however, have secured their advantages by excluding—by economics, neighborhood, achievement scores, or racial codes—those who represent the other half (or more) of children.

This unhappy resolution remains in force today. International assessments reveal that America's schools are among the most unequal in the industrialized world in terms of spending, curriculum offerings, and teaching quality (Educational Testing Service, 1989, 1991; McKnight et al., 1987) and are only slightly less disparate today than when Arthur Wise wrote *Rich Schools, Poor Schools* (1972). Differential spending ratios of more than 10 to 1 appear most vividly in the quality of teaching children experience (Educational Testing Service, 1991). These disparities create differences among students' educational opportunities as a function of race and socioeconomic status as well as geography. As Taylor and Piche (1991) noted in a report to Congress;

> Inequitable systems of school finance inflict disproportionate harm on minority and economically disadvantaged students. On an *inter*-state basis, such students are concentrated in states, primarily in the South, that have the lowest capacities to finance public education. On an *intra*-state basis, many of the states with the widest disparities in educational expenditures are large industrial states. In these states, many minorities and economically disadvantaged students are located in property-poor urban districts which fare the worst in educational expenditures. In addition, in several states economically disadvantaged students, white and black, are concentrated in rural districts which suffer from fiscal inequity. (pp. xi–xii)

Minority students are still largely segregated in American schools: More than two thirds attend schools that are predominantly minority (Orfield, Monfort, & Aaron, 1989). In these schools, on every conceivable measure children of color have less access to high-quality curriculum offerings; qualified teachers; computers, libraries, and laboratories; small, personalized classes; clean and safe facilities; and environments that support a humane and caring educational experience (Darling-Hammond, 1995).

The fact that the U.S. school system is structured such that students routinely receive dramatically unequal learning opportunities based on their race and social status is simply not widely acknowledged. Despite widespread stark disparities in school funding and radically different levels of educational quality available to students, the prevailing view is that if students do not achieve it is both their fault and their sole burden to bear.

The costs of this inequality are increasingly high for our society as a whole and for the individual young people placed at risk by their schools. For those who cannot find a productive place in an increasingly competitive economy, who cannot find a way to connect to and become a part of the community in which they live, personal tragedy translates into social tragedy. Growing rates of crime, incarceration, structural unemployment, homelessness, drug use, and social dysfunction increasingly victimize those trapped in a growing underclass and all those who pay—financially and socially—for its costs to the broader society. In many and increasing ways, unequal access to education threatens the foundation of democracy.

There is a long legacy to overcome. In 1857, a group of African American leaders testified before a New York state investigating committee that the New York board of education spent $16 per white child for sites and school buildings, whereas the comparable figure per black child was 1¢ (Tyack, 1974). This kind of inequality continued with segregation and unequal funding of schools in nearly all the South and much of the North, with white schools generally allocated 5 to 10 times as much money as black schools and with higher-education institutions almost entirely closed to nonwhites until the 1960s. An analysis in New York State found that on every tangible measure—from qualified teachers to fiscal resources—schools serving greater numbers of students of color are significantly poorer than schools serving mostly white students (Berne, 1995).

Not only do funding systems allocate fewer resources to poor urban districts than to their suburban neighbors but schools with high concentrations of low-income and "minority" students also receive fewer instructional resources than other schools within these districts. In addition, tracking systems exacerbate these inequalities by segregating many low-income and minority students within schools, allocating still fewer educational opportunities to them at the classroom level, with fewer and lower-quality materials, less qualified and experienced teachers, and less access to high-quality curriculum (Darling-Hammond, 1995).

Jonathan Kozol's *Savage Inequalities* (1991) describes the striking differences between public schools serving students of color in urban settings and their suburban counterparts, which typically spend twice as much per student for populations with many fewer special needs. *Savage Inequalities* is replete with familiar but poignant stories: for example, MacKenzie High School in Detroit where word-processing courses are taught without word processors because the school cannot afford them and East St. Louis Senior High School, whose biology lab has no laboratory tables or usable dissecting kits. Meanwhile, children in neighboring suburban schools enjoy features such as a 27-acre campus, an athletic program featuring golf, fencing, ice hockey, and lacrosse, and a computer hookup to Dow Jones to study stock transactions.

The students notice. One New York City 16-year-old notes of his school, in which holes in ceilings expose rusty pipes and water pours in on rainy days, in comparison with others (Kozol, 1991),

> You can understand things better when you go among the wealthy. You look around you at their school, although it's impolite to do that, and you take a deep breath at the sight of all those beautiful surroundings. Then you come back home and see that these are things you do not have. You think of the difference. (p. 104)

His classmate adds:

> People on the outside may think that we don't know what it is like for other students, but we *visit* other schools and we have eyes and we have brains. You cannot hide the differences. You see it and compare. (p. 104)

The message is clearly conveyed: Some children are worth less in the eyes of society than others. The intricacies of school funding formulas and state-level politics do not take away the sting or lessen the effects. The disparities in physical facilities are just the tip of the iceberg. Inadequate funds make it difficult for urban and poor rural schools to compete in the marketplace for qualified teachers or to offer the kinds of mathematics, science, and foreign language courses needed to go to college. It all adds up.

Much has been made in recent years of the relatively low performance of U.S. students on international assessments, especially in mathematics and science. Still more striking is the finding from the Second International Mathematics Study that, for U.S. students, the spread of achievement—and of measured opportunities to learn—was many times greater than that of other industrialized countries and was comparable only to the level of disparity found in developing nations that do not provide universal access to education (McKnight et al., 1987).

A growing body of research illustrates that the vast differences in curriculum opportunities across U.S. schools are the single greatest source of differences in outcomes among students. Studies during the past decade have repeatedly found that students from different groups who take similar courses and have access to equally rich curriculum and equally well-qualified teachers perform similarly (Jones, 1984; Jones, Burton, & Davenport, 1984; Moore & Smith, 1985; Oakes, 1985).

This kind of equal access is, however, rare. As Robert Dreeben (1987) found in a comparative study of first graders across seven Chicago schools, with the same kind and quality of teaching, African American and white students had comparable reading achievement. The quality of instruction received by African American students, however, was on average much lower than that received by white students, thus creating a racial gap in achievement over time even for those who started out ahead of their white counterparts in other schools.

Another study examined African American high school youth who were randomly placed in public housing in the Chicago suburbs rather than in the city.

Compared to their comparable city-placed peers, who were of equivalent income and initial academic attainment, the students who were enabled to attend largely white and better funded suburban schools had better educational outcomes across many dimensions: They were substantially more likely to have the opportunity to take challenging courses, receive additional academic help, graduate on time, attend college, and secure good jobs (Kaufman & Rosenbaum, 1992).

These examples are drawn from carefully controlled studies that confirm what many other studies have suggested: Much of the difference in school achievement found between students of color and white students is due to the effects of substantially different school opportunities and, in particular, greatly disparate access to high-quality teachers and teaching (Barr & Dreeben, 1983; College Entrance Examination Board, 1985; Darling-Hammond, 1990; Dreeben & Barr, 1987; Dreeben & Gamoran, 1986; Oakes, 1990).

Perhaps the most important differences in what happens to children at school depend on their teachers: what they understand about children and about learning, what they are able to do to respond to the very different approaches and experiences children bring with them to the learning setting, and what they care about and are committed to as teachers. An "equity pedagogy"—one that makes knowledge accessible to all students—requires teachers who are able to connect the diverse experiences of their students to challenging curriculum goals and who can marry a deep understanding of students and their learning to a wide array of strategies for bringing knowledge and critical discourse to life.

Recent studies confirm that teacher expertise is one of the most important predictors of student achievement, and that children of color have the least access to highly qualified teachers (Darling-Hammond, 1992, 1997). One large-scale study found that, controlling for socioeconomic factors, large differences in the expertise of teachers available to students in Texas explained virtually all the difference in black and white students' achievement scores (Ferguson, 1991). Another found that for schools of similar demographic populations in New York City, differences in teacher qualifications accounted for 90% of the variance in students' mathematics and reading scores (Armour-Thomas, Clay, Domanico, Bruno, & Allen, 1989).

Because of short-sighted licensing and hiring policies, unequal resources, and lack of attention to teacher recruitment, however, at least 50,000 teachers annually are hired without adequate preparation for their jobs primarily to teach disadvantaged students in cities and poor rural schools (National Commission on Teaching and America's Future, 1996). In high-minority schools, students have less than a 50% chance of being taught by a mathematics teacher who has a license and a degree in the field (Oakes, 1990). Many students are taught throughout their entire school careers by a parade of inexperienced, underprepared, and unsupported novices, many of whom stay less than a year in the classroom, alternating with substitutes who also come and go. For students in the most impacted schools, there is little continuity and almost no expertise brought to bear on their learning, year after year after year.

Studies consistently find that, with little knowledge of learning or child development to guide them, teachers who lack preparation are less effective with students. They are more reliant on rote methods of learning; more autocratic in the ways in which they manage their classrooms; less skilled at managing complex forms of instruction aimed at deeper levels of understanding; less capable of identifying children's learning styles and needs and less likely to see it as their job to do so, blaming students when their teaching is not successful (Darling-Hammond, 1992).

A lack of skills can also exacerbate racism. Teachers who enter teaching without adequate preparation often begin to resent and stereotype students whom they do not understand, especially when these teachers' lack of skills render them less successful. One student who was just completing her year of preservice teacher training told me about the advice she received from two young teachers who had previously been hired at a school in Washington Heights through Teach for America, a program that sends college graduates into urban and rural classrooms after only 3 weeks of training. They told her, "The first thing you need to understand is that you have to yell at these students. It's the only thing they understand." Another recruit from the same program described how she found herself experiencing the tendency to blame her students before she left teaching to enter a teacher preparation program:

> I found myself having problems with cross-cultural teaching issues— blaming my kids because the class was crazy and out of control, blaming the parents as though they didn't care about their kids. It was frustrating to me to get caught up in that . . . . Even after only three-fourths of a semester in my teacher education program at Berkeley I have learned so much that would have helped me then.

Even decent people who want to do good work can be sabotaged by their lack of knowledge and skill. Also, when underprepared teachers are routinely assigned to the most vulnerable students, these students are doubly disadvantaged by their teachers' lack of technical competence and by the negative attitudes this underpreparation can breed toward students. For all these reasons, and others described later, poor and minority children continue to encounter significantly less supportive, engaging, and effective learning experiences than their more advantaged peers (Darling-Hammond, 1995; Dreeben, 1987; Oakes, 1985).

## How Schools Structure Inequality

Within schools, inequality is structured in a variety of subtle and not so subtle ways. Like manufacturing industries, modern schools were designed at the turn of the last century as highly specialized organizations—divided into grade levels and subject matter departments, separate tracks, programs, and auxiliary services—each managed separately and run by carefully specified procedures engineered to yield standard products.

The school structure created to implement this conception of teaching and learning is explicitly impersonal. Students move along a conveyer belt from one teacher to the next, grade to grade, and class period to class period, to be stamped with a lesson before they pass on to the next. They have little opportunity to become well-known during a sustained period of time by any adults who can consider them as whole people or as developing intellects. Secondary school teachers may see 150 students or more each day, precluded by this structure from coming to know any individual student well. Teachers work in isolation from one another with little time to work with others or share their knowledge. Students, too, work alone and passively, listening to lectures and memorizing facts and algorithms at separate desks in independent seatwork. Rarely will teachers have the opportunity to work with any group of students for longer than a daily 45-minute period or for more than a year of their school careers. This is an important difference from many European and Asian schools in which teachers stay with their students for more than 1 year, and teaching them multiple subjects as well as serving as counselors (Darling-Hammond, 1997). These strategies help them to know their students well enough to teach them effectively.

This kind of connection between students and their teachers is most markedly absent in the large urban schools most students of color attend. These schools are run like huge warehouses, housing 2,000 or more students in an organization focused substantially on the control of behavior rather than the development of community. With a locker as their only stable point of contact, young people cycle through a series of seven to nine overloaded teachers and get "personal advice" from a counselor struggling to serve the needs of several hundred students. In this setting, students struggling to find connections have little with which to connect. Heavily stratified within, and substantially dehumanized throughout, most students are likely to experience such high schools as noncaring, even adversarial environments where "getting over" becomes important when "getting known" is impossible.

Students perceive that the system is structured for not caring. A New York City dropout from a large, comprehensive high school described his experience as follows (as quoted in Carrajat, in press):

> At one time school was important to me. I liked getting good grades and making my parents proud of me. (But in high school) I never felt part of the school. It didn't make no difference if I was there or not. The teachers just threw me aside, probably because I was Spanish. I felt like I was being ignored, like I wasn't important.

Another dropout offered the following sophisticated analysis of the problem (as quoted in Carrajat, in press):

> I had passing grades when I decided to drop out, but nobody tried to stop me. Nobody cared . . . . None of the counselors paid any attention to me. The only time I ever saw the principal was when I got sent to him, which I never stayed around for. The individual classes were too big for students to learn. Students should have longer exposure to individual teachers. If students could have the same subject teachers throughout their high school careers, this would allow teachers to get to know students better. . . . No high school should have more than 400 students max and all on one floor. Who needs seven floors in a school?

A California high school student stated more succinctly, "This place hurts my spirit" (as quoted in Poplin & Weeres, 1992, p. 11). An administrator in the same school voiced the poignant dilemma of caring educators caught in the squeeze between mandates and children: "Yes, my spirit is hurt, too, when I have to do things I don't believe in" (p. 23). In a study in which teachers and students shared their views of schooling, the dilemma emerged in full force. Poplin and Weeres (1992) note,

> Teachers perceive themselves to be very caring people who went into teaching to give something to youth. Teachers were initially shocked at the degree to which students felt adults inside schools did not care for them. Teachers struggled as they read student comments, trying to articulate how their attention had been focused away from students. Teachers felt they were pressured to cover the curriculum, meet bureaucratic demands, and asked to do too many activities unrelated to the students in their classrooms. There is little time in the day to actually relate with students. Teachers and others felt the size of their classes and numbers of students they saw each day, particularly in middle and high schools, made it difficult to care. (pp. 21–22)

When teachers have little opportunity to come to know their students well, and students have little opportunity to relate to any adult in the school on an extended, personal level, it should not be surprising that large secondary schools of the kind that predominate in central cities create virtual chasms of the cracks into which students can fall.

Schools communicate to students their "place" in society and their relationship to learning and achievement. One way they do this is through tracking—the allocation of different course-taking opportunities to different students. Research has found that schools serving African American, Latino, and Native American students are "bottom heavy"—that is, they offer few academic programs and more vocational education programs that tend to train specifically for low-status occupations (College Entrance Examination Board, 1985; Oakes, 1983; Pelavin & Kane, 1990). In racially mixed schools, the tracks are color-coded. Honors or advanced courses are reserved primarily for white students, whereas the lower tracks are disproportionately filled with students of color (Oakes, 1992). Here, too, differentials in teacher qualifications are part of the story. Evidence suggests that teachers are also tracked, with those judged to be the most competent and experienced and those with the highest status assigned to the top tracks (Davis, 1986; Finley, 1984; Oakes, 1985; Talbert, 1990). Students in the lowest tracks are most likely to be assigned teachers who are underprepared, unlicensed, inexperienced, and out of field (National Commission on Teaching and America's Future, 1996).

Efforts to make a rich curriculum available to all children can be stymied by uneven teacher capacities. In one desegregated, "magnet" elementary school, for example, I noted that the primary-grade classrooms were distinctly identifiable by race. Although the school was predominantly minority, classes for "gifted and talented" students were largely white. The mathematics classes were most distinct. In two classrooms teaching a highly conceptual curriculum, the Comprehensive System of Mathematics Program (CSMP), there were no students of color. In the remaining classrooms, a memorization-based, rote-oriented curriculum emphasizing lower-order skills was being taught. It was clear even in first grade which students were being prepared for algebra, trigonometry, and calculus.

I learned from the principal that the CSMP curriculum was reserved for "highly gifted" students. When I told her it had been developed with inner-city students in St. Louis and should be available to them all, she emphatically agreed. She later secured resources so that the curriculum could be offered to all students the next year. And it was. However, three years later, when I returned to the school, the old tracking system had been reinstated. When I asked what happened, the principal replied that most of the teachers found the more conceptual curriculum too difficult; they lacked the mathematics and teaching skills needed to use it well. Therefore, tracking for students was revived, primarily as a means for dealing with unequal capacities of teachers.

Although test scores and prior educational opportunities are one basis for students' differential placements in tracks, race and socioeconomic status play a distinct role. Adam Gamoran's (1992) research found that race and socioeconomic status determined assignments to high school honors courses even after test scores were controlled. This occurred because of prior placements of students in upper tracks in earlier grades, in part due to counselors' views that they should advise students in ways that they believe are "realistic" about students' futures and in part because of the greater effectiveness of parent interventions in tracking decisions for higher socioeconomic status students. Race and socioeconomic status also affect students' placements in vocational and academic programs and more or less challenging courses within them (Oakes, 1992; Useem, 1990). At every level of the system, educational resources are differentially allocated and further rationed, and at every level of the system, students of color and low-income students are least likely to secure the benefits of high-quality education.

Tracking also reduces the extent to which students have the opportunity to develop a broad social understanding from actually participating in a democratic community and gaining access to multiple perspectives. In *Democracy and Education*, John Dewey (1966) noted that "a democracy is more than a form of government; it is primarily a mode of associated living" (p. 87). He stressed the importance of creating circumstances in which people share an increasing number of interests and participate in an increasing number of associations with other groups. He noted,

> In order to have a large number of values in common, all the members of the group must have an equitable opportunity to receive and to take from others. There must be a large variety of shared undertakings and experiences. Otherwise, the influences which educate some into masters educate others into slaves. And the experience of each party loses in meaning, when the free interchange of varying modes of life experiences is arrested. (p. 84)

In this respect, too, the factory-model school undermines democracy. It does so by enforcing a single, official knowledge, by segregating groups of students by track and social class, and by encouraging disengagement, silence, and separation where intense communication, inquiry, and connections are needed. Both student tracking and teacher isolation undermine inclusive forms of community building and shared discourse. These practices heighten divisions among groups and prevent most young people (and teachers) from becoming active social participants in the life of their school.

Students placed in lower tracks are exposed to a limited, rote-oriented curriculum and ultimately achieve less than students of similar aptitude who are placed in academic programs or untracked classes (Gamoran, 1990; Gamoran & Mare, 1989; Oakes, 1985, 1990). Teacher interaction with students in lower-track classes is less motivating and less supportive as well as less demanding of higher-order reasoning and responses (Good & Brophy, 1987). These interactions are also less academically oriented and more likely to focus on behavioral criticisms, especially for minority students (Eckstrom & Villegas, 1991; Oakes, 1985).

## Interactions, Expectations, and Identity

Jacqueline Irvine's (1990) review of 36 studies of teacher expectations found that most studies conclude that teachers hold more negative attitudes about black children's personality traits, ability, language, behavior, and potential than they do about white children, and that most black students have fewer favorable interactions with their teachers than do white students. Other studies have found that children of color are more likely to be punished for offenses that white students commit without consequence, and that black students, particularly males, are more likely to be suspended from school than are whites (Carter & Goodwin, 1994; Fine, 1991; Nieto, 1992).

Perhaps most disturbing are the results when students fail to conform to school expectations. In one study (Rubovitz & Maehr, 1973), 66 white student teachers each worked with two white students and two black students. One student of each race was identified to the teachers as gifted. The study found that the "gifted" black students, especially boys, received less attention, praise, and encouragement and more criticism than any of the other students.

Young people are very observant. They note these patterns, and they understand when they have been identified as not deserving or requiring a rigorous and humane education. It is little wonder that in settings such as these, African American students often create an identity that is oppositional to school—one in which, as Signithia Fordham (1988) found, achieving means "acting white" or disidentifying from one's racial group.

The not uncommon response that being black, Latino, or Native American means rejecting the norms and mores of school is a sign of what Joel Spring (1997) calls resistance to deculturalization. Schools deculturalize in many ways, including (a) segregation and isolation of minority students; (b) forced change of language; (c) a curriculum whose content and textbooks reflect the culture of the dominant group; (d) a setting in which dominated groups are not allowed to express their culture, customs, or religion; and, (e) the use of teachers exclusively from the dominant group. Acceding to these forces produces the psychological phenomenon Fordham (1988) identified as racelessness. She notes that black students "enter school having to unlearn or, at least, to modify their own culturally sanctioned interactional and behavioral styles and adopt those styles rewarded in the school context if they wish to achieve academic success" (p. 55).

As Robert Carter and Lin Goodwin (1994) noted in their seminal work on racial identity and education, the racial identity development of educators undoubtedly influences how they perceive and treat visible racial and ethnic group children. To be empathic and effective with all their students, educators need to also develop a sense of themselves as racial and cultural beings and to also develop a sense of their students' experiences. This requires a conscious effort to understand and embrace diverse perspectives. Lisa Delpit (1995) reminds us that "we all interpret behaviors, information, and situations through our own cultural lenses; these lenses operate involuntarily, below the level of conscious awareness, making it seem that our own view is simply 'the way it is' (p. 151). Educators must develop a keen awareness of the perspectives they bring and how these can be enlarged if they are to avoid what Edmund Gordon (1990) calls "communicentric bias—the tendency to make one's own community the center of the universe and the conceptual frame that constrains thought" (p. 19). This bias limits understanding of those whom we teach and thus renders our exchanges less educative. The ability to appreciate perspectives is an important aspect of both cognitive and social functioning; it is one of Piaget's indicators of higher stages of cognitive development and a goal of socially responsive education.

Finding what we have in common requires that we communicate from the vantage points of our separate, but increasingly related, interests. Each of us has to find a way to express and locate our own experiences within our education to be validated as learners and human beings and to connect with new knowledge and with the experiences of others. We also need a way to find and understand the experiences of others so that we can communicate with them in an educative manner. Thus, all of us need a multicultural education to be citizens together.

Far from encouraging separatism, acknowledgment of diverse experiences help's create new associations. A communication that is, in Dewey's (1966) words, "vitally social or vitally shared" is one that allows one person at least partially to experience the perspectives of another and by this connection to develop understanding and appreciation for that person's experience and understanding of the world. Crossing boundaries is essential to social learning. This is true for learning across disciplines and methodologies, for learning across communities and cultures, for learning across ideas and ideologies, and for learning across the many groups of individuals—parents, teachers, staff, and students—who comprise a school. Educative institutions actively strive to construct and manage diversity rather than trying to suppress it.

## Culturally Responsive Pedagogy

A growing body of recent research suggests that effective teachers of students of color form and maintain connections with their students within their social contexts. Such teachers do not shy away from issues of race and culture; with students of varying language backgrounds, they allow the use of multiple languages; they are familiar with students' dialects even though they instruct in standard English; and they celebrate their students as individuals and as members of specific cultures (Cochran-Smith, 1995; Garcia, 1993; Irvine, 1992; Murrell, 1991; Nieto & Rolon, 1996; Strickland, 1995), asking students to share who they are and what they know with the class in a variety of ways.

Successful teachers of students of color exhibit a culturally responsive pedagogy. Connections to community are one important variable. Studies of exemplary African American, Latino, and Native American teachers consistently illustrate how they use their knowledge of community and culture to advance student learning. Michelle Foster's (1993) studies of exemplary African American teachers found that these teachers express feelings of connection, affiliation, and solidarity with the pupils they teach. Like the successful teachers, both black and white, of African American students studied by Gloria Ladson-Billings (1994), they link classroom content to students' experiences, focus on the whole child, and believe that all their students can succeed. They see themselves as part of the community and view teaching as giving back to the community.

Irvine (1992), Ladson-Billings (1992), and Eugene Garcia (1993) have all summarized research finding that effective teachers of students of color, who include white teachers and members of minority groups, are passionate about content and use an active, direct approach to teaching: demonstrating, modeling, explaining, writing, giving feedback, reviewing, and emphasizing higher-order skills while avoiding excessive reliance on rote learning, drill and practice, or punishment. They see the teacher-student relationship as fluid, humanely equitable, and characterized by a sense of community and team. Their classrooms feature cooperative learning strategies, participation, and acceptance, and they deemphasize competition. They also often seek to incorporate familiar cultural and communication patterns, such as call-and-response, in their teaching.

The literature contains many examples of such culturally responsive practices that make a difference for student achievement. For example, Katherine Au (1980) documented how the use of familiar cultural communication patterns that resemble the Hawaiian "talk story" are a key feature of a school program that has successfully raised reading achievement levels of Native Hawaiian students. Sonia Nieto (1992) describes how Hispanic teachers create a sense of intimacy and trust with students in ways that resemble the students' family interactions and support greater student learning. Chinn and Wong (1992) describe how Asian American communities often perceive schooling as a very formal process in which parents expect teachers to practice with authority. Awareness of these expectations provides a basis for building communication and eventual trust.

Teachers do not have to be members of the same racial or ethnic community as their students to learn to teach them well. The fundamental idea of the common school was to create a public space within which diverse people could communicate and forge a joint experience that would allow them to build a broader community. The early university was designed to bring people together from throughout the world who could build knowledge by sharing different cultural experiences and areas of study. There is no doubt that this is uncomfortable and problematic: It is easier to talk with those who think as we do, who have had common experiences, and who agree with us. This is one appeal of homogeneous neighborhoods, private schools, and tracking systems. It is essential to try to expand our associations and experiences beyond the boundaries that initially define them, however, if we are to create new and larger common ground. Democratic schools seek out diversity in people, perspectives, and ideas and construct educative means to learn from these multifaceted experiences and expertise.

## Building Democratic Schools

An increasing body of research illustrates that children of color, and other children, are succeeding in many new small schools featuring communitarian structures that foster more cooperative modes of learning, less departmentalization and tracking, a more common curriculum for students, stronger relationships between teachers and students that extend over multiple years, greater use of team teaching, and participation of parents, teachers, and students in making decisions about schooling (Braddock & McPartland, 1993; Darling-Hammond, 1997; Fine, 1994; Lee, Bryk, & Smith, 1993; Wehlage, Rutter, Smith, Lesko, & Fernandez, 1989). This participation appears to be most productive when schools create many opportunities for developing shared knowledge among teachers, administrators, parents, and community members, and when they create joint work in which this knowledge can be used and deepened.

In our work at the National Center for Restructuring Education, Schools, and Teaching at Teachers College, Columbia University, we are studying how these features are sustained in city schools that produce dramatically unexpected outcomes for low-income and minority students and for others typically labeled "at risk." Many of these schools are affiliated with the Coalition of Essential Schools. (Case studies of these schools are included in Darling-Hammond, Ancess, and Falk [1995] and Darling-Hammond et al. [1993]). If these students, most of whom are African American and Latino, attended the comprehensive high schools in their neighborhoods, more than half would drop out and very few would go to college. Instead, in the high schools we are studying, more than 90% of students graduate and continue on to postsecondary education, and the vast majority of them succeed at college.

Following an untracked common core curriculum, students are challenged to meet high standards embodied in graduation requirements requiring research papers, scientific experiments, mathematical models, essays and literary critiques, and oral defenses of their work—the kind of work these same students in most schools would be presumed unable to attempt much less master.

We have tried to understand what enables them to meet these standards and what enables their teachers to help them do so; in other words, how their schools support powerful teaching and learning. Rather than asking, "What are the correlates of marginally greater success within the parameters of traditional schools?" we are asking, "What entirely different parameters for schooling appear to enable far greater numbers of students of all kinds to succeed in ways that are not found within traditional schools?"

We have identified the following factors that seem to be important:

1. *Structures for caring* that enable teachers to know students well and to work with them intensely: In addition to the personalization made possible by smaller school size, all these schools cluster students and teachers together in ways that allow teachers to work for longer periods of time over the day, week, and years with a smaller number of the same students. These structures range from interdisciplinary clusters to multiyear advisories, but they all allow teachers to know more about how their

students think and learn, to come to know them as people, and to come to know their families, to undertake more ambitious chunks of curriculum work, and to have the time to develop difficult performances that require intense work and sustained effort. These structures are especially important for more challenging and indeterminate forms of learning that ask students to construct knowledge rather than simply feeding it to them. Our analysis suggests that to manage the risks of teaching for understanding, teachers need school structures that provide them with more extended time with individual students, enabling deeper knowledge of students' learning and stronger relationships that can leverage motivation and commitment.

2. *Shared exhibitions of student work* that make it clear what the school values and how students are doing: Symbolically, the walls of these schools are literally plastered with student work. Student writing, designs, models, and artwork cover hallways, classrooms, and offices . This sends out the message that students "own" the school; the school's major purpose is to support and celebrate students and their work. Teachers work collectively to create assessments, set standards, and to document and evaluate student learning within and across classrooms. This serves to decentralize information about student learning and about teaching in other classrooms. As teachers look at the work of their own students, they learn what is working as they had hoped and what is not. As they look at the work of other teachers' students, they have a window into the curriculum and teaching strategies used in other classrooms. When some teachers succeed with students, this creates norms for other teachers to learn to do so.

3. *A multicultural curriculum* that connects school work to students' experiences both culturally and personally: The curriculum enables students to find themselves in their education and thus to develop new skills and abilities and handle new curricular material with a sense of grounding in what they already know. The projects in the portfolios that students prepare for graduation include the following titles: "What Is Education?" (clearly a personal connection for a student); "The Internship Blues" (based on a student's internship experience in a local community organization); "Education in South Africa and Cuba"; an essay on "*Down These Mean Streets*"; "Slavery: The Struggles and Hardships of Black Women"; and, "African American Intraracial Prejudice." Treatises on Shakespeare and Mozart and scientific studies are also included. Furthermore, students' work is evaluated on the extent to which it demonstrates that they can appreciate a range of viewpoints, an ability to see connections among different ideas and points of view, and an ability to seek out and evaluate evidence on all sides of a question. As students develop their own voice, they also develop an appreciation for other perspectives.

4. *Structures that support teacher collaboration* focused on student learning: The higher levels of skill and expertise required by teachers to do this work must be continually developed. A very strong organizational feature of many of these schools is that faculty work in two kinds of teams: one that focuses on curriculum planning within subject areas and another that focuses on a shared group of students and their needs. In houses, teams, or divisions, groups of teachers assume common responsibility for a number of students, work with them across multiple subjects and counseling them during a period of several years. These structures allow teachers to become more accountable for student success. They also motivate teachers by increasing their expectancies of success: As team structures increase teachers' reach over students' lives and their control over the total learning process, they reduce/uncertainty and thus increase teacher willingness to invest even more effort (Darling-Hammond, 1996). The schools have also constructed shared curriculum and assessment work that cuts across teams. This work includes/collective assessments of student learning and analyses of student progress that require teachers to focus together on academic issues that affect the entire school. All these strategies help to develop knowledge about students and about subjects, and they help to develop shared standards of practice and incentives for ongoing change.

5. *Structures for shared decision making* and discourse about teaching and learning among teachers, students, and parents: Teachers are engaged in hiring their colleagues, developing evaluation systems, conducting peer reviews, making curriculum decisions, setting standards for assessing student and teacher work, and deciding on professional development. Students and parents are frequently included in these activities. Each school has articulated its own set of educational ideals that is a touchstone for organizational decisions. This provides coherence and a basis for shared action. Because the schools are deliberately small, governance engages teachers, parents, and students; this enables the collective decision making that provides a sense of empowerment and enables access for more voices. These in turn create a greater sense of shared purpose, commitment, and effort and allow education to function as democracy. The legitimization of each voice, each perspective, and each view is a central feature of student success and is essential for our entire society.

As James Baldwin (1963) noted in the essay "A Talk to Teachers,"

> The purpose of education, finally, is to create in a person the ability to look at the world for himself, to make his own decisions, to say to himself this is black or this is white, to decide for himself whether there is a God in heaven or not. To ask questions of the universe, and then to live with those questions, is the way he achieves his own identity. But

no society is really anxious to have that kind of person around. What society really, ideally, wants is a citizenry which will simply obey the rules of society. If a society succeeds in this, that society is about to perish. (pp. 678–679)

To create an empowering education for all of our children, it will be essential for us to confront the legacy of discrimination and inequality that is woven into the warp and woof of our institutions, including schools. Schools can make a difference if they create a public space for diversity and develop strategies for consciously building on the strengths of each child in a context that explicitly honors democratic values.

# PART II

# Organizational and Institutional Settings

# 6

# Families in Their Cultural and Multisystemic Contexts

*Nancy Boyd-Franklin*

In American society, as in many others throughout the world, the most basic organizational unit is the family because it serves as the primary link to all institutions in the society. It might seem odd to have a chapter about families in a book about culture and organizations. The family, however, is a key organizing unit for the transmission of culture and for the interactions with other organizations that one encounters throughout his or her life.

In the past 40 to 50 years, there have been dramatic changes in the organizational structure of families in the United States (Goldenberg & Goldenberg, 1994). This has been in response to many cultural, social, and political influences, including the immigration of families from disparate cultures to the United States; the high rates (50%; Peck & Manocherian, 1988) of family dissolution through divorce and separation; the increasing number of single-parent families; the significant growth of family reformation through remarriage (McGoldrick & Carter, 1988); and recognition of alternative family formations, such as gay and lesbian couples and families (Laird & Green, 1996).

Before specific family structures can be discussed, three key concepts must be explored: (a) families as organizational systems; (b) families in their cultural, racial, and socioeconomic contexts; and, (c) families within their multisystemic framework.

## Families as Organizational Systems

Families as organizational systems is not a new concept, only the specific terminology is recent. Minuchin (1974), in his model of "structural family therapy" described different family organizational structures and explored strategies for "restructuring" or reorganizing the family to maximize effective family functioning. He described family structure as a "set of functional demands that organizes the ways in which family members interact" (p. 51). This organizational structure is defined by a series of rules that determine who participates in family functions and how (i.e., decision making, disciplinary measures, etc.). These rules are called "boundaries." Minuchin's analysis of family structures was strongly analogous to the corporate workplace. For example, he discussed the family as a hierarchy and defined the parental unit as the "executive system" of the family.

Aponte (1980, 1994) elaborated on Minuchin's (1974) structural family model by including areas such as boundary alignment and power. The attention to power dynamics is also reminiscent of the organizational psychology literature (Alderfer, 1994).

Although this chapter will address the complexity and diversity of families as organizational systems and offer an overview of the important trends in family structural systems in recent years, it is not intended to be an extensive discussion of these issues or an exhaustive review of the literature on each topic.

## Families Within Their Cultural, Ethnic, and Racial Contexts

Cultural influences or ethnicity or both are in many ways the "heart and soul" of a person's life (Cujllar & Glazer, 1996). In keeping with the precedent established by many authors (Cujllar & Glazer, 1996; Linton, 1945; McGoldrick, Giordano, & Pearce, 1996), the terms *ethnicity* and *culture* will be used interchangeably in this chapter to describe a "sense of commonality transmitted over generations by the family and reinforced by the surrounding community" (McGoldrick, et al., 1982, p. 4). McGoldrick et al. explain that ethnicity

> involves conscious and unconscious processes that fulfill a deep psychological need for identity and historical continuity (Giordano & Giordano, 1977). Ethnicity patterns our thinking, feeling, and behavior in both obvious and subtle ways. It plays a major role in determining what we eat, how we work, how we relax, how we celebrate holidays and rituals, and how we feel about life, death, and illness. (p. 4)

Carter (1995) defines race as "a concept that refers to a *presumed* classification of all human groups on the basis of visible physical traits or phenotype and behavioral differences" (p. 15). Pinderhughes (1989) elaborates on this concept, emphasizing the difference between race and ethnicity:

> [R]ace constitutes a different level of cultural meaning than ethnicity. Originally carrying a meaning that referred to biological origin and physical appearance, the concept of race was always more inclusive, embracing a number of ethnic groups within a given racial category. Over time, race has acquired a social meaning in which these biological differences, via the mechanism of stereotyping, have become markers for status assignment within this social system. (p. 71)

The introduction of the concept of race increases the complexity of these variables. The history of slavery and the legacy of segregation, discrimination, and prejudice have created a very charged atmosphere regarding race in the United States. Racism is a forceful presence in the lives of African Americans and other persons of color. It influences the way in which members of this group view themselves and the perception and behavior of others toward them (Boyd-Franklin, 1989; Carter, 1995; West, 1993).

## Families Within Their Multisystemic Framework

Broadly, each family is influenced by the norms and values of the country in which it resides. In the United States, the societal ideal is expressed as conformity with "mainstream" or "family" values. Each family is also influenced by its own cultural, racial, or religious group and the mores, values, and expectations of that group. In addition, families must be viewed within the context of their particular multisystemic system. Examples of multisystemic levels include individual, family, extended family, neighborhood, community, faith membership (i.e., church, synagogue, or mosque), schools and educational institutions, workplace, and government bureaucracies that impact their lives, such as the social welfare (i.e., public assistance and child protective services) and criminal justice (i.e., police, courts, probation, and prisons) systems.

The multisystems model has a strong legacy as a conceptual approach and as a sound intervention strategy. Proponents of this approach include Bronfenbrenner (1979), who conceptualized these issues within a social ecology model, and Aponte (1994), Minuchin (1974), and Minuchin, Montalvo, Guerney, Rosman, & Schumer, 1967), whose structural and ecostructural models provided intervention strategies for working with poor urban families. Henggeler and Borduin (1990) provided a viable family therapy treatment intervention program. Empirical research and outcome studies have substantiated the validity of this approach in working with families, particularly poor urban families, coping with multiple complex psychosocial problems, such as juvenile delinquency (Henggeler, Melton, & Smith, 1992), adolescent aggression (Henggeler et al., 1992), and substance use and abuse in a juvenile offender population (Henggeler et al., 1992).

Many authors have stressed the need for development of interventions addressed specifically to African American families and communities (Akbar, 1974, 1981, 1985; Boyd-Franklin, 1989; Nobles, 1985, 1986). Boyd-Franklin (1989) provided an application of multisystems theory to the treatment of African American families. This "Afrocentric" approach focuses on the strengths of families, including cohesive extended family bonds, spirituality and religious orientation, and educational orientation.

Some individuals and families, because of their ethnicity, minority status, race, religion, sexual orientation or gender or both, are vulnerable to bias within society expressed through racism, sexism, anti-Semitism, homophobia, and so on.

Persons with special challenges or disabilities may also experience discrimination in society.

The multisystems model expands on the structural family therapy approach of Minuchin (1974) incorporating many of its basic techniques and interventions. It goes beyond the structural approach, however, by providing a way to conceptualize the family within the context of its societal, cultural, and socioeconomic reality. It is an important framework in viewing all families. As practitioners become more involved with poor families, however, it becomes essential to include a multisystems framework because these families are often less able to protect the boundaries of their family from intrusion by the many outside systems and agencies mentioned previously. It would therefore be a grave error to include only the family members in an analysis of their presenting issues and problems.

Socioeconomic factors play a major role in the number and intrusiveness of multisystems interventions in the life of a family. Families of wealth and privilege are often insulated from the power that government agencies and institutions exert on poor families. Poor families are far more likely to be intruded on and to feel their privacy violated by schools, courts, police, child welfare departments, housing authorities, hospitals, and so on. A very striking illustration of this phenomenon is suspected physical or sexual abuse. Poor families are more liable to be reported to child protective services than are middle- and upper-class families because those who suspect that abuse has occurred (e.g., teachers and administrative staff in schools, social workers, doctors, nurses, and neighbors) are fearful of lawsuits, a device infrequently resorted to and largely unavailable to the poor.

## Different Family Organizational Structures

### Two-Parent, Nuclear Families

Two-parent, nuclear families have received the most attention in the family literature despite the changing family dynamics and organizational patterns within the past four decades. Some authors have suggested the need for a "paradigm shift" (Harway & Wexler, 1996) away from this outdated stereotype to include the wide range of organizational structures that currently exist.

The traditional nuclear family has not been immune to significant changes in recent years. For example, Harway and Wexler (1996) point out that the typical nuclear family of the 1950s included a mother who was primarily a homemaker, a father who went to work, 2.5 children, and traditional gender role distinctions. The impact of the women's movement, combined with economic necessity, has led to an increasing number of women in the workforce (Mirkin, 1994) and the commonality of dual-earner households. These households face new challenges in role overload, the "super parent syndrome" (Mickin, 1994), and the need for custodial support of children such as day care.

The family life cycle model proposed by McGoldrick and Carter in their classic 1980 book, *The Changing Family Life Cycle*, described the following life cycle stages: (a) unattached young adult, (b) the joining of families through marriage, (c) families with young children, (d) families with adolescents, (e) launching children and moving on, and (f) the family in later life. In their second edition published in 1989, they widened their concept of family from the child-centered, two-parent nuclear family in response to the diverse family organizational structures that had become more widespread in the United States, such as the single-parent family.

**Single-Parent Family**

Seibt (1996) and Sporakowski (1988) showed that the number of single-parent families with one or more children has been increasing significantly since the 1970s. In fact, the number of single-parent families almost tripled (3.8 million to 9.7 million) between 1970 and 1990 (Seibt, 1996; U.S. Bureau of the Census, 1991). This increase is related to many factors, including the increased number of out-of-wedlock births and the high rate of divorce and separation (Norton & Glick, 1986; Seibt, 1996). In addition, adoption of children by single individuals has become more prevalent (Miller, 1992).

The demographic and gender experiences of these different types of single-parent families can vary considerably. For example, a poor, inner-city teenager may have one or more children outside of marriage and support her family with a low-paying, often minimum-wage job, by public assistance, or through a combination of both a low-wage job and public support (e.g., food stamps and subsidized housing). Separated or divorced or both single-parent families can vary in terms of gender (i.e., mothers or fathers) and in terms of socioeconomic level. Both men and women risk significant financial hardship, although single-parent mothers frequently experience greater financial instability (Seibt, 1996; Taeuber, 1991). The pressures of inadequate child care (Hofferth & Phillips, 1987; Turner & Smith, 1983) and role overload result in attempts to become "Supermom" (Burden, 1986; Quinn & Allen, 1989) or 'Superdad" (Grief, 1988). Single working parents share the universal burden of trying to balance family obligations with the need to spend time with their children (Risman, 1986). An important challenge for the adults in many of these families is the task of countering isolation and loneliness and the need for adult companionship (Seibt, 1996).

**Extended Family**

There are many forms of extended families. Boyd-Franklin (1989) described a variety of extended families within African American culture that may include a single parent, children, grandparent(s), and other blood relatives and "nonblood" kin who are close friends of the family living in the same household or in different households. In Italian and Hispanic families, often there are complex and involved interactions of extended family members between different households (McGoldrick et al., 1982). Similarly, many immigrant families (e.g., Latino, West Indian, and Asian Indian) have large extended family households in which newly arrived family members may live until they secure a job and a home of their own (McGoldrick et al., 1982). Many extended families, particularly from non-Western cultures, are extremely interdependent and rely on the family for support and help (e.g., African American, Latino, and most Asian cultures). Also, child rearing is often shared (Boyd-Franklin, 1989; Harway, 1996; McGoldrick et al., 1982).

## The Separated or Divorced Family

One of the most dramatic changes in the past 30 years has been the large increase in divorce, with almost 50% of couples divorcing (Peck & Manocherian, 1988). This trend, accelerated by the institution of "no-fault divorce" in which neither party has to establish cause or blame (Miller, 1992; Seibt, 1996), has created a "divorce climate" (P. Guerin, personal communication, 1980) in which divorce is sought much more quickly by today's couples than it was by those of the 1960s. Many authors view divorce as a transitional phase for families that is ultimately resolved by the establishment of a one-parent household or a remarriage (Ahrons & Rodgers, 1987).

Research on the impact of divorce on children has increased in recent years (Blau, 1994; Francke, 1983; Goetting, 1983; Kalter, 1990; Skolnick & Skolnick, 1983; Wallerstein & Kelly, 1980; Walsh, 1993). The literature has documented many emotional reactions in children of divorce, including reunification, feelings of responsibility for the divorce, divided loyalties, lack of power and helplessness, abandonment, hurt and sadness, confusion and frustration, anger, and embarrassment and relief (Ahrons & Rodgers, 1987; Blau, 1994; Peck & Manocherian, 1988; Seibt, 1996; Wallerstein & Kelly, 1980). Although studies show variable findings on the impact of divorce on children, many stress the diversity of children's responses, the fact that divorce is not a one-time event, the importance of the parents' response and its effect on the child, and the fact that initial adjustments are often not easy. Hetherington, Law, and O'Connor (1993) pointed out that "many children show some problems in the first 2 years following their parents' divorce. . . . 20% of children are showing extreme levels of behavior problems beyond the crisis period" (pp. 222–223).

Authors have indicated that children experience the impact of divorce differently at different life stages (Peck & Manocherian, 1988; Wallerstein & Kelly, 1980). Therapeutic literature has focused on helping to lessen the emotional trauma of divorce for parents and children (Blau, 1994; Peck & Manocherian, 1988; Seibt, 1996). Most authors agree that children fare much better in families in which the adults are able to cooperate in their role as coparents.

## Remarriage and Stepfamilies

The increasing divorce rate has resulted in a concurrent increase in remarriage rates for men (70%) and women (65%) (Glick & Lin, 1986). Remarriage is not a new phenomenon and has always been a factor in the United States. It is only in the past century that remarriage has occured not primarily as a result of the death of one parent (Cherlin, 1983) but because of divorce. Glick (1991), in a national survey of families, found that 33% were living in a "step" family. Glick and Lin (1986) predicted that stepfamilies will be the most common form of family by the Year 2000.

Visher and Visher (1979, 1988, 1993) emphasized that stepfamilies face many challenges related to factors such as societal expectations and unrealistic myths, ranging from the "wicked stepmother of Cinderella" to "instant love." Many researchers have also explored stage theories in the evolution of stepfamilies (Papernow, 1993; Seibt, 1996) that range from an initial stage of high hopes and expectations to a middle stage of confrontation and to a later stage of varying degrees of unification. All these authors stress, however, that "each family is unique," and this progression rarely occurs in a "neat and orderly fashion" (Seibt, 1996, p. 57).

Many authors have discussed ways to support and help these families (McGoldrick & Carter, 1988; Seibt, 1996; Visher & Visher, 1988, 1993). Rutter (1994) cited recent research (Hetherington et al., 1993) that states that "80% of children of divorce and remarriage do *not* have behavior problems, despite the expectations and challenges" (p. 33). Seibt (1996) builds on this point and emphasizes the need for flexibility and compromise.

## Gay and Lesbian Couples and Families

Defining families as limited to those with children has been challenged by many authors (Laird & Green, 1996; Skolnick & Skolnick, 1983). Laird (1993) and Walsh (1993) used the term *family* to include same-sex couples without children and gay and lesbian single parents and same-sex couples with children (p. 282). All the authors who have explored gay and lesbian couple and family relationships caution against stereotyping and emphasize the diversity of these family units (Carlson, 1996; Laird & Green, 1996). Carlson (1996) proposes a triangular model in assessing gay and lesbian families with children: (a) family genesis or how the family originated (i.e., heterosexual divorce, artificial insemination, or adoption); (b) the stage in which the family is in regarding the gay/lesbian life cycle; and (c) each member of the couple's homosexual identity formation (DeCecco, 1984) and each member's stage in the "coming out process."

For gay and lesbian couples, issues related to each member's coming out process and degree of identification with the gay and lesbian community influence the development of the couple's relationship. Some gay and lesbian couples have had the support of their families of origin; others have had to develop supportive "families of choice" following emotional cutoffs (Bowen, 1978) from their biological family members.

Gay and lesbian families with children face unique challenges in all the family life cycle stages discussed previously. First, having a child is not a simple process—it may involve custody issues, artificial insemination, or adoption—and may in itself become a stressor in gay or lesbian family life. Second, as Carlson (1996) has shown, "the dominant culture generally assumes that parents are heterosexual" (p. 66), which may create difficulties when gay and lesbian parents interact with their child's world in school and leisure activities (e.g., play dates, scouts, sports, dance classes, and camps). Third, the adolescent period in which teenagers typically distance themselves from their parents may be especially hard for gays and lesbians, who may experience this as rejection due to their sexual minority orientation.

Carlson (1996) emphasizes that bias and discrimination (Adelman, 1977) and internalized homophobia exist in the lives of all gay and lesbian individuals, couples, and families. Laird (1993) noted,

> Today, in spite of the fact that many researchers believe gays "come out" to a much more tolerant society, it is clear that they continue to face social approbation isolation and public humiliation. Their relationships lack legal sanction, and they are not afforded many social protections heterosexual people take for granted. Their families face threats of dissolution through child removal, their families of origin may disown them, and some are subjected to violence. (p. 287)

Many authors have also stressed the importance of developing a supportive community, particularly in cases in which a cutoff has occurred from the family of origin (Carlson, 1996; De Vine, 1984; Laird & Green, 1996; Warren, 1974), to promote positive adjustment, family bonding, and emotional health.

## Couples Who Are Childless by Choice

The family literature contains a bias toward parenthood and the value of having children (Skolnick & Skolnick, 1983; Veevers, 1983). There is little written on couples who are childless by choice. Even the term "childless" evokes a value judgment that these couples are somehow "less" for choosing not to have children.

Veevers (1983) identified two paths or "careers" by which couples "come to define themselves as voluntarily childless" (p. 539):

One route to childlessness involves the formation by the couple, before they are even married, of a definite and explicitly stated intention never to become involved in parental roles; a second and more common route is less obvious, and involves the prolonged postponement of childbearing until such time as it was no longer considered desirable at all. (p. 540)

Many of these couples feel "stigmatized by their unpopular decision to avoid having children" (Veevers, 1983, p. 541). Veevers (1983) reported that childless couples receive pressure from their families and friends and sanctions from society regarding having children. Women particularly have suffered from societal stereotypes and have been characterized as "abnormal, selfish, immoral, irresponsible, immature, unhappy, unfulfilled, and nonfeminine" if they do not have children (Veevers, 1983, p. 541). Unfortunately, this view persists today.

Adoption is often considered by couples who have unsuccessfully tried to have children. For some couples, however, adoption sometimes remains a symbolic rather than a viable alternative (Veevers, 1983). The prospect of adopting at some indefinite time in the future allows the couple to avoid feeling that they have made an "irreversible decision" (p. 543).

Bradt (1988) attributes childlessness in couples to a broad variety of sociopolitical factors:

Changes in educational and job opportunities for women, the increased necessity of women being in the workforce, and the use of birth control and legalized abortion are contemporary factors influencing the decision as to whether to have a child. The divorce statistics, affirming the uncertainty of a lasting marriage and our nation's low priority on working parents and on children, add to the conflict about having children. (p. 241)

Many couples believe that their lives are complete without children and prefer to devote their time to their careers and activities they can pursue as a couple. Bradt (1988) offers the following perspective on the trend of childlessness for some middle- to upper-middle-class couples: The quest for "self-actualization, self-potential, self-fulfillment has been a counterforce along with the great worldwide economic uncertainty against having children" (p. 241).

It is also worth noting that trends to postpone motherhood in view of educational and career opportunities may result in more couples facing an unintended childless future because fertility decreases with a woman's age. Many couples who experience infertility go to great lengths and expense in attempting to have children (e.g., fertility drugs, *in vitro* fertilization, and surrogate motherhood). If these methods are unavailing, many couples desiring children find adoption to be their only alternative.

## Adoptive Families

Adoptive families, like other families, are heterogeneous. Many complex variables distinguish such families from each other and from biological families (Anderson, Piantanida, & Anderson, 1993; Schwartz, 1996). The first distinction is related to demographics. The "traditional" adoptive parents are "typically infertile white couples who want to adopt a healthy same-race newborn" (Kadushin & Martin, 1988, p. 542). The second group are single individuals (usually women, although there are an increasing number of men) (Anderson, et al., 1993; Feigelman & Silverman, 1977) who may be single by choice (Anderson, et al., 1993) or single women who had hoped to be married before becoming mothers but are facing the tolling of the "biological clock" without having found a mate. Third, increasingly, gay and lesbian individuals and couples are choosing to adopt children (Carlson, 1996; Laird, 1993; Laird & Green, 1996).

The second distinction concerns the adopted children. Prior to the 1960s, the typical child available for adoption was white, healthy, and an infant. This is no longer the case: "Changing norms regarding female sexuality and the concomitant acceptance of birth control, adoption, and a single woman's right to keep and parent her child" (Anderson, et al., 1993) have resulted in a scarcity of healthy white newborns. Coincidentally, the rising incidence of infertility among white couples (Menning, 1977; Salzer, 1986) has increased demand. The confluence of these trends has forced adopters to pursue alternatives.

Some sought to adopt children from foreign countries, particularly overpopulated and poor countries in Latin America and Asia. Others sought to adopt African American, Latino, or Native American children from the United States (Berlin, 1978; O'Rourke & Hubbell, 1990; Small, 1984; Tizard, 1991). Others adopted "older" children (e.g., 2–5 years old) or children with mild disabilities (e.g., cleft palate, club foot, correctable heart defects, blindness, and deafness) (Anderson, et al., 1993, p. 257). These forms of adoption are not without controversy, however. Many authors have raised questions about transracial and transcultural adoptions, particularly in terms of the adoptive family's ability to instill a sense of racial, ethnic, or cultural pride and identity in the adoptive child (Koh, 1988; Ladner, 1977; McRoy, Zurcher, Lauderdale, & Anderson, 1984; Pahz, 1988).

Changes in child welfare and foster care laws in the past two decades have also had a significant impact on adoption practices (Anderson, et al., 1993; Chambers, 1970; Triseliotis, 1991). Legislation, such as the Adoption Assistance and Child Welfare Act of 1980, attempted to ease the financial burden of parents willing to take on the responsibility of "special needs" children who are older, minority, had physical or emotional difficulties or both, had spent years in foster care (Glazer, 1993; Groze & Rosenthal, 1991; Schwartz, 1996), or wanted to remain together as a sibling group (Anderson, et al., 1993; Schwartz, 1996).

Prior to 1980, adoption records were typically sealed. Recently, there has been a move toward allowing biological parents or adopted children or both to locate one another. Schwartz (1996) presents a helpful overview of the controversy of reuniting birth parents with adopted children that has resulted from this process.

## Conclusion

This chapter examined the complexity of today's evolving families. It explored their organizational structures, their cultural, ethnic, and racial diversity, and their multisystemic and socioeconomic contexts. Although many different family organizational structures have been discussed (nuclear, extended, single-parent, divorced or remarried, or both, gay and lesbian couples and families, childless couples, and adoptive families), it is important to acknowledge the existence of other family structures beyond the scope of this chapter, such as adults who are single by choice (Cargan, 1983; Skolnick & Skolnick, 1983); childless, cohabiting couples who are not married; aging adults in later life (Hess & Waring, 1983; Walsh, 1993); poor families and inner-city families (McGoldrick & Carter, 1988; Hines, 1988); dual-career families (Piotrowski & Hughes, 1993); foster families (Kinney, Haapala, & Booth, 1991); ethnic minority families (Boyd-Franklin, 1989; Comas-Dias & Griffith, 1988; McGoldrick et al., 1982, 1996); and families living with disabilities or serious illness and loss (Boyd-Franklin, Steiner, & Boland, 1995; Edminster, 1996; Rolland, 1993; Strozier, 1996).

The heterogeneity of these "families," their ever-changing organizational structures and complexity, and even the debate as to what constitutes a "family" are issues that are sure to occupy researchers in the fields of social sciences, mental health, family studies, and sociology for many decades in the future.

# 7

# Teachers as (Multi)Cultural Agents in Schools

## A. Lin Goodwin

Since common schools were begun in the mid-1800s, the question of how to balance collective, mass education with the unique needs of individuals has been perennially perplexing. On the one hand, schools serve a socializing function. They are intentionally organized in ways that guide and shape students— individuals who exhibit a wide range of diversities—so that they adopt the dispositions and acquire the skills necessary to the smooth functioning of society. On the other hand, they are seen as serving an emancipatory function whereby individual development is supported and each person gains the knowledge, tools, and self-confidence necessary to achieve self-actualization. Conformity versus self-determination and the common good versus the good of the individual—these are the dichotomous goals schools have been asked to attain. The dilemmas that these contradictory goals present are further exacerbated by political battles over the control of the common school curriculum. The struggle over the purpose of schooling, what is most worth knowing and therefore teaching, and who schools represent has defined educational history. The reality is that schools have not served all individuals and all groups equally well. Indeed, contests between what is best for all and what is best for some have occurred along racial, religious, gender, language, ethnic, political, and socioeconomic lines, with various groups demanding that schools respond to their own different and particular needs, sometimes at the expense of and sometimes in concert with other groups.

In the midst of these ideological conflicts is the teacher. Teachers lie at the heart of educational service delivery. What is or is not accomplished in schools and who is served well or poorly is often a consequence of the actions teachers do or do not take and the preparation they are afforded. Although they work within national, state, and local arenas that uphold and forward certain educational policies, teachers play key roles as implementers of policy and educational agendas. Teachers become, in essence, cultural agents who help to translate public notions of the educated person into practice. As cultural interpreters, teachers are responsible for forging links between home and school cultures and for integrating what children bring to school with them, regardless of their background and histories, into the curriculum. Yet, teachers bring their own beliefs and values into the classroom, implicit theories that shape their own conceptions of the ideal student. Within the cultural crucibles we call schools, teachers become gatekeepers (Thornton, 1991, pp. 237–248 ) who make key decisions about and for children in terms of what is taught and who experiences success. Therefore, in any examination of schools and the role they play in acculturation, in ensuring educational equity or in determining notions of cultural worthiness, teachers become a critical unit of analysis.

Using teachers and teaching as conceptual lenses, this chapter examines culture and how it is defined, celebrated, or silenced within organizations called schools. As indicated earlier, not all groups or children have been served equally well by schools. Indeed, children who are considered linguistically and culturally different as well as poor children typically have not been the recipients of all that schools have to offer. The acculturating function of schools has been shaped by common conceptions of who is "American"; by a national legacy of slavery, xenophobia, and racism; and by a diverse citizenry that has fought for civil rights and for the right to determine what is best for their children. This chapter examines the initiation of public schooling and its attendant aims, and then it provides a discussion of the structure of schools and the struggle to create not simply a universal system of education but an inclusive one. This historical analysis serves as a backdrop that enables us to see parallels between the intersection of diversity and culture and schools in the past and what is currently occurring in schools. This chapter then turns specifically to the idea of teacher as cultural agent—a discussion that focuses on the issue of teacher preparation and how well today's teaching force is able to work with multiracial, multicultural students. Finally, the chapter offers recommendations for practice—what educators can and should do to ensure that schooling is a multi- and not a monocultural experience.

## Universal Schooling: Out of the Many, One?

The architects of the common school had "total faith in the power of education to shape the destiny of the young Republic" (Cremin, 1961, p. 9). Horace Mann, viewed by many as the father of universal schooling, envisioned a school that was common to all people as the "great equalizer" of men and the instrument whereby a common value system necessary to social progress and nation building could be inculcated. Although Mann perceived the diversity of the American people as an asset and was a supporter of the abolitionist movement, "one misses, too, the sense that common schools should embrace all *races* as well as all classes and denominations" (Cremin, 1957, p. 25). Thus, although the majority of the states had established public school systems by 1860, blacks, Chinese, and other people of color were routinely excluded (and relegated to either segregated or private schools, both of which were minimally supported and depended on the "charity" of benevolent donors) (Takaki, 1989; Tyack, 1974). In the late 1800s, this exclusion was written into law whereby a segregated, dual system of education was formally established (Baptiste, 1979):

> The doctrine of "separate but equal" based on the decision in *Plessy vs. Ferguson* (1896), sanctioned the existence of segregation that maintained its strongest bastion in the area of education. A dual system of education based on race was entrenched in the American educational system. (p. 5)

The years following the Civil War saw the rapid growth of urban areas accelerated by the country's transformation from an agrarian to an industrial society. Census rolls swelled as a huge influx of immigrants from Ireland and southern and eastern Europe, drawn by the promise of economic advancement, poured into cities. The cities also drew people from farming communities; in the wake of mass production and the mechanization of labor, people gravitated toward the cities in which jobs were available (Cremin, 1961; Degler, 1984; Tyack, 1974). Schools found themselves "faced with thousands of children eager for education and too few teachers and classrooms to serve them" (Cremin, 1961, p. 19) as "young immigrants from a dozen different countries swelled the tide of newly arriving farm children" (p. 21). Educators "called upon the school to train newcomers to American ways of life and thought" (p. 66) and "saw a new vision of schooling suitable to the demands of an industrial age" (p. 33). Thus, public schools became mechanisms whereby immigrants could be both "appropriately" inducted into American society and contained. Seeking systematization, educators adopted mass-production principles from industry and applied the factory model to schools. During the second half of the nineteenth century, superintendents worked to create a bureaucratic model of schooling "in which directives flowed from the top down, reports emanated from the bottom, and each step of the educational process was carefully prescribed by professional educators" (Tyack, 1974, p. 40). Superintendents such as William T. Harris in St. Louis and William Harvey Wells in Chicago and principal John Philbrick in Boston became powerful and vocal proponents of standardized and efficient schooling. Harris (as quoted in Tyack, 1974, p. 43) said, "The first requisite of the school is *Order*: each pupil must be taught first and foremost to conform his behavior to a general standard." Wells was instrumental in designing the graded school by prescribing both content and instruction for each grade level, whereas Philbrick argued convincingly for the "egg-crate school" that would physically structure and organize massive numbers of students.

Thus, in the early days of public schooling, the desire for uniformity and efficiency overshadowed any notions of individuality or differentiation. Immigrants from Europe, along with their cultures, religions, and languages, were expected to conform. The process of Americanization became a process of homogenization (Tyack, 1974):

> Amid the pluralistic politics of interest groups, the cultural conflicts of
> Catholic and Protestant, immigrant and nativist, black and white, the
> position of school*men* [italics added] was an anomalous one. For the
> most part, they held a common set of WASP values, professed a
> common-core (that is, pan-Protestant) Christianity, were ethnocentric,
> and tended to glorify the sturdy virtues of a departed rural tradition.
> They took their values for granted as self-evidently true—not subject to
> legitimate debate. (p. 109)

The majority of teachers were white, unmarried females who were viewed as
docile and easily controlled by superintendents who were overwhelmingly male
and white. They were expected to follow the prescribed curriculum and abide by
the policies set by school officials. As cultural agents, teachers were to offer
instruction in English and became responsible for "assaulting all forms of cultural
difference" (Tyack, 1974, p. 235). Although there were many teachers who were
themselves first- or second-generation immigrants, these individuals were often
extremely zealous about mainstreaming immigrant children and obliterating their
differences so as to ensure their success (Tyack, 1974). Meanwhile, black
teachers, who were in abundant supply, were generally only allowed to teach in
separate schools for black students or in cites where the black student
population was large (Tyack, 1974). Therefore, the early days of public schooling
were characterized by segregation and cultural conformity, with teachers serving
as monocultural agents. "Multicultural" education was nonexistent.

## Responding to Race: Initial Attempts by Schools

Two major events disturbed the status quo of monocultural schools. First, the
country experienced severe race riots as African and Mexican Americans
competed with European Americans for jobs generated by the war effort (Banks,
1993). In addition, African American soldiers returned "home" after the war to a
country that denied them basic rights; in turn, they began to demand change.
Education was seen as the way to ameliorate racial tensions, and leading
educators of the time, such as Hilda Taba, created the Intergroup Movement
(Ramsey, Vold, & Williams, 1989).

Using curricula designed to guide students to explore cultural differences and
resolve conflict, the goals of the Intergroup Movement were to raise cultural
sensitivity and promote interracial harmony. To implement these curricula,
classroom teachers were trained in the human relations approach (Sleeter &
Grant, 1987), which emphasizes interpersonal relations and cooperation,
particularly in urban areas in which racial conflicts were most evident. The
movement, however, experienced limited success because it "only partially
recognized the connections between ethnic group conflict and cultural
differences" (Olneck, 1990, p. 153). Thus, although schools and teachers tried to
"celebrate" cultural differences, they failed to address the serious inequities

experienced by people of color. In essence, the Intergroup Movement targeted the effects and not the cause of racial disharmony.

The second major event was the 1954 *Brown v. Board of Education* court decision that dismantled segregated schooling and was the beginning of the Civil Rights movement. As the Intergroup Movement faded in the wake of legislated school desegregation, teachers were again viewed as critical to the smooth functioning of schools that were to be integrated and, ostensibly, more equal. Baptiste and Baptiste (1980) noted, "Federal legislation established desegregation centers to prepare inservice teachers to teach effectively in cross-cultural settings" (p. 45), and college programs were created to prepare teachers for multiracial classrooms (Caliguri, 1970; Jackson & Kirkpatrick, 1967). This training typically consisted of isolated, self-contained workshops that focused on helping practitioners develop intercultural awareness. This awareness usually emphasized children's differences and conceptualized them as deficient. Disparities in economic, social, and cultural experiences became explanations for apparent achievement differences among the races (Carter & Goodwin, 1994). The prevailing opinion was that poor children, especially those of color, required remediation to enable them to acquire the experiences and skills deemed necessary for success within schools and, subsequently, mainstream society (Boyd, 1991; Passow, 1991). Ornstein (1982) noted that:

> educators [became] increasingly concerned with the need to study the problems of the poor, especially the black poor, in order to remedy their plight. The term "disadvantaged" and its derivative terms "deprived" and "underprivileged" began to appear with reference to the children and youth of lower-class and minority groups. (p. 197)

As cultural agents, teachers were to provide "culturally disadvantaged" children with those background experiences that would enable them to travel within a society dominated by a culture that was not theirs but was one that, nonetheless, defined the norm. Education for poor and black children, perceived as different and deficient, was compensatory in nature, designed to fill their "cultural gaps."

The mid-1960s fueled racial and ethnic groups' calls for curriculum reform and community school control (Banks, 1988). African Americans and other marginalized groups struggled for relevant curriculum materials and diversity among teachers and school administrators. The civil rights era witnessed the creation of ethnic studies programs on college campuses and greater diversification among faculty. It was marked by experimentation and exploration in the nation's schools and by legislation that provided funds for a profusion of teacher training offerings, conferences, and materials designed to build self-pride among specific ethnic groups.

Although these changes appear to indicate that schools were indeed responding to cultural differences, an analysis of these responses to "culture" from World War II through the late 1960s reveals that schools yielded only to pressure from external forces, such as legislation, civil unrest, and the politicization of visible racial/ethnic group peoples. Schools operated from a reactive stance characterized by an ameliorative ideology. Their goal in terms of "multicultural" education was to "fix" children of color who were perceived as disadvantaged. The coupling of a reactive posture and an ameliorative mind-set resulted in hastily conceived educational reforms that lacked conceptual depth and intellectual coherence (Banks, 1988; Baptiste, Baptiste, & Gollnick, 1980; Ramsey et al., 1989). Designed specifically for "minority"[1] students, these changes became curricular appendages that left the core of American education, with its attendant white, middle-class values and perspectives, undisturbed. Thus, teachers, despite cultural training, continued to function within a Eurocentric framework. In addition, cultural training was deemed most appropriate for inservice rather than preservice teachers. Consequently, teachers entered the profession with minimal understanding of how to respond to culturally diverse students.

## Preparing Teachers to Be (Multi)Cultural Agents

The Civil Rights movement did, however, help to spark a growing awareness that teachers needed to be prepared to work with diverse populations **before** they entered the profession. The following landmark statement, issued by the American Association of Colleges for Teachers Education (AACTE) (1973), advocated the inclusion of cultural diversity training in preservice teacher education programs:

> Multicultural education programs for teachers are more than special courses or special learning experiences grafted onto the standard program. The commitment to cultural pluralism must permeate all areas of the educational experience provided for prospective teachers. (p. 264)

The idea of specific teacher preparation to work effectively with multicultural populations gained a foothold as the profession began to articulate goals and curricula in keeping with this notion (Banks, Carlos, Garcia, Gay, & Ochoa, 1976; Baptiste & Baptiste, 1980; Baker, 1974; Gay, 1977; Gollnick, 1977; Klassen & Gollnick, 1977; Ramsey et al., 1989). Concerted efforts to integrate multiculturalism throughout teacher education programs attended to governance issues, faculty and student representation, curricula, and evaluation (Gollnick, Osayande, & Levy, 1980; Klassen, Gollnick, & Osayande, 1980). The multicultural movement also affected legislation so that by the late seventies, "[twenty-eight] states ... [had] state provisions regarding multicultural, bilingual, and/or ethnic studies programs for elementary and secondary school programs. Seven or more [required] specific training in multicultural education for teachers to be certified" (Gollnick, 1977, p. 57).

During this period, multicultural teacher education appeared to be well established. However, school enrollments began to fall precipitously, resulting in a teacher glut and simultaneous sheer drops in teacher education program enrollments. In a climate of budget crises, schools of education scrambled to stay afloat, and multicultural programs, often supported by soft money, were usually the first programs to be reduced or eliminated. Shifts in the political climate of the country had an even more devastating impact on multicultural education so that the late 1970s and early 1980s witnessed "societal and educational emphases on basics, conservatism, fundamentalism, and the cost-effectiveness of human services . . . not conducive to educational ideas that run counter to the status quo" (Gay, 1983, p. 563).

Although the future of multicultural teacher education seemed dim in the early 1980s, a series of events changed the prognosis dramatically. In 1983, the publication of *A Nation at Risk* (National Commission on Excellence in Education) "helped to bring key educational issues to the forefront of public consciousness" (Brown, 1992, p. 2) and initiated a period of comprehensive school reform that continues today. Encompassing curriculum change, teacher quality and professionalism, and teacher preparation (Darling-Hammond & Goodwin, 1993), this reform effort coincided with burgeoning visible racial/ethnic group populations, especially in schools ("Today's Numbers," 1986). These demographic shifts revitalized the multicultural teacher education movement because the need to effectively instruct these diverse children became paramount.

## The Demographics of Today's Schools: History Repeats Itself

America is again in the midst of an immigration flood. Statistics about new majority "minority" populations are commonplace and are further confirmed by 1990 census data. Between 1980 and 1990, the Asian American population doubled, the Latino population increased by 53% and African Americans increased by 13%. In contrast, European American numbers declined by 3% (Espiritu, 1992). California is already a "minority" majority state and is fast being joined by New York, Texas, Florida, and New Jersey, among others (Garcia & McLaughlin, 1995). Many of these majority "minorities" speak languages other than English. Estimates indicate that by the Year 2000, there will be 40 million people whose maternal language is not English; at least 3.5 million of these will be school-aged children who will be considered limited English proficient (Trueba, 1989). To provide a sense of how rapidly these numbers are rising, it is helpful to know that the 1980 census estimated those numbers to be 30 million and 2.4 million, respectively.

It is important, however, to bear in mind that population increases among Asian Americans, African Americans, and Latinos are not due simply to increased levels of immigration but also to high birth rates. These groups are generally younger with higher percentages of individuals in their child-bearing years compared to the European American population, which is aging, postponing marriage and childbirth, and choosing to have smaller families. It is also important to be aware of the fact that Spanish speakers constitute 80% of the linguistic "minorities," and many of these represent "in-country ethnolinguistic minorities" (Trueba, 1989, p. 5)—that is, individuals who are American-born but speak a first language other than English.

Nowhere are these demographic changes being felt more keenly than in the schools (American Council on Education and the Education Commission of the States, 1988; Commission on Minority Participation in Education and American Life, 1988; Gonzalez, 1990). It is anticipated that by 2020, children of color will constitute 46% of the public school population (National Center for Education Statistics [NCES], 1991); currently, 30% of all public school students are children of color (Banks, 1991), and these children comprise more than 70% of total school enrollments in 20 of the largest school districts (Center for Education Statistics, 1987). Schools in central cities, such as New York and Los Angeles, are bursting with new arrivals, and it is not uncommon to find teachers facing classes of students who speak a dozen or more different languages and dialects.

If there was ever a time that a heterogeneous teaching force was needed, that time is now. The converse is true, however; teaching ranks are not characterized by diversity and remain predominantly white (Dilworth, 1990; Fuller, 1992; Goodwin, 1991; King, 1993; Research About Teacher Education Project, 1990). Three-fourths of teachers are female, and approximately half speak English only; teachers of color represent little more than 10% of all teachers (Zimpher & Ashburn, 1992). (Note: The same is true of teacher education faculty who, according to recent AACTE surveys, are more than 90% white but overwhelmingly male [AACTE, 1990; Zimpher & Ashburn, 1992]. In fact, one report found that during the 19871988 school year, 50% of schools had no teachers of color (NCES, 1992). Despite numerous efforts mounted during the 1980s (and currently) to attract more candidates of color to teaching, the field has lost its "captive" labor pool. Given expanded vocational opportunities, women and people of color are no longer limited professionally and have expanded their horizons beyond the teaching, clerical, and nursing jobs to which they were traditionally confined (Darling-Hammond, Pittman, & Ottinger, 1987).

This analysis of the current demographics of schools reveals a very diverse school population, on the one hand, and a racially and culturally homogenous teaching force on the other. Dramatic changes in school demographics are occurring that are analogous to the sweeping changes witnessed at the turn of the twentieth century. Schools are again responsible for embracing and instructing children who bring experiences, traditions, ways of knowing and family backgrounds that are often unfamiliar to teachers and under-represented in the curriculum. Although it cannot be assumed that teachers of color are inherently equipped to work effectively with children of color, it is important to realize that these teachers "represent surrogate parent figures, disciplinarians, counselors, role models, and advocates" (King, 1993, p. 121) for culturally and linguistically diverse students. Children's sense of themselves and their ideas of what is possible and about power and control are affected by the adults they see around them and the roles that adults assume. When children of color are surrounded in schools by powerful adults who do not represent their communities or families, it is likely that their perceptions of schooling and their feelings of affiliation are negatively affected. Equally as important as a racially heterogeneous teaching force is one that is culturally responsive. Indeed, whites teaching non-whites is a growing phenomenon (Dilworth, 1990; Grant & Secada, 1990, pp. 403–422), a trend that can only continue given the strong likelihood that teachers of color cannot be recruited proportionately to the increasing number of pupils of color. Thus, it can be argued that culturally responsive teachers are what we should be trying hardest to achieve.

## Schools, Teachers, and Culture: Maintaining or Disturbing the Status Quo?

Currently, as a result of renewed interest and attention to the needs of children of color and greater understanding of how culture mediates learning, there are some positive changes occurring. First, there is an increasing realization that "to continue to define the difficulty as inherent in the raw materials—the children— is plainly to blame the victim and to acquiesce in the continuation of educational inequity in America" (Ryan [1971] as quoted in Gay, 1983, p. 561). Researchers and multiculturalists are challenging the notion of cultural difference as synonymous with deviance or deprivation (Banks, 1991; Baratz & Baratz, 1970) and have reconceptualized the relationship between culture and schooling by studying the various educational, psychological, and social variables associated with specific cultural experiences. Consequently, the field has begun to articulate the idea of pedagogy that is multicultural or culturally responsive (Estrada & Vasquez, 1981; Irvine, 1991b; Ladson-Billings, 1994; Nieto, 1992; Ramsey, 1987) and "addresses students' cultural knowledge, history, personal style, language and dialect, cognition and learning styles, as well as their parents and community" (Irvine, 1991b, p. 17).

The notion of culturally responsive pedagogy is grounded in numerous investigations into the mediating influence of race and culture on visible racial/ethnic group children's ways of knowing and sense making. It is theorized that the differential school experiences and academic achievements of children of color may be attributed to a mismatch between the culture of the school and the home cultures of pupils (Cummins, 1986; Irvine, 1991a; Nieto, 1992). These theories raise the possibility that culturally and linguistically diverse children may learn in culture-specific ways and require instruction that capitalizes on their learning styles and strengths rather than emphasizes their "deficits." Carter and Goodwin (1994) note that the manner in which children of color receive, manipulate, transform, and express knowledge, as well as their task and modality preferences and the ways in which they interact and communicate with others, may not be well explained by mainstream learning theory traditionally grounded in White children's ways of knowing (p. 319).

The growing body of evidence that supports the idea of culturally grounded learning styles notwithstanding (Gay, 1991; Irvine, 1991a; Ramirez & Castenada, 1974; Shade, 1982), it would be unwise for teachers to use these theories as rigid indicators of how culturally diverse children learn simply because much of what we now know is inconclusive and untested (Carter & Goodwin, 1994; Ladson-Billings, 1994). The lessons that teachers can and should take from this body of literature is the idea that they will need to build cultural bridges that span home and school communities so that children experience greater continuity between these two contexts and are not forced to "enter school having to unlearn or, at least, to modify their own culturally sanctioned interactional and behavioral styles and adopt those styles rewarded in the school context if they wish to achieve academic success" (Fordham, 1988, p. 55). One of the best examples of this is the Kamehameha Elementary Education Program (KEEP) in which ethnographic data gathered from Hawaiian children's home communities were used to achieve "cultural compatibility . . . a school program compatible with the culture of Hawaiian children *in ways that . . . make the program educationally effective*" (Jordan, 1985, p. 109). Substantive research documenting this effort indicates that Hawaiian children's achievement levels rose as a consequence.

Finally, there have also been positive changes at the level of teacher certification policy such that states, (e.g., California and New York) have mandated that new teachers be prepared to work effectively with linguistically and culturally diverse children. As a consequence, many teacher preparation programs now must attend to the idea of multicultural education. Movement in teacher education has also been spurred on by changes in National Council for the Accreditation of Teacher Education standards that specify that programs seeking accreditation must show evidence of preparing teachers for culturally and linguistically diverse classrooms.

Concurrent with these positive indicators, however, are numerous indicators that not enough is being done; children of color are still not receiving equitable, high-quality schooling. Numerous studies have documented the negative experiences that seem to characterize the school lives of children of color (Aaron & Powell, 1982; Fine, 1991; Garibaldi, 1988; Nieto, 1992; Simpson & Erickson, 1983), and they reveal that these children are more likely to be assigned to the lowest academic or special education tracks (College Board, 1985; Goodlad, 1984; Hilliard, 1990; Oakes; 1985), and to be subjected to intellectually impoverished curricula (Collins, 1982; Garcia & Pearson, 1991; Moll, 1991; Oakes & Lipton, 1990; Walsh, 1987). Implicit in the labels currently assigned to children of color (and their families)—at risk, limited English proficient, disadvantaged, developmentally delayed, dysfunctional, and underclass—is the notion that these children are still viewed as deficient. This perception of deficiency is evident in studies that have examined the relationship between teacher expectations and student achievement. For example, Irvine (1991a) found a correlation between race and teacher behavior. Her analysis revealed that "teachers had more negative attitudes and beliefs about black children than about white children in such variables as personality traits and characteristics, ability, language, behavior, and potential" (p. 57). Her review also showed that white students received more favorable treatment than black students, and that black children, especially black boys, received less praise and more criticism than did their classmates. Fine (1991) and Nieto (1992) found that children of color were more likely to be punished for offenses that white children could commit without consequence, whereas other studies (Cardenas & First, 1985; Garibaldi, 1988) demonstrated that blacks, particularly black males, are suspended from school at higher rates compared with whites.

In addition, "schools generally do not value skills in any language but standard American English" and perceive "languages spoken by subordinate groups [as] inferior or 'broken' versions of [the] dominant-group language" (Au, 1993, pp. 128–129). In fact, the inability to speak standard English is often equated with low levels of cognitive functioning; linguistically diverse children are often then relegated to the lower or nonacademic tracks and offered watered-down curricula (Moll, 1991) even while their bilingualism is used as a "scapegoat" for their poor academic achievement (Cummins, 1995).

Teachers' beliefs about and attitudes toward visible racial/ethnic group children do not occur in a vacuum. One need only examine the current political climate to know that teacher attitudes cannot help but be affected by general public opinion and by changes occurring in society at large, including the current backlash against affirmative action and against immigrants, the passing of Propositions 187 and 227 in California, conflicts regarding the implementation of multicultural curricula, and racial riots in various parts of the country. Studies have also shown that culturally responsive teaching is more an ideal than a reality, and that the nation's classrooms fail to include the experiences of culturally diverse children (Goodwin, 1997; Goodwin, Genishi, Asher, & Woo, 1997). Finally, an examination of teacher education programs reveals that despite the more explicit multicultural standards in accreditation mentioned previously, teacher education programs continue to fall short of comprehensive multicultural teacher preparation (Gollnick, 1992).

Therefore, it appears that after 100 years of public schooling, little has changed. Besides the fact that blacks and other children of color are now legally allowed into public schools, the socializing function of schools continues to be preparing children to fit into mainstream society, with mainstream defined as white, Protestant, and middle class. The history of public schooling also reveals that, in truth, the idea of teachers as cultural agents is long-standing. Values, beliefs, knowledge, and behaviors (i.e., culture) sanctioned by society are funneled into schools and are in turn purveyed by teachers to students. Schools are supposed to efficiently produce citizens who are productive, well functioning, and literate and to give children the preparation they will need to support and take their place in society. History also indicates, however, that teachers have primarily acted as monocultural versus multicultural agents. Culture was (and continues to be) defined by the majority and by those who held political and economic power, namely, the white, Anglo-Saxon, middle class. The aim of schooling and, it follows, of teachers has been to inculcate these values; the collective educational consciousness still does not fully embrace linguistically and culturally diverse children.

## Recommendations for Practice: Seeking Substantive Change

Teachers can be multicultural agents only if they truly believe that children who are culturally and linguistically diverse can and must learn, are fully capable, and will benefit from instruction that is meaningful and rich with powerful ideas. Families and communities send the best children they have to schools; children enter kindergarten curious and ready to learn; mothers and fathers believe in their children and in their potential to achieve; and teachers have to share these beliefs and assume responsibility to make positive things happen for children in school. Too often, children are blamed for their own failures, for their poverty, and for their lack of facility with English; too often, poor, working-class parents are defined as uncaring, unsupportive, or disinterested in education. Teachers can and do find many convenient reasons for children's lack of success unless they closely and critically examine themselves and their own practices and assume first that they are the ones who must do something differently if children are not learning.

Teachers must believe in **all** children's inherent capacity to learn and achieve academic success, in students' communities and families as rich resources and equal partners in the educational process, and in the ultimate responsibility of education professionals and institutions to advocate for educational equity and access for all children, notably poor children and children of color. If educators subscribe to deficit views of children and their families, attribute learners' shortcomings to social or background variables, and fail to be accountable for the academic progress and development of all children, then schooling will continue to be a process whereby children of diverse cultures fail and are silenced.

What does this all mean in terms of practice? Primarily, it means that teachers must take it upon themselves to immerse themselves in diverse communities and must define the classroom as an extension of the community as opposed to apart from it (Goodwin & Macdonald, 1997; Smith & Goodwin, 1997). It also means that teachers must allow children's families and caregivers to teach them about the children they send to school. Too often, schools and educators establish themselves as the sole experts about children and learning, and they forget that the children they teach are connected to an entire group of people who know the children best and to a way of life that is important to each child. In addition, teachers who engage in culturally responsive practice understand that different ways of knowing can be nurtured and supported only by different methodologies, a wide range of activities, differentiated instruction, deep caring for the uniqueness of each child, and the creation of an inviting classroom family (Purkey & Novak, 1984) that values the contribution of each member. Finally, if teachers are to be multicultural agents, they must employ curricula that incorporate the cultural experiences of children. Typically, however, this is taken to mean adding ethnic heroes and literature to an immutable curriculum grounded in European American cultural and intellectual traditions or disconnected and isolated celebrations of "ethnic" holidays (Banks, 1988; Goodwin, 1997). In contrast, a curriculum that embodies cultural inclusion and social activism is "developmentally appropriate and culturally authentic ... integrate[s] multicultural education into different academic disciplines ... creates an awareness of how student evaluation and assessment is interpretive and contextual, and it includes parent participation" (Grant & Gomez, 1996, p. 10). Sleeter and Grant (1987) term this approach "education that is multicultural and social reconstructionist" because it uses the lives of students and of visible racial/ethnic group people as starting points for discussions about oppression and emphasizes the empowerment of learners to bring about social change in their own lives and the lives of others.

To be multicultural agents, teachers must work at providing culturally and linguistically diverse children with multiple opportunities to explain their world through movement, art, talk, storytelling, building, creating, and so on. They must reconfigure the classroom so that a variety of interactional styles can be accommodated and children are encouraged to communicate without the discomfort of being singled out (Au, 1993; Duran, 1994; Jordan, 1985). Finally, teachers must also be explicit about cultural capital—the ways of speaking and behaving that this society prizes and that enable academic and economic success (Delpit, 1995).

Although research into multicultural teacher education is weak and limited (Grant & Secada, 1990; Irvine, 1992), it is known that single courses, short-term interventions, and student teaching placements in culturally diverse settings are ineffective or produce mixed results (Grant, 1981; Grant & Koskela, 1986; Haberman, 1991; Henington, 1981; McDiarmid & Price, 1990; Washington, 1981). Clearly, the challenge for teacher education is the development of comprehensive programs to produce a teaching force that is culturally diverse in both composition *and* professional orientation. Past practice provides the field with some direction and highlights mistakes or difficulties to avoid. Educating preservice teachers solely about the artifacts of visible racial and ethnic peoples' culture has not proven useful in the production of culturally responsive educators. Also, add-on programs to "multiculturalize" teachers have had limited results. Multicultural teaching is not an act but rather a way of perceiving and thinking about one's craft. Previous attempts to implement multicultural teacher education concentrated on changing what teachers do; they have focused on the tangibles of the teaching act. Now, there is greater credence given to the idea of changing teachers from the inside to affect how they think and conceptualize the world and the many people in it. This idea of guiding preservice teachers to look inward to examine their own implicitly held beliefs about culture (their own and others) as a precursor to working responsibly and effectively with children of color is gaining support (Banks, 1991; Carter & Goodwin, 1994; Goodwin, 1977; Ramsey, 1987). Although this is not necessarily a new concept, the idea that self-knowledge should precede content and strategies approaches to multicultural teacher education is gaining prominence. Sleeter (1992) suggests that educators "spend time developing [their] own understanding of the issues underlying multicultural education, to reconstruct [their] own daily [lives] and work to affirm equality and to engage in support of social movements led by oppressed people" (p. 213). Her statement raises questions about teachers' understanding of multicultural education and issues: the right of every child to a rich and meaningful education; the responsibility of schools and teachers to interrupt negative and harmful patterns of behavior in educational and societal contexts that demean and marginalize children of color; the role that schools must play in introducing children, especially poor children and children of color, to "cultures of power" (Delpit, 1995); and the basic worthiness of all children.

## Note

1. The term "minority" is used because it is commonplace and readily accessible to readers. Quotation marks are used to acknowledge the problematic nature of this term, however, and the fact that those designated as "minorities" in the United States are really in the majority when considered globally.

# 8

# Cultural Dynamics and Issues in Higher Education

*Raechele L. Pope and Corlisse D. Thomas*

Culture has increasingly become a lens through which members of society are asked to view experiences, work, education, and themselves. Although culture has always been present in all aspects of our lives, it is not always consciously identified or applied (Fried, 1995). The acknowledgment and use of culture as a lens for examining the dynamics of organizational and societal behaviors radically transforms basic epistemological assumptions about organizations and society.. Using this lens creates a clearer awareness and understanding of underlying assumptions and cultural values (Carter, 1995).

Elizabeth Minnich (1990) emphasized the importance of deconstructing the unexamined and habitual cultural assumptions and values that exist in organizations and society. She posited that most of the dominant paradigms, which typically drive the values and practices of most organizations, are unrecognized and unchallenged. It is vital to clarify the dominant paradigm and its underlying cultural values to recognize that other perspectives and values exist. Moreover, Minnich stated that without clarifying the dominant paradigm, conceptual errors will occur in the definitions and assessments of our organizations and our work. Conceptual errors are those thoughts and ideas that derive from the use of a single cultural experience as the standard for all. This chapter examines the underlying cultural assumptions of higher education as an institution and explores strategies for addressing culture in higher education.

## Culture in Higher Education

There are 3,688 colleges and universities in the United States (*Chronicle of Higher Education*, 1996). They consist of small liberal arts colleges, large research institutions, the Ivy League, women's colleges, community colleges, historically black colleges and universities, and a host of other types of schools. This multitude of institutions seek to educate a total enrollment of more than 14 million students (*Chronicle of Higher Education*, 1996). These colleges and universities offer students the necessary preparation for their aspirations toward leadership and professional employment in society. In addition to this initial preparation, colleges and universities offer students a wide range of information in a variety of subjects (e.g., literature, science, and history) outside of a student's selected major that is needed to exist as a educated person in the current world. College and university life, however, is more than the everyday classroom experience. Boyer (1990) discussed the qualities that he believed every institution should aspire to possess. His description of a purposeful, open, just, disciplined, caring, and celebrative community conveys the goal of intellectual and personal growth and understanding for every member of the college community. As society becomes increasingly complex, higher education is faced with the issues that this complexity produces. Soaring costs, advancing information technology, affirmative action, and social problems are societal issues that are replicated within the context of colleges and universities. Changing demographics, another major societal consideration, clearly impact the college and university environment. Approximately 27% of the total enrollment of college and university students comprises Native American, Asian, black, and Hispanic, and another 3% comprises foreign students (*Chronicle of Higher Education,* 1996). This represents a 10-year increase of more than 38%. This increasingly culturally diverse population creates an atmosphere on college and university campuses that requires heightened attention to cultural dynamics.

Higher education is not immune to the amorphous nature of the word "culture." According to *Webster's Ninth New Collegiate Dictionary* (1987), *culture* is defined as "the integrated pattern of human knowledge, belief, and behavior that depends upon [one's] capacity for learning and transmitting knowledge to succeeding generations" (p. 314). Similarly, from a higher-education perspective, a broadly stated definition of culture often encompasses the largest and the smallest aspects of college and university life. Kuh (1993) defined culture within the higher-educational context as

> the collective, mutually shaping patterns of institutional history, mission, physical settings, norms, traditions, values, practices, beliefs, and assumptions which guide the behavior of individuals and groups in an institution of higher education and which provide frames of reference for interpreting the meanings of events and actions on and off campus. (p. 2)

This overarching perspective of culture addresses the variety of ways in which higher education influences and is affected by the members of its environment. Kuh, adopting Schein's (1985) framework, focuses on cultural "outcomes" to explicate his definition. Kuh identifies *artifacts* (the tangible aspects of culture), *perspectives* (shared rules and norms), *values* (ideals that serve as a basis for judgment), and *assumptions* (beliefs that define members' roles in organizations), as the four aspects of culture existing within the higher-education environment. According to Kuh, artifacts may be physical (e.g., particular campus locations [the campus green at the University of Virginia], or structures [the Alma Mater statue at Columbia University]), verbal (e.g., words, phrases, and names used within the campus community), or behavioral (e.g., institutional rituals and ceremonies). Perspectives are customs (e.g., expected attire in certain settings, and methods for conducting meetings) that illustrate an institution's culture. Values may be exhibited by institutional commitments (e.g., a college's commitment to community service as evidenced by widespread student and faculty participation in ongoing service projects). Assumptions are manifested by artifacts, perspectives, and values. They publicly identify an organization's beliefs with respect to its relationship to the environment, its perceptions of truth, and its belief in the capacity of human nature and human relations (e.g., Judeo-Christian beliefs that serve as a foundation for an institution's mission statement). These four facets of culture are evident on both the institutional and the individual levels. Thus, a university's academic and administrative structures are reflected in its artifacts and by its values, perspectives, and assumptions, while simultaneously its faculty, staff, and students reinforce the community's culture by their exhibition of these same cultural characteristics. For example, a competitive academic culture that is supported by grading procedures and classroom dynamics (the institutional level) is further evidenced by students who do not participate in study groups or are only attentive to their own interests in their attempt to attain the highest grades or both (the individual level). Within the overall university culture, a variety of groups exist that have their own cultures, including student organizations, residential groups, sports teams, faculty groups (e.g., assistant, associate, and adjunct), administrators, support staff, and others (Kuh, 1993).

Another view of higher-education culture is offered by Bergquist (1992). His research has asserted that there is not one culture but four distinct cultures in higher education: *collegial, managerial, developmental, and negotiating.* He believed that each of these cultures has its own history, perspective, and values. According to Bergquist, the *collegial* culture focuses on faculty, values scholarship, and ensures and emphasizes rationality. In addition, it identifies the institution's mission as the generation and dissemination of knowledge and the development of tomorrow's leaders. The *managerial* culture emphasizes goal-oriented work, values effective supervision and fiscal responsibility, and assumes that the institution can effectively define and measure its goals. It identifies the institution's mission as encouraging students to become responsible citizens. The *developmental* culture focuses on the personal and professional growth of all members of the campus community, and values service to others, curriculum planning, and institutional research. It assumes that all individuals strive toward personal growth and identifies the institution's mission as encouragement of the growth and maturation of students, faculty, staff, and administrators. The *negotiating* culture emphasizes establishing fair policies and procedures for the institution, values fair bargaining among management, faculty, and staff, and assumes power is a reckoning force in the institution. It identifies the institution mission as reaching new and more equitable social attitudes and structures.

In essence, Kuh (1993), Bergquist (1992), and other scholars of higher-education institutions and culture opt to deal with the nebulous nature of culture with attempts to reify it to study and write about it (Fried, 1995). As Morgan (1986) warned, however,

> Our understanding of culture is usually much more fragmented and superficial than the reality. . . . Too often culture is viewed as a set of distinct entity with clearly defined attributes . . . such as beliefs, stories, norms, and rituals, that somehow form a cultural whole. (p. 139)

Fried attributes this superficial view of culture to the positivist objectivist paradigm that focuses on outcomes or assumes objective observation. She suggests that constructivist researchers are less apt to view culture as object and instead focus on the interaction of the study, the studied, and the studier. Fried states, "All meaning is constructed by people who are involved in events, observing them, participating in them, and reflecting on them" (p. 41). This perspective of meaning making and the complexity of culture has been rarely explored in the higher-education literature.

The literature purporting to examine the culture of higher-education organizations historically and, to a great extent, currently defines culture as if it exists in a vacuum devoid of the notions of race, ethnicity, gender, and class. Instead, culture is defined purely as an organizational concept with limited reference to the underlying cultural assumptions of race, ethnicity, gender, and class. The conceptual error, as Minnich (1990) would define it, in this literature is the a priori assumption that colleges and universities are acultural with regard to concepts such as race, ethnicity, gender, and class. Missing in this literature is an examination of how higher education, like most organizations, is steeped in a cultural value system that is white, Anglo, male, and middle to upper class (Fried, 1995; Morgan, 1985).

When higher-education researchers attempted to address issues of values, beliefs, assumptions, and perspectives particular to the race, ethnicity, gender, age, religion, class, and sexual orientation of its many participants, a separate body of literature that focuses on issues of multiculturalism was created. Although this attention to multicultural issues has been very important to higher education and has filled a large gap in knowledge and practice, this same literature has failed to use this "multicultural" lens to explore the issues of what has been traditionally regarded as organizational culture.

Rarely have higher-education scholars attempted to fuse the concepts of multicultural and organizational culture. This chapter will incorporate both these concepts of culture by examining the organizational culture of higher education, which includes the underlying values, norms, traditions, practices, and assumptions of its academic and administrative structures, and the culture of underrepresented or multicultural groups in colleges and universities. It is important to explore both these conceptualizations of culture because they are interconnected and ultimately affect the organizational structures of colleges and universities and the individual experiences of all who participate in higher education.

Significant to any discussion of cultural dynamics in organizations is the recognition of two fundamental characteristics of culture. First, organizational culture is enduring in that it is inherited by the current and future generations from those preceding them by implicit and explicit means. Second, to the degree that culture is created by people, it can change as determined by the people within the culture's context (Fried, 1995; Kuh, 1993; Schein, 1985; *Webster's Ninth New Collegiate Dictionary,* 1987). These features are particularly meaningful for higher education in view of the changing demographic picture of the United States' population. The often unexamined culture or cultural values within the institution are called into question as increasing numbers of white women and people of color become members of higher-education communities. These populations introduce a variety of cultural beliefs, assumptions, values, and perspectives that differ from those of the prevailing cultural system. Membership in these groups within the higher-education community requires a review and revision of the current cultural norms.

Higher education has a unique position in the United States as a home of scholarly endeavor and new knowledge. It values the concept of academic freedom and thereby the assurance that conflicting ideas and concepts are welcomed and debated as a means to enhance intellectual study (Rudolph, 1977). In addition, society looks to higher education to create leaders who ultimately will manage and direct society's present and future. With these preconceptions and expectations bearing on its existence, plus the shifts in U.S. demographics, it follows that higher education should be the forum that intimately understands, accepts, and integrates a variety of cultural perspectives into its structural framework. Most of the institutional cultural components of higher education, however, are manifestations of white culture. Katz (1989) comprehensively delineated the values and beliefs of white culture that dictate the cultural norms within many higher-education contexts. According to Katz, these attitudes and beliefs are demonstrated in various ways, including an orientation toward winning and competition; a desire for mastery and dominance over nature; a hierarchical approach to decision making; an emphasis on individualism; an adherence to quantitative, "rational" approaches to problem solving; the use of the European immigrant experience as the historical reference point; and a belief in Christianity as the accepted form of spiritual expression. These expressions of white culture are manifested in the administrative structures, academic departments, curriculum, staffing, student activities and organizations, and residential life of colleges and universities. Moreover, these cultural values and beliefs are perpetuated on an individual level by students, faculty, and staff. Daily interactions, conversations, attitudes, and behaviors within and among these groups exhibit the values, norms, and beliefs of the dominant white culture. Because a majority of U.S. colleges and universities may be characterized as predominantly white institutions both individually and institutionally, it appears that an entire higher-educational system is largely Eurocentric.

The ethnocentric character of white culture combined with the controlling role that it plays in higher education creates oppressive and racist institutional structures and individual attitudes (Katz, 1989). Pope, Ecklund, and Mueller (1989) demonstrated the way in which the dominant culture is manifested and maintained within the higher educational context using the Higher Education Impact (HEI) model. The HEI is a conceptual model designed to demonstrate the potential for higher-education administrators to change the current organizational structures and systems that reinforce and perpetuate racism. The authors of the HEI model believed that higher education is an extremely influential socializing element in American society. Furthermore, the authors suggested that the content of higher education, which is taught in both overt (e.g., college courses, lectures, and research) and covert (e.g., policies, procedures, values, and hiring practices) ways, has significant and cyclical impact on the other societal institutions (e.g., religion, government, business, and other educational systems), societal values, personal impressions, and articulations.

The authors used the HEI to depict the cyclical practice in which a university's homogeneous structural and staffing components help perpetuate societal values, personal impressions, and articulations that are racist. Positive reinforcement of these white values, impressions, and articulations, to the exclusion of other cultural values (which are translated as racism), then causes these structures to persist. Conversely, the HEI demonstrates that diverse structures and staffing may be created and reinforced by introducing values, personal impressions, and articulations that value diversity. The abiding expression of the dominant culture within higher education deeply affects the administrative and academic components of an institution and the diverse constituents of a university community. Moreover, the values and belief systems that exist in universities play a pronounced role in the shaping of the values of society (Pope, et al., 1989). Exploring the pervasive effects of the dominant culture in each of these areas will provide a clearer understanding of higher education's current structure and the ways in which it can be changed into a more inclusive and culturally sensitive environment.

**Culture and the Administrative Structure**

Higher education's administrative structure consists of those offices, bodies, and committees within the academy that create operating policies, formulate philosophical direction, allocate and spend funds, determine what programs will occur, and select the environment's physical makeup. Barr and Strong (1988) offered a comprehensive list of the institutional policies and practices that can reflect administrative cultural dynamics. Their list included the following areas that may help or hinder multicultural inclusion: hiring and promotion practices for faculty, staff, and administrators; admission practices; financial aid policies and procedures; budget decisions; library acquisition policies; management of institutional investment portfolios; and the selection of extracurricular activities, including speakers and entertainers. In addition, other administrative areas that incorporate cultural content in their policies and procedures may include alumni affairs, athletics, public relations, student discipline, multicultural affairs, counseling and advising, institutional research, and residential life. These areas can affect every facet of campus life.

Consider the implications of administrative structures that are not culturally inclusive. When disciplinary proceedings involve racist or sexist matters, are campus structures equipped to fully understand these matters, address them from a disciplinary standpoint, and address their existence in the student population at large? Are student discipline decisions made by campus constituents who are able to address the disciplinary violation being reviewed, and is any culturally specific content or meaning within this situation being reviewed if necessary? Are faculty review, tenure, and promotion decisions made by faculty committees and administrators sensitive to the unique experiences and cultural realities of faculty of color? Are these committees diverse in their membership and the criteria used. Do these committees understand and appreciate the scholarly work, particularly when it relates to multicultural issues? Do alumni affairs programs and outreach efforts address the interests and needs of alumni of color and women alumnae? Are counseling and advising staff representative of the diversity of the campus student body? Are counseling and advising staff knowledgeable of the variety of cultural perspectives existent in the student population, and do they incorporate this knowledge into their practice as counselors and advisers? Also, what of the residential life environment that seeks to provide students with a living and learning environment that encourages positive growth but that is staffed by resident directors and assistants of a single culture and sponsors programs that do not take into account the diversity of preferences, interests, and viewpoints that are represented within a multicultural residential population? The answers to these questions can illuminate whether college and university administrative structures are culturally inclusive. The way in which campuses respond to questions such as these teaches students, faculty, administrators, and others the institution's accepted cultural values.

Although higher education has a long-standing reputation for collegial decision making (Birnbaum, 1988), seeking consensus does not necessarily coincide with the inclusion of various cultural perspectives. Institutions have a choice as to whether they will or will not incorporate multicultural perspectives administratively. Barr and Strong (1988) astutely questioned institutional commitment to change when they stated that "the structure of higher education is a well-oiled, rationalized, inherently racist system providing many privileges to the dominant group. Why would anyone who benefits from this system want to change it?" (p. 87). The comfort level at which many administrators exist may lead to limited change. Often, an examination of the cultural assumptions underpinning administrative structures is on a piecemeal and isolated basis rather than a systemic approach (Pope, 1993). Although the sincerity of administrators organizing structural change efforts is usually not in question, institutions may be stymied in their quest for multicultural inclusion by various conceptual, programmatic, and personal impediments. These hindrances may include endless study, review and discussion of the problem without movement toward the goals, programs motivated by guilt that lead to ill effects when the guilt is not assuaged, a refusal to forge ahead when powerful community members' lives are disrupted or altered by change, the dilution of pertinent issues by attempting to address all issues simultaneously, and the idea that limited change efforts will solve multicultural inclusion issues (Katz, 1989).

These blocks to administrative and institutional change assist in maintaining monocultural higher-education settings. Student, faculty, and administrative participants in the change effort learn from the lack of change that desiring change may be acceptable, but producing change is a difficult process that may be avoided in many ways. A review of higher education's administrative structures can reveal basic cultural assumptions based on who and what are valued in the institutional setting. Administrative structures, however, are not the only window from which to view cultural dynamics within higher education.

**Culture and the Curriculum**

Undoubtedly among the greatest challenges facing higher education is the reflection of culture in the curriculum. The structure of a college curriculum on many campuses centers around what is commonly known as a core curriculum or general education. These courses are required of every student as an institutional response to the question, "What must students graduating from this college or university know to be considered an educated person?" Previously unquestioned Eurocentric, male-oriented course content and teaching methods are being questioned, discussed, and, in some cases, revamped at many higher-education institutions (Levine & Cureton, 1992). Fueled by the call from several constituencies within the academy—most often and most loudly from students—to see various cultural perspectives reflected in the curriculum, the debate over whose perspectives are to be included is often the cause for bitter separation among academics and the spark that ignites student protests. This issue has also been the topic of numerous volumes dissecting curriculum issues from every angle, including the history of the current curriculum, the advantages and disadvantages of infusing other perspectives into a Eurocentrically oriented core, and the means and methods employed by some institutions of higher learning to achieve curricular adjustment (Minnich, 1990; Rudolph, 1977; Schlesinger, 1992; Simonson & Walker, 1988). Notably, curricular debate is often heard in its extremes. Levine and Cureton (1992) looked beneath the dichotomous character of the public debate to reveal what they term a "quiet revolution" in curricular practices. In a random sample survey of 270 institutions, they found that institutions no longer question whether multiculturalism has a place in their curricular offering but rather focus the debate on the issue of how multiculturalism will be incorporated. Their findings noted that one third of the 270 higher-educational institutions surveyed offered ethnic and gender studies, and that more than one half reported having multicultural content within departmental courses.

Although Levine and Cureton's (1992) findings indicate that multiculturalism is being discussed in the academy, a deeper and more meaningful question focuses on the content of discussion. Much of the discussion regarding culture and the curriculum appears to be occurring at a superficial level for fear of the change that the recognition and inclusion of multiple perspectives requires (hooks, 1994). This infusion of multiculturalism is not a neat and simple process. Minnich (1990) and others (Butler, 1991; hooks, 1994) involved in this process call for a deep and multifaceted critical examination into styles of teaching, choices of works to be studied, and appropriate levels of classroom comfort for both teacher and student. Adherence to the traditional Eurocentric, male-oriented curriculum, however, which has been advocated as a means of maintaining unity and common interests (Bloom, 1987; Schlesinger, 1992), has served to preserve an accepted and comfortable way of life for many.

hooks (1994) cited a common misconception regarding the call for multiculturalism in the curriculum as the belief that multicultural perspectives must and are supplanting the current canon. Levine and Cureton (1992) also refuted this claim by pointing out that most of the curricular revisions they discovered were "add-ons" rather than replacements. Minnich (1990) also disputed the notion that multicultural perspectives are in any way replacing the current European focus of the curriculum. She extensively outlined the deep-rooted and exclusive conceptual foundations of the current curriculum as ample evidence of its dominance in higher-educational thought. In addition, arguments against the infusion of multicultural perspectives are based on the assumption that advocates of the integration of multicultural content primarily seek to bolster the self-esteem and self-identity of students of color (Schlesinger, 1992) rather than use this content as a vehicle for valid academic discourse worthy of critical examination and deconstruction. Although self-esteem may be a by-product of this inclusion, hooks (1994) contended that the acceptance of varied cultural perspectives into a scholarly forum calls for constant critical examination of all modes of thought. Likewise, Minnich (1990) challenged the academy to engage in a paradigmatic review of the core cultural assumptions and thinking patterns on which the curriculum is based.

Among the significant changes called for by this infusion is a move away from what Friere (1970) defined as the "banking system" of education, one in which the student passively receives information from an all-knowing teacher. He supports a "problem-posing" approach that requires a student to question and respond to classroom material—in effect to "interact" with the curriculum. This educational approach requires that a student be a participant rather than an object, acting on his or her own behalf, consciously creating his or her own reality and learning, and acting based on this learning (Freire, 1970; hooks, 1994). From this viewpoint, learning stands in sharp contrast to the current cultural standard in education that not only perpetuates monocultural content but also relies heavily on white culture's value system with respect to a belief in the scientific method, a hierarchical system of decision making, and measures of status and power (Katz, 1989).

hooks (1994) provided a revealing account of the painful process experienced by white faculty as they addressed the question of multicultural inclusion within the curriculum at Oberlin College. She described the resistance on the part of white faculty to acknowledge the political role that "the isms" (racism, sexism, heterosexism, etc.) played in curricular decisions. She also described faculty who willingly accepted the need for curricular revision but spoke of the difficulty of actually making the change and the need for a forum to discuss how and why change was being made. Milem and Astin (1993) concurred with this point in their review of changes in faculty racial and gender composition and changes in faculty attitudes toward diversity during the 17-year period from 1972 to 1989. They found that faculty are more aware of multicultural issues and the need to address them. Milem and Astin also concluded, however, that based on the fact that little has changed with respect to hiring practices and the representation of faculty of color at U.S. colleges and universities, although attitudes may be changing, practices are not. It appears that the paradigmatic shift that includes unlearning deeply embedded exclusionary cultural values that ultimately drive practice is much slower to occur.

## Effects of Culture on Higher Education's Participants

The academy's expectation that students from diverse cultural backgrounds assimilate into the established cultural milieu has not met the needs, desires, or expectations of those students (Livingston & Stewart, 1987; Woolbright, 1989). Popular and higher-education literature reports continual tension between students and the colleges they attend involving the students' desire to be recognized culturally by academic and administrative structures. These students enter collegiate environments seeking promised educational and postgraduate rewards only to confront feelings of isolation and hostility (Livingston & Stewart, 1987). Other problems identified by these students encompass a variety of administrative and academic structures, including sparse financial assistance; a lack of multicultural faculty and staff mentors and role models; inadequate or undesirable social opportunities; difficulty adjusting to majority culture values, customs, and academic life; and, a lack of academic advising (Livingston & Stewart, 1987).

In her landmark study, *Blacks in College*, Jacqueline Fleming (1984) addressed the effect of the environment at predominantly white institutions on the educational attainment of black students. Among the most significant findings she cited was the lack of academic success experienced by these students. Fleming found that, "the stress of racial tension and inadequate social lives borne by black students in white schools generates feelings of alienation that often lead to serious adjustment problems. These stresses lead to a psychological withdrawal that impairs academic functioning" (p. 3). Fleming suggested, as do others (Howard-Hamilton, Owens, & Robinson, 1993; Tinto, 1993), that the lack of significant and consistent faculty-student contact negatively affects a student's college experience. Cultural barriers, however, often keep this essential contact to a minimum (Ayvazian, 1996). Ayvazian cited fear on the part of white faculty members about how well equipped they are to deal with racial issues as a major barrier to developing cross-cultural mentoring relationships. According to Ayvazian, white faculty are afraid of making a mistake, being misunderstood, being labeled "racist," and revealing that they do not know everything with respect to racial issues. Another significant barrier that she discussed is the "collision" of racial identities between students and faculty members. This occurs when students and faculty are at disparate stages of racial identity awareness and consequently clash in their interactions. This mismatch between students and their potential mentors can prove to be an overwhelming obstacle when the combination of the two identity levels prevents honesty or results in self-protection without regard for the other's developmental needs. Ayvazian argued that students are most often the losers in this collision because they may be more vulnerable or less experienced in the academic environment or both.

The limited acceptance of the cultural reality of students of color directly affects student retention rates in an overwhelming number of higher-educational environments. Tinto's (1993) longitudinal model of institutional departure cites the incongruence (mismatch between student and institution) and isolation (lack of contact between students and social and academic subcultures) experienced by students whose cultural values, beliefs, and norms differ from those of the institution that they attend as primary factors leading to attrition. In Tinto's view, it is essential to consider student attrition within the context of the university's influence on a student's experience from a social and intellectual perspective. Although he does not claim that a student's values must perfectly match those of an institution for retention to occur, he does note that a mismatch of values is a precursor to attrition.

People of color and white women who are faculty and staff may have experiences of alienation similar to those of students of color and white female students in the academy. Hall and Sandler (1984) described unwelcoming university environments as those that ignore the needs and perspectives of women. Moses (1989) found that black female students, administrators, and staff do not believe that they are integrated into the mission and goals of higher-educational institutions. Phillip (1994) expounded on the difficulty that male faculty of color experience in seeking the ultimate academic acceptance—tenure. In addition to regularly assigned duties and responsibilities, staff and faculty of color, although typically small in number, are often expected to carry the added responsibility of mentoring and advising students of color (Smith & Davidson, 1992) because of an institution's inability to relate to the diverse experiences of students of color. This responsibility or expectation is often unspoken and rarely acknowledged or compensated.

The entrance and socialization of faculty of color into the professoriate is an area of higher education that clearly portrays the tension that exists within cultural dynamics in the academy. Moore (1988) posited that control of access, discriminatory practices, and a focus on race are factors that account for the small numbers of black faculty at predominantly white colleges and universities. He argued that the merit system, which is often put forth by many campuses as the means for hiring and promoting faculty members, is rarely the only factor used to determine entry into faculty ranks. The power of the faculty is conveyed by what he defined as the "gatekeeper" role played by faculty search committees that are usually and primarily composed of white faculty. He states,

> The gatekeepers determine who is qualified and who is not; what rules to apply, break, or modify as it suits their objectives. . . . The candidate is likely neither to have advocates on the search team nor to be a recipient of the academic patronage of the "old boy" system. (p. 118)

Various authors (Aguirre, Martinez, & Hernandez, 1993; McCormick, 1998; Sands, 1992; Turner & Thompson, 1993) have documented the lack of mentoring experienced by graduate students of color preparing for careers as faculty. This mentoring is described as an essential function that welcomes the new professional into academic life and socializes new members into the values, beliefs, perspectives, and assumptions of the field. In addition, reports indicate that faculty of color are often marginalized within academic departments with respect to decision making and research projects unrelated to multicultural areas (Reyes & Halcón, 1990; Mitchell, 1990).

To mediate the effects of higher education's difficulty in addressing cultural dynamics, such as those highlighted previously, various scholars, theorists, and practitioners have proposed and employed strategies to implement change and address issues of organizational culture. How one conceptualizes and perceives organizational culture greatly affects not only how one attempts to implement change but also whether or not one believes that change is possible. For example, Kuh and Whitt (1988) stated that an anthropological perspective on culture indicates that institutional culture is unalterable. Other theorists and practitioners, however, such as those in organization development, believe that the underlying structures and dynamics of organizations can, and often must, be changed (Morgan, 1986; Ray & Rinzler, 1993; Senge, 1990). This perspective is echoed by those in higher education who are committed to making colleges and universities more multiculturally sensitive. Although some in higher education (e.g., Cheatham, 1990) believe that multicultural change efforts have been uneven, there is increased sentiment that to be effective, multicultural change efforts must be focused on the organizational or institutional level (Barr & Strong, 1989; Manning & Coleman-Boatwright, 1991; Pope, 1993, 1995).

## Strategies for Addressing Cultural Issues in Higher Education

During the past decade, an increasing number of models and tools have become available to address multicultural and organizational culture issues in higher education. Some of these perspectives are derived from literature that emphasizes creating organizational change (Barr & Strong, 1988; Pope, 1993, 1995; Stewart, 1991), whereas others are focused more generally on creating higher-education institutions that are more affirming and welcoming to diverse cultures and groups (Wright, 1987).

To create change in the culture of higher education, these conceptual models and tools must be translated into practice. In proposing her model for multicultural organization change, Pope (1995) stated that such models could be used to create multicultural campuses in three primary areas: (a) assessment, (b) strategic planning, and c) curriculum transformation.

Assessment is a necessary foundation for any change effort. Before attempting to create change, it is vital to assess how individuals within the environment perceive, experience, and evaluate the environment. Most of the models available for assessment do not appear to have instruments that have been evaluated for their validity and reliability, but rather they have more of a heuristic value in their ability to conceptualize the cultural dynamics and realities of the environment. Before strategic planning or curricular transformation can occur within an institution or unit, some assessment must be completed. An example of an assessment tool that is heuristic in nature is a cultural audit that, according to Kuh and Whitt (1993), can be used to "systematically identify artifacts, values, and institutionally relevant assumptions about matters, such as the nature of teaching and learning, the reward structure, students' efforts, relationships between faculty and students, and collaboration and cooperation in the academy" (p. 103).

Several developmental models also exist that highlight specific developmental phases necessary to create multicultural organizations or campuses. These models can be used to assess or diagnose where a given institution or division, department, or unit within the campus lies on the developmental continuum. According to Katz (1989), once the system has been diagnosed, one can develop appropriate interventions to help move the institution or unit further along the continuum. Katz offered a developmental model that "outlines how organizations can move developmentally from being a monocultural system, whose goal is to maintain a white cultural system, to being an inclusionary, multicultural system, which seeks and values diversity" (p. 9). Katz's model for developing culturally diverse organizations specifies stages that range from conceptualizing organizations as exclusionary (the club) to focusing more superficially or symbolically on incorporating multiculturalism (the symbolic difference organization) to an emphasis on increasing the diversity of their environment (affirmative action). The final stage of the model occurs when "multicultural values and norms are institutionalized as racism and sexism once were, and being multicultural is fundamentally connected to the organization's business, mission, values, and purpose" (p. 12). Katz also highlighted specific interventions for each of the four stages and suggested that true organizational transformation might take 3 to 5 years. This model can be used for both assessment and strategic planning.

A similar model, which can be used for assessment and strategic planning, was developed by Manning and Coleman-Boatwright (1991). According to Manning and Coleman-Boatwright, the Cultural Environment Transitions Model based on the Katz model (1989) is "a means to assist institutional members to define and work toward the goals of multiculturalism" (p. 369). Their model identifies three steps and two plateaus that organizations must experience to become multicultural. Similar to the Katz (1989) model, the Cultural Environment Transitions Model begins with an acknowledgment of the monocultural nature of the organization or institution (Monocultural). The next step involves an Awareness with Inability to Change and Height of the Conflict in which institutions are beginning to struggle with creating change. The final step focuses on Institutional Rebirth Reflects Multicultural Goals and the creation of a Multicultural campus. Manning and Coleman-Boatwright also offered indicators and possible initiatives for each step or plateau of the Cultural Environment Transitions Model.

Pope (1995) offered another conceptual model based on the concepts of systemic planned change and multicultural organization development that can be used for either assessment or strategic planning within a higher-education institution. The Multicultural Change Intervention Matrix (MCIM) provides a framework for codifying the range of activities used to address multicultural issues on a given campus. The MCIM offers six different ways to conceptualize and structure multicultural change efforts. Within the MCIM, there are three different targets of change (Individual, Group, and Institutional) and two different types of change (first- and second-order change). According to Pope (1995), "by increasing one's understanding of the range of targets and goals that may be used, the types of activities, strategies, and tools can more easily be expanded" (p. 243).

All the previous models can be used for institutional strategic planning. According to Pope (1995), "strategic planning is an essential tool in the creation of multicultural campuses" (p. 245). The MCIM and other models can be used to conceptualize the multicultural change efforts currently being used (and the overall status or developmental phase of the institution), to set goals and priorities, and to design future change efforts.

In terms of curricular transformation, some of these models, especially the MCIM, have the potential to be used to infuse multicultural issues into a specific academic program, department, or the entire academic unit of a campus. The MCIM offers a useful framework that can be used to assess the type and level of multicultural education in the classroom and within the overall curriculum. Reynolds (1996) described how to use the MCIM as a way to conceptualize multicultural teaching in counseling psychology training programs.

All these models have the potential for creating institutional change in higher education and infusing culture and making cultural dynamics more conscious, acknowledged, and actively chosen. The potential for change is great with these models because they focus on both structural and cultural aspects of institutions that are necessary for creating lasting change (Katz, 1989; Pope, 1995). It is also important, however, to remember that, as Manning and Coleman-Boatwright (1991) stated, "the all-pervasive presence of the dominant culture in the organizational structure works against progress toward multiculturalism" (p. 371). They also stated that the dynamic process of creating institutional change "requires constant educational processes and vigilance to reward nondominant cultural styles, structure, and behaviors" (p. 371).

## Conclusion

In general, the literature examining higher education has failed to fully explore the issues of institutional culture particularly as it relates to the issues of race, ethnicity, gender, class, and the existing cultural values. Instead, most of this literature examines the culture of higher education from a purely organizational and structural context with occasional references to some of the interpersonal dynamics that occur. This literature rarely, if ever, acknowledges that higher-education institutions are steeped in a cultural value system that is white, Anglo, male, and middle to upper class. Higher-education institutions might be better served with a more inclusive and more complex understanding of institutional culture. A more inclusive concept of culture might involve the conceptual linking of the literature of higher education and multicultural issues with the institutional culture literature. This new conceptualization of higher-education culture requires more than merely adding content to the existing literature; instead, what is needed is an integrated multitheoretical perspective that incorporates theories and ideas from established fields and translates them to the higher-education context. The writing by Katz (1989) provides a good example of the conceptual work that needs to be done. Furthermore, the research and writing of Carter (1995) provide an excellent reminder of the need to make culture a central and visible issue.

# 9

# Mental Health

## *The Influence of Culture on the Development of Theory and Practice*

### *Barbara C. Wallace*

The field of mental health represents an institution that reflects the culture in which it has developed and evolved. The various organizational settings in which the counselor, researcher, and teacher work closely reflect the larger dominant culture. Within these settings, not only is harm done to clients, research subjects, and students who experience invisible, covert forms of violence, but also professionals effectively role model for and condition the next generation of professionals in how to perpetrate violence. In this manner, the culture of the field of mental health closely parallels and mirrors the historical reality of the United States' being a culture of violence (Wallace, 1993). Historically, the U.S. culture of violence oppressed Native Americans and African slaves, and nativism and xenophobia have fueled violence against new immigrant arrivals (Wallace, 1996). In contemporary times, this dominant culture of violence may be criticized as patriarchal, racist, sexist, and homophobic, perpetuating oppression of various groups, historically, through overt violence, and through covert forms of violence in contemporary times. It has been argued that professionals may actually engage in invisible, covert forms of violence when they project negative and low expectations on clients, talk down to clients as though they are inferior, and pose as superiors working with inferiors who are "below" them (Wallace, 1994, 1995). To engage in overt, invisible forms of violence is to participate in the oppression of others—whether clients, research subjects, or students. Thus, those settings in which the counselor, researcher, and teacher work, within the larger field of mental health, need to be critically examined and transformed so they no longer closely mirror the dominant society in the perpetuation of oppression.

The field of mental health is currently faced with an imperative. The field must evolve well beyond its cultural roots, given the goal of pluralism and the presence of a multicultural society. Members of ethnic, racial, gender, sexual orientation, and class groups once subjugated, oppressed, and shaped to accept domination and control in past historical eras demand that society and the field of mental health implement a new cultural paradigm that guarantees their humanity and "does no harm." A transformation is absolutely essential in both professionals as individuals and in the culture they create in the settings in which they practice. This involves transforming the personal paradigms that counselors, researchers, and teachers employ, thereby changing the prevailing cultural paradigm in their work settings and the paradigm that inevitably influences the development of theory and practice within the field of mental health.

The goal of this chapter is to stimulate in the current or future counselor, or both, researcher, and teacher four simultaneous processes: (a) gaining critical insight into the influence of culture on the development of theory and practice in the field of mental health, (b) becoming multiculturally competent (or more so), (c) transforming one's personal paradigm, and thereby (d) transforming the guiding paradigm that helps to create and sustain the prevailing culture in the settings in which that individual works. In addition to an analysis of the influence of culture on the development of theory and practice in the field of mental health and exposure of the forms of covert, invisible violence, a model for training how to become multiculturally competent is also presented. Such training is vitally important, given the "call to the profession" by Sue, Arredondo, and McDavis (1992) for "some sort of formal training on cultural differences" (p. 480) that responds to the reality that counselors without "training or competence in working with clients from diverse cultural backgrounds are unethical and potentially harmful" (p. 480). A larger audience of current and future professionals in the mental health field, including not only counselors but also researchers and teachers, need exposure to training that helps them attain multicultural competence. This chapter seeks to foster multicultural competence in this larger audience by meeting the following need articulated by Sue et al. (1992):

> What is needed is for counselors to become culturally aware, to act on the basis of a critical analysis and understanding on their own conditioning, the conditioning of their clients, and the social political system of which they are both a part. Without such awareness, the counselor who works with a culturally different client may be engaging in cultural oppression using unethical and harmful practices. (p. 480)

Thus, the training provided in this chapter seeks to foster multicultural competence by shifting beliefs and attitudes and transmitting skills necessary for ethical conduct toward the goal of ending practices consistent with cultural oppression. The resulting awareness may constitute a new body of knowledge that produces new cognitions that guide the exercise of new behaviors.

# Shifting Beliefs and Attitudes

The first part of training in multicultural competence strives to shift the beliefs and attitudes held by professionals in the field of mental health. If professionals continue to adhere to false beliefs about their current status and the nature of their performance in the settings in which they work, the need for training in multicultural competence may easily be denied. Attitudes that clients, research subjects, and students have that support the status quo also need to be challenged, especially because many clients, research subjects, and students in the field of mental health become professionals in this field. It is all too easy to continue to hold on to the attitude that the status quo is acceptable.

## Examples of Oppression in Mental Health Settings

Several examples of how all is not well within the field of mental health within counseling, research, and teaching settings may begin the process of shifting beliefs and attitudes. Case examples reveal how oppression and invisible, covert forms of violence reign across diverse organizational settings in the field of mental health.

### *The Setting of Inpatient Hospitalization*

The case of Mr. D., an African American master's-level educated professional with a chemical-dependence problem, illustrates a common experience for many clients, especially minorities and women, who enter treatment in the inpatient hospital setting. Once an outpatient, Mr. D. spoke angrily of spending $32,000 of his insurance plan funds on the one and only inpatient hospitalization stay his plan would permit, making even more tragic his one negative experience with month-long inpatient hospital chemical-dependency treatment. Throughout the month of treatment, he was not taught relapse prevention strategies even though he was told that relapse was "practically inevitable." He also spoke of several examples of being treated in group counseling in a manner that suggested that he was also perceived as having a poorer prognosis. Mr. D. also believed he was treated poorly relative to other clients by professionals in the facility, and that these professionals lacked the cultural competence for treating an African American male client such as he. Toward the end of his month-long treatment, an African American female joined him in integrating the inpatient unit.

This case example exposes the need for those working within the field of mental health, including those who may have relatively less frequent contact with minority patients, to obtain multicultural competence. Without training in how to be multiculturally competent, professionals may unwittingly foster not only bad feelings and negative memories of treatment in clients such as Mr. D. but also poorer treatment outcomes.

*The Setting of the Field Researcher*

The field researcher enters the community in which research subjects are to be found, often insensitively violating their privacy and imposing on them a pernicious cultural paradigm rooted in the U.S. culture of violence. Often, research subjects feel violated and oppressed in their very own community. For example, as an African American researcher in the field within an urban residential therapeutic community in which clients lived, worked, and received treatment, I encountered the anger of several African American and Latino residents in a research planning meeting that was specifically designed to create a culturally sensitive process of introducing research into this field setting. Two residents angrily spoke of not wanting to be treated as "guinea pigs." Their views and feelings were taken seriously, and the voluntary nature of their participation, their right to discontinue participation at any point, and the potential uses of the data collected and benefits of participation to future residents in the therapeutic community were explained in the meeting. How many researchers, however, have provided a forum in which minority research subjects could articulate their anger for past research experiences and their fears regarding participation in a current research project?

Prior to becoming a researcher, as an undergraduate, graduate student, and postdoctoral fellow, I, too, often felt anger at how poor, minority research subjects were perceived and treated by researchers. These residents were asking a question I had struggled with myself: What made me different from this legacy and tradition as a researcher of color? Second, how was my research going to be different from a large body of deficit-oriented or blame-the-victim research? This body of research typically concluded that the deficit or blame for one's condition could be located within the individual minority subject or his or her families, citing some inherent weakness or vulnerability. Research findings from a deficit-oriented or blame-the-victim perspective may also serve to spread misinformation and myths about a poor, oppressed group.

*The Classroom Setting in Academia*

As an undergraduate and graduate student, as well as a teacher in academia, I have experienced and witnessed the manner in which hierarchical relationships threaten students into passivity, silence, and submission, especially when students are abruptly cutoff, spoken down to in a demeaning manner, publicly accused of not doing reading assignments, or otherwise humiliated in the classroom. This regularly occurs in classrooms purporting to train the next generation of counselors, researchers, and teachers.

*Debunking Myths to Shift Beliefs and Attitudes*

Shifting beliefs also necessitates debunking several myths, including the following: (a) Counselors do no harm and are ethical and competent, (b) researchers engage in value-neutral objective science, and (c) teachers promote free speech in academia.

*Debunking the Myth That Counselors Do No Harm and Are Ethical and Competent.* The myth that counselors do no harm and are ethical and competent must be debunked because mental health professionals operate in ways that closely parallel the dominant culture. Pinderhughes (1989) examines how "cultural perceptions and experiences related to ethnicity, race, and power affect people's sense of themselves, as well as others, their feelings and attitudes" (p. 2) and the behavior they manifest; moreover, all this appears in service delivery. Heyward (1993) tries to "help sharpen awareness among healers and those seeking healing and liberation" (p. 1). Her goal is to expose how "an immutable 'power-over' dynamic that does not move us toward a more shared connection serves to diminish and mute the human spirit—even in well-intended, carefully structured professional situations such as psychotherapy" (pp. 1–2). She appreciates the way in which those of us who have been socialized in this culture have been exposed to a "white-dominated, male-defined, profit-driven militaristic society organized to maintain and increase the power of those who historically have been white, economically privileged, ostensibly heterosexual males" (pp. 4–5). Furthermore, she spells out how her experience included what women "are shaped to experience by heterosexist patriarchy: abusive social relations" (p. 15). In this regard, Heyward (1993) asserts the following:

> Psychotherapy is a class privilege. I do not believe that, as a privilege, psychotherapy is inherently unethical, wrong. But something is wrong—ethically, psychologically, spiritually, and politically—when therapists or other helpers approach pain as if it could be treated more or less independently of the social forces, including the privilege, that often have created it and always have helped hold it in place. (p. 13)

Pedersen (1994) explains that counseling as a source of help has a "bad reputation for taking the side of the status quo" in forcing individuals to adjust or adapt to the institutions of society, despite the reality that the client is "right and the system is wrong" (p. 49). As West (1993) states, "the enemy is oppression and exploitation" and it is "legitimate to abhor and hate oppression and exploitation" (p. 107)—as many clients who left harmful counseling surely did.

West (1993), however, also states that "we cannot lose sight of the humanity of those who are perpetuating" oppression and exploitation (p. 107). After all, professional training has had serious deficits historically, and the delivery of training in multicultural competence is challenging. Pinderhughes (1989) argues that the ability to become comfortable with "culturally different others and to recognize the relativity of one's own values" are critical elements in professional training but are quite difficult to develop (p. 5). At the same time, the fears evoked when teachers, counselors, and others "are asked to shift their paradigms" (hooks, 1994, p. 36) must be recognized. Carter and Qureshi (1995) assert that counselors who enjoy the benefits of dominant group membership or have a vested interest in the status quo "seem to have no interest in working toward developing consciousness of the inequities inherent in the status quo" (p. 254).

LaFromboise, Foster, and James (1996, p. 48) focus on the need for ethical guidelines that address the appropriate behavior of counselors and psychologists in public agencies, academic settings, private practice, and industrial and business sites. According to Lafromboise et al. (1996), the resulting "multicultural ethics" must be forged in an environment that considers it unethical not only to serve clients from culturally defined backgrounds when a counselor is not competent to work with that cultural group but also to deny clients professional services because the staff is inadequately prepared (p. 49). This dilemma underscores the valuable contributions made to the field of multicultural counseling through the publication of multicultural competencies and standards (Sue et al., 1992), guidelines for operationalizing these competencies (Arredondo et al., 1996), and by many authors (Ponterotto, Casas, Suzuki, & Alexander, 1995) offering multiple perspectives and guidelines for multicultural training in many settings (Berg-Cross & Chinen, 1995; Brown & Landrum-Brown, 1995; Carter & Qureshi, 1995; Pope-Davis & Dings, 1995; Reynolds, 1995). The purpose of training is to prepare counselors to deliver services in a variety of settings without doing harm while being ethical and competent. In the absence of wide-spread training in multicultural competence, however, the historical reality of inadequate training necessitates debunking as myth that counselors who currently deliver services are doing no harm and are ethical and competent.

*Debunking the Myth That Researchers Engage in Value-Neutral Objective Science.* Whether called cultural psychology (Shweder, 1995), cross-cultural counseling (Pedersen, Draguns, Lonner, & Trimble, 1996), multicultural counseling (Ponterotto et al., 1995), or a global, international psychology (Greenfield & Cocking, 1994; Kitayama & Markus, 1995), the new "fourth force" in psychology (Pedersen et al., 1996) provides compelling evidence of the pernicious influence that culture has had and continues to have on the area of research. Moreover, writers within this new area debunk the myth of a value-neutral objective science.

Ingleby (1995) suggests that psychologists have tended to downplay the problem of ethnocentrism, explaining how "paradigms" or "research programmes" contain fundamental propositions that are never put to the test (p. 109). He posits that psychology as a science is "deeply entangled with its own object, the inhabitants of the modern western world" (p. 111). Moreover, Ingleby poses the central question for psychology that is the basis of this chapter's analysis: "[C]an it disentangle itself sufficiently in order to open up to us the reality of other cultures?" (p. 111) Further exposing the nature of the dilemma, he points out how the notion that scientific theories were grounded "exclusively on objective data gave the theories the kind of absolute authority formerly enjoyed by the bible or the Pope" (p. 115).

Shweder (1995) provides a critique of general psychologists, attacking how once in the experimental laboratory it is "quite fantastically and against much evidence" assumed that "we can physically enter a transcendent realm where the effects of context, content, and meaning can be eliminated, standardized, or kept under control" (p. 49). In support, Kitayama and Markus (1995) identify the "readiness to assume that the processes revealed in our studies are universal and the product of relatively invariant computer-like human processors" (p. 379). Psychologists have to face the reality that "our current mainstream psychology is in many senses a 'local' psychology that is rooted in a Euro-American culture, and as a consequence, it is not yet a fully comprehensive psychology" (Kitayama & Markus, 1995, p. 380). As psychologists move toward rectifying this predicament, they need to embrace the challenge of becoming more international and global; this requires "moving forward while simultaneously reexamining many of the assumptions, frameworks, and theories that have been the basis of our previous work" (p. 380). For example, Kitayama and Markus (1995) found that "virtually the only model of the individual, of the person, or of the self in psychology, or indeed, in any of the social sciences is that of the rational, self-interested actor" in which the individual emphasizes one's "own inner attributes and not being unduly influenced by others" (pp. 366–367). On the other hand, "this model of the self is quite simply not one held by the majority of the people in the world;" the Japanese, for example, emphasize "relations— fitting-in and harmonious interdependence with others" (p. 367).

As additional illustration of the need for reexamination of psychological research and theories, Cushman (1995) probes deeply into the research by Stern (1985) involving infant development of the self that was warmly embraced by self psychologists. Cushman questions Stern's conclusions regarding how the infants had control over self-generated action, which Stern described as the characteristic of individual agency. Cushman argues that Stern could have emphasized in his conclusions the concepts of "cooperation with and dependence on others" or social dependence (p. 395). Cushman explains why reexamination of this and other research is important:

> If psychologists are going to do more than support the status quo and reproduce the current forms of power and privilege in the world, we must situate our work historically, situate the current concept of self, and study how that self is constructed and how it fits with and reproduces the current sociopolitical forms and structures of our world. We will have to decide whether we approve of that fit and whether we want to contribute to it. . . . Those who "own" the self control our world. That is, those who are accorded the right to define, describe, understand, and heal the self are in a powerful, prescriptive position. . . .

> Therefore, the battle over the self—who knows it, who is responsible
> for it, who can heal it—is a central aspect of this era's struggle for
> power and hegemony. . . . Decontextualized theories, creative, soothing,
> and eloquent though they may be, in the end prevent people from
> facing the political consequences of this era and developing structural
> solutions that might lessen the suffering that is all around us. (pp. 412–
> 413)

Others foster the search for structural solutions in the field of developmental psychology, attempting to free it from a narrow perspective, one that is "ethnocentric" and "dominated by a Euro-American perspective" (Greenfield, 1994a, p. ix). Greenfield observes how at international conferences, "all too often, colonial and other hierarchical power relations are replicated at the intellectual level" (p. ix).

Greenfield (1994b) critiques the manner in which developmental psychology has been guilty in theory and research of "mistaking the particular for the universal" (p. 1). She recognizes how developmental psychology, and psychology as a whole, has attempted to conform to the scientific method, thereby reifying objectivity as opposed to subjectivity. The corollary of this scientific value is that "the less involved you are in a psychological phenomenon, the more accurately you can study it" (p. 23). Greenfield (1994b) exposes this view as naive at best and asserts that in studying their own culture, "psychologists or other social scientists are unacknowledged insiders" (p. 23). Recognition of this fact permits seeing how the advantage for research "is that methodological procedures and interpretations of data are unconsciously adapted to the culture of the subjects" (p. 23). Greenfield and Cocking (1994) seek to redress the situation wherein many groups and societies throughout the world "have been studied almost exclusively by European and Euro-American outsiders" (p. 23). In their edited volume, a body of quantitative and qualitative research from throughout the world illustrates how psychologists are all too often completely unaware "that we are imposing assumptions about conditions, values, and pathways of socialization and development that are foreign to the people being studied" (pp. 23–24). Several conceptual steps are put forth to remove ethnocentric bias and foster scientific recognition that different cultures value different developmental trajectories that arise as adaptations to different ecological niches (p. 29).

Drawing on evidence in the literature, Greenfield (1994b) cites, for example, how European and Euro-American scientists have assumed that independence and school-based cognitive development are universal goals of development, with implicit value judgments concerning the superiority of the independent individual. As a result, respect for elders and the socialization of practices that support this respect have been given a negative evaluation in developmental psychology and labeled as a lack of initiative and authoritarian child rearing (p. 30). Ethnocentric bias is inherent when developmental psychology assumes the goal of an independent individual and studies the development of self-regulation "rather than other regulation, of independence training rather than interdependence training, when we study the child's acquisition of information from books rather than from people" (p. 31). This ethnocentric bias also prevails when researchers concentrate study of communicative development on a "dyad in which the mother focuses exclusively on the child" (p. 31). Instead, researchers might study the child in a communication network that includes a third party (p. 31), such as a father, and a larger family setting.

Similarly, Greenfield (1994b) provides a compelling reexamination of field independence and how it has been positively evaluated, whereas field dependence has been devalued. Field dependence, however, could be reconceptualized as a dimension of field sensitivity. In this manner, Greenfield (1994b) draws on a body of research and literature to expose the reality that developmental psychology is not a "value-neutral science" (p. 31). The myth of value-neutral objective science must be debunked as a critical step toward fostering the development of research, as well as theory which guides research, so that it is a relevant domain of inquiry in a multicultural society.

*Debunking the Myth of Free Speech in Academia.* For those teachers within the field of mental health who teach the practice, theory, and research of psychology, all too often reified as value-neutral science, it is essential to follow hooks (1994) in understanding the "difference between education as the practice of freedom and education that merely strives to reinforce domination" (p. 4). Based on Greenfield's (1994a) analysis, far too many teachers have unwittingly practiced a form of education that subtly reinforced domination—merely by using information in the standard publications and journals in the mental health field.

Also, a clear boundary exists between the dominant, powerful teacher, and the passive, subordinate student. Educators need to follow hooks (1994), who celebrates "teaching that enables transgressions—a movement against and beyond boundaries" (p. 12). It is necessary to transgress those boundaries that would confine each pupil to "a rote, assembly-line approach to learning" (p. 13), as hooks (1994) explains:

> Caring about whether all students fulfill their responsibility to contribute to learning in the classroom is not a common approach in what Freire has called the "banking system of education" where students are regarded merely as passive consumers. Since so many professors teach from that standpoint, it is difficult to create the kind of learning community that can fully embrace multiculturalism. . . . It has been as a teacher in the classroom setting that I have witnessed the power of a transformative pedagogy rooted in a respect for multiculturalism. Working with a critical pedagogy based on my understanding of Freire's teaching, I enter the classroom with the

assumption that we must build "community" in order to create a climate
of openness and intellectual rigor.(p. 40)

hooks (1994) points toward an important guiding philosophy, especially as we
come to appreciate how the classroom and academic community as a whole still
comprise an environment characterized by authoritarian, hierarchical
relationships wherein a chain of command involves superiors talking down to
subordinates: Financial officers and trustees tell administrators what to do,
administrators tell faculty what to do, and faculty tell students what to do and
think. Homogenizing tyranny too often reigns, revealing, as does Taylor (1994,
p. 51), how the programming of a general will occurs. There is pressure to talk the
party line, at least in public discourse, condemning the academy into being an
oppressive regime that falsely claims to embody the principle of free speech. A
reorganization of academia is vitally needed that strives to avoid top-down
communication, and the subtle exercise of the abuse of power and that follows
the values of a new cultural paradigm.

   In light of the decentering of the West globally, while embracing
multiculturalism, educators must be compelled to focus attention on the issue of
voice, inquiring "Who speaks? Who listens? And Why?" (hooks, 1994, p. 40).
An answer to hook's question, "Who Speaks?" is that too often teachers
prevent students from exercising free speech by talking down to them,
dismissing and demeaning them for any independent, autonomous thinking, and
confining them to the role of the passive, silent student who must memorize by
rote what professors tell them is "right knowledge and thinking." An answer to
hook's question, "Who listens?" is that many educators have yet to learn how to
"truly hear" the diverse voices of students. The myth of free speech reigning in
classrooms and in academia must be debunked. Finally, an answer to hook's
question, "Why?" is that educators must recognize an ethical imperative to
genuinely foster free speech in academia because only a free-flowing dialogue
will permit students, faculty, and the institution to reach their full potential.

## Transmitting Skills

Consistent with a paradigm shift, the transmitting of new skills to current and
future counselors, researchers, and teachers needs to occur to foster
multicultural competence. It is difficult to shift attitudes and beliefs and produce
the awareness that "all is not well" in the field of mental health and the status
quo must change. It is hoped that this awareness will constitute a new body of
knowledge, producing new cognitions. Ideally, new cognitions lead to the
production of new interpersonal behaviors. The production of new interpersonal
behavior, however, often requires the transmission of specific interpersonal
skills.

## Interpersonal Skills for Effective Communication

Several authors have described, using various language, the ideal combination of good listening skills, accurate empathy, and the process of reflecting back to the communicator what has been heard and perceived. Heyward (1993) uses a term that captures the process dimension of this skill, directing professionals to "hear to speech" those who seek counseling services. Heyward explains: "[T]here is in each of us a need to be heard to speech. This need is the root of all genuine healing and the source of all creative revolutionary movement. It is the wellspring of our redemption, and it is the hope of the world" (p. 192). An individual who is "heard to speech" will speak and hear aloud their own truth. As Miller (1995) suggests, "as I hear myself talk, I learn what I believe" (p. 95).

Similarly, from the "fourth force" in counseling, Pedersen et al. (1996) describe the skill of being able to deploy "cultural empathy," performing the basic skill of which Heyward speaks. Wallace (1993) describes this same fundamental skill, referred to as culturally sensitive empathy:

> The deployment of this culturally sensitive empathy requires that I merely sit across from clients, listen ever so keenly to their tales with my observing ego in full operation, and feel empathy for their inner self experience. The next step is to gently hold up a mirror and reflect back to clients what we have felt and experienced empathetically as perhaps their inner feelings. I may now label and identify such feelings and encourage the client to talk about that feeling or situation further. To the extent that clinicians do this with some success, clients who look across from us, seeing us and our overt differences, will feel genuinely understood and validated. Their inner self feels gratified that another real self has felt their pain and validated their private, inner experience as genuine, real, valid, and acceptable—without conveying any judgment, criticism, or condemnation. (p. 19)

This description of a culturally sensitive empathy is compatible with Heyward's (1993) term, being heard to speech. Cultural empathy, culturally sensitive empathy, and being heard to speech are all reminiscent of the concept of active listening and reflection with empathy put forth by Carl Rogers (Miller & Rollnick, 1991). Although the field of counseling may have historically placed a premium on active listening skills, along with the use of empathy and reflection, researchers and teachers need to value and deploy these same skills. As a field researcher in the residential therapeutic community, I sought to be culturally sensitive by having an orientation meeting before I introduced research into that setting with an African American and Latino population. By actively listening to residents, I heard to speech those who spoke of not wanting to be guinea pigs, also attuned to their feelings of anger from past experiences in which they were taken advantage of by others. Similarly, as teachers, the task is to hear to speech students who share what they think about a reading assignment or concept. The teacher may also attune to what a student seems to be feeling, perhaps electing to reflect back to that student what he or she senses the student is feeling, or the teacher may listen and observe as other students join in the dialogue. In this manner, the actions that the counselor typically performs as an active listener who attunes to the inner affects of clients must be regularly practiced as essential skills by the researcher and teacher to foster and sustain a new cultural paradigm and so that the researcher and teacher are multiculturally competent.

The acquisition of interpersonal skills tends to be cumulative; individuals master and deploy one or two skills (such as active listening and being genuinely empathic) and then begin practicing another skill. The next step is to combine active listening, reflection, and empathy with the pointing out of discrepancies in clients' cognitions or between a cognition and a behavior; this tends to create a state of cognitive dissonance, causes a new feeling or affect to surface, and increases motivation to engage in behavioral change. The term *empathic mirroring* (Wallace, 1991, 1996) captures the cumulative process of engaging in active listening, empathy, reflection, and pointing out discrepancies between cognitions or cognitions and behaviors—with the result of producing cognitive dissonance, affects, and a state of readiness and motivation to change. This change may include a shift in one's cognitions or behavior.

Empathic mirroring has been summarized as having four critical steps: (a) empathy—be empathic and not confrontational; (b) cognitive dissonance—point out discrepancies in the client's thinking or between thoughts and behavior; (c) mirroring—reflect or mirror back to the client, after intensive listening, what he or she is saying and feeling; and (d) self-determination—ask the client what he or she thinks should be done about the problem, conflict, or condition. In addition, by using this skill, one seeks to instill a sense of empowerment and restore hope (Wallace, 1996, p. 257).

Empathic mirroring (Wallace, 1991) is identical to Miller's term or concept (1983; Miller & Rollnick, 1991) of motivational interviewing (Wallace, 1996). It is interesting that independent practitioners discovered and described an identical technique in separate work with crack cocaine-dependent clients and alcoholics, respectively—populations oppressed insofar as they are dependent on a chemical substance and stigmatized and rejected by society. The search and discovery of practical techniques that "work" with oppressed populations (Miller & Rollnick, 1991; Wallace, 1991, 1996) is not unlike the search for a pedagogy that works for the oppressed. Freire (1970), in helping to substantiate how the multiple acts of reflection inherent in empathic mirroring may indeed be valid instruments of liberation from oppression, states the following:

> This pedagogy makes the oppression and its causes objects of reflection by the oppressed, and from that reflection will come their necessary engagement in the struggle for their liberation. . . . In order for the oppressed to be able to wage the struggle for their liberation, they

must perceive the reality of oppression not as a closed world from which there is no exit, but as a limiting situation which they can transform. This perception . . . must become the motivating force for liberating action. (pp. 33–34)

Empathic mirroring is a skill that fosters the perception in clients that they are in a situation that they can transform, and this perception becomes the motivating force for liberating action from oppression. Empathic mirroring may result in the perception of options for ending a limiting dependency or addiction.

## Research Supporting Nonconfrontational, Nonhierarchical Techniques as Effective

Empathic mirroring has also been described as nonconfrontational and nonhierarchical. Often, alcoholics and drug users have been harshly confronted with the facts of their addiction and disease and been forcefully educated to accept the label of alcoholic or addict. Research has found, however, no beneficial effect from educational lectures and films (Miller et al., 1995, p. 31). In addition, no outcome studies have provided support for the effectiveness of confrontational approaches in controlled studies with alcoholics (Miller et al., 1995, p. 27). Moreover, confrontation may be seen as the conceptual opposite of Carl Roger's client-centered therapy (Miller & Rollnick, 1991), which when used with alcoholics was found to compare favorably with alternative approaches in three of four studies; it was the only form of individual psychotherapy for people with alcohol problems that yielded positive findings (Miller et al., 1995, p. 27). Motivational interviewing has been found in several controlled evaluations to produce significant evidence of efficacy with problem drinkers (Miller, 1995). In a meta-analytic study of 211 controlled alcohol treatment studies, as a result of its cumulative evidence score motivational interviewing ranked third in efficacy compared to 29 other treatments; in addition, brief interventions, such as motivational interviewing, accomplished the greatest level of efficacy (Miller et al., 1995). A motivational counseling approach that relied on the "authority" of the physician did not produce better results than an uncounseled control group (Miller, 1995).

Exposing a typical action of an authoritarian figure, Miller (1995) explains that "[d]irective, confrontation tends to increase resistance. Reflective, supportive counseling tends to minimize resistance" (p. 96). He acknowledges that motivational interviewing is a confrontational process, and that the meaning of the word is literally "to bring face to face." When confrontation is used correctly, however, as in motivational interviewing, the result is an effective therapeutic technique for use with alcoholics and substance abusers. Rollnick and Bell (1991) empowered primary care workers—family doctors, nurses, social workers, probation officers, members of the clergy, and visiting nurses—to use brief motivational interviewing. Others have asserted that Miller and Rollnick (1991) actually present a counseling style or an overall way of interacting with clients (Saunders, Wilkinson, & Allsop, 1991, p. 279), if not with all humans. Recognizing the utility of this innovation, others have applied this highly effective counseling style to other challenging populations, such as adolescents (Tober, 1991) and sex offenders (Garland & Dougher, 1991), and for risk reduction of HIV (Baker & Dixon, 1991).

Hence, the cumulative process of combining the skills of active listening, empathy, reflection, pointing out discrepancies, creating cognitive dissonance, and empathic mirroring (or motivational interviewing) may lead to the production of new cognitions and new behaviors, even when these skills are delivered by a variety of professionals and paraprofessionals to individuals with varied needs and problems. Given the supportive research, it is appropriate to encourage current and future counselors, researchers, and teachers to adopt this combination of skills to be able to engage in effective communication in the settings in which they work in the field of mental health. The goal is to engage in a meaningful dialogue, suggesting the hope of transforming the field of mental health and ushering in a new guiding paradigm.

Freire (1995) also offers a pedagogy of hope, emphasizing he has always been concerned with raising consciousness, or *conscientizaçao*, whereas "the dogmatic, authoritarian leaderships have no reason to engage in dialogue with the popular classes. They need only tell them what they should do" (p. 104). Empathic mirroring and motivational interviewing promote a nonhierarchical dialogue that not only empowers the formerly oppressed to engage in self-determination but also raises the consciousness of those engaged in the dialogue. The nature of the dialogue necessary to raise consciousness must be understood. It involves empowering clients to decide what they should do (Miller & Rollnick, 1991; Wallace, 1991, 1996) or, for example, permitting research subjects to articulate their anger about potentially being treated like guinea pigs or having students in academia exercise free speech in the classroom. As Miller and Rollnick (1991) explain, the dialogue recommend is a radical departure from the confrontation that has occurred in counseling settings in the past:

> Some of the confusion in this area probably arises from the multiple ways in which people have used the term "confrontation." In one sense it connotes ... heavy-handed and coercive tactics. ... It suggests uneven power—an authoritarian one-up pounding the truth into a defiant one-down. This is a style that complements personal or societal attitudes of anger toward the one-downs, and individual needs for power or abasement. ... Yet in a different sense, confrontation is a goal of all counseling and psychotherapy, and is a prerequisite for intentional change. ... More generally, the purpose of confrontation is to see and accept reality, so that one can change accordingly. ... To see one's situation clearly is a first step in change. This is the goal of confrontation. (p. 13)

The goal is not to have the counselor tell the individual how to run his or her life, have the researcher dictate to the subject to silently submit and cooperate with any procedure, nor have the teacher tell the students what and how to think. Instead, responsibility for change "is left with the individual" client (Miller & Rollnick, 1991, p. 52), research subjects actively share responsibility for their participation, and students actively self-determine what they come to think and know. Hence, multiculturally competent professionals no longer pose as "an authoritarian one-up pounding the truth" or their version of reality into others. Also, within the settings in which they practice, professionals foster others coming to see and accept a reality that is actively created by clients, research subjects, and students. Meanwhile, multiculturally competent professionals who no longer engage in covert, invisible forms of violence may reflect on how they have helped to create the prevailing climate in those organizational settings in which clients, research subjects, and students come to realize their potential for self-determination. Multiculturally competent professionals help to create settings within the field of mental health that are conducive to others feeling empowered to self-determine their own cognitions and behavior by promoting and sustaining a new cultural paradigm in their work settings.

## Conclusion

This chapter provided a critical analysis of the influence of culture on the development of theory and practice in the field of mental health and also exposed how the organizational settings in which the counselor, researcher, and teacher work reflect the pernicious influence of the larger culture. To break the cycle of violence and oppression, counselors, researchers, and teachers need to stop role modeling and conditioning harmful behaviors and cognitions in the next generation of professionals. Toward this end, the chapter discussed multicultural competence training specifically designed to shift attitudes and beliefs as well as to transmit skills necessary for ethical conduct.

As we enter a new millennium, the multitude oppressed by racism, sexism, homophobia, and other forms of violence have demanded that society and the field of mental health implement a new cultural paradigm that guarantees their humanity and does no harm. It is imperative that mental health professionals engage in ethical behavior that serves to empower the historically oppressed. Oddly, by actively speaking aloud and demanding their liberation, the oppressed create the conditions for liberating the oppressors in the field of mental health from bondage to the old cultural paradigm rooted in the culture of violence in the United States. The consciousness of both the oppressed and the oppressor is raised through constructive dialogue. Even more odd is how by giving up their power responsibly and letting it be transformed by the power of mutuality (Heyward, 1993) while also seeking to empower the oppressed, the former oppressors also gain liberation. As equal cooperative creators of a new reality, under a new cultural paradigm, both the formerly oppressed and their oppressors may celebrate liberation and finally benefit from conditions conducive to all realizing their highest potential.

Within the overall process of expanding consciousness, or Freire's (1970) conscientizaçao, "learning to perceive social, political, and economic contradiction, and to take action against the oppressive elements of reality" (p. 19) is essential, as Ivey (1995, p. 54) also argues. Both the formerly oppressed and their oppressors may feel empowered to take action against the oppressive elements in the larger societal reality.

It has been asserted that a pedagogy of the oppressed and a pedagogy of hope must be made and remade (Freire, 1970) through multiple acts of reflection. Beginning with the use of empathic mirroring or the skills inherent in motivational interviewing, the formerly oppressed and their oppressors may engage in civil discourse. As a consequence, they may cooperatively create reality, experience the power of mutuality, and proceed to remake, again and again, the pedagogy for keeping society free from oppression and for sustaining hope for the future. The goal of not only continually expanding consciousness but also constantly creating reality is then earnestly pursued. Earnestly pursuing this goal, professionals entering the new millennium may be seen as functioning within a revitalized field of mental health that is evolving toward its highest potential as they work in diverse organizational settings. Counselors may be seen as engaging in the delivery of ethical and multiculturally competent counseling to foster liberation in clients (Ivey, 1995; Wallace, 1996). Researchers may be appreciated for internationalizing theory and research in psychology so that we understand the diversity of human behavior through the lens of a global psychology that respectfully engages research subjects throughout the world (Greenfield, 1994a; Kitayama & Markus, 1995). Teachers may be respected for practicing the art of teaching to transgress boundaries, making education the practice of freedom (hooks, 1994). Also, society benefits from ethical practice in diverse organizational settings. It is toward realization of these goals that this chapter has analyzed the influence of culture on the development of theory and practice in the field of mental health.

# 10

## The House of God
### The Fallacy of Neutral Universalism in Medicine
#### Vivian Ota Wang

*If there is any possible means of increasing the common wisdom and ability of mankind it must be sought in medicine.*

—Descartes

Behind medical practices are overt and covert values that must be brought to light and examined if one desires to gain a clearer understanding of the attitudes and behaviors held by medical practitioners and the organizational culture that sustains them. For this to occur, a critical analysis of how the medical organizational culture is manifested, influenced, and connected to other sociocultural institutions and traditions must be considered within the context of the attitudes, beliefs, and behaviors of those who teach and practice. Clearly, the cultural assumptions underpinning medicine held by people and society strongly shape each facet of the medical enterprise—education, practice, medical-legal, economic, and social. These premises also influence clinical decision making and attitudes of health care professionals and the image(s) they hold of themselves and those they treat. Burns and Engelhardt (1974) suggested that at the core of medicine are issues concerning the value and purpose of being:

> Science and technology presuppose value judgments and issues of purpose. Just as such facts enable purposes to be accomplished, purposes cause facts to cohere in terms of expectations and meanings. We gather the world around us in terms of what is markedly the case with the central concepts of medicine: health and disease.... They sketch the limits and values of the human condition. (p. ix)

## The Culture of Medicine

Overall, medicine is a discipline based in the natural sciences. Using sophisticated scientific technology, the value of biological phenomena is upheld by empirically validated measurements of natural phenomena. Although it is true that medical practitioners depend on evidentiary scientific knowledge to understand disease and well-being, how they use this knowledge also governs their hypothesis formulation and refutation, decision making, and critical thinking skills. Reductionism through empirical quantification is the means to the end of informing the practitioner of how to formulate, validate, refute, and treat problems; thus, it fundamentally influences the type of knowledge sought and valued (e.g., a patient's self-report of information is viewed as less reliable than a empirically measured chemical on a laboratory report). In this regard, Descartes's empirical reductionism has greatly influenced how scientific knowledge is pursued. In seeking connections between physical symptoms and diseases, practitioners are expected to understand the etiological agents and pathological mechanisms of illness, thereby reducing disease into its elemental components. The visible is credible, measurable, and neutral, whereas the invisible is prone to suspect.

The medical universalistic tradition emerges from this positivist-empirical model and presumes that what is measurable reflects a universal aspect of human life. To this end, individuals who do not "fit" along the statistically "neutral" normal distribution are equated as deviant. What universalistic values are embedded in the medical culture, and where and how do these microcultural values intersect in people's lives? Medical researchers and practitioners understand people according to the canon of the basic sciences; Individuals are generic, human, and universal. Medical practitioners adopt this universal approach focusing on shared experiences (e.g., illness or well-being), deductive reasoning (e.g., growth hormone deficiency vs. malnutrition as a diagnosis), validation through verifiable and reproducible means (e.g., X rays and weight gain), and treatments under controlled conditions (e.g., hospitals and medical clinics). They consider this decision-making process parsimonious and unfraught with the influences of social class, religion, race, and so on that are regarded as more scientifically ambiguous.

Western science fundamentally influences the character, methods, practices, ethos, ethics, and ideology of medicine and has nurtured a medical paradigm that is based on the fragile infrastructure of universality and neutrality. In this regard, the cultural values of white American, middleclass, and able-bodiedness are considered the universal normative standard. Unfortunately, the effects of blindly applying these universal norms in research and medical practice to women and visible racial-cultural people across a variety of social class, age, and physical ability groups results in real-life predicaments often leading to damaging or deadly consequences.

In general, these ideas and values of universality and moral neutrality are the primary sources used to justify the expectations and behavior of medical professionals, their patients, and society. Never have the conceptual bases of medicine had a greater impact than they do currently, and the need has never been more urgent to critically examine the underlying values of the medical culture given the issues of access inequity to medical services today. To understand how the culture of medicine influences physicians and the treatment of those who seek its relief, a brief historical overview illustrates how encultured assumptions of universality and neutrality have influenced the practice of medicine. How medical culture and physicians embody the dominant culture will then be examined to illustrate how universalism and neutrality foster an illusion of impartiality, minimize physicians as racial-cultural people, and sterilize the structure and functions of hospital organizations to individualistic enterprises. Multicultural medical education will be discussed as a vehicle of change, and how the mere examination of multicultural issues may threaten the cultural fabric of medicine will also be discussed.

## Medical Culture: Past and Present

The Western cultural tradition of medicine and the recognition of specialized practitioners as an independent profession were established through the Hippocratic school in the fifth century B.C. The Hippocratic method of inquiry focused on subjective observations of individual patients by physicians to determine diagnoses, treatments, and prognoses. These personal observations, unaccountable by empirical findings, were used by physicians to understand and achieve well-being (Edelstein, 1967). Hippocrates, in this regard, presumed physicians possessed special observational and healing skills that could be ideally practiced universally. In this respect, he likened the physician to a demigod (Pellegrino & Thomasma, 1981). Unfortunately, in absentia, his writings neglected to explore how the physician's observations were heavily skewed by personal experiences, feelings, values, the selectivity of what was chosen to observe, and how he or she understood the observations.

In the past century, the influence of Descartes' reductionism changed medicine from a discipline based on philosophical epistemology to one of deductive empirically based reasoning. Thus, the medical paradigm shifted from individual subjective observations to understanding a person's existence by universal, concrete, and measurable bodily functions. According to Pellegrino and Thomasma (1981), this transition freed physicians and the practice of medicine from religious influences to a more mechanistic Socratic natural philosophy. This shift profoundly influenced the quintessence of medicine by firmly grounding its new paradigm in a universalistic, reductionistic mode of reasoning. Not unlike other professions and institutions, these philosophical foundations have shaped the questions asked, the research funded, and the people treated.

The culture of medicine values caring for the physical body. Pellegrino and Thomasma (1981) noted, "[Medicine] is used to promote health and healing, and thus becomes an intervention into an individual human life" (p. 101). It would seem for those who are concerned about the caring needs of "human life" that the essential ontological propositions of science, values, culture, and sociopolitical influences should be accounted for in the complexity of any persons' existence. In medicine, however, the caring for people to some restored quality of functioning is largely influenced by the reductionistic empirical premises of the natural sciences. This pragmatic reliance of the scientific method is heightened by a second critical theme: Medical knowledge from which practices are based is value laden. Therefore, one might ask, what influence does reductionism have in medical institutions (e.g., hospitals) and on the attitudes and beliefs of medical practitioners who apply this knowledge?

## The Values of Medicine

Ahronheim, Moreno, & Zuckerman (1994) and others (Hafferty & Franks, 1994; Pellegrino & Thomasma, 1981) have characterized the medical culture as a moral community guided by the Hippocratic oath and a physician's duty to his or her patient. What is notably absent, according to Pellegrino (1993), is the sense of the physician's individual obligation to society and the professions' collective obligation for the health of all members of society.

In medicine, illness is the primary manifestation of deviancy. Using this frame of reference, members of the medical community typically understand that a standardized criteria of human pathology operates universally and does not vary given differing social and cultural factors. This existence of common or even universal illnesses testifies not to the absence of a normative framework for judging pathology but to the presence of widespread, invisible norms (e.g., individualism, autonomy, and moral neutrality) that Katz (1985) eloquently described. Thus, the understanding of illnesses by medical professionals emanates from perceived or real differences in behaviors and feelings embedded in the social norms of value neutrality, individualism, and universality.

Unfortunately, in practice, these social norms remain invisible, uncritically examined, and often carelessly taken for granted within the realm of personal, social, scientific, and cultural values of patients and practitioners. This is not unlike how whites operate in the dominant society (Katz, 1985; McIntosh, 1992). Boone's (1988) statement, "The claim that science is ethically neutral is accurate" (pp. 11–12), relays the message that illness and health are individual and neutral. One can only become more suspect of this glaring invisibility.

In the broadest sense, illness occurs when a person has been unable to achieve certain socially constructed goals that are derived and supported by the framework of the dominant culture (Kleinman, 1980). One needs only to examine the history of paradigm shifts for alcoholism and schizophrenia to determine that these changes have been sensitive to the medical culture's social and economic barometer. For example, the previous examples share a history of changing etiological paradigms from personal (e.g., self-motivation) to environmental (e.g., parents) to biochemical and genetic (e.g., neurotransmitter deficiencies and gene mutation). They have also shared and benefited from a larger cultural arena of economic and political support. For example, if alcoholism and schizophrenia were to have higher incidence rates among visible racial-cultural groups, would research and resources have been so vigorously pursued? Some would say no. This argument parallels the criticisms of the medical community's lackluster response to HIV that many believe has been slow and inadequate because of the higher prevalence of HIV in people deemed more "socially undesirable" (Shilts, 1988).

What implications do mechanism and reductionism have on professional attitudes, institutions, and policies? One outcome is an inherent belief held by the medical community that pain and suffering of individuals can simply be understood by reducing diseases to mechanistic models of biochemistry and genetics. Another unspoken effect is conformity to dominant white cultural norms. Across various cultural groups, visible racial-cultural patients and practitioners alike are often defined by whites and estranged from the process of self-definition. Because they do not know themselves or are unable to answer the question "Who am I?," whites tend to feign cultural universality and neutrality. One consequence is that visible racial-cultural people become particularly vulnerable to experimentation (e.g., Tuskegee syphilis experiments) and labeling (e.g., *mutant*, as recently used in the name of the repository, the Human Genetic *Mutant* Cell Repository of DNA for genetic research at the National Institute of General Medical Sciences, that "contains both male and female specimens from... Adygei, Amerindian, Ami, Ayatal, Cambodian, Chinese, Druze, Japanese, Malaysian, and Pygmy ... " [American Society of Human Genetics, 1996, p. 972].

Some visible racial-cultural people adopt the dominant culture's answers to questions and call them their own. Although some external messages can be helpful, they do not emanate from within, thus disempowering visible racial-cultural people by creating a dependence on dominant white cultural norms (e.g., universalism, neutrality, and individualism) for self-definition and validation. Dependent people often feel powerless and are unlikely to oppose the status quo or existing power structures (Pinderhughes, 1989). In turn, organizations whose members have benefited from privileges conferred on them due to their race may nurture misguided wishes for neutrality and universalism by minimizing cultural connections and thus promoting self-alienation and psychological separation for those unlike themselves. Thus, by maintaining the status quo of universalism and neutrality and "not rocking the boat," the dominant white culture's general intolerance for differences is maintained.

For example, this perspective was shared by Charles Epstein in his presidential address to the American Society of Human Genetics in which he expressed dismay at the "cultural" clouding of the genetic research community's morally neutral, mechanistic worldview lens. Advocating for "rational discourse," he cited as an example a meeting titled "The Meaning and Significance of Research on Genetics and Criminal Behavior" at which the implications of current genetic research of violent, antisocial, and criminal behavior were presented. He disparaged the arguments raised by opponents at the meeting about behavioral genetic research and possible abuses resulting in the enslavement of an underclass (that would particularly adversely affect visible racial-cultural people) and potentially place restrictions on those deemed genetically irredeemable. He concluded that if one reacts to these concerns, "we are in danger of tying ourselves in knots and of embracing policies and regulations that will only serve to impede the progress of human genetics" (Epstein, 1997, p. 8).

This example illustrates how professionals in the medical culture place value on understanding illness within the boundaries of the physical body in isolation from the sociocultural context in which people live. Thus, physicians attempt to understand who their patients are through a morally neutral lens using physiological arguments based in scientific and abstract terminology. Unfortunately, the medical practitioners' adherence to beliefs of moral neutrality and universality ultimately strips the patient and the physician from the social and cultural milieu in which they live. This limited understanding coupled with Descartes' empirical reductionistic reasoning often leaves physicians with overly simplistic explanations of the complex disease processes of their patients.

## The Practice of Medicine: Physicians and Beneficence

*I will keep [the patient] from harm and injustice.*

—Hippocratic oath

Bound by the Hippocratic oath, a physician has a prescribed duty to a patient's health and well-being (Curzer, 1993; Marsh & Yarborough, 1990). This well-being is accomplished through the physician's ability to restore "normal" body functioning; the body is regarded as the primary conduit when creating hypotheses about illness, health, and well-being. To accomplish this task, physicians base their medical decision making on universal assumptions that link scientific knowledge with qualities "believed" to be found in all people. For example, disease categories, etiological agents, and healing principles are often reduced to universal "objective" common characteristics. Within this context, healing is viewed as an implicit application of general biomedical knowledge. Pellegrino and Thomasma (1981) noted,

> When a body objectifies its disease and a physician compares this with general classifications of diseases common to human bodies, the search for a scientific explanation takes place . . . to explain the etiology of the

disease and to understand its pathology as a general condition of human experience. (p. 111)

It is life that makes the biological norm a concept of value. Thus, the culture of medicine encourages physicians to objectify their patients' illnesses and well-being through scientific, quantitative data. Unfortunately, the consequence of the physicians' capacity to objectify the body also allows the body to define a person. Thus, rather than a patient's identity being found within his or her inner experience, personal identity depends on a biological descriptor or laboratory result. It is not an uncommon practice for a patient to become objectified as his or her diagnosis (e.g., the cardiac) rather than the diagnosis being used as a description of the patient (e.g., a patient with Down's syndrome).

In hospitals and clinics, the physician is ultimately held responsible for the scientific, medical, legal, and moral implications of medical decision making and treatment of patients. In fact, since the late nineteenth century, physicians have been the primary practitioners of health care, thereby establishing and maintaining the current medical cultural value system of beliefs, attitudes, and practices (Marsh & Yarborough, 1990; Pellegrino & Thomasma, 1981). As Lipkin (1974) has argued, "the practice of medicine is to a large extent what the individual doctor is. His ideas of what illness is and how it is caused determine the first steps in his deciding what to do for his patient" (p. 35).

To this end, the acceptance of individual responsibility emanates from a dominant cultural value system that believes in personal control or mastery and meritocracy (Freire, 1972; Katz, 1985) and values self-determination and autonomy. For the physician who is in a position of power, this poses few dilemmas. For those in less powerful positions (e.g., patients and visible racial-cultural people), however, this individualism can become a dominant cultural gag interfering with their ability to ask, be heard, and receive help.

*Medicine is practiced among people who are essentially strangers.*
—Veatch (1983, p. 188)

The physician, the central practitioner of medicine (Marsh & Yarborough, 1990; Pellegrino & Thomasma, 1981), is viewed in society and within medical culture as the health expert promoting well-being through individual self-determination (based on autonomy) and the knowledge of etiology, diagnosis, treatment, and prognosis of illnesses. Physicians have derived a powerful position in society from the fact that they command "valued" knowledge used to explain diseases and possess skills that can eradicate, reverse, or placate suffering. Beneficence couched in the words "do no harm" has been the moral framework giving physicians power to make judgments for others. Despite the fact that a physician's technical training does not equip him or her to make overall best-interest judgments concerning the good of the patient (Christakis & Feudtner, 1993; Hickson et al., 1994; Leape, 1994; Richmond & Fein, 1995; Valenstein &

Howanitz, 1995), patients often rely on the physician to provide advice, make recommendations, and serve as proxy in these issues. Thus, under the auspices of neutrality and beneficence, physicians practice in a wide latitude of discretionary space.

For example, regarding new federal regulations allowing researchers to enroll unconscious patients in some medical research studies without informed consent (Kolata, 1996), the patient has no option but to rely on the physician's judgment on what he or she believes is best. In support of this change, medical researchers have argued that medical progress has been stymied due to the stringent requirements of informed consent. They suggest that, in fact, a greater harm may exist for patients if they are denied participation in research studies due to the difficulties of obtaining informed consent. This change of participating in research without voluntary consent to date is the only exception of the Nuremberg Code since its inception. The message is clear: It is more important for scientific research to proceed than for the patient to have the right not to be an experimental subject. Thus, as Pellegrino (1973) states, within the physician-patient relationship, the physician's role becomes one of a

> benign, paternalistic figure who [has] . . . rational capabilities. He determines what was good for his patient and discloses only so much of his reasons or his art as he thought appropriate. He is assumed moral as well as a technical authority, declaring his relationship with the patient as sacred precinct—guarded by confidentiality and not to be intruded upon by anyone beyond the patient or his family. (p. 133)

Given the ambiguous nature of working with people and their diseases, physicians also learn to cope with uncertainty by developing strategies of "rational" detachment (Fox, 1989; Hafferty, 1991). As Veatch (1983), stated, "[M]edicine is practiced among people who are essentially strangers" (p. 188). In fact, a belief exists that if this professional detached role is compromised, the quality and efficacy of medical treatment will be in jeopardy, thus "caus[ing] serious problems for both the caring and for the cared" (Curzer, 1993, p. 55). For example, under the guise of moral neutrality, a physician learns to maintain a detached stance by guarding himself or herself from the dangers of becoming too involved, reflective, or introspective by focusing on the concrete functions of his or her patient's body. There is no room for anything else (e.g., racial, cultural, and social variables). What complicates this professional detached stance of caring is the physician's own internal dialogue as a racial-cultural person who is realistically more involved and less neutral than the medical cultural mores allow. After all, Pellegrino and Thomasma (1981) argued that caring is a moral activity. Caring does not operate in a vacuum but rather through a personal interrelationship in which the physician and patient are coparticipants interacting, each in his or her own sociopolitical-cultural moment.

The inherent power differential between the physician and the individual he or she treats, however, often causes the patient to modify his or her behavior to conform with the physician's recommendations or advice or both. Physicians can ask and expect within the first 15 minutes of meeting a patient that he or she reveal personal information, take off clothing, and allow a virtual stranger to freely touch and examine any part of his or her body without adverse consequences. These actions occur because the relationship between the physician treating the physical body before him or her and the patient as a whole is ideally constrained by a fiduciary responsibility of physician beneficence. The physician is presumed to help and not harm, thus advocating for the "good" of the patient at all times. This moral axiom of beneficence rests on the presumption that the physician is a morally good and neutral person who "knows best." This position of power is not unlike the international health relief efforts of industrialized countries to developing countries they deem worthwhile to assist.

Unfortunately, patients are not always viewed by physicians as objects of fiduciary responsibility. Often, they are transformed into objects of work and sources of frustration, and they are misnomered as "hits," "gomers," "geeks," and "dirtballs" (Leiderman & Grisso, 1985; Mizrahi, 1986; Shem, 1978). Patients who are judged to be different, to be difficult, to have little to no "value" in our society, or all three become objectified targets, with physicians feelings justified in their use of negative labels and corresponding behaviors.

Babbie (1970) argued that the physician-patient relationship, like other social relationships, reflects the general values of human morality in a given society. The professional values are founded on basic ontological beliefs about man's nature and that of society. Although Pellegrino and Thomasma (1981) suggested that the healing relationship is based on mutual responsibility between a physician and a patient, the healing relationship is also the source of the division of labor from which physicians and patients derive rights, duties, privileges, and other forms of approval from the dominant society. Due to the imbalance of value and importance placed on scientific knowledge, physicians consider themselves to have a greater degree of responsibility and power than do the patients. Within this context, medical judgments are based on the physician's frame of reference; diagnosis, prognosis, and treatment are conditional on the biological functioning of the body. The physician's professional motives and skills are inclusive of scientific explanations of disease and, specifically, an understanding of illnesses. Several assumptions are embedded in these medical judgments: (a) The physician is committed to the patient's well-being, (b) the physician is morally and value neutral, and (c) the judgments and decisions are established on empirical-inductive reasoning based on the physician's "imaginative preconception of what the truth might be" (Pellegrino & Thomasma, 1981, p. 67).

For example, when making clinical judgments, physicians have one specific purpose—to heal. A clinical decision is based on a series of deductive and inductive inferences, serially modified by "facts" and observations used to evaluate and interpret, resulting in specific recommendations for what a particular patient should do. These criteria of the scientific method are most clearly pursued in making the diagnosis and selecting treatments. The physician is judged, however, by the end product—a healthy person. Although medical practices encourage physicians to strip people out of their social, cultural, and political environments and recontextualize them within scientific empiricism under the guise of neutrality and rationality, medical decision making is irretrievably personal.

What should be done when medical treatment becomes a situation of counterpositions of what the physician thinks is appropriate versus what the patient will accept as good and worthwhile? For a physician, the scientific evidence and the probability statements about diagnosis, prognosis, and treatment become arguments for or against a choice of alternatives. Once the positions of a physician and patient are explored, a decision is made based on the belief that the choice made should take preference to all other alternatives. In making the most appropriate decision with an individual patient, however, the physician must also consider personal, social, and cultural factors. Is neutrality possible? How much coercion and cultural arm twisting by the physician is done in the physician-patient relationship? Does the physician's scientific recommended action take priority?

The intersection or collision of a physician's and patient's values and worldviews can often create tensions in this reductionistic cultural milieu of medicine, science, and the dominant society at large. Arguably, the physician's overt and covert power can directly influence the patient's choices and values. Who has power and who remains powerless is illustrated by a situation in which a person who is a Christian Scientist receives a court-ordered medical procedure after rejecting medically recommended treatment because of his or her religious beliefs.

Thus, clinical decisions are made by the physician's criteria of what he or she will accept as justification for a particular action. Medical decisions are made and conclusions drawn that are based on "acceptable" probabilities for outcomes. Additionally, decisions are also made and conclusions drawn that are "scientifically defensible" (e.g., an acceptance of biochemical assay results and biopsies or an X-ray examination justifying a "right action" ). What implications does this have for a client who believes that her child's birth defect was caused by her seeing a horrific accident while she was pregnant? She will probably receive a supportive head nod and an extra 5 minutes of psychoeducation on the Western scientific explanations about the birth defect. If her "abnormal" thoughts persist, a referral to a psychologist may be recommended. By focusing on a diagnosis and laboratory results, physicians have systematically deemphasized the relevance of social and cultural macroentities, such as families, communities, organizations, and institutions, in their lives and the lives of their patients.

## The House of God

Given the increasing expense of medical technological advances, physicians, in an entrepreneurial spirit, historically pooled their financial and professional expertise into medical organizations, primarily hospitals, to practice medicine and generate revenues. Thus, the increasing technical complexity of medicine dictated the need to establish hospitals as central locations in which expensive equipment, access to operating rooms, nursing, pathology, and other services that make the scientific and business enterprise of medicine possible could be located. As a community, voluntary, or nonprofit organization, a hospital, or "House of God" as aptly named by Shem (1978), is believed to be available to all, and its self-interests are subservient to those of the surrounding community, thus reflecting the dominant cultural value of universal equality of all.

Until a few decades ago, physicians dominated the institutional life of the hospital and were responsible for its planning, establishment, operation, and financing. In this context, physicians established and perpetuated the medical decision-making model administrators, directors, dominant figures on boards and executive committees, and medical educators. Within the past few years, however, physicians in hospitals have experienced dramatic institutional changes. For example, in the spirit of health care cost containment, clinical decisions in hospitals and medical clinics have been changing and are more often driven by economic models such as health maintenance organizations and preferred payment organizations. As noted by Marsh and Yarborough (1990),

> In 1986, health care spending rose to $458 billion, an increase of 8.4 percent over the previous year... to $498 billion in 1987. ... By 1990, 12 percent of America's gross national product will be spend on health care. Yet the number of untreated poor and uninsured (in many cases the middle class) continues to grow. (pp. 3–4)

A shift in the administration of hospitals toward nonphysician professional outsiders trained specifically as medical administrators has also created a tier of nonphysician middle managers who are responsible for the management and coordination of all the services that physicians use in the hospital. This fact, coupled with the move to multidisciplinary teams, has often resulted in physicians believing that untrained (meaning non-MDs) health care professionals are impinging on their professional discretionary space.

Ideally, in hospitals the roles of hospital administrators and physicians are clearly defined. Hospital administrators are responsible for the bureaucratic decisions—those affecting efficiency, equity, and allocation of resources; physicians are responsible for the personal dimensions of caregiving. Caring, the domain of the physician, is always under the watchful eye of the administrator's vision of efficiency and equity, however. Thus, physicians are obligated, ex post facto, to the institutional framework and culture that modulates the health care of their patients.

Pellegrino and Thomasma (1981) argued that the institutionalization of medicine has placed the hospital in a relationship with a physician that is not very different from a physician's traditional patient relationship. Within this context, the hospital has been personified. What occurs when conflicts between the medical and dominant culture arise? Crane (1975), in her classic study about medical decision making and the decisions physicians make in the care of the critically ill, showed that considerable disparity between official medical positions and dominant and personal cultural norms existed. In the case of comatose patients, although the medical culture's position held the view that treatment should continue until the patients were physiologically nonfunctioning, in actual practice many physicians took personal liberty with the interpretation of the Hippocratic oath of "to do no harm" and discontinued treatment based on their judgment of when the possibility of meaningful social interactions for the patients became nonexistent. Given how medical culture and physicians embody a high-status position in society that values dominant culture norms—rational, objective, selflessness, and trustworthiness—the physician has tremendous influence and power in the decision-making process.

This hidden power differential, guised in the cloak of neutrality and equity, is also present in the increasing number of changes in hospitals toward multidisciplinary medical teams. Multidisciplinary medical teams are transitory social systems comprising an aggregate of health workers directed to meeting certain needs of a patient, family, or community. Thus, although the medical teams may appear to be cooperative and interdependent and contradict the dominant culture's value of individualism, this collectivist facade fades when disagreements among medical team members occur; it is clear who the captain is—the physician.

## Multicultural Medical Education

The medical culture is grounded in a problem-focused, biologically based universal worldview. Medical education is one vehicle that socializes and indoctrinates medical students into medical culture. Supported by the dominant culture's general intolerance for differences, some medical educators who have been paralyzed by their own universalism and false sense of neutrality have recently begun to cautiously see the value of multicultural issues in health care. They have tried to introduce multicultural issues in clinical care and medical education. When teaching this "new" multicultural education within the rubric of the universalistic medical paradigm, however, the lessons have typically focused on learning about specific visible racial-cultural groups. Unfortunately, this teaching strategy perpetuates the false notion that race and culture reside exclusively within members of visible racial-cultural groups and not within practitioners. In this respect, medical educators have assumed that multicultural competence is found externally from oneself, thus distancing themselves and simultaneously preserving the universal and neutral values so carefully attended to in their medical training and socially supported by dominant cultural norms. Carter and Qureshi (1995) stated, "The universal approach does not deny the existence of culture as such; rather it calls for an intense focus on shared human experience while incorporating culture-specific knowledge" (p. 245). This universal approach attempts to transcend the meanings of differences by focusing on the similarities among people as an approach to disaffecting oneself from what the differences mean in a social, cultural, and political context. For example, to address multicultural issues in medical practice, administrators have provided physicians with reading lists or have invited guest speakers to teaching rounds as "spokespeople" of specific racial and cultural groups. Use of these approaches is ultimately a disservice to medical practitioners and patients. Analyzing a few examples to "highlight" differences and clinical difficulties when treating these cultural others only encourages physicians to develop different treatment standards for visible racial-cultural people, thus creating a hierarchical tiered system of health care delivery. As a result, the reliance on the universal approach ultimately promotes the idea that culture belongs to specific "other people" rather than to the physician as a racial-cultural participant in a health care delivery system. Thus, medical educators discount the importance of the physician's awareness that he or she is a racial-cultural being who is a social and cultural product shaped by the larger dominant culture and the medical socialization process. This choice to ignore physicians and physicians-in-training is similar to the way in which whites operate in the dominant society by choosing to ignore or objectify others in the dominant society.

Like the four blind men who described the proverbial elephant as discrete anatomical structures (e.g., trunk, leg, body, and tail), medicine has only begun to examine in a piecemeal fashion how culture influences medical research, practice, and training. Instead of understanding the elephant in its ecological context (Bronfenbrenner, 1979; Bronfenbrenner & Weiss, 1983) as a whole elephant living with other elephants in a herd within an environment with accommodations and dangers, medicine has chosen to study "characteristic" and culturally narrow pieces of knowledge as its approach to multicultural issues. In reality, however, people who interface with the medical community are more than biological specimens. They are racial-cultural individuals who live in families within a community that has institutions that function independently, competitively, and in concert (e.g., schools, social services, and hospitals) with each other. These individuals interact with the medical system within a social, cultural, and political history.

## Conclusion

Education is one form of socialization. In this sense, a person's mind is being shaped within a framework that transmits notions of rightness and wrongness, and appropriateness and inappropriateness. Traditionally, this point of view has had little receptivity among professionals in medical settings who view science and the practices of medicine as objective and value neutral (Fox, 1989; Giroux & Purple, 1983; Hafferty & Franks, 1994; Self, Baldwin, & Olivarez, 1993). This may be the result of the physician's worldview of science and technology that he or she is selectively taught to see and not to see coupled with the press for conformity to dominant cultural norms. The repercussion of this selective "blindness" is foreboding. Because physicians subscribe to a universalistic, neutral, scientific worldview, they are taught and personally empowered in the beneficent decision making they practice. They are also more disinclined to acknowledge that nonbiological social and cultural influences truly matter to the well-being of their patients.

Thus, a hidden curriculum exists in medical education and operates in several different areas that introduces, reinforces, and normalizes an uninvolved and falsely neutral stance. This false sense of self, developed against the fear of becoming too involved and introspective, defensively relies on a reasoning process that emphasizes inductive rather than deductive reasoning. Within the classroom, instructors of biochemistry and other natural science courses transmit not only information about metabolism and biochemical pathways but also messages about the nature of science, including the presence or, more aptly, the absence of uncertainty and ambiguity in medicine.

Although teachers of the medical curriculum may focus on fundamental components of **what** comprises a person, these facts are erroneously viewed synonymously with the issue of **who** comprises a person. For example, the individual case study method used in medicine is prone to conveying images that perpetuate gender, racial, cultural, and disability stereotypes (Finucane & Carrese, 1990; Shem, 1978). Thus, introducing racial-cultural variables as relevant issues into medical curricula and practice will require changes in medical school curricula and the organization's overall climate. Without these changes, integrating multicultural issues into the medical professional's identity will not be recognized as important or necessary. Failure to make these changes will result in physicians who are armed with limited culture-specific knowledge and techniques but have little awareness of the meaning and place for these tools.

To remediate the lack of attention placed on multicultural issues in medicine, medicine as a cultural worldview must also be examined. The presence and influence of messages embedded in the medical culture must become more overt and openly discussed so that covert, invisible cultural norms can be honestly examined. Only then can people combat the institutional reproduction of cultural values associated with racism, sexism, classism, and oppression. Successful efforts will require the acknowledgment of the presence of unacknowledged and privileged value systems underlying institutional and professional policies as well as the recognition that changes will take time and require participatory support from leadership and management. The focus must be not only on individual attitudes and related behaviors but also on identifying how the organizational structure and overall milieu of the medical setting may in fact foster undesirable values, attitudes, behaviors, or all three. Thus, attention must be paid to "macro" issues (e.g., those affecting groups, institutions, and the general public) as distinguished from traditional "micro" issues (e.g., those affecting individual patients and practitioners).

The trend toward multicultural inclusion will reflect an increasing recognition that racial and cultural issues cannot be conceptualized in isolation from the broader social context from which they arise. Thus, medical school curricula and postgraduate training (e.g., residency programs) need to address their charge of including multicultural issues in clinical practice seriously and move beyond simple and static stereotypical images of visible racial-cultural groups and the cultural values that these groups are believed to hold. They must replace their exclusive notions of a universal and neutral "racial-cultural homunculus" and linear causal relationships with ecological models of dynamic systems and invest in training physicians to understand themselves as a racial-cultural people who have developed in a social, cultural, and political context. Ultimately, physicians must recognize that to embrace racial-cultural issues into research and practice means allowing for the complexity and ambiguity of the sociopolitical, emotive, cognitive, and behavioral components to be integrated into a more realistic understanding of themselves and their patients.

Medical professionals have a duty to assume leadership roles in confronting social issues that affect their patients. The medical milieu must nurture, educate, and prepare its future physician leaders to reform social policies to improve the health and well-being of their communities. For multicultural influences to be a transforming force in medical institutions, several steps must be taken. First, the content and effects of the "hidden curriculum" need to be identified and addressed with a consortium of faculty, students, and outside consultants whose specialty is in multicultural curriculum development and evaluation. Ideally, the goal should be to address, understand, and implement education and training in a contextualized ecological model.

Second, students and professionals need to be given "real-life" opportunities to appreciate the relevance of multicultural issues in medicine at the organizational level. Organizations such as medical schools, hospitals, and clinics are not often considered cultural entities. The benign neglect of practitioners and administrators considering medicine as a organizational entity is compounded by the fact that within medicine, multicultural issues are framed most often at the individual and not at the organizational level. In this regard, even when topics such as allocation of resources are discussed, the frame of reference is often at the level of the patient and health care practitioner (e.g., which patients should be seen, by whom, and for how long) rather than at the institutional level (e.g., referral networks, budgets, CPT codes, and insurance reimbursement). Similarly, broad issues, such as abortion, reproductive technologies, and genetic manipulation, are often discussed through the concerns of individual patients with little attention paid to what steps organized medicine, as a legally enfranchised profession, might take in addressing and remedying cultural and ethical issues in these areas. Although organized medicine may occasionally take a stand on public policy matters, such positions are often weakened by medicine's long-standing position that individual physicians cannot be expected to act contrary to their own neutral moral beliefs.

An acknowledgment by medical organizations that they are indeed cultural entities is particularly problematic because such awareness and disclosure may call for a degree of insight that has been precluded by medicine's almost exclusive focus on culture using the universal and "cultural other" perspective. Thus, addressing issues of culture at the organizational level requires that steps be taken regarding the following areas:

1. Administration: Agents of change within the organization must be identified and empowered, particularly within the administrative, teaching, and research areas.

2. Medical curriculum: Curriculum committees must become involved in developing a culturally inclusive medical curriculum for **all** didactic, laboratory, and clinical courses.

3. Admissions: Admission material and advertising brochures need to highlight medicine and medical education as cultural entities. In addition, admission interviews should profile medicine from the vantage point of medicine as an ecological cultural entity, thus beginning an enculturation process at the point of a student's first institutional contact. Therefore, admission committees can begin to view their deliberations as grounded in an overall ethic of social responsibility.

4. Financial aid programs can underscore issues such as the fundamentally moral and fiduciary nature of medicine at both the organizational and the individual practice levels.

These recommendations are based on the premise that faculty and administrators are willing, trained, and able to function as positive cultural agents and role models. This is frequently not the case. Sometimes, the opposite is true. For example, basic science faculty may argue that multicultural issues have no place in the teaching of biochemistry. The clinical faculty may criticize and question the value of an inclusive multicultural curriculum that does not theoretically or researchwise or both emanate from medicine but rather from other disciplines, such as psychology, anthropology, and sociology, that they may consider to not deal with the "realities" of medical practices. The relatively invisible profile of multicultural issues in medicine thus constitutes a "curriculum in absentia," with its invisible content reinforcing the message that multicultural issues most appropriately reside peripherally as an adjunct to the "essential" scientific and medical work or to those who are members of visible racial-cultural group affiliations or both.

The existence of a hidden value-oriented curriculum needs to be examined in the medical community from the top down. From all medical organizational strata, there must be a recognition that a nonneutral stance of morality and culture is ubiquitous to the organization and the practice of medicine. Medical practitioners have a culturally rooted sense of what is right and wrong. What dominants the culture of medicine, in addition to the hidden curriculum that supports it, is not good intentions but rather a structurally ambiguous training process characterized by double messages (e.g., physicians are trained to believe they are practicing a caring profession but are told that when they "care" they are overinvolved and unprofessional).

Merely offering more pedagogically sophisticated courses, however, is not the answer. Even the development of an exquisite, multidisciplinary, formal multicultural curriculum, staffed by the best role models and funded with considerable financial resources, will afford students with little more than a temporary haven and the profession a quick fix. The hidden curriculum cannot be supplanted or replaced by dedicated pedagogy or "new and improved" learning experiences.

At a minimum, institutions of medical education have a responsibility to facilitate a student's development of critical thinking skills, to teach the student to value self-reflection, and to facilitate the student's development of a meaningful awareness of the distinctions between oneself and the roles he or she occupies and a sensitivity to and knowledge of structural factors, social situations, and cultural contexts that influence his or her participation in medicine and those who seek its relief. Training in multicultural issues must begin early and continue throughout all course work, including the basic and clinical sciences. Faculty members committed to including multicultural issues in research and practice and acknowledging their own strengths and limitations will immeasurably enrich the professional development of their students as ethically, culturally, and socially competent physicians. In addition, faculty, administrators, and students will need to establish working partnerships to identify the hidden and unspoken curriculum that permeates their institution and, in turn, implement remedial solutions best suited for their situation. As a medical faculty strives to teach and understand multicultural issues, it will find its own perspectives regarding the nature of science and medical work challenged. In these ways, faculty and students will become linked in an effort to ensure the professional development of each other.

Therefore, medical education (and thus medical educators as cultural workers) must adopt a new, more activist role within the culture of medicine. First, the basic science faculty must take on a broader responsibility for the training of medical students by making more explicit the aspects of the hidden curriculum in research methodology that operate and shape knowledge acquisition and critical thinking. Medical professionals need to examine the fundamental principles that define and drive research and practices and to determine whether they are truly consistent with the purposes and goals of medicine. They will need to reevaluate concepts of the profession and the nature of professionalism, including the embodied core of technical expertise and service orientation.

Second, the medical profession needs to rethink whether maintaining a facade of neutrality should remain pivotal when understanding professional and clinical dynamics. A related issue involves the concept of medical uncertainty and the ambiguity of medical work. Does scientific knowledge reduce the amount of uncertainty present in a system or will such advances create a new arena of uncertainty? The profession needs to examine how the notions of science and uncertainty are being created and being driven by effectiveness research and how these assumptions are related to issues of health, disease, and medical work.

Less well-understood, and in many cases completely unexamined, is the organization of medical work and research. How do notions of expertise and altruism intersect in different political, social, and economics environments? This fundamentally questions the very notion of whether multicultural issues are to be considered a necessary or sufficient condition for the practice of medicine. Those who are satisfied with or paralyzed by the status quo may argue that, regardless of the individual, mere exposure to multicultural awareness training is the best medical education that can be provided. Nevertheless, instituting a multicultural curriculum about awareness of racial-cultural issues is not a wholly sufficient or satisfying strategy. It is a necessary and beginning step for the practice of ethically and culturally competent medicine, however. Multicultural competence based on awareness must be integrated with self-exploration and critical thinking skills. Researchers, teachers, practitioners, administrators, and the organizational structure as a whole must recognize their obligations to train culturally competent health care professionals. Who will change? What will change? The rhetoric is plentiful. Only time will tell.

# 11

## And Justice Is Blind
## (To Race and Ethnicity):
### That Is Not Good!

*Curtis W. Branch*

Race is omnipresent in American society; its reality confronts us in all our daily activities. The historical legacy of race relations challenges us in the execution of our daily professional activities. Attitudes about race often make it difficult for friendships to develop across racial group boundaries. Impacts of race occur on individual and institutional levels. Institutions such as religious worship communities (e.g., churches, mosques, and temples) are not exempt from its influence; this is evidenced in part by the racially homogeneous makeup of most religious communities. Are there no places in which the influences of race are not felt in America? Branch and Carter (1996) suggest that the answer to this question is no. They contend that race has a pervasive influence in the lives of Americans throughout their lives, influencing their individual, cultural, and institutional behaviors. According to Branch and Carter, race is a vital component in the development of a sense of personal identity, thereby influencing the filters that an individual uses to focus on work and personal life matters. In some ways, the two are inseparable. Who we are personally influences how we perform our jobs.

If personal life and workplace boundaries are fluid and inseparable, performing job duties in an objective and racially unbiased way can pose a special challenge for workers. This is especially true in work settings that are predicated on functioning in a color-blind and equally objective way, providing services to all consumers in the same unbiased manner. The justice system and its auxiliary components (e.g., probation and parole departments), are the prototype of an institution founded on the ideals of equality and justice for all. In principle, such an articulation sounds awe inspiring. Is this reality? More simply, can such an ideal evenhanded dispersing of justice occur in a larger societal context in which racialistic thinking and behavior are integral parts of the daily lives of many people? This complex question raises the issue of how objective an agency can be if it is composed of individuals who have been immersed in a social environment that is not idealistic or even fair-minded. It appears that the resolution of questions associated with this issue requires that there be a systematic analysis of the questions of objectivity factors that sustain the questions in their current form, and creative solutions that can realistically be accomplished. Indeed, it is not enough to generate workable solutions; there must also be a methodology for evaluating the effectiveness of the interventions.

Because the justice system and its supportive services are critical factors in the contemporary life of American society, it is necessary to examine the role of race in the activities of probation and parole departments. The investigations in this context will focus on how racialistic thinking occurs in decisions regarding consumers and the clinical activities of probation and parole officers. For simplicity, the term *probation* is used to refer to both probation and parole offices. The functions of the two offices are both similar and dissimilar. The overwhelming similarity, that both offices deal with a disproportionate number of people of color as consumers, is substantial. It dictates that a discussion regarding race as a theme in the life of probation departments should occur.

## Helping Troubled Youth: Historic Notes

Youth in need of supervision is a pronounced problem in American society. This is not a new problem. There are historic precursors to the current epidemic that if carefully examined, provide some clues to the reasons for the increase in numbers of young people in need of special support services. The history patterns also offer some poignant insights into the social issues present in our society and the overly simplistic linear solutions that have been offered to overcome them. First, the history of special interventions on behalf of troubled youth can be traced to social factors (e.g., economics and acculturation processes) that competed for the attention of children and adolescents in the late nineteenth century. Specifically, as public education became mandatory, many young people opted to not attend school out of financial necessity. The last 20 years of the nineteenth century were also punctuated with a huge wave of immigration. A result of this immigration was that many young people lived outside the law because of the divided loyalties between cultural imperatives of the old country, economic struggles intensified by their immigrant status, and an internal motivation to be become acculturated (i.e., fully Americanized). A variation of this pattern is evident in the history of criminal justice systems in New York City.

In the late 1920s and 1930s, the typical adjudicated delinquent was Jewish, Italian, or a member of some other group that had recently immigrated en masse. A similar pattern was noted in other parts of the country in the 1960s and 1970s, consistent with recent immigration patterns. This pattern of statistics is interpreted to mean that youth from recently immigrated groups are more likely to be identified as delinquent than others, and that minority group-status youth are also likely to be perceived as more at risk and delinquent than others. The absoluteness and truthfulness of both interpretations are debatable.

Another significant event in the development of special supports for troubled youth was the creation of the child guidance movement and its emphasis on the development of clinics in the 1920s. Child guidance clinics were originally founded to help troubled youth and their families in a setting that was facilitative of restoring family relationships. The clinics operated on an interdisciplinary model, suggestive of a belief that the problems experienced by the youngsters they were serving were the results of multiple factors.

Belief in a multifaceted approach to the problems of young people and their families also indicated the need for different types of interventions. A multifaceted approach recognizes that there are different dimensions of the identified problems that can be examined in a variety of ways. One dimension is the idea that youthful offenders are different from adults, and that they have special needs that are related to their psychological developmental status. Family courts and probation departments were established, in part, to meet the unique needs of young people. Much of the impetus for the establishment of youth probation departments and courts was a belief that youthful offenders are similar to but different from adult offenders.

## The Denver Court System

There is a division of the court system for the city and county of Denver known as municipal court. Its mission is to hear cases of individuals who are accused of violating municipal codes. Because of a dramatic increase in the number of youthful offenders in the 1970s and 1980s, a juvenile probation department was added to the municipal court in 1987 for the purpose of serving first- and second-time adolescent code violators. The assumption was that the young offenders referred to the municipal court would not also have citations against them in the state and federal court systems. As originally conceived, the juvenile probation department was the arm of the municipal court designated to provide support services for adolescents. Three probation officers were assigned to the department, and it was planned that cases would remain active with the department for 6 to 12 months. It was expected that the probation officers would provide guidance for troubled youth and their families. Intense participation in alternative social service systems and minimal court involvements were expected to be the outcomes of referrals to the municipal probation department. The model on which the probation department was founded continues to be followed, but the realities of shrinking budgets, shifts in behavioral patterns among adolescents, and the epidemic of youth violence and sociopathy have dramatically altered the probation department.

Despite the centrality of the mission of the juvenile probation department to the court system, there has been a 66% reduction in the number of probation officers. One worker is now responsible for supervising 500 to 600 clients per year. The situation is made even more grave by the tremendous increase in the number of minors who are tried in municipal court each year. When the juvenile section of municipal court was founded, it heard complaints of loitering, unlawful assembly, noise violations, and so on. It still hears these types of cases, but it also frequently hears complaints related to possession of firearms, assault and battery of police officers, and other similar offenses. The number of summons issued to youthful offenders has quadrupled since 1987. Some cases still remain active with the department for less than 1 year, but recidivism is quite common. A pattern that has emerged in the past year is that for some clients there are also charges pending against them in state and federal courts. This was not a reality that the court had anticipated. As these cases have become more frequent, the municipal court has developed a policy of deferring to the higher courts in situations in which a youngster has multiple summons. Theoretically, it is impossible to be sentenced to jail for a municipal court offense except in the case of a charge of "failure to appear in court."

There has been a tremendous increase in the number of failure to appear in court citations and other contempt of court citations issued to juvenile municipal court clients within the past 3 years (Abdullah, 1997). A result of this change is that the juvenile detention facilities, state-operated facilities, are overcrowded with adolescents who are there not because of the offenses that originally brought them to court but because they disregarded the orders of the court.

One of the missions of the probation department is to help families improve the quality of their lives. Ironically, there are no family or mental health services housed in the municipal courts. Probation officers are expected to refer families to outside professionals who can provide the specialized services that are needed. The process of referring families in need of special services often uncovers dormant racial issues that are operating among the probation workers and families of clients. The following questions are examples of frequently encountered issues: What should be done when families specifically request a therapist from their own racial or ethnic group? How should youngsters who are attributing all their legal system problems to racism (e.g., racist police, racist legal system, and racist judges) be handled? What, if anything, should probation officers do to convince families that they are culturally sensitive?

## Clinical Examples

During 5 years of working with the probation department, I have had several opportunities to observe how racial and ethnic issues find expression among probation officers. In the following sections, I discuss four patterns that I have observed. The similarity of these patterns to their counterparts in the real world will be discussed later.

**"How Important Is Race?"**

The relative importance of race in the lives of probation department clients varies dramatically. Workers also vacillate about how they make attributions that are racial in nature to families. This seems to work in two ways. One approach is to avoid seeing the families in racial terms: "I just see people as people." The logical opposite to this position is to racialize everything about the families. Such an approach dictates that everything is seen in racial terms. It also attributes all the family members' variance in behavior to the fact that they are members' of a specific racial group. A brief examination of both of these postures shows that it is often the worker's issue with race that is an issue and not the family's racial attitudes or identity.

In discussing probation families, it is necessary to record demographic data about the family and try to determine the relative importance of these data in shaping the family's behavior in the present. Gender, income, age, and race are common characteristics identified on forms and reports. Unfortunately, the ways in which these pieces of information are used are frequently very superficial. There is rarely an exploration of how specifically these dimensions have contributed to the psychological and behavioral evolution of the clients. Rather, a determination that the dimensions have been important in the client's life is made uniformly. In some ways, this is a gross generalization about a subcategory of individuals to include the client. For example, gender attributions that note that women are likely to have received socialization toward passivity are made frequently. These are so common that such an interpretation of gender role socialization is often made without questioning it. Nearly everyone accepts the axiom to be true. Of course, there are many situations in which women have not been socialized toward passivity. What, then, is an interviewer to make of the woman whose life experiences do not fit the stereotypic pattern?

The same dynamics of overinterpreting the impact of race on development occur with great frequency. Typically, this occurs when workers note the racial designation of a family and then make sweeping generalizations about their experiences that can be attributed to race. At an extreme level, this may take the form of assuming that all people of color have had horrific experiences with racism or assuming that, because a person is categorically a minority individual, he or she has grown up in poverty. In some ways, this is stereotyping that interferes with a genuine appreciation of the client's understanding of the contributions to his or her evolution that can be attributed to race. Bronfenbrenner (1979) calls this type of superficial treatment of demographic characteristics social address labeling. He uses this phrase to note that such quantification of individuals on the basis of physical characteristics such as race does not begin to address the meaningful ways in which these characteristics have shaped the life of the individual. Bronfenbrenner and Crouter (1983) note,

Among the most common "social addresses" appearing in the research literature are the following: social class, family size and ordinal position, rural vs. urban residence, differences by nationality or ethnic group, and more recently, what I have referred to as the "new demography." (p. 373)

Bronfenbrenner and Crouter caution that to simply use a demographic trait (e.g., race) as an explanation for the various behaviors and attitudes that an individual may be expressing is an oversimplification:

One looks only at the social address, that is, the environmental label—with no attention to what the environment is like, what people are living there, what they are doing, or how the activities taking place could affect the child. (pp. 382–383)

In the case of race in the lives of probation department clients, it is often assumed that knowing the racial designation of a family gives some ready-made insights into the developmental history of the members. Without significant exploration of the family's reconstruction of the racial ambiance in which it has functioned, there is no way to fully understand the significance of race to the family.

### "But These Families Won't Participate"

Efforts to stage the Family Intervention Project immediately precipitated conflicts for some workers. The struggle seemed to be whether such an approach would make a difference with this population or whether a more directive and structured intervention should be pursued. At a more basic level, some workers questioned whether or not any attempts to work with families should be undertaken with this client group. No specific rationale for such reservations was offered other than the casual observation that many juvenile delinquents come from families whose members are not available to assist them or to participate in any type of remediation program. This pattern of disbelief in the client's family to work on the family problems is not uniquely racial in nature. It is, however, a statement about the probation workers' attitudes about the client's family. In the context of working on the FIP, the level of lack of faith in the family increased exponentially if the family was an ethnic minority. It is difficult to explain exactly how the doubts would be expressed, but small subtle messages that the probation officer did not expect the family to be compliant were often heard. Sometimes, there were even intellectual disclaimers, such as "they don't make use of mental health services, you know" or some variation to explain why the probation officer did not feel confident that the family members would avail themselves of the opportunities presented by the FIP.

To further mask the insidious nature of their comments, some workers would qualify their statements by suggesting that an alternative source of help (e.g., minister or priest) should be considered for some families. The nature of the work to be performed in the workshops was very clear to the probation workers. They had been involved in helping to develop the program.

It has never been entirely clear to me whether the belief that the families will not participate is based on generic observations or a pervasive disbelief in parents of youngsters involved in the criminal justice system. In either case, it is not a strong statement about the parents. At the very worst, it represents a jaded and somewhat unflattering image that probation workers have developed about families. Clinically, there are several dynamics that often operate in such work relationships with parents of adjudicated delinquents. Workers who share the same racial and ethnic identities as the clients often feel conflicted because they want desperately to help the client. When the client does not respond in a manner consistent with how the clinician believes her or she should respond, the client is often characterized as being unmotivated or unappreciative of all that is being done for him or her. In either case, the expectations and hope that the worker has for the family are not realized. Clinicians sometimes refer to this as overidentification with the client. Doing so usually precipitates countertransference reactions (Heimann, 1950/1981; Kernberg, 1965/1981. 1976; Little, 1951/1981; Reich, 1951/1981; Tower, 1956/1981) that, if left unaddressed, can threaten the work relationship. The term *countertransference* is borrowed here from traditional psychoanalytic usage, in which it refers to the reactions of the analyst toward the patient. It is used here to refer to the reactions toward the client harbored by the probation officer. A second very common reaction to clients that might explain the "but they won't participate" reply is more complex. It involves work dyads when there is a racial mismatch between the worker and the client family. This pattern of mismatch is very common in the criminal justice and mental health systems because of the underrepresentation of people of color as professionals and the overrepresentation of people of color as consumers. The mismatch is potentially problematic because of views and behaviors that both the client and the helping professional may bring to the relationship. Here, our interest is exclusively in what the professionals bring to the relationship.

Many very good intentioned white probation workers want to help their clients and are willing to do practically anything to assist in the process. Unfortunately, such unbridled good intentions are often the professional's countertransference reactions at work. Vontress (1968) referred to this as "the great white father syndrome." He apparently was referring to white workers who verbalize a desire to help clients of color but who unknowingly infantalize their clients in the process.

One of the most pervasive beliefs held about the families of gang-affiliated youth was that their families were not available for participation in the intervention project. This was most frequently expressed as a fear that the parents would not attend the sessions with no evidence to support such a conclusion. The validity of the conclusion of parental nonparticipation was never directly discussed. This was often considered as being necessarily true.

### "We Need More Minority Facilitators"

In the early stages of the development of the FIP (Branch, 1997), a clinical intervention program for use with gang adolescents and their families, members of the probation department staff were active participants. They had knowledge of the rationale underlying the program and the intended outcome. A comment that was often made by probation officers in response to the trial runs of the program was "we need more minority facilitators." It was not entirely clear at the time that the statement was being made what the officers were really saying. Significant discussion in response to this frequent comment, however, revealed several findings that are perceived as being indicative of probation officers' feelings (e.g., ambivalence and discomfort) about working directly with issues of race and diversity.

The statement that we need more minority facilitators suggests that the facilitators who were actively involved were not doing an adequate job of being sensitive and working with the families involved in the FIP. It should be kept in mind that the majority of the families involved in the FIP comprise people of color. A careful review of the comment of needing more minority facilitators also suggests three plausible interpretations: the workers who are currently involved are doing an adequate job; viewpoints in addition to those offered by the current workforce are needed if the FIP is to be maximally effective; and having more people of color involved in the implementation of the FIP reduces the likelihood that white workers will have to interact in a very direct way when issues of race and diversity become very pivotal in the clinical proceedings.

The idea of needing more minority workers to make the FIP more effective suggests that the current workers are not getting the job done. Either the task is complex and beyond their level of competency or the job is so large that more hands are required. Perhaps both interpretations are true. These sentiments were never verbalized directly. Rather, they found expression in covert statements in several trial runs of the FIP. Finally, workers were confronted directly. Not getting the job done did not merely mean that the workers were incompetent. It is also a metaphoric way in which the complaining parties noted that they believed the facilitators were not responding to issues of diversity in a way that was acceptable. In a covert way, questions were being raised about the facilitators' level of racial and ethnic consciousness. Many of the probation officers were of the opinion that families and the adjudicated adolescents needed to be directly confronted as opposed to being approached in a more traditional psychotherapeutic manner. That is not to say that the workers were not sensitive or empathetic, but rather they were not in full support of an indirect and "soft" approach to confront inappropriate behavior. This difference in professional style gave rise to the comments of needing more minority workers. Also, the constant request for more minority workers indicates how the probation officers attribute much of the variance in the dynamics with the families to racial and cultural differences. They appear to be suggesting that having more workers would decrease the likelihood that some cultural variation would be misunderstood and not responded to in an appropriate manner. Such a failure implicitly compromises the effectiveness of the FIP because it reduces the credibility of the facilitator in the eyes of the families.

Another interpretation of the "we need more minority facilitators" comment is that the probation workers involved are incompetent in their analyses relative to cultural diversity. The specific comments of the probation officers who are people of color appear to be of special clinical significance. Focusing on minority status as a characteristic of workers that is likely to enhance the quality of the work relationship with the minority clients appears to be implicit. This type of within-cultural group match between consumer and service provider has a long tradition in the cross-cultural counseling and psychotherapy literature. Some writers have suggested that a within-racial or -ethnic group match is the optimal pairing when dealing with clients who are people of color. This is an ideal situation, but one that is not likely to occur if the pattern of minority underrepresentation within the mental health field continues. Within-racial or -ethnic group pairing also has the potential of being counterproductive to new service providers learning about cultural diversity. Continuing to assign people of color to service providers of color, as a preferred approach, reduces the likelihood that issues of race and ethnicity will be explored by many service providers (e.g., therapists, social workers, and probation officers). This same dynamic was at work in the FIP when probation workers, white and nonwhite, were quite persistent in their belief that minority facilitators are most likely to be effective with clients who are people of color. The psychotherapy literature concerning cross-racial clinical introductions does not support the widely held belief that reducing cultural barriers increases the effectiveness of the intervention. This does help, but the relationship is not a simple linear progression. Within-racial or -ethnic group counseling, relationships do have the potential for complicating the work relationship. Most notably, the perception of progress may be altered because the counseling is intimately acquainted with the cultural niches within which the client operates. Occasionally, there is an overidentification with the client. Finally, there is the possibility of a strong countertransference on the part of the counselors that renders them helpless to be of assistance to the client.

## "I Know You Will Think This Is a Stupid Question, But _____"

A very revealing behavior often occurred when the facilitators and probation officers attempted to analyze the events that occurred during one of the trial sessions of the FIP. Invariably, some client behavior would be highlighted for discussion. Sometimes, the behavior would be identified as a variant on a cultural theme. Other times, the behavior in question would be identified as inappropriate behavior. On other occasions, behaviors would be noted as cultural variations but inappropriate for the context in which they were being emitted. The final interpretation was the one least likely to be invoked. In retrospect, it appears that such was the case because no one wanted to run the risk of being labeled as being insensitive or, at the very worst, "a racist." After several clinical reviews of the FIP sessions, some workers became more comfortable with the idea that not identifying contextually inappropriate behavior was another form of stereotypic behavior that served only to deceive clients. Not confronting maladaptive and inappropriate behavior positively reinforces the behavior and encourages clients to persist in such behaviors. The major task of helping probation officers become more proactive in identifying and questioning behaviors led to some interesting dynamics of self-deprivation. "I know you will think this is a stupid question, but _____" became the qualifier that many workers would use to introduce an inquiry, especially if it concerned race and diversity matters.

The disclaimer served several purposes, none of which were facilitative of personal growth and development of the person asking the question. First, such a statement has the impact of an apology for a lack of knowledge. Clinically, this could be interpreted as an indicator of anxiety and fear that the listener will be negative toward the speaker. It also has the impact of diverting attention away from the real issue—the question. Conversely, the statement also makes a projective interpretation, "I know that you will think...." In some ways, the speaker is then presuming to have an awareness of how the listener will respond even before the question is asked. In both these situations, the qualifier almost invariably had a distracting effect. Listeners often were diverted into explaining why the person asking the question should not apologize for his or her lack of information. Dynamically, the disclaimer frequently forced the listener into the role of caretaker, making the questioner feel better about himself or herself.

The larger dynamic caused by a disclaimer or apology is that the person asking the question continued to feign ignorance. Rather than directly asking the questions, much energy was spent in being circular and avoidant of one's genuine need to have an answer for the question at hand.

Another interpretation of what is accomplished by the disclaimer is that the speaker creates a hierarchy involving self and the listener. The listener is elevated to a status higher than that of the person asking the question, "I know you will think...." In an absolute sense, such a status attribution can be viewed as a negative statement about the listener. The listener is seen as being negatively judgmental about the person who is asking the question. Of course, this is not necessarily true, but it is the speaker's anticipation of what will happen.

In many ways, the disclaimer is a critical clinical indicator of the person about to ask a question. It reveals something of the speaker's level of anxiety and fear of rejection by others, and it also speaks to the anticipated reaction to the question about to be asked. Perhaps as important, the disclaimer is revealing of how the speaker finds it necessary to seek information from a position of self-deprecation. It is interesting, however, that similar apologies are not made when seeking information about issues unrelated to race and diversity. What does all this mean? What implication for staff training are inherent in such behavior?

The interpretations of such behavior needs to be idiosyncratic to the individual engaging in such behavior, as is always the case. There are, however, some issues associated with such behavior that are repeated in all settings in which the disclaimer is verbalized. Individuals who use the disclaimer invariably are wanting to dilute any response when they ask their question. More telling in the anticipation is the idea that the speaker expects the reaction to be negative. Implicit in the disclaimer is some type of indication that the speaker bears no responsibility for potentially having the information he or she is seeking. Discussions of why the speaker finds it necessary to apologize for what he or she does not know often reveal that speaker does not feel a sense of responsibility to know about racial and cultural matters, especially those related to groups other than his or her own. This pattern of claims of lack of knowledge and, hence, an apologetic stance is especially pronounced among whites, who are at a low level of racial identity development (Carter, 1995).

The "I know you will think this is a stupid question, but _____" scenario was observed in interactions between facilitators and probation officers. It is not clear whether the same behavior presents itself as probation officers interact with parents. If so, one has to wonder how distracting and confusing it must be for parents who wish to obtain assistance from the probation officer. This does not mean that the probation officer has all the answers. It does suggest that the officer should not use the occasion of interacting with parents as a way to act out his or her own anxieties, ignorances, and avoidant behaviors about racial matters.

The previous examples are drawn from some of the interactions that occurred with the probation officers while piloting the FIP. They represent a cross section of issues that point to how to work with probation officers regarding race and diversity as developmental issues. They also demonstrate the level of understanding of probation officers about issues of race, ethnicity, and human relating. In many ways, the attitudes of the probation workers, reflected in their verbal behaviors, provide a wonderful microscopic view of larger society racial and ethnic attitudes.

## How Do Race and Ethnicity
## Impact the Probation Department Setting?

The views of probation workers whom I encountered while developing and piloting the FIP mirror larger society's thinking about race and ethnicity. Much of their behavior is not conscious or even mean-spirited. It simply is naive and self-serving of their own private agendas and is consistent with societal behavior and attitudes that have been documented in the professional literature. Among the probation workers and the client families, there is an ambivalence about the significance of race as an explanation for attitudes and behaviors. For example, race is rarely identified directly in discussions. Instead, it is talked about but never identified by name. When it is called by name, there are many disclaimers and qualifiers associated with the discussion. Here, I have highlighted those discussions with the examples of "I know you will think this is a stupid question but _____" and the illusion of racelessness that allows workers to pretend that the justice system is truly color blind. The opposite of ambivalence occurs when a worker attributes all a client's behavior to racial factors. Every inappropriate action that the client took is explained on the basis of him or her being a minority group member. Another troubling feature of the racial ambivalence relates to the observation that many probation workers are willing to talk about race only when it is applied to others. This finding matches a similar finding noted by Hirschfeld (1997), who observed that in much of his fieldwork with white children they were willing to talk about race only when it referred to the race of someone else. Among probation workers, there was a pronounced tendency to not note their own race and how it influences their interactions with others. In the case of juvenile probation clients, I think the impact of race on relationships with families is likely to be considerable. The race dynamics (same race interactions and cross-racial interactions) often solidify or seriously compromise the probation officers ability to be helpful to a troubled youngster and his or her family.

The "more is better position," exemplified here by "We need more minority facilitators," also demonstrates a racialistic posture that exists in the larger society. The probation workers who kept insisting on the need for more workers, apparently to reflect more views, appeared to be engaging in this type of behavior as a creative way to avoid dealing directly with the families and also as a ploy to express dissatisfaction with the work that was being done. To do the latter significantly increases the risk of being charged with being racially insensitive. It should be noted that all the facilitators are mental health professionals. There is a great likelihood that the complaining workers were also having difficulty with competent minority mental health professionals. In so doing, they were giving voice to their hitherto unconscious displeasure and nonacceptance of minority group individuals who did not match the stereotype of minority group persons. Rather than directly confront this possible interpretation, the workers found it easier to simply ask for more facilitators.

## How Do Racial Dynamics Enter the Justice System? Or, Isn't Justice Blind?

Many of the values reflected in the comments and questions of the probation workers are reflective of attitudes developed in the world outside the probation department. Workers inculcate these attitudes without giving them much thought. Specifically, beliefs about troubled youth become internalized very quickly. A common belief about the youth is that their families are not available to help them nor do their families really care about what happens to them. This has been illustrated here by the oft-repeated phrase that "these families won't participate." The assumption of the nonparticipation of families creates an atmosphere in which workers feel the need to be paternalistic to the adolescent probation clients. Behaviors associated with such a posture include violation of personal space boundaries. Clients are sometimes considered surrogate children and treated as if they are obligated to cooperate with the probation worker out of a sense of gratitude. This type of infantalizing usually erupts into volatile relationships in which clients resent the intrusiveness of workers and workers resent the "lack of gratitude of the clients."

The probation workers appear to introduce into policy and behaviors the belief that parents of color are inadequate to provide for the well-being of their children. This is observable in the rate at which adolescents are referred for mental health or other specialty assistance, and the parents are not involved in the decision or the service delivery. This occurs with young people being sent for counseling, but no equivalent help is provided for families. All this indicates that the parents are being ruled out as possible allies to the young persons who must overcome the developmental tasks that they face. It also gives the message of parental inadequacy.

Perhaps the most profound way in which race and ethnicity are introduced into the proceedings of the probation department is through legislation designed to counteract youth crimes by creating tougher sentences for individuals convicted of crimes. The logic for such thinking is that stiffer penalties will serve as a deterrent to future offenders. This has not turned out to be the case. Rather, the rates of juvenile crimes have been increasing rapidly during the past 10 years, most rapidly for girls (Poe-Yamagata, 1996). For example, between 1986 and 1995, the number of arrests involving female juveniles increased by 50% compared with an 26% increase in arrests of male juveniles. As a result, the female proportion of all juvenile arrests increased from 22% to 26% during that time.

A final way in which societal attitudes about race and ethnicity find expression in the probation department concerns the belief that cultural variations are nonexistent and that all people should be treated the same: "People are people .... We're all the same." This type of logic, quite pronounced among workers and policymakers in the Denver Municipal Court , helps to foster a belief that equality means color and culture blindness. Treating everyone the same, in my opinion, means keeping things the way they have always been. The powerful remain powerful, and the powerless continue to be marginalized and disregarded. The contention of color blindness and egalitarian treatment for all means that subtle variations in community resources and cultural patterns that could aid in the development of effective community prevention programs are also lost.

The blindness of justice also eliminates helpful components of the probation officers. Frequently, the ability to identify maladaptive patterns for additional exploration is lost because workers are afraid to ask questions that might be construed as being racial. Workers also fail to develop to their fullest capacity because they learn to overlook the obvious, disregard elements of themselves that could have a positive impact on their relationships with clients and their families, and pretend that the blindness to realities confronting the probation department is good. Collectively, these features suggest that the blindness of justice in this case, when there could be sight, vision, and growth, aids in the ineffective functioning of a system that could have an overwhelmingly positive impact on its clients and itself.

# PART III

# Interventions and Applications for Training

# 12

# Classic Defenses:
## *A Critical Assessment of Ambivalence and Denial in Organizational Leaders' Responses to Diversity*

### Samuel D. Johnson

As a trainer, teacher, and executive in higher education, I am aware that psychoeducational professionals have spent more than 40 years studying and analyzing our national experiments with desegregation, affirmative action, and diversity. Change has been painfully slow. As a society, we have passed laws, conducted millions of hours of training, supervised thousands of studies, and employed legions of attorneys only to be continually impeded by a refusal to acknowledge diversity as an issue.

It is my intention to provide a critique of leadership responses to race, culture, and gender issues in terms of the psychological constructs of ambivalence and denial. The central roles that leaders play in the construction and maintenance of organizational culture will be reviewed with regard to their impact on relationships with consultants. Awareness of the social impact of these shifts on the workplace has provided impetus for many leaders to attempt to adopt specific goals and objectives for their managers and other employees under the banner of accommodating diversity. This effort has encompassed a wide array of organizational contexts, including schools, social service agencies, hospitals, and the corporate sector. Obviously, no single approach to the content of this work is universally appropriate.

This chapter is for the practitioner, instructor, and advanced student of the applied psychology of human difference who aspire to work as diversity consultants. Each must address the theoretical and intellectual basis of their work and confront the moral and ethical consequences of ambivalence and denial on the part of those who engage them.

Central to the current position is the premise that organizational leaders are first and foremost creators and managers of the organizational culture. Their behavior defines standards of conduct and value that become norms (Morgan, 1997). Thus, consultants to leaders of organizations take their direction from these norms and the vision that the leadership is able to articulate. For example, General· Electric, a major multinational organization, incorporated diversity objectives in its vision statement (Capowski, 1996): "GE developed a vision statement for diversity: 'To be recognized as one of the world's most competitive companies due to our ability to value and fully utilize contributions of all employees from all cultural and social backgrounds'" (p. 19).

## Cultural Differences

During the past 40 years, as leaders became aware of disparity among race and gender in salary, rank, and career path, the easiest and most obvious response was to recruit more women and visible racial-ethnic group members. Under the broad rubric of "diversity issues," leaders supported several strategies for identifying and confronting the consequences of racial, ethnic, and gender difference in the workplace.

The first strategy has to do with access of visible racial-ethnic group members to the organization. It suggests that simply increasing the number of visible racial-ethnic group members in the organization is enough to address the letter of affirmative action. Approaches that measure success through demographics alone constitute a basic component of this "mix and stir" structural integration strategy. Denial and ambivalence help maintain the implicit assumption that simply increasing interaction will solve the problem. In the beginning of our experiments with desegregation, our focus was principally on race. In the intervening years, other protected classes have been added to the list through force of law. Leaders are now accountable for managing organizations that are complex social structures comprising gender, professional, linguistic, ethnic, racial, and cultural diversity. One response to this complexity has been an increasing acknowledgment of the role and influence of leaders on organizational culture. It has begun to impact their approaches to managing diversity. In some circumstances, it seems that complicating the mix made matters worse. Those of us who lived through the early days of race-based desegregation can attest to the experiences of social isolation, racial conflict, rage, and "blaming the victim" (Pierce, 1969, 1970). Descriptors such as culturally deprived, culturally different, and diversity have served to provide support for leaders' and others' collective projection of "the problem" onto visible racial-ethnic group members. Much of this conflict, I believe, can be attributed to the denial of the role of personal and cultural values in organizational and interpersonal interactions. Leaders and consultants began to focus on how people interacted. Naturally, efforts to impact these interactions began to emerge in training.

A second strategy has to do with helping individuals, typically whites, develop sensitivity to visible racial-ethnic group members. This strategy is variously referred to as sensitivity training, diversity training, and antiracism training. Often, training of this type is conducted after an organization has begun to diversify through integration or in response to affirmative action or after a leader's experience with the difficulty of effectively managing visible racial-ethnic group members ("minorities"). Issues with performance, job satisfaction, or filed Equal Employment Opportunity complaints focused leaders on monitoring intergroup and personal intercultural interactions. Tolerance and understanding of the minority experience emerged as explicit and implicit objectives. The focus for whites and males continued to be on the "other" rather than on themselves in action. The task of understanding was disconnected from the goals of the organization and its work. The "minority problem" was viewed as "make-work" to whites and males and victim blaming to visible racial-ethnic group members and women.

Taken together, these approaches have one commonality—an almost exclusive focus on groups of visible racial-ethnic group member people or on training whites to be more aware of their perceptions of visible racial-ethnic group members. In each instance, there is little focus on the racial or cultural characteristics of the majority group or on organizational values related to difference. Whites typically only have to learn to tolerate and get along with others who are different. In this way, it is theorized that destructive racial stereotypes can be altered through training.

Whites were encouraged to explore their ethnic background, whereas visible racial-ethnic group members talked about their race. Denial by leaders and trainers can allow whites to avoid talking about themselves as racial beings. Whites were allowed to deny their race and maintain the belief that whites do not have a race. Consequently, the false impression that only people of color have race and, by extension, issues with race, is implicitly maintained. Confronting their denial and framing a white racial identity are critical objectives for each white member of the organization. They must understand how race and their identification with it influences their feelings, perceptions, and behavior. This will not happen by accident. Intentional management of diversity requires structure and purpose (Jamieson & O'Mara, 1991).

A third strategy is designed to operationalize organizing for diversity as suggested by Morrison (1994). It structures contact and managed tasks across racial and cultural lines within organizational units. The organizing for diversity strategy involves structuring situations in which people of different racial and ethnic groups will actually work together in an environment that is managed with attention to intergroup and interpersonal interactions. Linking organizational goals and outcomes to success in overcoming traditional patterns of discrimination added formal legitimacy to diversity initiatives. In this strategy, everyone has a race and a culture. The notion is that actively managed contact with one another will help break down racial barriers. Thus, if racially different people work together in an environment that supports their success in collaboration, they will discover their similarities, learn to appreciate their differences, and work in mutually supportive ways. The exposure strategy accounts for process and outcome.

Reorganizing for diversity (Morrison, 1996) has become an issue for the leadership of educating organizations. Ann Morrison of the Center for Creative Leadership defined the leader's role in the results of her study of leadership diversity. She has documented the "glass ceiling" that racial and ethnic group members confront as they approach leadership-level positions in organizations. Her recent project "Guidelines on Leadership Diversity," speaks to the issues for educating organizational leaders in ways that I find quite compelling. In her view, organizing for diversity is a leadership issue, leaders need to be from diverse backgrounds, and effective leaders of culturally diverse organizations must develop ways of achieving the maximum potential of people regardless of the cultural form which it takes.

Morrison's (1994) research of corporate America identified five steps in addressing diversity issues from the position of an organizational leader: *Discover or rediscover current problems, strengthen top management commitment, choose practices carefully, demand results, and build on past successes.*

Discovering or rediscovering current problems requires an institutional audit to define problem areas, assess perceptions of the organization, and identify barriers to advancement across diverse groups; identify problems of prejudice, poor career development, poor work environment, isolation, no mentors, less knowledge, skills, organizational savvy, comfort with own kind, career versus family; and identify real versus assumed problems. For example, an assumed problem such as women leaving professional positions due to conflicts between career goals and family life can serve to mask a real problem of professional women leaving positions for the same reasons as professional men—a perceived lack of career opportunities.

Strengthening top management requires top management support to proceed. At the least, top management needs to be tolerant of changes. Data must be given to senior executives to define problems. No news does not equal good news. Top managers need to be active and concerned.

Choosing practices carefully recognizes that practices are many and varied. They need to match the data and the apparent culture of the organization to be viable. Work toward a strategic balance of practices such as recruitment (scholarships and programs), development of education and training, and accountability, clear targets and goals with performance review and compensation, education to change attitudes slowly, enforcement to change behavior, and exposure to structure change at the personal level. Managers need to be challenged and then recognized and supported.

Demanding results suggests that data and numerical goals are required. Despite issues with quotas, develop and use numerical goals, include other measures of success (e.g., morale and job satisfaction) and expect what managers can deliver.

Building on past successes means leveraging prior successes. Add diversity to diversity to include gender, race, ethnicity, international issues, and issues concerning the physically challenged. Acknowledge the powerful role of group identity in organizational interactions (Morrison, 1996). Successfully organizing for diversity is a core issue for the leadership of modern organizations. The capacity to effectively engage and facilitate the reduction of denial and ambivalence among organizational leaders is firmly at the heart of defining success in training and development in support of organizing for diversity.

## Denial and Ambivalence

Denial has proven to be an effective defense in the campaign against race and gender barriers in the workplace. Organizational leaders hold fundamental roles in the development and management of an increasingly diverse workforce. Leaders who deny or are ambivalent about race and gender issues risk ineffectiveness by perpetuating status quo corporate culture in their organizations. They increase frustration for others who have different cultural, personal, and political values.

Ambivalence means being inconsistent or contradictory in one's recognition of and response to diversity issues. In psychoanalytic theory, Fenichel (1945) proposed that "some persons feel inhibited when they have to greet people or show any other social amenity. The root of this inhibition is in ambivalence" (p. 184). Some of the most inhibiting social amenities to perform are conducting interracial and intercultural interactions. These interactions are fraught with social anxiety. Emotional responses to the racial or cultural other that are framed in anticipation of race-related social anxieties contribute to the push and pull of ambivalent posturing. Such interactions are difficult for most individuals and an insurmountable challenge for many others. Ambivalence clearly plays a part in the inhibited, uncomfortable quality that seems initially characteristic of interracial relationships. The introjection of anticipated anger on the part of blacks, for example, could account for the social anxiety that supports ambivalence in cross-racial interactions. Fenichel (1945) illustrated ambivalence psychoanalytically as follows:

> A consideration of the reactions of the environment to one's actions plays a large part in all human relationships. And indeed, in a hundred ways every individual's existence depends on his taking other people's reactions into account. This can be called the rational component of social fear. It is very well founded. Social anxiety of this kind may represent ... a reprojection of the superego onto the environment.... Exaggerated social anxiety must be regarded as a corollary of increased ambivalence. He who hates everyone must fear everyone. Compulsion neurotics are frequently particularly polite, accommodating, and considerate. This is an expression of reaction formations that oppose aggressive tendencies.... The original instinctual conflicts between the

patient and the person whose introjection gave rise to the superego are reflected again in the conflicts between the patient and the persons whose judgment he fears. (p. 519)

Ambivalence is the consequence of exaggerated social anxiety associated with disquieting affect toward visible racial-ethnic group members. The social fear of the racial other is reprojected into the environment and the visible racial-ethnic group members that inhabit it.

Denial in the current context means a refusal to acknowledge or simply saying no to diversity as an issue. Fenichel (1945) posed the following psychoanalytic view:

Sometimes the external world is warded off, not to avoid the mobilization of an instinct but to deny the idea that the instinctual act may be dangerous or cause pain; that is the prohibitive character of the external world may be warded off. In general, this type of denial cannot be carried too far in neuroses because the reality-testing function of the ego prevents too obvious a falsification. (p. 101)

Warding off the emotional discomfort, anticipated rage, and hostility of the racial other is at the root of denial in this context. Denial in response to the racial other may be less effectively modulated by reality testing due to limited effort at reality testing. Neither ambivalence nor denial is a new response to diversity issues, such as race and gender. Consistently challenging the acceptance of these defenses of leaders and consultants as responses to diversity would be a new response.

Executive vision provides the foundation for the development of effective training that complements local initiatives (Capowski, 1996). Trainers are hired and paid by managers from the ranks of executive, senior, and upper-middle management. In many respects, the leaders of the organization are the clients of origin. Success in large measure can be contingent on convincing organizational leaders that "diversity" is an issue, and that training can be effective as part of a response. The classic counselors' dilemma of "Who is the client?" comes directly into play if the trainer believes his or her employer executives are in denial. The act of hiring a consultant does not automatically suggest that the leader in question is not in denial. Often, consultants are recommended and hired by subordinates and introduced to leaders who are ambivalent or in denial. Do we treat the leaders and possibly lose the work or train the company employees as requested with full awareness of the flaws in the leader's vision?

## Training Is Only as Effective as Leaders Permit It to Be

Since the 1980s, sensitivity to the demographic shifts in the workforce and interest in and commitment to multicultural organizational interventions have increased rapidly (Brady, 1996; Capowski, 1996; McCune, 1996 Paskoff, 1996). Johnson (1987), Johnson and McRae (1992), and Carter and Block (1992) critically assessed the character and methods of organizational interventions in the workplace. In most cases, the interventions they reviewed were less than ideal because they did not take steps toward achieving objectives that could be framed as competence in applying cultural knowledge. Since then, many activities have been conducted in the service of effectively managing an increasingly diverse workforce.

Leaders of organizations in the United States have either voluntarily or through force of law sought to expedite the effective participation of visible racial-ethnic groups (visible racial-ethnic group members; i.e., a generic term used to refer to members of groups typically considered minorities) in the workplace (Brady, 1996; Capowski, 1996; McCune, 1996; Paskoff, 1996). Recent reports have documented the shifts in racial and ethnic makeup of the workforce. According to Gordon (1996), "The corporate enthusiasm for managing diversity was born of the 1987 *Workforce 2000* report. It was suckled on the milk of global economics and fattened by the desire to do business in foreign countries" (p. 27). Some training activities create more problems than they solve due to flawed analyses by client-managers whose ambivalence and denial have not been addressed. These client leaders compromise trainers effectiveness by becoming a significant part of the organization's problem (Gordon, 1996). Ambivalence has made it difficult to determine the problem. Is it a white problem, a minority problem, or is it a problem in the way we interact? Taking responsibility for solving problems that they have been allowed to deny (by both their company and society at large) becomes an emotionally tainted assignment for many white, male executives. When confronted with training delivered by visible racial-ethnic group members that is not linked to organizational culture and leaders, many white members can invoke denial as a defense. Gordon (1996), citing Daniels, illustrates the underlying problem:

> The [black] leader was operating from the assumption that, "I speak for blacks; I can tell you how we're treated and what you think about blacks." ... The whites were merely antagonized and learned nothing.... That leader went away saying "Well, there it is—and when you show it to them, they deny it." (p. 29)

Here, denial is noted as a response to flawed training that was poorly linked to organizational culture and the leaders that manage it.

## Applying Denial and Ambivalence to Organizational Assessment

There are many excellent examples of ambivalence and denial among top organizational leaders in Texaco, The Citadel, and the army. The Citadel, having lost an expensive fight to keep the student body all male faces charges of harassment by two of the four female cadets admitted in its second year of coeducation. The Citadel's "zero tolerance" policy is framed in terms of standards of conduct so that the quickest way out of the college is to behave in an inappropriate manner toward one of the female cadets. The Citadel admitted four female cadets out of 1,700. The Citadel is managed by white soldiers in denial. They have lost in court, and are complying with the letter of the law by enrolling four women. First, it must be acknowledged that The Citadel is coeducational in fact but not in spirit. How do its managers really feel about their loss in court? How much conviction is there in the institutions acknowledgment of the need for change? As academic managers, how, if at all, did they seek to learn from other institutions that have faced similar challenges? What is the real cost of failure to comply?

It is apparent that all the early 1950s struggles in higher education with racial desegregation and coeducation have not informed the leaders of The Citadel since they seem to have adopted a 1950s "letter of the law" approach to coeducation. I expect that the efforts to establish coeducation at The Citadel will be very expensive. It will cost the careers of some young men and women and hundreds of thousands of dollars in legal fees and settlements. The similarity of current events to news reports of the 1950s race desegregation stories is painful. I like to believe that we should not have to repeat the same ineffective strategies we attempted in the 1950s, but a close examination of the current level of response at The Citadel would suggest otherwise.

In the corporate sector, Texaco's recent losses in court have served as a benchmark for other multinational corporate entities. Beamon (1997) stated,

> Texaco will have plenty of company in making that positive transition since its record $176 million settlement with black employees hangs in the air as a warning to other companies that they must promote minority managers fairly or else. And few employers will want to follow Texaco's poor example of sitting through a class-action suit, a multimillion dollar settlement, a 2-year federal investigation, and tape-recorded proof of white managers disparaging blacks before they open their executive suites to minorities. (p. 8)

The cases of The Citadel and Texaco provide telling evidence of the inadequacy of the force of law and zero-tolerance policies as comprehensive approaches to effecting positive change in organizational practice. These cases also illustrate that ambivalence and denial, when used in response to emergent diversity issues, are problematic and counterproductive.

Today, we can hold leaders much more accountable for the equitable management of organizational processes. The current climate is the result of broad-based political and social support for issues of fairness and equity coupled with 40 years of wide-ranging efforts to address gender and race issues in education and the workplace. The federal government has muddied the water by revising laws governing affirmative action and civil rights litigation in the shift from Democratic to Republican leadership in the White House. Nonetheless, corporate leaders have been guided by federal policy in ensuring low vulnerability to litigation.

Why is it that so many leaders don't get it? Quite simply, they refuse to acknowledge it. They are in denial. Only denial could account for the failure of the leaders in these organizations to learn from similar cases. Why did these leaders not learn from our recent history with desegregation? How did the leaders of The Citadel miss all that was learned from earlier efforts in integrating single-sex institutions? It seems improbable that no one in these organizations saw the big picture. Someone at Texaco must have known how those offending executive leaders truly felt and taken umbrage. Being offended by manifest corporate cultural values while participating in the organization's defense illustrates ambivalence. In most circumstances, the organizational impetus to address diversity issues has derived its momentum from corporate responses to federal affirmative action policies (Brady, 1996; Capowski, 1996; McCune, 1996; Paskoff, 1996).

Meeting the required minimum in defining affirmative action goals became the excuse for a wide range of loosely coordinated training activities designed to address problems related to minority groups. Recently, awareness of the strategic consequences of America's changing workforce has led leaders to address issues that had been framed only in terms of public opinion and political liability. These efforts can be undermined by ambivalence and denial among leaders in all organizational contexts. In this regard, denial takes the form of projecting onto members of visible racial-ethnic groups rather than acknowledging the guilt and anxiety white male leaders experience in interaction with them. Denial among white male leaders is an effective defense. It functions as an "offensive mechanism" that puts off and deflects minority assertions of injustice (Pierce, 1969). In fact, Pierce noted a denial, dilution, and projection sequence as a key defense paradigm for whites in avoiding issues of racism. Ambivalence can evolve from feeling pressured to accept the importance of affirmative action and the implicit mandate of personal responsibility in creating a solution. These classic defenses and offensive mechanisms can induce organizational leaders and those they direct to interrupt their own efforts toward acknowledging diversity. Ambivalence can result from a leader's demand for collaboration with visible racial-ethnic group members and the concomitant guilt and anxiety regarding acknowledging race and sex discrimination. Also relevant is the predictable rage regarding having to experience guilt and anxiety associated with dealing with visible racial-ethnic group members. Projected onto the social other (visible racial-ethnic group members), it emerges as "the problem with minorities."

There is empirical evidence of ambivalence in a recent survey of educational leaders conducted by McGarraghy and Thompson (1995). Their survey of a wide range of institutional types found that more than 90% of college and university presidents rated the management and fostering of diversity as having importance. These authors noted, however, "when asked to list the top three strategic issues facing their institutions over the next 3 to 5 years, diversity was not among the most frequently mentioned issues." (p. 2). Ambivalence at the highest levels of educational management can undermine leaders' capacity to effectively manage the processes they are obligated to direct. Ambivalence can also impair decisions about training designs and outcome assessment, thus powerfully affecting the perceived results of training activities. Respondents viewed themselves as relatively more effective in promoting diversity with students and administrators than with faculty. Fewer than 20% said they were very effective in promoting diversity with students, and less than 10% said they were very effective in promoting diversity among administrators and faculty. By their own assessment, the majority of the participants in this sample rated themselves as ineffectual at managing aforementioned core issues in diversity (McGarraghy & Thompson, 1995). Future research must analyze the role of ambivalence in manifest ineffectiveness. Trainers working with a college or university should bear in mind the possibility that the upper levels of management believe that training for diversity is important but simultaneously believe that it is likely to be ineffectual. It appears that the president of The Citadel would be placed near the peak of the curve in this survey.

## Denial and Ambivalence in Organizational Culture and Identity

The idea of a organizational culture and a consequent identity is intended to invoke the powerful social influence of organizations on their members. It is a convenient metaphor for the values, beliefs, and attitudes that are reinforced by the leaders who control the reward system and create the culture (Morgan, 1997). Texaco's protracted legal fight and massive settlement are testament to denial on the part of their senior decision makers. Denial can impair leaders' capacity to acknowledge their roles as active creators and keepers of the corporate culture. Ambivalence can undermine the capacity to frame effective policies and practices in response to the natural consequences of diversity.

What is organizational identity? How is it manifest through management as an aspect of corporate culture? What policies and practices could move The Citadel's coeducational initiative forward? What can top management do? What formula could the leaders of The Citadel have used to derive the number of women for their first coed class? Was it careful planning or was it a hasty response to an unexpected loss on the part of a group of military educational leaders blinded by their denial of diversity?

The Citadel has an overwhelmingly male-centered identity derived from a hypermasculine military culture. If any inferences can be made about The Citadel's strategy for integration based on its strategy for coeduction, I hypothesize that is still has a white-centered identity. The leaders of The Citadel have decided to satisfy the letter of the law while actively denying the "spirit of the law." This ambivalent response often results in a solely legalistic approach to organizational change. Responses such as zero tolerance and the ubiquitous "War on . . .[drugs, sexism, racism, poverty, sexual harassment, etc.]" frame regulations and consequences with little regard for the psychosocial complexity extant in organizations. Lacking shades of gray, members of the organizations respond with ambivalence and rage to the double message, "Masculinity rules and we will absolutely not tolerate sexual harassment." What is perceived by some men to be an appropriate and persistent assertion of interest in a woman can be experienced as sexual harassment. Organizational support and mechanisms for managing such natural conflicts are necessary to avoid extended controversy.

Ultimately, organizing for diversity must become a cultural value for the organization. All the previously referenced guidance is vulnerable to leadership's defenses. Morrison (1996) provides a useful strategy that has its genesis in leadership. What kinds of interventions might a consultant suggest to leaders at Texaco or The Citadel? Keep in mind that both organizations endured long legal battles and extensive investigations to defend themselves against alleged discriminatory practices. Suppose the leaders of Texaco or The Citadel contact you. The man that calls you is an executive vice president who says, rife with ambivalence, "We'd like you to do some diversity training for us but we do not want to start any controversy or conflict." What do you do? Attempt to get leaders to see and feel the things they do not want to or press them to understand valuing diversity as an alternative to their ambivalence and denial?

In my view, no training should proceed until the leadership is equipped to handle the consequences of training. The representative that called you must understand why it is not possible to comply with his initial request. Controversy and conflict are natural consequences of diversity. Leaders cannot be led to believe that they are exempt from the treatment intervention. In fact, once the consultant is gone, they will have to maintain and manage the treatment. Leaders cannot be allowed to interrupt their own objectives by maintaining their belief that diversity is not an issue and the consultant is solely responsible for the outcome. Failing that, any intervention is vulnerable to leader's unanalyzed ambivalence and denial.

# 13

# Enhancing Diversity Climate in Community Organizations

*Roderick J. Watts and Arthur Evans*

This chapter presents a practical model for consultants seeking to enhance the racial and ethnic climate of diverse nonprofit organizations. The elements of the model are presented in Figure 13.1. At the center is "common ground," the ideal organizational state in which all racial and ethnic groups in the organization make a contribution to the organization's operation, and all feel equally respected and valued. The "feeling" or phenomenological dimension of common ground is akin to the concept of organizational climate. In this chapter, we are concerned with the view that employees develop of the racial and ethnic characteristics of the organization, which we and others (Kossek & Zonia, 1993) call *diversity climate*. An organization that has reached common ground has a very positive diversity climate. On the basis of our experience, a wide range of elements influence diversity climate. The elements range from the organization's demographics and the competencies of its staff to its mission, policies, practices, and distribution of authority. All these elements surround common ground in the model. In the discussion of climate, we show how these surrounding elements influence the settings, transactions, and events that in turn shape diversity climate and the prospects for reaching common ground. The discussion of the model will emphasize the practical aspects of organizational diagnosis and assessment in a way that can aid organizational consultants.

Increasingly, organizations are launching initiatives to enhance the psychological and the demographic aspects of diversity (Kossek & Zonia, 1993). Consultants are called on to design appropriate interventions in this area on a wide range of topics. Projects include "managing diversity" (i.e., helping managers promote effective working relationships in a multicultural staff), training on cultural sensitivity or cross-cultural skills, and resolving organizational crises believed to be related to race. The first step in any of these is assessment—the focus of this chapter. Assessment is the diagnostic phase, but it also sets in motion a reflective process on the part of employees that constructs the "problem" and confirms its existence. Next is intervention design, the intervention, and then crystallizing the intervention so that the organization

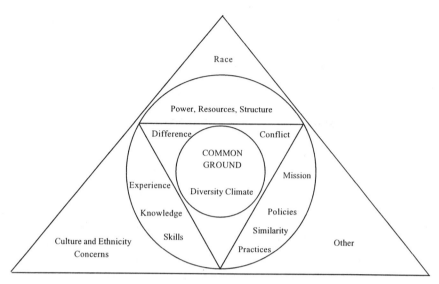

**Figure 13.1.**   Elements of Diversity Climate

does not revert to its previous patterns of behavior. Lewin described this succinctly as unfreezing, changing or intervening, and refreezing (Lewin, 1947; Marshak, 1994). Unfreezing is part of the assessment process in which the fluidity and the capacity to change is introduced in the system. Following the intervention, it is necessary to refreeze the system so that changes will be institutionalized. In this chapter, we discuss some experiences from our work that can guide intervention design.

The examples used in this chapter are nonprofit human-service organizations with a community focus. Human interaction, internal and external to these organizations. is of particular importance. All organizations depend on good human relations, but the social mission of these nonprofits makes human relations especially important. Helping people is the animating principle rather than producing profit and enriching investors. People give to nonprofit agencies for mutual benefit (e.g., the American Automobile Association) or as a charitable contribution (e.g., the United Way). Foundations and governments award grants to nonprofits because they expect the organization to improve society or in some way further shared nonfinancial interests. In none of these cases can contributors expect any monetary profit from their contribution. Running a successful nonprofit organization can be even more challenging than running a successful business because nonprofit organizations must remain financially solvent *and* fulfill their social mission. Businesses, however, have only to attend to their financial goals. The life of a social-service nonprofit organization is further complicated by its symbiotic relationship with its patrons, who may have fiscal (e.g., tax deductions) and public relations reasons for supporting the organization. The mission and operation of the nonprofit must be sensitive to these concerns if it expects to attract resources and thrive. All these distinctive attributes of nonprofits that arise from a social mission and multiple stakeholders require excellent internal and external communication. Tensions that occur due to differences in social and cultural values (especially in the context of limited resources) can undermine an agency's operation.

In the current social climate, in which the political pendulum has swung in the conservative direction, governments are seeking to reduce their role in the promotion of human welfare. Nonprofits are expected to make up the difference, and politicians urge businesses to take more proactive roles in their communities. A consideration of the feasibility of nonprofits and charitable organizations attracting sufficient funding to address the broad range of human needs is beyond the scope of this chapter, but it is fair to say that nonprofit organizations are playing and will continue to play an increasingly important role in serving those in greatest need. Social and economic inequities in the United States mean that many people in need of human services are people of color. The disproportionate social and economic power of whites in the United States means that in nonprofit organizations, especially large ones, many whites are in positions of authority, even when the clients of these organizations are predominantly people of color. Even in organizations in which people of color are in leadership positions, the mission and worldview often reflect European American cultural perspectives (Perkins, 1975). As other racial and ethnic groups gain power in organizations, clashes in worldviews will become increasingly likely.

## The Common Ground Model

The common ground model is presented in Figure 13.1. As an introduction to the model, all the sectors will be described briefly and linked to concepts from the literature. Next, the elements in each sector will be described in greater detail, with an emphasis on organizational assessment and with some examples from actual consultations.

The common ground model deals with race, culture, and ethnicity. There are almost as many definitions for these terms as their are theorists (Birman, 1994; Lonner, 1994), but for the purposes of this chapter *culture* refers to a group that shares a distinctive history, geography, behavior, heritage, lineage, and identity. There is often significant heterogeneity, however, as there is in U.S. culture. Ethnicity is the origin of this heterogeneity. Ethnic groups, such as Mexican Americans in the United States, are part of a larger cultural fabric, but they retain some distinctiveness as they interact with others in the culture. The term *ethnicity* is preferred when interactions between groups are of interest, whereas culture is used to described the larger amalgam of ethnic groups. The word cultural can also be used to denote the distinctive patterns of difference associated with an ethnic group's culture of origin. Race is often associated with ethnicity, but it is primarily a sociopolitical construction with sociopolitical consequences influenced by physical appearance and stereotypes (Helms, 1994).

At the center of the diagram in Figure 13.1 is the goal: The creation of a shared psychological space in which all racial and cultural groups that make up an organization's staff believe that the organization is supportive of their group. In parlance useful for applied work, this space is called *common ground*. It is a space in which there is effective cross-cultural communication, and members of all racial and cultural groups feel comfortable and are invested, and equally able to develop and use their abilities in the service of organizational goals. As its position in Figure 13.1 suggests, common ground is supported by an assortment of organizational structures and functions and by the capabilities and characteristics of individuals and their membership groups. These various structures, functions, characteristics, and capabilities can act as barriers or promoters to reaching common ground. As discussed in the following sections, understanding the interplay of these entities is crucial for the consultant working with nonprofit organizations on diversity issues.

The notion of common ground is related to the construct of organizational climate as articulated by Glick (1985) and others (Howe, 1977; Powell & Butterfield, 1978). As climate, common ground is group-level perceptions of the racial and ethnic atmosphere of the organization. Kossek and Zonia (1993) called this "diversity climate," in which climate is defined as "the influence of work contexts on employee behavior and attitudes, which are grounded in perceptions" (Schneider & Reichers, as quoted in Kossek & Zonia, 1993, p. 63). Common ground exists when each of the organization's principal racial and ethnic groups make meaningful contributions to the agency and view the climate as supportive of their racial and ethnic group. This perception is shaped by settings and events in the organization that contribute to perceptions of diversity climate (Table 13.1). According to Schneider and Reichers (as quoted in Kossek & Zonia, 1993, p. 63), climate is shaped by these experiences because "people attach meaning to or make sense of clusters of psychologically related events." Meetings and tasks such as performance appraisal are the experiential raw material for constructing perceptions of climate. Such events are important subject matter for assessment and key targets for intervention.

Immediately surrounding common ground is a triad of intergroup dynamics that accompany intergroup contact—differences, conflict, and similarity. Many authors have argued that population differences exist based on culture or race (Helms, 1994; Jones, 1991; Ramirez, 1983; Sue & Morishima, 1982) Conflict may emerge when cultural patterns of difference are associated with superiority or inferiority. Common ground is advanced when interethnic conflict and differences are managed properly by organizational and personal elements in the outer circle of the model. For example, cultural knowledge can help employees communicate better. Employees who know that differences in emotional expression can be an ethnic variation are better prepared to prevent difference from becoming conflict when communicating with associates who are ethnically different from themselves. Similarly, diversity-conscious policies that reward group and individual achievement (another cultural variation) contribute to similarity and complementarity in the organization's operation.

Surrounding the triad of differences, conflict, and similarity are three sets of organizational elements. One set is the personal qualities of the staff—experience, knowledge, and skills—that allow them to successfully work through the conflicts and differences present in a multicultural organization. Contemporary diversity training typically focuses on these three areas (Geber, 1990). The second set includes more abstract elements of the organization—power, resources, and structure—that are not a function of staff behavior. It is through this second set of elements that things get done. Examples of these elements are formal institutional and budgetary authority, chain of command, and the deployment of the organization's resources. The last set of elements comprises three important governors of organizational behavior—mission, policies, and practices. The mission determines the goals and objectives, and policies and practices regulate organizational processes. Policies and practices are subject to the will of power holders and their control over resources. Coherence of mission, policies, practices, rewards, and sanctions may shape a climate that is supportive of common ground.

The final, outermost elements of the model are race, culture and ethnicity, and organization-specific concerns. The interactions among these groups and in the organizational problems that prompted the consultation become clearer as the assessment unfolds. It is common that groups of women, African Americans, or Latin Americans will meet regularly but informally to discuss race-related policies or events in an organization. These groups and their leaders can become important informal components of an organization.

In the following sections, we discuss each set of elements in the model in detail and the major questions and themes in the assessment process. Trigger points for organizational change are also highlighted.

## Race, Culture and Ethnicity, and Other Concerns

### Institutionalizing Proactive Diversity Through Identity Groups

When decision makers in an organization are perceived as ignoring the concerns of a racial group or supporting policies that affect it adversely, group members may respond by forming an informal organization. In other instances, these groups form to provide mutual support and assistance. These groups are called identity groups because the glue holding them together is psychological identification. Groups ranging from the Congressional Black Caucus to Latin American case-work supervisors who meet monthly over breakfast fit this category. Sometimes, culture- or race-based identity groups are known to the organization's leadership, and sometimes they are nearly invisible. As part of the assessment, the consultant identifies and communicates with these groups. In consultations in which the aim is to develop racially diverse leadership from within, the assessment may focus on ways of institutionalizing these groups and developing mentoring activities. Another assessment question regards their function: Is it reactive, supportive, proactive, or a combination? Although reactive bodies can help leadership gain a new perspective on events that triggered the reaction, reactive groups can be too narrowly focused and emotionally charged to produce long-term change. Nonetheless, the perspectives such groups can bring to an organization are invaluable if the larger organization can establish constructive lines of communication. Supportive groups often function to blow off steam, commiserate, and provide sounding boards. They may never seek to influence an organization's operation. Proactive groups hold the most potential because they tend to take a wider view of the organization's operation.

The following is an example of a reactive identity group in a university that evolved into a proactive and supportive group with help from leaders in the organization. The organization began when graduate students of color organized and confronted department leaders with their dissatisfaction over the training on cultural and racial issues. Although this began as a reactive effort by the students, those with power and resources in the department ultimately supported the group and its leader by hiring her to lead the group and advance its concerns. One of the group's accomplishments as a proactive body was the creation of a new course on racial topics in the field. It was available to all students in the department, and thus it contributed to the roster of common-ground events. Mostly, however, it was a support group in which students could discuss their work and the department. Hiring the leader served to turn a reactive group into an asset, but it also co-opted the group to a degree. The leader was supervised by a faculty member and subject to university regulations. The department's solution to the original issue stabilized the situation, but it also probably blunted the potential future contribution to the organization. Nonetheless, it strengthened a point on the outer circle, and it produced a new resource for students of color that could potentially positively influence common ground. As part of the assessment, a consultant can create case histories of such groups in preparation for the design of an intervention.

The "other concerns" or organizational-specific point on the outer triangle in Figure 13.1 reminds the consultant of other group memberships that interact with culture, ethnicity, or race. Gender, sexual orientation, profession, age, and many other attributes may complicate the racial and cultural dynamics of an organization. During the assessment phase, the consultant identifies all groups in the organization, cultural or otherwise, that have influenced its operation in a meaningful way. Interviews with formal and informal leaders with a long tenure in the organization often reveal historical information useful in this regard. These groups may provide unique or organization-specific dynamics that affect common ground. For example, in an organization to which A. Evans consulted, educational status interacted with race and ethnicity to form a unique organizational climate. In this organization, it was difficult to determine if problems in the organization were due to educational status or racial and ethnic patterns of difference because many of the African American staff had lower status. Often, in their quest to work on cultural diversity issues, consultants may have to attend to the issues that these other group memberships raise. This includes events in the agency's history that often take on larger symbolic meaning in the minds of staff. For example, the firing of a well-regarded employee that was thought to have racial overtones can exert a continuing influence on diversity climate.

## Power, Resources, and Structure:
## The Forces of Change

Power and resources, via policies and practices, translate vision and mission into operating procedures. These elements, in combination with the qualities of the staff, shape the organizational climate (Glick, 1988). The prerogatives of the powerful are important: Without buy-in and follow-through by leadership, a consultation is unlikely to produce changes in the climate.

In an assessment of racial climate as seen by African American civil servants, Watts and Carter (1991) found that the absence of African Americans in positions of power and the lack of upward mobility were most strongly associated with institutional racism. In a survey designed to define the components of institutional racism, the respondents singled out circumstances in which few African Americans were in positions of authority and when upward mobility to these positions was restricted. Thus, demographics, power, and mobility are important. When the leadership of an organization is racially and ethnically homogeneous, it will probably be suspect in the eyes of the racial and ethnic out-groups.

Thus, one specific question for assessing power asks: Is formal and informal authority fairly distributed among representative members of significant groups? Employees may have a ready answer, but the consultant must listen carefully to the reasoning that produced the conclusion. The examples employees give provide useful information about the climate. The perceived racial or ethnic identity of those in power is also important. A demographically diverse leadership group is necessary but not sufficient for an organization that wants a diversity of ideas *and* physical types. Barker (1992, as cited in Hanover, 1993, p. 1) notes, "It is our diversity as a [work] group that lets us deal with complexity of the world *through the application of many paradigms* [italics added]. And that makes the group much more capable." Similarly, Jones (1994) argues,

> Affirmative diversity addresses the possibility that collectivities or groups are strengthened by the diversity of their individual members. It seeks to develop strategies for implementing institutional decision

making consistent with that proposition; that human diversity is a
positive value in institutional development and performance. (p. 43)

Without the many paradigms, there is no diversity. During an assessment, it is
useful to examine similarities and differences in the worldview of institutionally
powerful people and the worldview of those in their reference group. Worldviews
are translated into action through the chain of command (structure) and through
the application of resources. In the resource domain, the consultant assesses the
extent to which resources have been devoted to diversity-related matters (e.g.,
recruiting a diverse workforce) and the resources available for an intervention.
Questions include the following: To what extent will leadership secure and
deploy the resources needed to create common ground? What has been done in
the past? As the previous university example illustrated, institutionalizing
diversity usually requires an investment. Communication occurs through the
organizational structure. Here, the consultant determines how information from
the identity groups can be communicated to other elements of the model so that
they can be a resource for the organization. Another key question is the
communication of racial and ethnic information through the organization. How
does it occur, and where does the information go? Has there ever been an
organizational conflict or crisis with racial overtones? What parts of the
organization were involved and in what way? Other structural questions concern
work groups or recurring activities that the organization has created to address
issues of race and ethnicity.

## Mission, Policies, and Practices:
## Standards and Traditions for Action

Organizational power typically operates within defined parameters. These
parameters serve as a focus for the deployment of resources. At the broadest
level, these parameters are set by the organization's mission. In the diagnostic
phase, the consultant examines documents and makes inquires about the cultural
and racial implications of the mission. She or he also investigates its relation to
policies, practices, and the likely influences on climate and common ground.

A mission statement may or may not have implications for diversity matter, as
the following two real-world examples illustrate:

The Peace Coalition is a partnership of organizations committed to
preventing violence and promoting peace. With a primary focus on
youth and violence, New City will take action to help existing violence
prevention efforts increase their visibility, share information, and
connect to policymakers, volunteers, and each other.

The Pro-Family Network (PFN) is dedicated to promoting policies and
strategies that support families, recognizing them as the basic

institution for developing and nurturing children. We acknowledge that families are adaptive, resilient, resourceful, and diverse. The PFN also strongly condemns all forms of violence in the family, including child abuse, domestic violence, and elder abuse.

The Peace Coalition does not use explicit diversity language in its mission; therefore, the consultant must determine through interviews, practices, and policy documents whether a value on diversity exists elsewhere. Usually, there is evidence of diversity concerns that can be build on in an intervention. In this instance, initiating a discussion on "existing violence prevention efforts" and the "partnership" can lead the organization to reflect on the racial and ethnic inclusiveness of its efforts. In the second example, diversity language is built in, so the assessment would focus on how the organization lives up to this aspect of the mission in its actions. The consultant might ask: How does the PFN "acknowledge" the diversity of families in its operation in a way that promotes its aims?

Policies and practices are the operating procedures for maintaining the organization and accomplishing its mission. If the Peace Coalition seeks to address youth violence, it needs to hire and retain staff experienced in this area. During the assessment, the consultant determines if hiring policies (such as educational requirements) unduly restrict eligibility for coalition jobs and thereby reduce its demographic diversity. Similarly, are there polices on staff development, affirmative action, and performance appraisal that promote the development of a diverse leadership? Organizations also have traditions and routines that are unwritten. These de facto policies are known as practices. Because they are not written down, they must be determined through a search for patterns of organizational behavior. A consultant assessing practices at the PFN may examine the organization's library of parenting resources for families to determine if it reflects a multicultural orientation. Both policies and practices should reflect the diversity-related concerns of an organization's mission.

Policies and practices are one of the most important areas of focus in diversity-related consultation because they have a broader and more consistent influence on diversity climate than employee skills and abilities. The following example illustrates how the absence of a policy to promote racial and ethnic diversity affected an organization's operation. R. Watts consulted to an international youth-welfare organization whose mission statement made no mention of racial or cultural issues. In recent years, it began experiencing a shift in the demographic characteristics of its service population from white to African and Latin American. The absence of diversity language in the mission left leadership with no direct guidance for improving the organization's responsiveness to clients of color. Racial and cultural considerations were also absent in one of the most important policies and practice-related tasks the organization performed—site visits . Teams of senior staff did peer reviews of sites throughout the world to determine if their operations conformed with the national organization's requirements. If diversity was a priority, one would have expected the site visit teams to investigate the cultural and racial aspects of the organization's operation. Although the two site visit reports examined were lengthy (approximately 3/4-in. thick), there were no direct questions about, and virtually no discussion of, racial or cultural issues. Moreover, neither of the recommendation sections mentioned racial or cultural issues.

The preceding example of an assessment finding shows how diversity related policy (or its absence) influences an organization's operation. It also reveals an intervention opportunity. On the basis of this information, the consultant could help the organization develop new site visit standards that could have a broad impact on the operation of its sites. Although policies and practices are powerful, they are only as good as their design and enforcement. To be beneficial, they must be well crafted and supported by key personnel. Then, they must be implemented and enforced by leadership through formal and informal channels.

In the absence of formal policies, the cultural competence of individual decision makers can sometimes promote common ground. These individuals rely on their personal experience, knowledge, and instincts. In the youth-service organization described previously, members of the national staff requested training on race and gender at their annual retreat. Although there was no formal affirmative action plan, the national organization also hired two African American executive directors and recruited an African American woman for their international board of directors. These practices, despite explicit mandates from the mission or agency policy, contributed to common ground.

Assuming that these practices installed people with worldviews reflective of those in their reference group, and assuming the positions held by the newly hired African Americans had "real" power and authority over resources and organizational operations, the symbolic and practical effect of the organization's personnel should move the agency closer to common ground. These "ifs" illustrate the interdependence of elements in the model: Power, resources, policies, practices, and climate interact to produce the organization's common ground.

## Skills, Experience, and Knowledge:
## The Competence of Individuals

To be competent, people need the skills, knowledge, and personal experience necessary for their jobs. Competence with racial and ethnic matters helps staff understand their own worldview and work effectively with those who are different. Developing skills, experience, and knowledge is the bread and butter of diversity consultation. The typical consultation request is for cultural skill building and sensitivity training (Kossek & Zonia, 1993). These issues are also the least threatening to organizations because they do not require fundamental changes in its mission, resource allocations, or function. Nonetheless, these elements are essential to the staff's ability to understand, empathize, respect, and work well with one another.

In the assessment process, the consultant determines what new skills staff need or believe they are lacking. Research and training work by Kochman (1981) and Pedersen (1993) are examples of skills assessment or development interventions. Information (knowledge) complements effective behavior (skills). Several questions are important: Does the staff have the knowledge needed to understand ethnic and racial differences and similarities and the role of diversity in the organization? Does everyone understand the links between diversity and the quality of products or services? Orchestrating a significant change in an organization's operation by simply declaring "it is the right thing to do" is unlikely to produce the needed commitment and motivation. The staff and management need to understand how common ground contributes to the organization's mission and goals. In our experience, human-service agencies tend to view diversity as a resource because they see a need to match their clients and service providers by ethnicity or race. A diverse staff can also create an affirming image (presumably accompanied by a reality) of cultural pluralism. Frequently, when the consultant asks the staff why staff diversity is important, the staff will make comments, such as "our kids need black role models." Much less frequently will the consultant hear more sophisticated comments, such as "religion plays an important part in the healing process for many of our black patients. We need staff who have personal experience with African American religious traditions." In assessing skills and knowledge, the consultant pays close attention to how staff think about their services in relation to diversity.

Life experience is the third element in this section of the model. Do the people in the organization have the life experiences needed as a context for new skills and knowledge? What kind of personal stories do they tell about interracial and interethnic communication? What are the memorable diversity-related experiences of staff members, especially those related to equality of opportunity, communication, conflict resolution, and product quality? Due to the United States' history of racial oppression and segregation, many white Americans grow up having few personal relationships with people of color. In contrast, people of color in predominantly white organizations have greater direct experience with racial out-groups than do whites. Without personal experience, people are forced to rely heavily on intellectual knowledge for cultural competency. As Jacobson (1988) argues in his discussion of cross-cultural competence for therapists, information is not enough; they need personal experience to put concepts and ideas in a real-world context. Short of this, Jacobson recommends a professional network that includes people experienced in the culture of interest. Moreover, Allport (1954) argued that not all cross-racial contact produces the same effect. In his view, equal-status contact was necessary for diminishing prejudice. Therefore, for those in authority and those who provide services to the disenfranchised, it is essential to develop relationships with culturally different peers. Equal-status peers are likely to contradict stereotypes and share their worldview with less fear of the consequences.

## Similarity, Difference, and Conflict: The Management of Intergroup Dynamics

Once the structural and functional supports for common ground are in place in the domains reviewed previously, the intergroup dynamics of culture and race can be managed in a constructive way. Group identity is based in part on the perception of a pattern of shared characteristics that is distinct from the pattern in other groups (Tajfel & Turner, 1986). The perception of differences can trigger intergroup conflict or, like left and right-handedness, it may be viewed as a benign dimension of human diversity. Groups may share a belief in hard work and the expectation of rewards (similarity) while differing in their expectations of supervisors. Conflict or discrimination may emerge when one group views its perspective as superior—for example, if white Americans believe their emotionally expressive style of discourse is superior to the more restrained style of Asian Americans. The experience of being devalued and of devaluing others may lead to intergroup animosity.

The organization's mission and the work group's tasks ideally form a new group identity that binds people together across ethnicity in an additive rather than substitutive way. The work group identity may keep the focus on problem-solving when perceived differences produce conflict and similarity.

Similarity describes the experience people have when they see commonalties between themselves or their reference group and members of other groups based either on shared personal experiences, attitudes, or values or on shared goals. This feeling of commonality can increase the permeability of racial and ethnic boundaries. Work-related transactions can bond people across ethnic group memberships, thereby encouraging a spirit of teamwork and strengthening the organization. With regard to similarity, an important assessment question is: People from various backgrounds work here, do you see any shared values or ideas that are important to getting the work done? A question to consider when observing organizational activities: During important transactions, do staff members of all racial and cultural groups participate comfortably?

Difference exists when people perceive dissimilarities, but these differences are not associated with feelings of superiority or acts of discrimination. Difference need not become a lightning rod for significant intergroup conflict. For example, in the international youth-serving organization mentioned previously, the white and black executive directors recognized that they tended to value community services, individualized services, and prevention work differently, in part due to their different perspectives on the role of their organization in the community. In terms of culture, this is analogous to the individualistic and collectivist difference that distinguishes cultures throughout the world (Nobles, 1986; Triandis, 1988). This difference did not precipitate a battle over the "proper" mission of the organization, however, or an effort to put forth one perspective as right and the other one as wrong.

As part of an assessment in this area, the consultant could ask the following: Do people perceive patterns of cultural difference? In what settings and circumstances do they see these differences? How do they feel about acknowledging cultural patterns of difference and openly talking about them?

In this model, conflict has two dimensions. The more benign but no less challenging dimension occurs when a cultural value such as improvisation in African American culture (Jones, 1991) clashes with a future orientation that emphasizes planning such as that in white American culture (Stewart & Bennett, 1991). Although many musicians appreciate the spontaneity of Jazz as much as they do the recital of Western classics, when the two styles converge on the common task of making music, conflict may result. In a nonprofit organization, this may mean that one staff faction wants to establish a drop-in program that meets the needs of people when they feel the need, whereas another wants to use those same resources and time slots to establish an appointment-based system of care that is structured and predictable. To resolve this conflict, compromise or fusion must occur. Although the process may be trying, it should be evident that highly creative integrations and eclectic combinations can result from the creative resolution of conflict.

The second type of conflict can be more damaging. It occurs when culture-based differences are associated with impaired communication, feelings of superiority or inferiority, or intergroup distrust. Staff may deny or denigrate group-based patterns of differences or view conflict purely as interpersonal strife. Alternatively, people may view the issues in question as evidence of personal or group incompetence rather than as patterns of cultural difference. These phenomena are classified as conflict rather than difference because a belief in the superiority of one's view is often associated with efforts to eradicate or neutralize the "inferior" perspective through new policies or practices. It is the basis of racist ideology. It can also set the stage for zero-sum struggles in which opportunities for creative resolutions are more limited.

The consultant can ask a variety of questions to elicit data on conflict, including the following: When Latin American (or white or black) staff get together, is there a lot of anger, frustration, or complaining related to race relations? Can you remember a conflict in this agency, major or minor, in which racial or ethnic issues played a role? Are there incident reports or other archival data that may document race or ethnicity as a feature of conflict among staff or between staff and its service population?

## Common Ground:
## Settings, Events, and Transactions That Shape Climate

According to Campbell, Dunnette, Lawler, and Weick (1970), as quoted by Werner (1993, p. 390), "[w]e might define climate as a set of attributes specific to a particular organization that may be induced from the way that the organization deals with its members and its environment." Common ground is an ideal form of diversity climate. Over time, the pattern of employee experiences in work settings and events shape diversity climate. Work activities maintain the organization's stability or produce its services, but the psychosocial context is also important. Common ground can also be viewed as the psychosocial or procedural context of work activity. This context is a patterned accumulation of work experience.

Diversity climate (Kossek & Zonia, 1993) is at the center of our model. A culturally competent organization, through attention to all the organizational elements discussed in this chapter, produces experiences that lead to a diversity climate supportive of all racial and ethnic groups in the organization.

### Common Ground Activities

Every organization has unique and recurring events that enable the work of the organization to be accomplished. From an open systems perspective, resources are the inputs, and throughputs are the settings, events, and activities associated with getting work done. Outputs are work "products" associated with the agency's mission and objectives. Table 13.1 lists examples of events and activities in the throughput phase. Rather than thinking of all of these events in isolation, a consultant assesses them from a transactional perspective. In the transactional worldview, key transactions (e.g., dialogue in a meeting that leads to a decision) influence the characteristics of future transactions (Altman & Rogoff, 1987). Therefore, the consultant attempts to discern themes and trends among events that may influence diversity climate. Although a transactional view is used less in understanding behavior than are trait or interactional views, its use is advantageous in understanding organizational behavior because organizational behavior involves a complex set of social and circumstantial processes that unfold over time with consistent groups of people and events in a shared setting. A challenge of assessment is understanding how elements of the common ground model interact and influence diversity climate.

### Applying the Common Ground Model to the Ridgeland Group

The following is a brief description of a nonprofit organization that has built a positive diversity climate and avoided destructive conflict on racial and cultural issues. For the purposes of this chapter, this organization is called The Ridgeland Group (TRIG). Important components of its operation, as they apply to the common ground model, are presented in Table 13.1. The Ridgeland Group is a coalition of municipal agencies, community-based organizations (CBOs), and constituent groups that formed to develop violence-prevention programming for a metropolitan area. It has its own staff, board, budget, and program activities.

**Table 13.1** Elements of Common Ground

*Settings, Events, and Transactions*

- Major planning meetings or retreats
- Recurring decision-making meetings
- Supervisory, debriefing and feedback transactions
- Presentations, training, discussion groups, and other learning activities
- Work that extends outside the organization
- Other, regular, task-related transactions between individuals that are related to the organization's products or services
- Informal ("water-cooler") transactions that may involve any of the themes above

*Power and Status Events and Transactions*

- Performance appraisal
- Policy implementation, and enforcement
- Resource (re)allocation, organizational expansion and contraction
- Establishing incentives and rewards; Sanctions and disincentives
- Promotions
- Conferring status symbols, status upgrades, and informal power
- Mentoring and grooming
- Developing and conferring professional development opportunities

*Social Activities*

- Celebrations
- Breaks, pauses, meals
- Off-hours recreational, entertainment, and mutual support activities

During the period when R. Watts and others provided consultation and technical assistance to TRIG, racial and cultural issues had not led to any destructive conflict. There is some evidence that the proactive stance the organization took in addressing racial and ethnic matters contributed to its success in managing these dynamics effectively. In particular, the group dealt with power, control, and representation very early on when one of the founders, a white male state legislator, supported the appointment of a politically experienced and well-respected African American man as an interim director. During his brief tenure, the legislator also hired staff and consultants from other important ethnic constituencies in the region. The interim director helped establish the fledgling organization and lent it credibility to all the major constituent groups in the target area. He then led the search for the permanent executive director, and he successfully recruited a woman of Mexican descent. The diversity, power, and authority of these leaders symbolically—and in their policies and practices—fostered a high level of credibility among people inside and outside the organization.

In its policies and practices, TRIG's watchword seemed to be inclusion. Rather than exclude others in ways that could be perceived as discriminatory or elitist, it expanded its structure to include a series of constituency bodies based on common ethnic or substantive interests. These bodies became resources for the overall organization. Some organizations make the error of ceasing their inclusion efforts once they sanction such bodies, or they delay new ethnic or race-related innovations until these bodies clamor for more influence over resources, policies, and so on. To a limited extent, the TRIG took a more proactive approach instead by immediately working to give voting representation to its youth constituency, many of whom were adolescents of color. TRIG made this decision early without pressure from the youth. Currently, external ethnic organizations are not voting members of TRIG, but they are part of the "constituent body" that meets with the board. TRIG also helped these CBOs obtain independent funding to pursue initiatives of mutual interest. Thus, TRIG made significant resources available to those in the organization with a cultural agenda. Note that age, another aspect of human diversity, became a concern in the organization, and it intersected with ethnicity. As such, age fills the empty point on the outer triangle in Figure 13.1 labeled "other concerns."

TRIG has not conducted any training or education on cross-cultural communication, but the youth constituency, through its youth forums, educated TRIG about racial and cultural aspects of violence ranging from conflict resolution to racist hate crimes. This is an illustration of how identity groups can influence policy and increase the sophistication of agency staff.

Members of TRIG were united by a belief that the violence problem was areawide and not municipality specific. This unity helped in the formation of a task-group identity and enhanced similarity. Although there was little evidence of conflict, there was some evidence of a tacit acknowledgment of differences. For example, racial groups tended to differ in their views on police integrity and behavior.

As part of his assessment, the senior author observed key events directly or through agency records. He searched for evidence of factionalism, racism, alienation, extreme cynicism, cultural miscommunication, stereotyping, and discrimination in the events and transactions of the agency. Early on, the youth, many of whom were people of color, were uninvolved and the least visible and influential members of the organization. TRIG largely corrected this problem through actions in identity groups and through leadership functions, such as resource allocations and policy. TRIG adjusted effectively to issues of race and ethnicity, but it will continue to face challenges as more "grassroots" community members join the group. Because street violence disproportionately effects people of color in the region, it is possible that differing experiences with it will cause polarization along racial or ethnic lines. TRIG must adapt to these challenges if they emerge. Currently, however, TRIG has maintained a spirit of inclusiveness and a shared mission. Its diversity climate is healthy, and a measure of common ground has been attained.

## Conclusion: Implications of the Model for Action and Research

Like human development, common ground is more of an ideal that is strived for than a destination that can be fully realized. The example given previously illustrates how an organization can work toward this ideal. To assist consultants in assessing and intervening in organizations, we summarized some of the key organizational characteristics that we believe are associated with common ground. All are related to elements of the common ground model:

1. The mission, goals, and objectives of the organization address diversity directly or acknowledge its importance implicitly.

2. There are written policies supporting the recruitment, retention, development, and advancement of a diverse workforce.

3. The racial and cultural distribution of people in the organization is equitable among members of the governing board and, among employees at the various power and status levels of the organization.

4. The racial and ethnic diversity of the agency is at least comparable to that of similar organizations, and it exceeds the average in fields with a particularly flagrant history of racism and discrimination.

5. Retention rates, promotion, and opportunities for development are comparable for all groups.

6. The practices and climate of the agency reflect the formal attention to diversity evident in policy.

7. Members of different racial and ethnic groups view the climate as equally supportive.

8. Staff has the racial and ethnic knowledge, experience, and skills to understand themselves and to work effectively with others.

9. Staff values diversity and understands its relationship to the production of goods and services.

10. Diversity is used as a resource to enhance the delivery of products and services.

11. The agency's external relations with its target communities and customers are positive and reflective of the common ground it has achieved internally.

In the future, we intend to use assessment data based on the previous points as the basis of empirical research. Many of these ideas can be operationalized as variables and investigated through the content analysis of documents, participant observation, and interviewing. Others items are statistical benchmarks or norms. Is the comparison of norms the best way to evaluate outcomes of common ground, or do fixed benchmarks make sense? Society does not have a compelling exemplar for the operation of racially and ethnically diverse groups at the agency, local, national, or international level. There is no consensus on what constitutes an inclusive, fair, and equitable organization system. As long as our society is multicultural, however, the need to construct and elucidate a model of common ground will remain.

# 14

# Social Diversity in Social Change Organizations:
## *Standpoint Learnings for Organizational Consulting*

### *Evangelina Holvino*

Compare the following mission statements taken from the strategic plans of two very different organizations:

> The mission of the Romero Institute for Research and Advocacy (RIRA) is to *promote Latino progress through research, advocacy, and leadership development.*

> *The mission of "X" (a Fortune 500 company) is to increase stockholders' wealth.*

There is major difference between the mission of a social change organization and that of a for-profit organization. Purpose is only one of the differences that exist between social change organizations and for-profit organizations. Because important differences exist between social change organizations and other organizations, our (i.e., those professionals who join with me in this endeavor) consulting theories must also differ. In addition, because we address the sociocultural differences in organizations in the context of these larger organizational differences, we must practice organizational consulting in a different way.

In this chapter, I reflect on my experience consulting with two social change organizations, the Eastern Cities Community Council (ECCC) and the RIRA, to identify new learnings about organizational consulting reflected in my approach to organization change. First, I discuss the challenges I faced when consulting to these organizations on issues of sociocultural differences and diversity. Three themes are explored: (a) social change organizations and their significance in the nonprofit sector, (b) the meaning of sociocultural differences and diversity in social change organizations, and (c) initial questions and challenges when consulting with social change organizations on issues of social diversity and differences.

Next, I report on two critical incidents in my consulting work with social change organizations. The analysis of these incidents reveals five learnings that challenge my knowledge about organizational consulting theory and practice.

Using sociocultural differences as a lens to diagnose and intervene in the organization is a fundamental aspect of this analysis. I use the term *sociocultural differences* to refer to differences in the ways of seeing, perceiving, being, and acting in the world that arise from one's social position. They are *cultural* because they are an expression of learned ideas, and they are called *social* because they are directly or indirectly carried out in sets of interpersonal and intergroup relations. One's social position is defined as a matrix of subjectivities determined, among other things, by one's belonging and claiming to belong to or in different sociocultural groups. These groups are politically and socially constituted, providing meaning to how race, gender, sexual orientation, and ethnicity are understood and experienced. My perspective differs from other theories of differences that understand a person's race, gender, and class as inherently (usually biologically) determined, essential, and immutable.

I conclude the chapter by advocating a standpoint approach to consulting in which the sociocultural differences of both consultant and organizational members are used to decipher and reconfigure organizational meanings and actions about organizations and organizational change. A standpoint approach transforms the theory and practice of organizational consulting.

## Diversity Consulting in Social Change Organizations: A Complicated Enterprise

Consulting with social change organizations on issues of sociocultural differences and diversity raises three important questions. First, what are social change organizations and how are they similar to and different from other organizations? Second, what does "diversity" mean in social change organizations, and how are issues of social and cultural differences and diversity addressed in these organizations? Finally, what specific challenges, if any, does consulting to social change organizations on issues of social diversity present to an organizational consultant? I explore each of these questions to set the context for the analysis of the consultations that follows.

Although I try to use the term sociocultural differences throughout the chapter, I believe that having social diversity in an organization—that is, an organization with members of different sociocultural groups based on their gender, race, class, nationality, sexual orientation, and other social differences— implies having to address sociocultural differences. Sometimes, I use the terms diversity, social diversity, social differences, and sociocultural differences interchangeably to avoid redundancy and repetition.

**Social Change Organizations: An Important Subset of the Nonprofit Sector**

There are 1 million nonprofit organizations in the United States that are recognized as a third, independent, and very important sector of the economy and society. Throughout the world, the increase in nonprofit organizations has been described as an "associational revolution that may permanently alter the relationship between the state and its citizens" (Salamon, 1994, p. 109).

Nonprofit organizations are defined as private, voluntary organizations pursuing public purposes outside the formal apparatus of the state and not dedicated to distributing profits to shareholders. They are incredibly diverse, with purposes as varied as providing health, social, and educational services; pursuing grassroots economic development; promoting culture and the arts; advocating civil rights; and performing philanthropy.

Nonprofit organizations are beginning to be recognized as organizations with their own characteristics and unique contributions to organizational theory and practice. When compared with for-profit organizations, they are more flexible and loosely organized, they are driven by their mission instead of money, they have more accountable and active boards, and they are more successful at motivating their staff (Drucker, 1989). They are considered to be an important social innovation with a unique role in promoting and protecting values of equity, security, efficiency, and innovation in the modern industrial world (Young & Hammack, 1993).

Social change organizations (SCOs) are an important subset of the nonprofit sector, but definitions of them are less numerous and less clear. SCOs are also referred to as social movement (Zald & McCarthy, 1979, 1988) and social justice organizations (Anner, 1996). Much of the literature focuses on the relationship between these organizations and social change movements, such as research on the impact of centralizing or decentralizing organizational structures on the ability to organize and mobilize constituencies to achieve societal change (Freeman, 1979; Young, 1991).

Brown and Covey (1989) define a SCO as "a private voluntary organization whose mission is to bring about social change" (p. 27). Some of the special characteristics that Brown and Covey identify in SCOs are "social change missions, emphasis on values and ideologies, multiple external constituencies, and relatively loose organizations" (p. 33). Cooperrider and Pasmore's (1991) work focuses on *global* social change organizations (GSCOs). The following is a summary of the criteria they propose to help define them: GSCOs serve as "agents of change in the creation of a healthier and more sustainable world," they "hold values of empowerment," and they "draw on resources from, or have membership across, three or more countries" (p. 765).

I define SCOs as nonprofit organizations whose mission is to change some aspect of the status quo to eliminate or redress a social injustice. In contrast to other nonprofit organizations dedicated to providing services or charitable deeds, SCOs emphasize the empowerment of disenfranchised groups, work to achieve societal change through activism or advocacy, and have a social justice agenda and rhetoric.

Because of their multiple constituencies and their public social justice agenda, SCOs have always had to address socially-based differences as part of their mission and work. In the 1990s, paying attention to differences such as race, gender, class, and sexual orientation has become an even more important issue reinforced by the attention to identity groups and the impact of social differences in both profit and nonprofit organizations. Sometimes referred to as multiculturalism or diversity, the management of sociocultural differences in organizations is becoming part and parcel of the work of organizations and organizational change consultants (Anner, 1996; Gordon, 1995; Gordon & Newfield, 1996; Jackson & Holvino, 1988). In the following section, I discuss the study of sociocultural differences in SCOs.

**Diversity in Social Change Organizations: Clarifying My Terms**

"Diversity" has become a popular phrase in organizations and organizational consulting. In for-profit organizations, diversity usually refers to one or more of the following three approaches to achieve change in the demographics and the culture of an organization: (a) increasing representation and equal treatment for previously underrepresented groups; (b) developing a business case for the inclusion and use of previously underrepresented groups; and, (c) valuing the differences that employees bring to the workplace, such as race, culture, gender, sexual orientation, personality style, individual preferences, and experience.

Diversity consulting has become a popular and recognized part of the management industry (MacDonald, 1993), and although consultants and consulting groups use different models and techniques for "managing diversity" (Cox, 1993; Jackson & Hardiman, 1994; Miller & Katz, 1995; Thomas, 1990), they all seek to achieve organizational change through long-term, planned, and expert-guided interventions. The models of change that support these efforts fit a human resource development, top management-driven, and organizational effectiveness paradigm. J. Palmer (1994) noted that diversity consultants help "to create a high-performance, smoothly running organization in which members are neither penalized nor rewarded for the type of person they are perceived to be" (p. 257).

Many SCOs have tried to address their social differences and diversity issues by importing corporate models of managing diversity—for example, by conducting diversity training, by sensitizing members of dominant groups to their biases, and by recruiting members of underrepresented groups in their boards of directors, staffs, or volunteer cadres. Because SCOs have unique characteristics and face dilemmas particular to their type of organization, however, it has been my experience that following these for-profit-based models is not always effective.

What are some of the differences between for-profit organizations and SCOs that impact how social differences and diversity are "managed" in these different kinds of organizations? One key difference is in the term *managing diversity*, which indicates that in for-profit organizations the managerial role is privileged. SCOs that are nonhierarchical or that seek to implement more democratic internal structures need to use a more appropriate term—I prefer *addressing social differences*.

I identify other differences from my practice and use them as a starting point to explore why other consulting models and principles may be needed to consult with SCOs on issues of social differences and diversity. Four questions stand out when comparing how social differences are addressed in SCOs and for-profit organizations: (a) Is there agreement on the need for achieving diversity? (b) Where does the pressure for change come from? (c) Who is responsible for initiating an organizational change effort? and (d) What are the knowledge base and skills that support a diversity change effort?

### The Need for Diversity

In for-profit organizations, one of the biggest challenges has been the need to demonstrate the relationship between diversity and the bottom line—that is, how does diversity contribute to augmenting profits and increasing productivity. Cox and Blake (1991) provide the following reasons for an organization to increase its diversity and skills in managing diversity: better use of human resources, increased productivity, ability to tap new market segments, cost reduction, gaining competitive advantage, and attracting and retaining the "best and the brightest." Articulating the specific reasons for why diversity should be part of the organization's agenda is a common first intervention in a corporate diversity change effort, and it is in the diversity consulting world as "making the business case for diversity."

SCOs, however, address social differences as part of their identity and task. Issues of equality and differences, such as race, gender, and class, are directly addressed in the organization's mission. Therefore, there is usually no need to spend time developing a business case for diversity because the case is already in the mission statement. In SCOs, the relationship between addressing social differences and the nature of their work or task is usually well established.

### The Pressure to Change

In for-profit organizations, the impetus for change usually comes from legal or economic pressures, such as a legal suit by a group of underrepresented employees or a need to target a particular market segment that the majority group in the corporation does not believe it can represent appropriately.

In SCOs, the combination of a moral commitment to justice and equality, together with pressures from external and internal stakeholders, usually supports an agenda for change. Consequently, the need to address social differences in a SCO as part of a change agenda is based on a perceived need to achieve more congruence between the organization's mission and values and the realities of the organization's internal culture and structures that may be oppressive and discriminatory to particular groups of people. For example, a SCO with a mission to empower a diverse population of gay youth will be strongly criticized if it continues to hire only white gay males.

*Initiating the Diversity Change Effort*

Most diversity efforts in for-profit organizations are initiated by the top leadership, and top management involvement is considered a requirement for success (Morrison, 1993). Because of the constituency-based nature of SCOs, however, managers may not necessarily be the driving force behind a diversity initiative. Usually, social differences become an issue because some external or internal identity group identifies a problem—for example, the lack of representation and influence of a particular identity group on a board of directors. This has the effect of expanding the ways in which the problem is conceptualized and thus the type of change interventions that can be implemented. For example, change efforts may require the inclusion of minority groups in the community and the support of informal organizational leaders in addition to formal leaders and managers.

*Knowledge Base and Skills About Social Differences and Social Issues*

Often, the staff of a SCO is involved in work that makes it more aware of dynamics of social differences at the individual and societal level, such as discrimination, identity, and intergroup conflicts. In many instances, the staff is familiar with at least one type of social difference, (e.g., gender and class) and possesses some skills necessary to address one of these differences. In addition, the staff is likely to have some knowledge about how oppression operates in society and how it relates to the mission of the organization. This is evident in many AIDS clinics, in which an understanding of the relationship between homophobia and the health treatment options available to people who are infected with the HIV virus or have AIDs has been a part of these organizations' work since their inception (Patton, 1990).

In summary, there are four differences between for-profit organizations and SCOs regarding how social differences are addressed in a diversity change effort: (a) the rationale for change, (b) the source of the initiative, (c) the pressure to change, and (d) the knowledge and skills base of the people involved. Because of these differences, I did not follow the corporate approach to address social differences in the consultations that I describe later. As a result of using a different approach, I was able to clarify the fundamental differences in the principles that guide my theory and practice of organizational development when consulting to SCOs and for profit organizations. Before engaging in this analysis, however, I discuss some questions and challenges regarding what it means to consult with SCOs in addressing social differences.

*Consulting With SCOs and Addressing Social Differences: Some Questions and Challenges*

Very little is known about planned organizational change in SCOs and the role of organizational development as a consulting approach with this type of organization. Powell and Friedkin (1987) provide a comprehensive analysis of organizational change in SCOs. Their work, however, is not focused on the effects of planned consultations on the organizations they studied but rather on the external forces that drive organizational changes, such as changes in the mission, the structure, and the organizational survival of SCOs. For Minkoff (1993), the mere organizational survival of a SCO contributes to social change. It seems that the strength and effectiveness of a SCO very much depends on chance and external forces.

Organizational development (OD) emerged in the 1970s as a form of organizational consulting to help organizations manage change through long-range planning and problem solving (Bennis, Benne, Chin, & Corey, 1976; Hanson & Lubin, 1995). Most organizational consulting based on this model assumes that the principles of corporate consulting are applicable to nonprofit and social change organizations (Drucker, 1990; Lakey, Lakey, Napier, & Robinson, 1995).

In contrast, Brown and Covey (1989) argue that SCOs require their own theory and practice of organizational change because of their unique characteristics. Similarly, in an effort to develop an approach to organizational change that responds to the social justice agenda of nonprofit organizations, Kelleher, McLaren, and Bisson (1996) suggest that "many of the old ideas about management need to be questioned" (p. xiii).

Because key differences exist between SCOs and for-profit organizations and organizational consulting is primarily based on premises derived from for-profit organizations, it follows that new principles and theories of organizational consulting with SCOs be sought. Young and Hammack (1993) pose the question, "What managerial methods and strategies used by for-profit business are transferable to nonprofit organizations, and which management principles and techniques from the nonprofit world can be usefully adopted by the business sector?" (p. 411). This exchange of new ideas, in turn, will generate new practices for both for-profit and nonprofit organizations.

In the next section, I discuss two critical incidents selected from my consulting practice with SCOs. I will demonstrate how analyses that focus on sociocultural differences as an integral part of the practice of organizational consulting with SCOs challenge received knowledge about organizational development and planned change. Also, these analyses serve to generate new insights about organizations and organizational change.

## Learnings From SCOs: Reflections on Two Consultations

Here, I reflect on two experiences of my consulting practice with SCOs in which paying attention to sociocultural differences was an integral and revealing aspect of the consultation. Describing and reflecting on one's own practice in a public form is difficult, however, the temptation for positive self-reporting is great, and the fear of appearing naive is high. Trinh Minhha (1989), reflecting on her practice, articulates well my dilemma as a woman of color:

> How do you inscribe difference without bursting into a series of euphoric narcissistic accounts of yourself and your own kind? Without indulging in a marketable romanticism or in a naive whining about your condition? Between the twin chasms of navel-gazing and navel-erasing, the ground is narrow and slippery. (p. 28)

The incidents and my reflections take me on an unexpected path as I struggle to integrate a social differences lens into my consulting work. I briefly profile the organization and then describe a critical incident that provoked an important confrontation between "old" learnings about consulting and my own approach. The insights derived from this confrontation challenge my own style of organization development consulting, and they suggest revisions in my practice and new conceptualizations about organizational change.

### The Eastern Cities Community Council:
### Stories, Disalignment, and Stakeholder Groups in SCOs[1]

The ECCC is a small organization sharing space in the basement of a church with its offspring organization, a housing development corporation. The ECCC's mission is to advocate on a variety of changing social issues in a very diverse and largely immigrant community in Hartford, Connecticut. Its multicultural board is composed of representatives of diverse constituency groups in the community: recently arrived immigrants, city professionals, and established community members.

The executive director, a white bilingual male, manages the affairs of the organization with a skeletal staff of part-timers and community volunteers. The organization is well respected and very influential.

I was asked to assist the ECCC board in becoming more sensitive and effective at managing cultural and language differences among its members. The board's monthly meetings were conducted in English and simultaneously translated into Portuguese, Spanish, and Khmer. The board members wanted to improve the way in which they worked together as a multicultural group and to become more effective as a board. They recognized the importance of learning more about how to manage their differences and to use them to perform their work and represent their community more effectively.

My partner, an ethnically English white male with international experience in addressing issues of language, and I decided on the following approach to address the board's request for consultation. We videotaped a regular board meeting and after the meeting we asked each board member (and his or her interpreter) to identify at least one critical incident that he or she observed in the meeting. We then followed up on the meeting by conducting a brief telephone interview with each member. Four critical incidents were identified—each lasted approximately 3 minutes. The videotape was edited so that these four incidents appeared sequentially. The edited videotape and the other information collected from the interviews were shared with the board during a 1-day retreat. At the retreat, board members discussed their perceptions of the board's strengths and weaknesses in managing its differences, and based on this discussion they developed action plans.

The following critical incident occurred during the board meeting that my partner and I observed and videotaped. The incident is reconstructed from my process notes of the consultation:

> The executive director is reporting on the month's key activities. One of the most time- and resource-consuming efforts has been providing orientation and assistance to community members about a new law which changes the immigration and residency requirements in the United States. Many families in the community are affected, and the ECCC staff has developed a program to assist individuals and families to fill out the appropriate forms to allow them to take advantage of a "grace period" set by the law before they are deported to their countries of origin. A discussion to clarify the need and scope of the services offered follows the report. Concern is voiced by various board members whether this activity fits the mission of the organization and if its utilizing too many organizational resources. Xu Yun, a Cambodian board member, raises his hand and asks to speak. Through his interpreter, he tells the story of his hardship and agony in coming to this country after being persecuted in Cambodia. In a moving description, Xu Yun tells how the past immigration laws saved him and his family; how important the ECCC's support was for his survival in this country, and how necessary it was that the ECCC continue to offer that assistance and support to others. A few seconds of silence follow his speaking. At the end of the meeting, all board members identify Xu Yun's speech as a critical incident because it got them in touch with the mission of the organization and their own commitment to working on the board. Support for the immigration assistance program was reaffirmed.

My reflections on this incident generate three insights: the importance of voice and stories, the positive meaning of organizational disalignment, and the need to consider the stakeholder groups that are based on social difference interests when consulting with SCOs.

### The Importance of Voice and Stories

Telling a story, having a voice (in this case, through an interpreter), and listening to a story, although not usually emphasized in theories of organization development, are important aspects of a multicultural interaction, an important form of communication across different languages, cultures, nationalities, classes, and educational levels.

Gabriel (1991) explores how stories serve as symbolic means by which passivity and powerlessness are turned into control and action by actors in an organization. In the ECCC, the personal story also became the representation of the organizational task. It was the "glue" that held together the members of this very diverse board, allowing them to reaffirm their commitment to the organization's mission and their work on the board despite funding difficulties, lack of resources, simultaneous translations, and long and complicated meetings.

### The Positive Meaning of Organizational Disalignment

Dominant definitions of organizational health and survival measure organizational success in terms of their "fit" and "alignment" with the external environment. These dominant perspectives on the relationship between the organization and its environment are challenged by SCOs such as the ECCC. The concept of alignment, which is key to current approaches to strategic thinking and management, is traceable to organizational metaphors of organism and machine in which the parts must fit each other and their environment. In contrast to fitting the environment, however, the ECCC incident shows that for SCOs to think strategically and socially about their missions and activities, they need to recognize that a fundamental "disalignment" with the dominant culture and external environment is the nature of their type of organization.

For the ECCC, what was required of the board the evening of the meeting was that it reaffirm its commitment to a program that went against dominant conservative immigration trends in the nation. The literature on workplace democracy, for example, recognizes the problematic consequences of this lack of fit between an organization's purpose and environment (Bernstein, 1983; Rothschild & Witt, 1986). In SCOs, organizational fit is further redefined and eventually means achieving a partial alignment with an environment that is deemed unjust and oppressive to a sociocultural "minority."

*Considering Stakeholder Groups Based on Social Difference Interests*

My understanding of stakeholder groups as a framework for organizational consulting was enriched by this consultation. The stakeholder framework is an organizational consulting and research approach based on the analysis of different actors or interested parties that are affected by and who affect an organizational phenomenon (Burgoyne, 1994). The model works to recognize, identify, and bring together the different interest groups that have a "stake" in the organization's business, its products, its future, or all three.

Most perspectives on organizational consulting assume that although certain differences of interest exist between different actors in an organization (e.g., managers, line staff, suppliers, and owners), all organizational members have the same level of investment and interest in the organization if the organization's supragoal is defined in terms of increased productivity and organizational effectiveness. It is also assumed that effective leadership can successfully channel the energy of all these different stakeholder groups to work together to increase the organization's bottom line. Therefore, if the organization is prosperous, then the implied promise is that the benefits will trickle down to all.

SCOs, however, work from a model based on a political framework (Bolman & Deal, 1991). Instead of assuming an underlying commonality of interests among different stakeholders, most SCOs recognize and engage differentiated interests in working for social change. The consultation with the ECCC board also suggests that sociocultural difference, such as racioethnicity, gender, and class, help frame stakeholder group interests. I borrow the term *racioethnic* from Cox (1990), who uses it to refer to biologically determined or culturally distinct groups or both. This usage is particularly appropriate for Latinos or Asians in the United States who may prefer to identify themselves as ethnic groups but whom the dominant culture identifies racially.

The discussion of the immigration assistance program tested the limits of the stakeholder framework around the ECCC's mission in a very real way; one could feel the tension in the room as the board members, also differentiated along race and class lines, engaged in the discussion. Paradoxically, it was a common and simple story that held these differentiated stakeholder representatives together at the board meeting. The power of the story was that it identified the stakeholder group in which the many identity groups represented on the board had a political interest—that of being an immigrant.

Recognizing that sociocultural identity influences the way in which a group claims its "stake" and recognizing how it affects the group's interests and position expands the use of the stakeholder framework. It also provides the possibility of applying the framework to address social differences and diversity in organizations in new and exciting ways. For the second critical incident, I explore in detail how dichotomies play a part in organizational consulting.

**The Romero Institute for Research and Advocacy: Challenging Oppositional Thinking**

The RIRA is located in a large midwestern city, a metropolitan hub for Latinos in the United States. The RIRA's mission is to promote Latino progress through research, advocacy, and leadership training. The board and staff of the RIRA are a highly talented mix of men and women of different racioethnic, national, educational, and professional backgrounds.

I assisted the RIRA board and management team in a strategic planning process. In a recent planning retreat, staff and board representatives produced a blueprint document geared toward organizational growth. Aware of the growth constraints that all nonprofit organizations face because of precarious funding, however, they wanted to engage in a planning process to help them assess more strategically how to maximize their organizational strengths and resources. For example, they wanted to consider whether to increase their focus on policy advocacy activities and reduce their involvement in basic research, an activity that some perceived as time-consuming and less impactful. They also knew that making decisions about how and where to focus their work would involve addressing considerable differences among them, specifically differences about the importance of particular issues for the community, methods of doing their work, and attitudes toward work, time, and family.

I contracted to work with the RIRA to help them develop a strategic planning process that the organization had already outlined. My role was to facilitate the planning process with the board and the management team, to help them engage with and manage the differences that arose as they discussed and developed the strategic plan, and to advise them about the process of strategic thinking and planning.

The critical incident I selected for analysis occurred while I was consulting with the management team that was developing the second draft of the strategic plan to be submitted to the board of directors:

> The management team is discussing its difficulty in saying "no" to requests. This has been identified as a major block in deciding what issues to focus on, what requests to respond to, and what activities to prioritize in future plans. Strategic planning, with its emphasis on organizational strengths and ability to respond to the demands from the environment, has made this a salient issue. The executive director explains how hard it is to say no, and consequently to focus the work of the RIRA. "We can't afford to say no," she exclaims. Her assistant, a younger Anglo-Saxon woman,[2] exclaims with some passion, "I don't understand what's so hard about saying 'no.' Other organizations do it all the time." As the process consultant, I point out that maybe it is no coincidence that these different responses about what one can or cannot do as a representative of the organization are being played out by the Latina director, a member of a subordinate group with deep-

learned attitudes about pleasing others and not saying no, and an Anglo-Saxon woman, a representative of the dominant group, with an attitude of entitlement and self-responsibility.

I identify two challenges to traditional principles of organization development consulting from my assessment of this incident: understanding the impact of oppressed-oppressor dynamics in organizational tasks and working the complexity of the relation between a SCO and its environment.

### *Understanding the Impact of Oppressed-Oppressor Dynamics in Organizational Tasks*

Little attention has been paid to race, gender, and class relations in the classic texts of organization development and change (Holvino, 1993). Organizational consultants are taught little, if at all, about the place of oppressed-oppressor dynamics in organizational life, possibly because the missions of for-profit organizations do not usually address such issues. SCOs, however, require consultants to consider and integrate oppression and issues of justice in the consulting process because of their social justice missions. The work with the RIRA offers some guidance about how to accomplish such integration.

The incident demonstrates how an oppressed-oppressor dynamic is expressed in what seems to be a "simple" interaction between two team members. The dynamic involved was also evident in the management team's group culture—one in which "we can't say no." I was surprised by how this inability to "say no" hindered the team's ability to move on the strategic plan. A variation on the oppression theme was the continuous reference among the team members to "the pain of making strategic choices." The needs of the community were so many, they kept reminding themselves, so how could they make choices and leave some needs unmet? They felt this struggle very personally, and it blocked the planning process. Identifying and examining these unconscious manifestations of the oppressed-oppressor dynamic at the individual, group, and organizational level was an important intervention in consulting with the RIRA.

This type of analysis expanded my understanding of how oppression and social differences relate to whether or not tasks are accomplished in organizations. For example, although the RIRA identifies with the "oppressed" in its mission, programs, and rhetoric, it also operates as a gatekeeper on behalf of the "oppressor"—the press, funders, policymakers, and the dominant white culture. In addition, the staff of the RIRA, like those of many other SCOs, are usually a mix of highly educated minority elites and grassroots and working-class members. Their boards of directors usually have a similar mix of members from diverse and differently positioned social class groups: professionals, working people, and small business owners. The simple dichotomy oppressed-oppressor does not help explain the complex individual, organizational, and environmental dynamics that occur when members of such a group interact.

Thinking and behaving in terms of simple dichotomies (men vs. women, black vs. white, profit vs. nonprofit, Latino vs. Anglo, and poor vs. affluent), however, is continually reinforced in SCOs by staff members' internalized images, their environment, and the consultant's theories of oppression that conceptualize "domination" in terms of an irreconcilable opposition between groups. In the RIRA, the key strategic choices in planning for the future required breaking these oppositional pairings (e.g., by deciding to provide two different kinds of services: one to the Latino business elite and another to the poor and working-class Latino community) instead of viewing these as incompatible choices (e.g., serving the oppressor or the oppressed along class dimensions).

Thus, I learned that consulting with SCOs requires acknowledging and consciously working with the paradox of managing both oppressed and oppressor polarities simultaneously and with the same people in real organizational tasks. This perspective was explored by Thomas and Ely (1996), who performed research while consulting with for-profit organizations on diversity issues. Their approach is in stark contrast to the dominant approaches to managing diversity in which race, gender, sexual orientation, and other sociocultural differences are addressed in the context of an educational workshop that does not engage the organizational task (the reason why these groups were originally brought together).

### Working the Complex Relation Between Environment and Organization in SCOs

My second lesson from this incident challenges the metaphor of an "organization as a system," a favorite in organizational consulting. The metaphor of a system evokes an imaginary boundary between an organization and its environment, helping to identify the key processes of exchange between them in the form of inputs, a transformation process, and outputs. In this model, the manager's role is to successfully control the exchange in ways that favor the organization (French & Bell, 1978).

It seems, however, that a more appropriate image in consulting with SCOs may be one that treats the sociocultural and political environment in which an organization operates as an integral part of that organization. Instead of using the image of more-or-less permeable boundaries to guide my understanding of how the RIRA team was managing the environment, as the metaphor of a system suggests, I found it more helpful to attend to how the staff was "enacting" a particular set of struggles in relationship to their environment (Prasad, 1991; Weick, 1979). In other words, the inside was simultaneously mirroring and challenging the outside, which in this case was the overwhelming needs of the Latino population. Therefore, I preferred to conceptualize the division between inside and outside (organization and environment) not as a dichotomy but as an interactive process in which organization and environment were mutually codetermined.

In the RIRA, the distinction between what was "in" and what was "out" of the organization was an important question to consider in the strategic planning process. Meeting all the needs of the Latino population was impossible, but closing themselves to this reality would have been a delusion for the management team. How the staff and board drew and redrew the boundaries between them and their Latino *compañeros* (colleagues) outside the institute had personal, social, and organizational consequences that were also socially determined and had both conscious and unconscious manifestations. In the end, the board and management team recognized that their anxiety of being unable to meet all the needs created by an oppressive system did not allow for progress in the planning process.

## A Standpoint Approach to Organizational Consulting: Meeting the Challenge of Consulting With SCOs

The challenge of reflecting on and writing about my experience consulting with SCOs is to turn the unsettling analysis of my practice and theoretical questions into learnings for the future. I learned from my professional development as an organizational consultant that I could apply organizational theories developed from the experience of consulting in for-profit organizations to all organizations, as if these theories were transparent and universal. Consulting to SCOs has challenged this basic assumption and has changed the way I think and practice organizational consulting. Two general principles shape this new approach to consulting with SCOs: (a) developing a standpoint approach to organizational consulting and (b) making social differences an integral dimension in the consulting process.

### Developing a Standpoint Approach to Organizational Consulting

The myth of the consultant's objectivity is strong among many, like me, who learned that organization development is an applied behavioral science. Debates are many and continuous about the meaning of science and objectivity, the role of values, and which values, if any, apply to the field of organizational consulting. The fact that the debate exists, however, only reflects the strength of this belief. Diversity consultants have been strongly criticized for bringing their own values into the systems in which they work and taking an "advocate" position. For example, they may advocate for the inclusion of previously excluded groups in an organization instead of assuming a more neutral stance in which they only support the making of "informed choices" in the client system (Freedman, 1996, p. 338).

Recently, the possibility of objectivity in science has been questioned on many fronts. Postcolonial and feminist theorists, among others, stress the importance of one's own particular position in performing any kind of work, be it research, theory, or practice (Alcoff & Potter, 1993; Calvert & Ramsey, 1996;

Harding, 1986, 1991; Mohanty, Russo, & Torres, 1991). These authors call for a "standpoint" approach that fosters the development of theories based on the researcher's own social location and recognizes the impossibility of neutrality in the production of knowledge. My experience with the ECCC and the RIRA supports using a standpoint approach in organizational consulting in which the consultant uses his or her social position, interests, and perspective to assess, interpret, and intervene in the organization.

The analysis of the two organizational consulting incidents suggests that my social position and social identity and how I use them are very relevant to the task of consulting. Instead of being denied and ignored, the consultant's social identity and location should be used as part of the consultation process. Psychoanalytic theories of organizational consulting have much to offer in helping us move in this direction (Alderfer, 1982; Hirschhorn, 1988).

In the case of the RIRA, I was able to locate myself in a network of power relations that included but was not limited to my social identity, my organizational role, and my politics.[3] The unique perspective produced by my complex social identities became relevant to the task—my Puerto Rican ethnicity, my mixed race, my professional class, and my being a woman. Instead of pretending that these identities had no bearing on the nature of the consulting relation, they were consciously used to interpret and offer a social perspective on what I was perceiving and doing as a consultant.

Consultants working with SCOs must position themselves at the intersection of racioethnic, gender, class, and other social groups to examine the organization and their own consulting work from the unique perspective that their social identities provide. Their social identities and the impact they have on the organizational work need to remain available for examination throughout the consulting process. When one uses a standpoint approach, the personal is both political and organizational. These relations, however, can never be fixed or taken for granted. It requires a fundamental shift in OD practice.

### Social Differences as an Integral Dimension of Organizational Consulting: Expanding the Meaning of Social Diversity in Organizations

Addressing sociocultural issues in SCOs means much more than transporting corporate models of managing diversity into the nonprofit sector. SCOs are committed to creating organizational structures that are nonoppressive (usually less bureaucratic) and to enacting social relations that are less oppressive (Staggenborg, 1995). The work with the ECCC highlighted the strong relationship between addressing the issues of social diversity and organizational structure.

After collecting the data at the ECCC and discussing it with the group, the joint analysis indicated that the too loose structure of the board meetings and the board's work were contributing to problematic interactions and a lack of equality in those interactions. New structures and processes were suggested to help the board run meetings in a more efficient manner. The proposed changes were supportive of the board members' efforts to address cultural differences through attention to language, class, culture, and other social differences. For example, I proposed that translated briefing sheets on the topics to be discussed be distributed prior to the board meeting and a glossary of nonprofit terms for new board members be developed. The goal of these mechanisms was to help equalize the verbal participation of all board members by reducing the language advantage of English-language speakers in expressing and interacting while increasing the ability of the non-English speakers to communicate on the topics specific to the board meetings.

I termed this challenge of linking the sociocultural and structural dimensions of organizational change the triple struggle to depatriarchalize, debureaucratize, and become multicultural. SCOs are teaching consultants that these struggles are connected, but on many occasions these three types of change efforts are disconnected from one another. Consultants need to do more to create transitionary spaces, structures, and processes that will allow SCOs to address this three-pronged struggle and to define more comprehensive organizational change agendas that support integrating these types of change efforts. Working on one in isolation of the others is not sufficient for SCOs or for any other type of organization.

Consulting about sociocultural differences with SCOs should be understood as helping organizations integrate their social agendas with their organizational requirements. This understanding has implications for organization development in general. In contrast to one of the classic definitions of organization development consulting as a long-term intervention "managed from the top to increase organizational effectiveness and health" (Beckhard, 1969, p. 9), I suggest a different definition based on my experience consulting with SCOs. Organization development consulting is a short-term collaborative relation and process established to generate new knowledge and skills required for increased internal and external organizational equality and justice.

Addressing sociocultural differences as an integral part of the consulting process and taking a standpoint approach that uses the consultant's and the organizational members' social identity in the consultation are two ways of performing organizational consulting with SCOs. As for-profit organizations become less bureaucratic and more socially diverse, maybe it is time that consultants start importing the learnings from working with SCOs into the corporation.

# Notes

1. The names and other identifying details of the organizations have been changed to protect confidentiality.

2. I use the term Anglo-Saxon to highlight ethnicity as a social identity dimension. As Klor de Alva, Shorris, and West (1996) note, one of the differences between Latinos and other groups in the United States (e.g., African Americans) is their emphasis on separating ethnicity and race and favoring ethnicity as the first category of self-identification. Members in the RIRA favored this usage.

3. This framework is borrowed from Arnold, Burke, James, D'Arcy, and Thomas (1991, p. 12).

# 15

## Building Institutional Capacity to Address Cultural Differences

*Thomas J. Gallagher*

"You can't get there from here!" This old aphorism captures the challenge of developing institutional capacity to address and cope with cultural differences. The focus of this chapter is on institutions in the largest sense, such as the institution of higher education. Other equivalent institutions in American society include the health system, criminal justice system, governmental system, entertainment system, and finance system. Thus, the focus of this chapter is at a scale higher than the familiar organization—the single financial institution (a bank) or a specific institution of higher learning (a single university or college).

In this chapter, the term "organization" is used when referring to discrete entities, such as a bank, a university, or other entity that is characterized by a formal name, leadership, and structure. The term "institution" is reserved for assemblages of organizations, such as the groups of universities and colleges and related organizations that comprise the "institution of higher education."

The challenge of building the capacity of such institutions to better address cultural differences is exceptional. The institutions of interest in this chapter are large, complex, and subtle in structure, activity, and product. They are difficult to understand and measure, and they are difficult to change. It is not possible to propose specific actions that will cause institutions to develop the capacity to respond to cultural differences; the theory and practice of organizational development, particularly at the institutional level, is not sufficiently developed. Rather, in this chapter I examine the nature of institutions through a systems perspective and offer several strategies and possible tools for analysis and action for this most important challenge.

The challenge is important because these large institutions play a major role in establishing and sustaining our society's values, principles, and norms of behavior. These large institutions, through their standards and authority, guide member organizations. Large institutions play a major role in supporting, or discouraging, organizations from addressing cultural differences.

In this chapter, I examine the nature of large institutions from a systems perspective, noting how they are embedded in the culture, express core values,

change in capacity, and react to change. This overview provides context for
discussion of the following strategies for increasing capacity: uncovering core
values, assessing characteristics of the system, providing opportunities and
incentives, using a test-review-revise process, and providing symbolic
recognition of cultural differences. Finally, I present more specific actions or
tools to consider: conducting a core value assessment, conducting an
institutional culture survey, and creating a "third culture."

The concepts and practices in this chapter are discussed as they relate to
institutions. They are, however, also applicable to large organizations in general.
The discussion, which is framed within an American context, draws heavily on
the author's experience in higher education and with cross-cultural aspects of
management in the Arctic.

## The Nature of Institutions

### Institutions as Systems

The large institutions of interest in this chapter are often referred to as
"systems" (e.g., the higher-education system and the health system). The term
"system" has become an accepted descriptor for these large, complex, and
diffuse entities, which include many organizations. In systems theory, the term
"systems" refers to combinations of two or more subunits that produce a
product that the smaller units cannot produce alone. In the institution of higher
education, the subunits are the many universities and colleges throughout the
nation as well as other cross-organizational entities, such as associations of
faculty, education policy groups, and organization membership groups.
Although the universities and colleges produce programs and graduates, which
are discrete and measurable, the larger institution of higher education (the
system) produces products that are much more subtle but nonetheless important.
These products include national-scale support for higher-education policy,
nationally accepted accreditation and testing, intercampus collaboration and
competition in instruction and research, and salary and performance norms for
faculty.

From the systems perspective, institutions are composed of parts (subunits)
that have connections. The number of parts and the strength of the connections
can be measured or described. The assessment of parts and connections
characterizes the system and provides insight into its behavior. In general, as the
number of parts increases, the system gains mass and inertia, and it becomes
harder to move it or change its direction. Similarly, as the connections grow in
strength, the system becomes more integrated and easier to communicate with
and possibly influence. As links become weaker, the system becomes more
diffuse and harder to influence, at least with a single stimulus or message.

Communication among parts of a weakly linked system requires extra energy and time.

From a systems perspective, the institutions of concern in this chapter are very large and weakly linked, at least compared to the organizations of which they are composed. Thus, the "institution of higher education" is much larger but much more weakly integrated than the various universities and colleges of which it is composed. This knowledge suggests institutions are harder to change than are the member organizations, and certain strategies (discussed later) are more appropriate than others.

## Institutions as Embedded in Society

Large institutions such as higher education are "embedded" in society. They are so large but subtle in their relationship to the individual that they are hard to recognize. For most members of American society, large institutions are simply "how the world is." They exist, and they are not optional or to be questioned. They are supported formally with constitutions, legislation, and regulations and informally through everyday decisions.

There are degrees of embeddedness. Higher education is old and deeply embedded in society. Although there are increasing attacks on the budgets of its individual universities and colleges, there is virtually no discussion of the propriety of the institution of higher education in our society. Other institutions, such as health care, are younger and subject to more debate about fundamental issues, such as whether health care is a public or private concern. The degree of embeddedness is useful information in developing strategies for promoting change. In general, those institutions that are most embedded are the hardest to criticize effectively. Criticisms aimed at such institutions are easily ignored or hotly defended. The embeddedness of institutions, like its systems characteristics, suggests certain strategies to build capacity.

## Institutions as Expressions of Core Values

Core values are those fundamental assumptions "about what is right, what is good, and what is conducive to the public welfare" (Gamble 1986, p 22). In the health care debate, core values are at the center of questions such as the following: Is health care a right or a personal responsibility? Should it be provided through public or private organizations? What are the rules of triage when funds are limited? Although there is no list of accepted American core values, such a list might include such oft-cited values as justice, equity, self-reliance, family, and compassion. If we expanded the list of core values, we would find more subtle values, such as the value of time (whether being on time is important) and risk (whether or not risk is accepted, encouraged, or treated with aversion). Recognition that institutions express core values, and that these values are often subtle, is useful in engaging in the discussion of building capacity.

Institutions may not recognize in any clear way what values they represent. Furthermore, institutions may not recognize that the values they express conflict with those of other cultures. A simple example from higher education is the use of the standardized class period and semester calendar for instruction. This time-structured system conflicts with most cultures, which have a more flexible time orientation (Hall, 1959). This is not to say the time-structured system is not effective and efficient; it may be effective and efficient, but the value the institution places on time may not be the same value as held by other people. Furthermore, it is unreasonable to believe that such a time-structured format is the only way higher education can occur, particularly in a culturally diverse world.

This example raises a central issue about values. It is not always the "higher-order" values, such as justice and equity, that cause conflict; often, the more subtle values, such as the value regarding time, territory, lifestyle, and behavior, and many other values (Harris & Moran, 1991; Samovar & Porter, 1988) lay the foundation for conflict.

**Institutional Capacity**

To speak of the "capacity" of an institution raises the question of how something as amorphous and structureless as higher education develops capacity. Most of the capacity of the institution of higher education rests in its member units—the many universities, colleges, and associations. As noted previously, however, all systems—whether at the institutional or organizational levels—produce products. This production involves internal functions and external effects, which both involve people and resources. It is through the execution of these functions and effects that institutions have the capacity to address and cope with cultural differences. Again drawing on an example from higher education, one product of the institution is nationwide, standardized testing used in the selection of student applicants. The capacity of the institution to address cultural differences is indicated by the functions of the organization that creates and scores the test, the functions of and effects on the organizations that use the test scores in their decision processes, and the effects on the students who take the test. It is the performance of these functions and effects that determines capacity; it is the adaptation of these functions to address cultural diversity that is needed.

The potential for an institution to change its capacity is determined, at least in part, by how well it understands its core values and institutional functions. Given that institutional values are often hidden and, moreover, that institutions are often hidden within the society, the potential for change is low.

An exception is found in the Arctic, where nurses found that traditional medical practices (functions) were not successful when working with the native, indigenous people. The nurses, using research from the University of Edmonton (Brink, 1984), adapted the normative institutional functions to fit the cultural perspectives of the people they were treating. For very traditional indigenous people, this included inviting a spiritual healer or shaman to participate in the conventional treatment. Although this example is from (literally) the edge of our society and represents the contact of two extremely different cultures, it demonstrates how institutions can adapt their functions and effects on others to address cultural differences. It is a credit to the nurses in the Arctic that they could adapt to the situation, which no doubt conflicted with the norms common to the institution of nursing.

## Institutions and Change

Unfortunately, large institutions, particularly those with a long history and tradition, typically resist change. New organizations, such as new high-tech companies, are often created around a culture of change. It is difficult, however, to maintain this prochange culture over time. The problem is people. Some people within a system resist change because they are dedicated to the original principles, whether stated or unstated, on which the institution is built. A person with a strong dedication to the principle of the institution, such as to the principle of higher education, is less likely to entertain criticism or proposed changes. Well-intentioned supporters of existing institutions are perhaps the strongest impediment to change.

In addition to those who argue against change on principle are those who argue against change to protect resources. As mentioned previously, from a systems perspective all systems represent a flow of resources. In most systems, the critical measure is dollars. Throughout the system are individuals and groups who tap this flow for salary and programs. These individuals have plans and dreams and quite probably children and mortgages. As the institution ages, the individuals become more obligated to the flow of resources. System changes that threaten the flow of resources, such as "downsizing," must overcome the defensive efforts of those who enjoy the status quo. Furthermore, individuals in old systems, such as higher education, tend to have little experience with change or with earning income outside the system and hence may be risk averse.

Large institutions may also be difficult to change because it is often a challenge to identify who benefits and how from the existing flow of resources. In many situations, the exchange is not directly in dollars but rather in votes, prestige, or authority. It is much easier to see the flow within an organization, such as a specific university or college. The challenge remains, however, to understand the institution, not just the organization, if there is to be real development of capacity to address and cope with cultural differences.

## Strategic Aspects of Building Capacity

The nature, or characteristics, of systems described previously suggests a variety of strategies to build capacity, five of which are discussed further. The strategies are ways of thinking about change and how to influence its direction.

### Uncover and Articulate Core Values

As discussed, institutions represent cultural values, particularly those at the core level. Largely because of the lack of a central office and administration, however, there are no "mission statements" describing core values for large institutions. Typically, the closest one can get to institutional values are mission statements of member organizations or broad statement of principles or codes of ethics from institutionwide commissions.

Although these various statements provide insight into what the organizations believe is important, such statements seldom go beyond the obligatory dedications to justice, equity, and knowledge. These statements rarely discuss subtle core values, which are no less important when considering cultural diversity. The issue of more subtle core values requires additional discussion and an example.

The mission of the University of Alaska, which provides higher education in a state that has 20% Native people, appropriately speaks of its concern for cultural diversity. The mission-directed instruction and research programs in the organization, however, restrict access to and success by Native students. Although the organization advertises and develops programs to attract Native students, the instructional and living format of the university are inconsistent with traditional Native ways of learning and living. Furthermore, instructional courses offered in the university largely ignore Native history, traditions and knowledge. A similar situation is found in research in which there are programs to engage Native students in research, but the research methods used ignore traditional ways of knowing or "Native science." In summary, Native students are invited to participate in higher education but only if they accept the norms, format, and message of the university. The institution strives to be equitable but will not or cannot address core values that require one way of learning, living, and conducting research.

In fairness, the organization has made an effort and some progress, but it exists within the institution of higher education that, through its formal accreditation program and informal peer review, discourages the flexibility of instructional format required in this situation. Some efforts to adjust delivery of higher education to better fit the culture of Alaska's Native people have been dismissed as "unacademic." Indeed, because of its relatively small size and limited reputation, the University of Alaska system is perhaps unnecessarily rigid in its programming as it strives to safely assure the world that it is indeed a real university.

The situation faced by the University of Alaska is not unique; indeed, I believe it is the norm throughout the nation. The larger institution constrains its member organizations within a set of behaviors that reduce exploration of alternatives. Only infrequently does an existing institution "break the mold" and take a leadership role in revising its fundamental structure of education. It is more often the case that a new college is created that incorporates new concepts from the start. This situation, of course, is not limited to universities or to Native people. It is also not restricted to cultures but rather is an issue for women (Gilligan, 1982), the disabled, the elderly, and many others in America.

The argument does not follow, however, that an institution such as higher education should abandon all that it stands for to address cultural diversity. Rather, the strategy should be to identify values that are essential and those that are unessential (typically the subtle values such as time orientation that vary across cultures) and to be creative and persistent in trying to find ways to address and cope with these cultural differences.

**Assess the System Characteristics**

Knowledge of values must be complemented by knowledge of the structure of the system. In theory, change can be initiated with less energy and with more effect if one knows which specific systemic connection to "tweak." In reality, systems are so complex that few are so easily changed by a single adjustment. Assessment is necessary, however, to understand the system—its parts, connections, and flow of resources. This type of assessment is needed if one hopes, when building institutional capacity, to physically alter systems in addition to change values. Without an understanding of who the players are and how they are served or not served by the current system, it will be difficult to change the parts, the connections, or the flow of resources through the system so that it will be sustained by the participants. Such assessments are difficult to conduct at the institutional level due to the lack of an oversight body with leadership and staff to undertake such an effort. Accordingly, assessments at the institution level are typically conducted by special commissions, thinktanks, legislative offices, and interest groups. When combined with a core values assessment, this strategy of conducting an assessment of the system can provide insight into who needs to be involved and what changes need to be made.

**Provide Opportunity and Incentives**

Because systems are resistant to change, another strategy that can be used is to develop creative opportunities and incentives for participants. Creative opportunities would ideally address cultural diversity while enhancing the overall institution. Incentives might be outright rewards or market-style feedback mechanisms to encourage supportive behavior. Ironically, by failing to address cultural diversity many organizations (both private and public) hurt themselves. Businesses in recent years have begun to recognize that they need to consider cultural diversity both in their market planning and promotions and in their hiring practices to stay competitive. Public organizations are perhaps reacting more slowly, but there are also new perspectives on the public sector (Osborne & Gaebler, 1993). The increasing pressure on public organization budgets could further limit programs that address cultural diversity, or they could have the opposite effect of encouraging the organization to broaden its "market" and service base. The institution, not just the organizations, must be supportive of this broadening or it will not occur.

### Test, Review, and Revise

Large-scale and abrupt change in large institutions is not likely and is seldom desirable. In rare cases, dramatic events such as legislation, or paradigm shifts, alter large systems relatively quickly (i.e., several years). Most institutions are changing to some degree in response to new computer and telecommunications services that are altering the linkages within and between systems. This change is very visible in higher education, in which computers and "distance delivery" have allowed the university to expand beyond the campus. Interestingly, although new technologies may instigate change in the institution, they may also raise issues of accreditability and may "harden" attachment to core values.

Change in response to technology often occurs rapidly because it does not require introspection. Institutions with enhanced technology continue to perform the same tasks as these performed before the new technology was incorporated, but they perform those functions over a larger area or more often. Change involving cultural differences, however, is hindered by the difficulty of developing self-awareness. Although institutional change can be very slow through the self-assessment process, small changes can be cumulative and effective in a shorter span than one might imagine. Furthermore, incremental changes may not appear to be direct assaults on the system, which can galvanize an institution's formidable defenses.

The proposed strategy is to conduct small tests, to review the results, and to revise and expand the range of tests. The tests might be pilot projects sanctioned by the institution that are undertaken by organizations within the system. This incremental—test, evaluate, and revise—process takes advantage of the many organizations within the institution to test a variety of alternatives. It leaves the core culture intact until specific changes can be developed and promoted.

Because the best solution to addressing cultural differences is not knowable, this incremental strategy provides a way to proceed with some certainty of eventually finding a solution or at least to test and reject for cause a wide array of options. This research strategy also helps to prepare the institution for change by building into the organizational culture the notion of continuous testing and learning. The strategy diminishes the notion that there is "one right way."

## Provide Symbolic Recognition

A final strategy in developing institutional capacity is to provide symbolic recognition of cultural differences. Symbolic recognition of cultural diversity may seem shallow and without substance. Symbols, however, are powerful. When an institution symbolically recognizes cultural differences, it makes an important first step in addressing the situation, defusing tensions, and providing the opportunity for communication. In most situations, symbolic recognition does not cost the institution any money, time, or effort—just some thinking, listening, communicating, and humility in admitting that it may not be doing everything correctly.

A simple form of symbolic recognition is the addition of a painting or statue that reflects cultural diversity. It might also be recognition among institutional leaders of noted individuals who have encouraged attention to cultural diversity. One of the simplest forms of symbolic recognition I have encountered occurred in the Arctic (Yukon Territory, Canada). There, the land management agency gathered the traditional, Native names of places and landmarks, such as rivers and mountains, and included them on its land maps below the English-language names. For the indigenous people, the traditional names are a source of pride and, in cultures that are losing their language, the publication of such important words helps to keep the language alive. The gesture cost the agency virtually nothing but built tremendous good will with the Native people who occupy the land. Of course, symbolic gestures must be followed with substantive action. If conceived well, however, which implies understanding how the symbol will be interpreted by others, a symbol has substance in the effort to develop the capacity to address cultural differences.

The previously discussed strategies are several of many, but they provide some direction on what actions should be taken. Perhaps the greatest value of these strategies is in initiating discussion of what specifically should be done. Several specific steps that institutions might consider taking are discussed in the next section.

## Specific Actions to Develop Capacity

### Conduct a Core Value Assessment

One method of conducting this assessment is to assemble a group of key individuals who are leaders in the institution to perform a core value assessment. These key individuals would typically be senior manages, leaders, policymakers, benefactors, and noted critics. The value assessment method I prefer begins with Kluckhohn Value Orientations method developed by the Kluckhohn Center for the Study of Values (Kluckhohn Center, 1995). The method, based on the scholarship of anthropologists Florence and Clyde Kluckhohn and Fred

Strodtbeck (Kluckhohn & Strodtbeck, 1961), examines five core values that, it is argued, vary among and characterize different cultures. The method serves to focus the discussion at the foundation—core values. It also is effective because it mixes core values, including some that are "higher order" and some that are more subtle. Thus, participants in the assessment develop a clearer view of the structure of values that their organization or institution holds. The method, if facilitated well, encourages instructive and candid discussion of cultural differences and can lead to an expanded list of institutional values.

The first value that the method examines is time orientation, which concerns the temporal focus of life: past, present, or future. In the past orientation, the emphasize is on preserving traditional teachings and beliefs; in the present orientation, the focus is on accommodating changes in beliefs and traditions; and, in the future orientation, the focus is on planning ahead. Each culture emphasizes these in a particular rank order. The second orientation is to human nature—whether humans are innately good, bad, or mutable. The third orientation is "person-nature," which concerns a group's view of the forces of nature; variations include mastery over, harmony with, and subject to nature. The fourth value orientation concerns the autonomy of the individual and includes the variations of individualism, collaterality (consensus oriented), and lineality (hierarchical). The final orientation concerns activity and the issue of mode of self-expression, from those who are satisfied with "being" to those who require "doing." The pattern of responses to these five orientations describes different cultures.

The method has been developed and used by the Kluckhohn Center for working between agency managers (mostly white Americans) and Indians of the Pacific Northwest. It has proven highly effective in helping groups in both cultures to understand each other. The differences in culture between the dominant white American culture and Indian American culture are substantial and important with regard to time orientation, relation to nature, and individuality. The differences explain much of the conflict between Indians and agencies responsible for forest management. Other differences among cultures have also been identified: Carter (1990) provided insight into African American and white American differences, and Ortuno (1991) provided perspective on the how the method has helped identify Hispanic and Angle differences.

The Kluckhohn method provides an excellent way to start a values assessment. It is highly effective at establishing the conditions necessary for a productive, candid cross-cultural discussion, and it provides the chance for a facilitated discussion from which a much longer list of values can be developed. This longer list develops easily from the basic five Kluckhohn orientations through a facilitated discussion.

## Conduct an Institutional Culture Survey

The Kluckhohn method can provide an introductory assessment of institutional values, but it cannot provide information on the overall culture, including such functional aspects of organizations as leadership, decision making, cooperation, communication, and evaluation. To assess the institutional culture, I prefer the Likert Systems Four assessment (Likert, 1967). The method uses a (Likert) scaled response to questions that address the various functional aspects. Responses place the culture in one of four categories: dictatorial/exploitive, authoritative/benevolent, authoritative/consultative, and collegial/participative. Although the Systems Four method was developed to evaluate the management style of an organization, it can be used at the institutional level by administering it to individuals with knowledge of the institution. The method also lends itself to expansion to address a wider range of institutional values such as risk, which is not on the current list.

The Likert method can be administered to different groups for comparison purposes, such as between management and staff and between management and a specific cultural group. It can also be used to help determine what various groups (cultures) believe to be the ideal organizational culture and to measure over time whether changes have made a difference. Furthermore, the method can be used to ask individuals inside and outside the institution if they believe it addresses cultural diversity.

## Create a Third Culture

The Kluckhohn and Likert methods can help an organization understand its core values and how they are expressed in the culture of the organization. Both methods help provide insight into how others of different cultures might be excluded, or even offended, by their values and culture. With this knowledge, the institution can begin the process of addressing cultural differences by opening a dialogue, which must be concerned with both process and content.

A key to the process is clear communication. Cultures, even those only slightly different from each other, can communicate quite differently. The differences can rest in the meaning of a word, norms surrounding communication form, and associated body language. A major issue in Alaska has been miscommunication between Native and non-Native (primarily Anglo) citizens, both of whom speak English (Gallagher, 1992). The meaning of words matters greatly. For example, both groups define "wilderness" as "land without people," but for Native people the word symbolizes non-Native efforts to keep them from land they have traditionally used. Communication is disrupted further by differences in speaking style and body language. Traditional Native people may pause for a second or more while speaking to make their point stronger. For non-Native people this is a queue to begin speaking. Hence, the Native speaker believes he or she has been interrupted, whereas the non-Native speaker believes the Native speaker cannot articulate thoughts well. Concerning body language, perhaps the most common difference is in the use of eye contact while speaking. The intense eye contact used in mainstream America can be considered aggressive by Native people, who prefer a more deferential, limited-eye contact discussion. Such differences in communication have caused serious problems in the classroom and in the courts.

The need in this situation is to develop a third culture that permits the groups to communicate without either group giving up its norms. Such artificial cultures, popular on science fiction shows when two civilizations make contact, are created to some extent in business and government when working across cultures (Harris & Moran, 1991). The third culture can be built from the appraisal of value differences developed from the Kluckhohn method with an organizational structure based on the components of the Likert method. Areas of differences can be articulated, and ways to "live together" can be formulated. Neither "side" gives up what it values, and where there are differences each moves from its norms to a new norm created for the situation. The effort forces self-examination and supports creativity and cooperation. The effort can be difficult, but it also can be enjoyable and is far superior to the typical conflict surrounding cultural diversity discussions.

## Conclusion

Moving institutions toward the objective of increased capacity to address and cope with cultural differences is difficult. This discussion provides a systems perspective of institutions that suggests a range of strategies and several specific ways to undertake the task. The process of changing major institutions is long and arduous, and it can easily consume a career and an individual. In this situation, it is important to emphasize that there is no one right way, and that the exploration must be critical, ongoing, and inclusive. Institutions with long histories of ignoring cultural differences will need to admit there is room for improvement. Long-standing conflicts that have kept groups at a distance will need to be set aside. All those involved will need to be more supportive and open and perhaps more aware that mistakes will be made and feelings will be hurt. The scale of institutions and the scale of the task demand that all parties commit to the process for the long haul.

# 16

## Cultural Issues in Organizations
### *Summary and Conclusions*
### *Robert T. Carter and Leah M. DeSole*

The journey you have just completed in reading about cultural issues in organizations has been broad and far ranging. It has focused on the role of culture in various types of organizations and institutions, including families, schools, the legal system, nonprofit organizations, and corporations. The preceding chapters have demonstrated how the current organizational climate is replete with issues germane to culture, such as threats to affirmative action policies; shifting ethnic and racial demographics in the workplace; and, wider sociocultural gaps between providers and receivers of services, supervisors and supervisees, managers and subordinates, and teachers, educators, and students. Nonetheless, as several of the authors in this book observed, very few comprehensive models or organization-specific analyses other than those offered for corporations currently exist. My intention in assembling this book has been to address this issue directly and move the discussion of culture in organizations and institutions beyond the corporate context.

The goal of this chapter is to highlight the objectives of the book and tie together some of the recurrent themes of the preceding chapters. First, I review the background and objectives of the volume. Second, I consider the core themes of each part of the book: Perspectives, Organizational and Institutional Settings, and Interventions and Applications for Training. Finally, as the journey winds to a close, I highlight the book's major themes and offer some concluding thoughts on cultural issues in organizations.

## Background and Objectives

The book's knowledge base draws, in part, from presentations given at the Teachers College Winter Roundtable on Cross-Cultural Psychology and Education. The contributors have extensive research and publication histories in psychology, education, and organizational consulting. In essence, they are scholars on the cutting edge of scholarship in their respective areas of expertise

who grapple with the manner in which various group memberships and cultural
contexts intersect and interact to produce particular outcomes.

What were my objectives in bringing together the work of these scholars into
a book about addressing cultural issues in organizations? My overall objective
was to raise awareness about a range of issues associated with culture that
influence the structure, functioning, and leadership of North American
organizations. I sought not only to provide a more comprehensive framework on
which to build an understanding of "generic" cultural issues in organizations but
also to illustrate the interaction of organizational type with issues associated
with culture as expressed through group memberships, such as race, class, and
gender.

Cultural issues in organizations are reflected in many ways and through
various reference group issues. The contributors note that cultural issues in
organizations are affected by the patterns and cultural preferences of the
dominant groups in our social system. This reality leads to particular reference
group issues becoming salient to organizational life. The patterns that determine
cultural trends in organizations stem from a history of access, opportunity,
exclusion, and group preference(s) that, as Clayton P. Alderfer pointed out, have
become embedded in the language and ideas used to discuss and frame racial
and cultural issues in our society. As a result, cultural issues in organizations
center around the relative power and influence of identity groups. Each part of
this book can be said to trace the impact of culture, vis-à-vis the relative power
and influence of identity groups, on the context of organizations. Next, I consider
some of the core themes addressed in Part I: Perspectives.

## Perspectives

Part I: Perspectives addressed how culture is expressed through reference
groups (ethnicity, race, gender, social class, age, and religion) in organizations.
In Chapter 1, Robert T. Carter defined terms and contextualized the basic issues
and assumptions that undergird the volume. Specifically, he defined racial
identity, discussed cultural patterns in organizations, and reviewed four
approaches to diversity in organizations. Subsequently, Chapter 2, by Clayton P.
Alderfer, addressed the way in which cultural values systems are expressed in
coded language by our national and corporate leaders. The use and imposition of
various language forms operates to derail and disguise the core issues and
serves to maintain the status quo. Clayton P. Alderfer illustrated his points
through an examination of issues that involve race relations between black and
white Americans.

In Chapter 3, Michelle Fine uncovered how white American cultural values are
hidden but determine access and opportunity on the bases of race, gender, and
social class. She revealed the unspoken and unexamined organizational polices
and practices that determine merit on cultural grounds, and she shed light on
how the preferences of white Anglo-Saxon, Protestant, middle-class culture is

embedded in our culture and reflected in the way social justice is experienced and understood—that is, how our organizations operate to prescribe many historically rooted cultural practices and preferences for particular group memberships and how other groups are taught and learn to hold their place in our organizations and in our social system.

Chapter 4, written by David Thomas and Karen L. Proudford, dealt with how race affects organizational functioning. These authors offered specific models for how to understand the complex influences brought on by race, and they also offered strategies that can be used to intervene and effectively cope with such influences. Chapter 5, by Linda Darling-Hammond, reminded us that our future is in the hands of our educational system. She argued that all our children have a right to learn. She described how our educational organizations, ruled by dominant cultural patterns, deny this right to children who are viewed by the dominant power group in our society as culturally deprived and inferior.

Overall, Perspectives focused on broad issues, such as how national and organizational leaders shape and influence the agenda regarding culture and how culture matters in the country's organizational life. The contributors provided insight on how language is used to frame and dominate the debate regarding cultural difference and how our organizational systems currently deny access to opportunity to those deemed "culturally" inferior. In addition, Perspectives centered on the notion that cultural diversity in and of itself may be not be sufficient to address many of the historically routed barriers in our organizations that seem to be associated with race and social class. Race as a cultural element in organizations, however, can be understood and addressed. In so doing, it can become an asset to an organization. Nonetheless, the premise of culture as an asset cannot be realized if organizational leaders, power holders, and members continue to deny an appropriate and critical educational foundation to the nation's children of color and lower social classes.

## Settings

In Part II: Organizational and Institutional Settings, the contributors focused on the way that organizations and institutions ignore wide variations in cultural patterns that exist in North American society. In Chapter 6, Nancy Boyd-Franklin described the organizational unit that is the primary communication vehicle for transmitting culture—the family. She also described the large differences that exist in family structures. One can determine from her descriptions that differences in family systems may have implications for how individuals are socialized. In turn, these differences may influence how people reared in different family configurations learn and express core cultural patterns. Understanding the role and impact of differing family systems is important in our effort to comprehend what cultural knowledge individuals bring to societal institutions. After all, the cultural messages that are embedded in our family systems influence our interactions, expectations, and behaviors in the organizations in which we learn and work.

Subsequently, in Chapter 7 A. Lin Goodwin shifted our discussion of cultural influences from the family to the context of schools. She helped us to see how the organization of schools is profoundly shaped by the cultural background of the people who make up its core components—teachers. She focused on the role that teachers play in transmitting culture in our society. Raechele L. Pope and Corlisse D. Thomas advanced this dialogue in Chapter 8 by presenting an analysis of how cultural influences operate in higher-educational organizations. They reinforced the notion that the first step in addressing cultural issues in organizations and institutions should be a systemic self-study. It seems essential for institutional and organizational leaders who seek to understand cultural issues in their organizations through a self-study or cultural audit that they first ask about the unexamined elements of their own culture before they attempt to understand the cultural contributions of other groups.

From schools, the setting shifted to mental health. Barbara C. Wallace demonstrated in Chapter 9 how unexamined cultural effects can actually be viewed as forms of violence in mental health practices. She offered ways to reduce the violence in mental health institutions in an effort to enhance these organizations' effectiveness. Moving from mental health to physical health, in Chapter 10 Vivian Ota Wang described the cultural assumptions that are inherent in organizations that are aimed at healing—medicine. Finally, Part II concluded with Chapter 11 by Curtis W. Branch, which described the role of cultural conflicts in one aspect of the criminal justice system.

Thus, Part II discussed a wide range of institutional and organizational issues in corporations and in the fields of education, health, and criminal justice. The authors demonstrated how too often the emphasis on cultural difference or diversity is other focused: People who are considered different from normal or mainstream groups are singled out for consideration, and the lens of the viewer is tinted with unexplained cultural norms, assumptions, values, and behaviors that shape and guide his or her perceptions. The contributors concur that it is time to shift the focus off of the other and onto the organization. Whether in the classroom or the boardroom, it is essential for institutional and organizational leaders who seek to understand cultural issues in their organizations to first ask about the unexamined elements of their own culture before they attempt to understand the cultural contributions of other groups.

## Interventions and Applications

Part III, Interventions and Applications for Training, focused on various organizational intervention strategies and discussed ways to help consultants assist organizational members to work more effectively with culture. In Chapter 12, Samuel D. Johnson discussed the types of defenses and resistances exhibited by organizational leaders that hamper efforts to intervene in organizations. In Chapter 13, Roderick J. Watts and Arthur Evans offered a road map for organizational consulting by outlining important steps and strategies that should be considered when working with nonprofit organizations.

Evangelina Holvino (Chapter 14) continued the dialogue about nonprofit organizations. She illustrated how traditional concepts about organizations that she learned during her training have not been useful in work with social change organizations that are culturally diverse. Finally, in Chapter 15 Thomas Gallagher outlined how institutions might approach and deal with cultural issues within a network of organizations. He shifted the focus from a single type of organization to an overall examination of how to help institutions develop the capacity to address cultural differences in many forms.

Part III, tells a story of complexity and challenge for organizations and their leaders as well as those who consult to them. It highlighted the role of the consultant and the type of learning that he or she must undergo to be effective in working with issues of cultural differences in organizations. As the contributors acknowledge, each organization has its own complex culture and is in turn influenced by the dominant cultural patterns of the society in which it resides. A leader, manager, trainer, or consultant to the organization must be able to describe an organization to its participants and to help its members to replace their simplistic ideologies with more complex constructs that include cultural referents. Consultants, trainers, and organizational leaders should act as reframers, translators, and organizational change agents so that they may provide consistent feedback about organizational processes and structures that is culturally linked to organizational decision makers.

## Conclusion

This book emphasizes and highlights the role of leaders in organizations in creating climates that foster or hinder the capacity of institutions to address issues of race, class, and culture. It is important to introduce complexity as part of this process when trying to first understand and then change organizations. More complex constructs force people to broaden the range of possible representations of difference and enable some people to stop and think before they act on unexamined culturally based assumptions, particularly those of the dominant group that typically remain implicit and are treated as the baseline against which all others are judged.

Leadership is clearly vital for an organization to successfully deal with cultural variation. Perhaps the most critical role of leaders is to convince each organizational participant to see the value of taking personal responsibility for consistently analyzing and explaining the ways in which cultural factors operate in organizational settings. The contributors challenge all members of society to address issues of culture in all organizations with which they associate.

Rising above the individual level, the dominant group values translate into distinct organizational cultures. These organizational cultures define the range of acceptable behaviors and establish the standards for what and who is rewarded within an organization. Given the increasingly diverse workplace, the most effective organizations will be those whose cultures make a strength of their diversity and are able to translate the varied backgrounds and experiences of their members into superior insight and responsiveness to their members, customers, students, clients, and patients.

# References

## Preface

Carnevale, A. P., & Stone, S. C. (1995). *The American mosaic: An in-depth report on the future of diversity at work.* New York: McGraw-Hill.

Cox, T. (1993). *Cultural diversity in organizations: Theory, research and practice.* San Francisco: Berrett-Koehler.

Johnston, W. B., & Packer, A. E. (1987). *Workforce 2000: Work and workers for the 21st century.* Indianapolis, IN: Hudson Institute.

Mandela, N. (1994). [A 1994 inaugural speech, written by Marianne Williamson].

## Chapter 1

Alderfer, C. P. (1986). An intergroup perspective on group dynamics. In J. Lorsch (Ed.), *Handbook of organizational behavior* (pp. 190-222). Englewood Cliffs, NJ: Prentice Hall.

Atkinson, D. R., Morten, G., & Sue, D. W. (1979). *Counseling American minorities: A cross-cultural perspective.* Dubuque, IA: William C. Brown.

Block, C., & Carter, R. T. (in press). White racial identity: Theory, research, and implications for organizational contexts. In A. Daly (Ed.), *Workplace diversity.* New York: National Association of Social Workers Press.

Carnevale, A. P., & Stone, S. C. (1995). *The American mosaic: An in-depth report on the future of diversity at work.* New York: McGraw-Hill.

Carter, R. T. (1990). The relationship between racism and racial identity among white Americans: An exploratory investigation. *Journal of Counseling and Development, 69,* 46-50.

Carter, R. T. (1991). Racial identity attitudes and psychological functioning. *Journal of Multicultural Counseling and Development, 19,* 105-115.

Carter, R. T. (1995). *The influence of race and racial identity in psychotherapy: Toward a racially inclusive model.* New York: Wiley.

Carter, R. T., & Qureshi, A. (1995). A typology of philosophical assumptions in multicultural counseling and training. In J. G. Ponterotto, J. M. Casas, L. A. Suzuki, & C. M. Alexander (Eds.), *Handbook of multicultural counseling and development* (pp. 239-260). Thousand Oaks, CA: Sage.

Chemers, M. M., Oskamp, S., Costanzo, M. A. (Eds.). (1995). *Diversity in organizations.* Thousand Oaks, CA: Sage.

Copeland, E. J. (1983). Minority populations and traditional counseling programs: Some alternatives. *Counselor Education and Supervision, 21,* 187-193.

Cox, T. (1990). Problems with research by organizational scholars on issues of race and ethnicity. *Journal of Applied Behavioral Science, 26,* 5-23.

Cox, T. (1993). *Cultural diversity in organizations: Theory, research and practice.* San Francisco: Berrett-Koehler.

Cox, T. (1994). *Cultural diversity in organizations: Theory, research, and practice.* San Francisco: Berrett-Koehler.

Cross, W. E. (1980). Models of psychological Nigrescence: A literature review. In R. L. Jones (Ed.), *Black psychology* (2nd ed., pp. 81-89). New York: Harper & Row.

Ferdman, B. M. (1995). Cultural identity and diversity in organizations: Bridging the gap between group differences and individual uniqueness. In M. M. Chemers, S. Oskamp, & M. A. Costanzo (Eds.), *Diversity in organizations.* Thousand Oaks, CA: Sage.

Hellriegel, D., Slocum, J. W., & Woodman, R. W. (1998). *Organizational behavior* (5th ed.). Cincinnati, OH: South-Western College.

Helms, J. E. (1984). Toward an explanation of the influence of race in the counseling process: A black-white model. *Counseling Psychologist, 12,* 153-165.

Helms, J. E. (Ed.). (1990). *Black and white racial identity: Theory research and practice.* New York: Greenwood.

Helms, J. E. (1995). An update of Helms' White and People of Color racial identity models. In J. Ponterotto, J. M. Cases, L. A. Suzuki, & C. M. Alexander (Eds.), *Handbook of multicultural counseling* (pp. 181-198). Thousand Oaks, CA: Sage.

Helms, J. E., & Piper, R. E. (1994). Implications of racial identity theory for vocational psychology. *Journal of Vocational Behavior, 44,* 124-138.

Johnston, W. B., & Packer, A. E. (1987). *Workforce 2000: Work and workers for the 21st century.* Indianapolis, IN: Hudson Institute.

Jones & Carter. (1996). Racism and racial identity: Merging realities. In B. P. Bowser & R. G. Hunt (Eds.), *Impacts of racism on White Americans* (2nd ed.) (pp. 1-24). Newbury Park, CA: Sage.

Katz, J. (1985). The sociopolitical nature of counseling. *Counseling Psychologist, 13,* 615-624.

Kluckhohn, F. R., & Strodtbeck, F. L. (1961). *Variations in value orientations.* Evanston, FL: Row, Peterson.

Kochman. (1989). Black and white cultural styles in pluralistic perspective. In B. R. Gifford (Ed.), *Test policy and test performance: Education, language, and culture* (pp. 259-294). Boston, MA: Klumer Academic Publishers.

Kovel, J. (1984). *White racism.* New York: Columbia University Press.

Marger. (1997). *Race and ethnic relations* (4th ed.). New York: Wadsworth.

Margolis, R. J., & Rungta, S. A. (1986). Training counselors for work with special populations: A second look. *Journal of Counseling & Development, 64,* 642-644.

Maznevski, M., & Peterson, M. F. (1997). Societal values, social interpretation, and multinational teams. In C. S. Granrose & S. Oskamp (Eds.), *Cross-cultural work groups* (pp. 61-89). Thousand Oaks, CA: Sage.

Midgette R. J., & Meggert S. S. (1991). Multicultural counseling instruction: A challenge for faculties in the 21st century. *Journal of Counseling & Development, 70,* 136-141.

Morrison, A. M., Ruderman, M. N., & Hughes-James, M. (1993). *Making diversity happen.* Greensboro, NC: Center for Creative Leadership.

Papajohn, J., & Speigel, J. P. (1975). *Transactions in families.* San Francisco: Jossey-Bass.

Ragins, R. (1995). Diversity, power, and mentorship in organizations: A cultural, structural, and behavioral perspective. In M. M. Cheners, S. Oskamp, & M. A. Costano (Eds.), *Diversity in organizations.* Thousand Oaks, CA: Sage.

Sackman, S. (Ed.). (1997). *Cultural complexity in organizations.* Thousand Oaks, CA: Sage.

Speigel, J. P. (1982). An ecological model of ethnic families. In M. McGoldrick, J. K. Pearce, & J. Giordano (Eds.), *Ethnicity and family therapy* (pp. 31-51). New York: Guilford.

Stewart, E. C., & Bennett, A. (1991). *American cultural patterns: A cross-cultural perspective* (2nd ed.). Yarmouth, ME: Intercultural Press.

Thomas, C. (1971). *Boys no more.* Beverly Hills, CA: Glencoe Press.

## Chapter 2

Alderfer, C. P. (1987). An intergroup perspective on group dynamics. In J. W. Lorsch (Ed.), *Handbook of organizational behavior* (pp. 190-222). Englewood Cliffs, NJ: Prentice Hall.

Alderfer, C. P. (1992). Changing race relations embedded in organizations: Report on a long-term project with the XYZ corporation. In S. E. Jackson (Ed.), *Diversity in the work-place: Human resource initiatives* (pp. 138-166). New York: Guilford Press.

Bateson, G. (1972). *Steps to an ecology of mind.* New York: Ballantine.

Berra, Y. (1998). *The Yogi book: "I really didn't say everything I said."* New York: Workman.

Carter, S. L. (1994). Foreword. In L. Guinier (Ed.), *The tyranny of the majority: Fundamental fairness in representative democracy* (pp. vii-xx). New York: Free Press.

Danforth, J. C. (1994). *Resurrection: The confirmation of Clarence Thomas.* New York: Viking.

Drew, E. (1994). *On the edge: The Clinton presidency.* New York: Simon & Schuster.

Guinier, L. (1994a). The tyranny of the majority. In L. Guinier (Ed.), *The tyranny of the majority: Fundamental fairness in representative democracy* (pp. 1-20). New York: Free Press.

Guinier, L. (1994b). The triumph of tokenism: The voting rights act and the theory of black electoral success. In L. Guinier (Ed.), *The tyranny of the majority: Fundamental fairness in representative democracy* (pp. 41-70). New York: Free Press.

Higginbotham, A. L., Jr. (1991). An open letter to Justice Clarence Thomas from a federal judicial colleague. In T. Morrison (Ed.), *Race-ing justice, en-gendering power* (pp. 3-39). New York: Pantheon.

Jaynes, G. D., & Williams, R. M., Jr. (1989). *A common destiny: Blacks and American society.* Washington, DC: National Academy Press.

Mayer, J., & Abramson, J. (1994). *Strange justice: The selling of Clarence Thomas.* Boston: Houghton Mifflin.

Morrison, T. (Ed.). (1992). *Race-ing justice, En-gendering power: Essays on Anita Hill, Clarence Thomas, and the construction of social reality.* New York: Pantheon.

Myrdal, G. (1944). *An American dilemma: The Negro problem and modern democracy.* New York: Pantheon.

Nordlie, P. (1972). Proportion of black and white army officers in command positions, In R. Alvarez, K. G. Lutterman, & Associates (Eds.), *Discrimination in organizations* (pp. 158-171). San Francisco: Jossey-Bass.

Swift, E. M. (1991). Reach out and touch someone. *Sports Illustrated, 75* (6), 54-58.

## Chapter 3

Banks, J. A., & Banks, C. A. M. (1989). *Multicultural education: Issues and perspectives.* Boston: Allyn & Bacon.

Biklin, S. K., & Pollard, D. (1993). *Gender and education.* Chicago: National Society for the Study of Education.

Bourdieu, P. (1991). *Language and symbolic power.* Cambridge, MA: Howard.

Delpit, L. (1993). The silenced dialogue. In L. Weis & M. Fine (Eds.), *Beyond silenced voices: Class, race, and gender in United States schools.* Albany: State University of New York Press.

Fine, M. (1991). *Framing dropouts: Notes on the politics of an urban public high school.* Albany: State University of New York Press.

Foucault, M. (1977). *Discipline and punish: The birth of the prison.* New York: Pantheon.

Frankenberg, R. (1993). *White women, race matters: The social construction of whiteness.* Minneapolis: University of Minnesota Press.

Gaertner, S. L., Davidio, J. F., Banker, B. S., Rust, M. C., Nier, J. A., Mottola, G. R., & Ward, C. M. (1995). Does white racism necessarily mean anti-Blackness? Aversive racism and pro-whiteness. In M. Fine, L. C. Powell, L. Weis & L. M. Wong (Eds.), *Off white.* New York: Routledge.

Gramsci, A. (1971). *Selections from the prison notebooks of Antonis Gramsci.* New York: International Publishers.

Guinier, L., Fine, M., & Balin, J. (1996). *Becoming gentlemen.* Boston: Beacon.

Guinier, L., Fine, M., & Balin, J., with Bartrow, A., & Strachel, D. L. (1994). Becoming gentlemen: Women's experiences at one Ivy League law school. *University of Pennsylvania Law Review, 143,* 1-110.

Hall, S. (1991). *Ethnicity: Identity and difference.* New York: Radical America.

Morrison, T. (1992). *Playing in the dark: Whiteness and the literary imagination.* Cambridge, MA: Harvard University Press.

Novick, M. (1995). *White lies, white power: The fight against white supremacy and reactionary violence.* Monroe, ME: Common Courage Press.

Oakes, J. (1988, January). Tracking: Can schools take a different route? *National Education Association,* pp. 41-47.

Rosenbaum, J. E. (1976). *Making inequality: The hidden curriculum of high school tracking.* New York: Wiley.

Schofield, J. W. (1982). *Black and white in school: Trust, tension, or tolerance?* New York: Praeger.

Scott, J. (1992). Experience. In J. Butler and J. Scott (Eds.), *Feminists theorize the political* (pp. 23-40). New York: Routledge.

Sleeter, C. E. (1993). How white teachers construct race. In C. McCarthy & W. Crichlow (Eds.), *Race, identity and representation in education.* New York: Routledge.

Weis, L. (1990). *Working class without work: High school students in a deindustrialized economy.* New York: Routledge.

Wells, A. S., & Serna, I. (1996). The politics of culture: Understanding local political resistance to detracking in racially mixed school. *Harvard Educational Review, 66,* 93-118.

Winant, H. (1996). Behind blue eyes: Contemporary white racial politics. In M. Fine, L. C. Powell, L. Weis, & L. M. Wong (Eds.), *Off-white: Essays on race, culture and society.* New York: Routledge.

## Chapter 4

Alderfer, C. P. (1977). Group and intergroup relations. In J. R. Hackman & J. L. Suttle (Eds.), *Improving life at work* (pp. 227-296). Santa Monica, CA: Goodyear.

Alderfer, C. P. (1986). An intergroup perspective on group dynamics. In J. Lorsch (Ed.), *Handbook of organizational behavior* (pp. 190-222). Englewood Cliffs, NJ: Prentice Hall.

Alderfer, C.P., & Smith, K. K. (1982). Studying intergroup relations embedded in organizations. *Administrative Science Quarterly, 27,* 35-65.

Alderfer, C.P., & Thomas, D.A. (1988). The significance of race and ethnicity for understanding organizational behavior. In C. L. Cooper & I. T. Robertson (Eds.), *International review of industrial and organizational psychology* (pp. 1-42). London: Wiley.

Alderfer, C., & Tucker, L. (1980). Diagnosing race relations in management. *Journal of Applied Behavioral Science, 16,* 135-166.

Alderfer, C. P., & Tucker, R. C. (1985). *Measuring managerial potential and intervening to improve the racial equity of upward mobility decisions* (Technical Report No. 6). New Haven, CT: Yale School of Organization and Management.

Bion, W. (1961). *Experiences in groups and other papers.* New York: Basic Books.

Cose, E. (1993). *Rage of a privileged class.* New York: HarperCollins.

Denhardt, R. (1987). Images of death and slavery in organizational life. *Journal of Management, 13*(13), 529-541.

Diamond, M. (1993). *The unconscious life of organizations: Interpreting organizational identity.* Westport, CT: Quorum.

Duleep, H. O., & Sanders, S. (1992). Discrimination at the top: American born Asian and white men. *Industrial Relations, 31,* 416-432.

Feagin, J., & Sikes, M. (1994). *Living with racism: The black middle-class experience.* Boston: Beacon.

Freud, A. (1946). *The ego and the mechanisms of defense.* New York: International Universities Press.

Freud, S. (1921). *Group psychology and the analysis of the ego.* New York: Norton.

Goldstein, A., Heller, T., & Proudford, K. (1995). *Who's on top: Unchanging demographic patterns in organizations.* Paper presented at the annual meeting of the Academy of Management, Vancouver, BC.

Greenhaus, J. H., Parasuraman, S., & Wormley, W. M. (1990). Effects of race on organizational experiences, job performance evaluations, and career outcomes. *Academy of Management Journal, 33,* 64-86.

Hirschhorn, L. (1988). *The workplace within.* Cambridge, MA: MIT Press.

Hirschhorn, L. (1990). Leaders and followers in a postindustrial age: A psychodynamic view. *Journal of Applied Behavioral Science, 26*(4), 529-542.

Hirschhorn, L., & Gilmore, T. (1992, May/June). The new boundaries of the "boundaryless" company. *Harvard Business Review,* 104-115.

Jacques, E. (1955). Social systems as a defense against persecutory and depressive anxiety. In M. Klein, P. Heimann, & R. E. Money-Kyrle (Eds.), *New directions in psychoanalysis.* New York: Basic Books.

Kanter, R. (1977). *Men and women of the corporation.* New York: Basic Books.

Kets de Vries, M. F. R., & Miller, D. (1984). *Neurotic organization.* San Francisco: Jossey-Bass.

Klein, M. (1959). Our adult world and its roots in infancy. *Human Relations, 12,* 291-301.

Klein, M. (1975). *The psychoanalysis of children.* New York: Seymour Lawrence/Delacorte.

Kovel, J. (1970). *White racism: A psychohistory.* New York: Pantheon.

Peck, M. S. (1978). *The road less traveled.* New York: Simon & Schuster.

Powell, G. N. (1969). *Race, religion, and the promotion of the American executive* (Monograph No. AA-3). Columbus: Ohio State University, College of Administrative Science.

Powell, G. N., & Butterfield, D. A. (1997). Effect of race on promotions to top management in a federal department. *Academy of Management Journal, 40,* 112-128.

Roediger, D. R. (1991). *The wages of whiteness: Race and the making of the american working class.* London: Verso.

Smith, K. K. (1989). The movement of conflict in organizations: The joint dynamics of splitting and triangulation. *Administrative Science Quarterly, 34,* 1-20.

Smith, K. K., & Berg, D. (1987). *Paradoxes of group life: Understanding conflict, paralysis, and movement in group dynamics.* San Francisco: Jossey-Bass.

Smith, L. (1961). *Killers of the dream.* New York: Norton.

Thomas, D. A. (1989). Mentoring and irrationality: The role of racial taboos. *Human Resource Management, 28,* 279-290.

Thomas, D. A. (1993). Racial dynamics in cross-race development relationships. *Administrative Science Quarterly, 33,* 169-194.

Thomas, D. A. (forthcoming). Beyond the simple demography-power hypothesis: How blacks in power influence whites to mentor Blacks. In F. Crosby, A. Murrell, & R. Ely (Eds.), *Mentoring dilemmas: Development relationships in multicultural organizations.* Hillsdale, NJ: Erlbaum.

Thomas, D. A., & Alderfer, C. P. (1989). The influence of race on career dynamics: Research and theory in minority career experiences. In M. Arthur, B. Hall, & B. Lawrence (Eds.), *Handbook of career theory* (pp. 133-157). Cambridge, UK: Cambridge University Press.

Thomas, D. A., & Ely, R. (1996). Making differences matter: A new paradigm for managing diversity. *Harvard Business Review, 74*(5), 79-90.

Wells, L. (1980). The group-as-a-whole: A systemic socio-analytic perspective on interpersonal and group relations. In C. P. Alderfer & C. L. Cooper (Eds.), *Advances in experiential social Processes II.* London: Wiley.

Wells, L. (1982). *Effects of ethnicity on the quality of student life: An embedded intergroup analysis.* Unpublished doctoral dissertation, Yale University.

Wells, L., & Jennings, C. (1983). Black career advances and white reactions: Remnants of Herrenvolk democracy and the scandalous paradox. In D. Vails-Webber & W. N. Potts (Eds.), *Sunrise seminars* (pp. 41-47). Arlington, VA: NTL Institute.

## Chapter 5

Armour-Thomas, E., Clay, C., Domanico, R., Bruno, K., & Allen, B. (1989). *An outlier study of elementary and middle schools in New York City: Final report*. New York: New York City Board of Education.

Au, K. H. (1980). Participation structures in a reading lesson with Hawaiian children: Analysis of a culturally appropriate instructional event. *Anthropology and Education Quarterly, 1*(2), 91-115.

Baldwin, J. (1985). *The price of the ticket: Collected nonfiction, 1948-1985*. New York: St. Martin's. (Original work published 1963.)

Banks, J. (1993). Multicultural education: Historical development, dimensions, and practices. In L. Darling-Hammond (Ed.), *Review of research in education* (Vol. 19, pp. 3-49). Washington, DC: American Education Research Association.

Barr, R., & Dreeben, R. (1983). *How schools work*. Chicago: University of Chicago Press.

Berne, R. (1992). Educational input and outcome inequities in New York State. In R. Berne & L. O. Picus (Eds.), *Outcome equity in education*. Thousand Oaks, CA: Corwin Press.

Braddock, J., & McPartland, J. (1993). Education of early adolescents. In L. Darling-Hammond (Ed.), *Review of research in education* (Vol. 19). Washington, DC: American Educational Research Association.

Carrajat, M. A. (in press). *Why academically able Puerto Rican high school students drop out of school*. Unpublished doctoral dissertation, Teachers College, Columbia University.

Carter, R., & Goodwin, L. (1994). Racial identity and education. In L. Darling-Hammond (Ed.), *Review of Research in Education* (Vol. 20). Washington, DC: American Educational Research Association.

Chinn, P. C., & Wong, G. Y. (1992). Recruiting and retaining Asian/Pacific American teachers. In M. E. Dilworth (Ed.), *Diversity in teacher education: New expectations* (pp. 112-134). San Francisco: Jossey-Bass.

Cochran-Smith, M. (1995). Uncertain allies: Understanding the boundaries of race and teaching. *Harvard Educational Review, 65*(4): 541-570.

College Entrance Examination Board. (1985). *Equality and excellence: The educational status of black Americans*. New York: Author.

Darling-Hammond, L. (1990). Teacher quality and equality. In J. Goodlad & P. Keating (Eds.), *Access to knowledge: An agenda for our nation's schools* (pp. 237-258). New York: College Entrance Examination Board.

Darling-Hammond, L. (1992). Teaching and knowledge: Policy issues posed by alternate certification for teachers. *Peabody Journal of Education, 67*(3): 123-154.

Darling-Hammond, L. (1995). Inequality and access to knowledge. In J. Banks (Ed.), *Handbook of research on multicultural education*. New York: Macmillan.

Darling-Hammond, L. (1996). Restructuring schools for high performance. In S. Fuhrman & J. O'Day (Eds.), *Rewards and reform.* San Francisco: Jossey-Bass.

Darling-Hammond, L. (1997). *The right to learn: A blueprint for creating schools that work.* San Francisco: Jossey-Bass.

Darling-Hammond, L., Ancess, J., & Falk, B. (1995). *Authentic assessment in action: Studies of schools and students at work.* New York: Teachers College Press.

Darling-Hammond, L., Snyder, J., Ancess, J., Einbender, L., Goodwin, A. L., & Macdonald, M. B. (1993). *Creating learner-centered accountability.* New York: Columbia University, Teachers College, National Center for Restructuring Education, Schools, and Teaching.

Davis, D. G. (1986, April). *A pilot study to assess equity in selected curricular offerings across three diverse schools in a large urban school district.* Paper presented at the annual meeting of the American Educational Research Association, San Francisco.

Delpit, L. (1995). *Other people's children: Cultural conflicts in the classrooms.* New York: New Press.

Dewey, J. (1966). *Democracy and education.* New York: Free Press.

Dreeben, R. (1987, Winter). Closing the divide: What teachers and administrators can do to help black students reach their reading potential. *American Educator, 11*(4), 28-35.

Dreeben, R. & Barr, R. (1987, April). *Class composition and the design of instruction.* Paper presented at the annual meeting of the American Education Research Association, Washington, DC.

Dreeben, R., & Gamoran, A. (1986). Race, instruction, and learning. *American Sociological Review, 51*(5), 660-669.

DuBois, W. E. B. (1970). Education and work. In P. S. Foner (Ed.), *W. E. B. DuBois speaks* pp. 55-76). New York: Pathfinder. (Original work published 1930)

DuBois, W. E. B. (1970). The freedom to learn. In P. S. Foner (Ed.), *W. E. B. DuBois speaks* (pp. 228-231). New York: Pathfinder. (Original work published 1949)

Eckstrom, R., & Villegas, A. M. (1991). Ability grouping in middle grade mathematics: Process and consequences. *Research in Middle Level Education, 15*(1), 1-20.

Educational Testing Service. (1989). *A world of differences: An international assessment of mathematics and science.* Princeton, NJ: Author.

Educational Testing Service. (1991). *The state of inequality.* Princeton, NJ: Author.

Ferguson, R. F. (1991, Summer). Paying for public education: New evidence on how and why money matters. *Harvard Journal on Legislation, 28*(2), 465-498.

Fine, M. (1991). *Framing dropouts: Notes on the politics of an urban public school.* Albany: State University of New York Press.

Fine, M. (1994). *Chartering urban school reform.* New York: Columbia University, Teachers College, National Center for Restructuring Education, Schools, and Teaching.

Finley, M. K. (1984). Teachers and tracking in a comprehensive high school. *Sociology of Education, 57,* 233-243.

Fordham, S. (1988). Racelessness as a factor in Black students' school success: Pragmatic strategy or pyrrhic victory? *Harvard Educational Review, 58,* 54-84.

Foster, M. (1993). Educating for competence in community and culture: Exploring the views of exemplary African American teachers. *Urban Education, 27*(4), 370-394.

Gamoran, A. (1990, April). *The consequences of track-related instructional differences for student achievement.* Paper presented at the annual meeting of the American Educational Research Association, Boston.

Gamoran, A. (1992). Access to excellence: Assignment to honors English classes in the transition from middle to high school. *Educational Evaluation and Policy Analysis, 14*(3), 185-204.

Gamoran, A., & Mare, R. (1989). Secondary school tracking and educational inequality: Compensation, reinforcement or neutrality? *American Journal of Sociology, 94,* 1146-1183.

Garcia, E. E. (1993). Language, culture, and education. In L. Darling-Hammond (Ed.), *Review of research in education* (Vol. 19, pp. 51-98). Washington, DC: American Educational Research Association.

Good, T. L., & Brophy, J. (1987). *Looking in classrooms.* New York: Harper & Row.

Gordon, E. W. (1990). Coping with communicentric bias in knowledge production in the social sciences. *Educational Researcher, 19,* 19.

Greene, M. (1982, June/July). Public education and the public space. *Educational Researcher,* pp. 4-9.

Greene, M. (1984). *Education, freedom, and possibility.* Inaugural lecture as William F. Russell Professor in the Foundations of Education, Columbia University, Teachers College.

Herrnstein, R. J., & Murray, C. (1994). *The bell curve: Intelligence and class structure in American life.* New York: Free Press.

Irvine, J. J. (1990). *Black students and school failure: Policies, practices, and prescriptions.* New York: Praeger.

Irvine, J. J. (1992). Making teacher education culturally responsive. In M. E. Dilworth (Ed.), *Diversity in teacher education* (pp. 79-92). San Francisco: Jossey-Bass.

Jones, L. V. (1984). White-black achievement differences: The narrowing gap. *American Psychologist, 39,* 1207-1213

Jones, L. V., Burton, N. W., & Davenport, E. C. (1984). Monitoring the achievement of black students. *Journal for Research in Mathematics Education, 15,* 154-164.

Kaufman, J. E., & Rosenbaum, J. E. (1992). Education and employment of low-income black youth in white suburbs. *Educational Evaluation and Policy Analysis, 14*(3), 229-240.

Kozol, J. (1991). *Savage inequalities.* New York: Crown.

Ladson-Billings, G. (1992). Culturally relevant teaching. In C. A. Grant (Ed.), *Research and multicultural education: From the margins to the mainstream* (pp. 106-121). Washington, DC: Falmer.

Ladson-Billings, G. (1994). *The dreamkeepers: Successful teachers of African American children.* San Francisco: Jossey-Bass.

Lee, V., Bryk, A., & Smith, M. (1993). The organization of effective secondary schools. In L. Darling-Hammond (Ed.), *Review of Research in Education* (Vol. 19). Washington, DC: American Educational Research Association.

McKnight, C. C., Crosswhite, F. J., Dossey, J. A., Kifer, E., Swafford, J. O., Travers, K. J., & Cooney, T. J. (1987). *The underachieving curriculum: Assessing U. S. school mathematics from an international perspective.* Champaign, IL: Stipes.

Moore, E. G., & Smith, A. W. (1985). Mathematics aptitude: Effects of coursework, household language, and ethnic differences. *Urban Education, 20,* 273-294.

Murrell, P. (1991). Cultural politics in teacher education: What's missing in the preparation of minority teachers? In M. Foster (Ed.), *Qualitative investigations into schools and schooling* (pp. 205-225). New York: AMS.

National Commission on Teaching and America's Future. (1996). *What matters most: Teaching for America's future.* New York: Author.

Nieto, S. (1992). *Affirming diversity.* New York: Longman.

Nieto, S., & Rolon, C. (1996). The preparation and professional development of teachers: A perspective from two Latinas. In J. J. Irvine (Ed.), *Defining the knowledge base for urban teacher education.* Atlanta: Emory University, CULTURES.

Oakes, J. (1983, May). Limiting opportunity: Student race and curricular differences in secondary vocational education. *American Journal of Education, 91*(3), 328-355.

Oakes, J. (1985). *Keeping track: How schools structure inequality.* New Haven, CT: Yale University Press.

Oakes, J. (1990). *Multiplying inequalities: The effects of race, social class, and tracking on opportunities to learn mathematics and science.* Santa Monica, CA: Rand.

Oakes, J. (1992, May). Can tracking research inform practice? Technical, normative, and political considerations. *Educational Researcher, 21*(4), 12-21.

Orfield, G. F., Monfort, F., & Aaron, M. (1989). *Status of school desegregation: 1968-1986.* Alexandria, VA: National School Boards Association.

Pelavin, S. H., & Kane, M. (1990). *Changing the odds: Factors increasing access to college.* New York: College Entrance Examination Board.

Poplin, M., & Weeres, J. (1992). *Voices from the inside: A report on schooling from inside the classroom.* Claremont, CA: Claremont Graduate School, Institute for Education in Transformation.

Rubovitz, P. C., & Maehr, M. (1973). Pygmalion black and white. *Journal of Personality and Social Psychology, 25,* 210-218.

Spring, J. (1997). *Deculturalization and the struggle for equity* (2nd ed.). New York: McGraw-Hill.

Strickland, D. S. (1995). Reinventing our literacy programs: Books, basics, balance. *Reading Teacher, 48*(4), 294-302.

Talbert, J. E. (1990). *Teacher tracking: Exacerbating inequalities in the high school.* Stanford, CA: Stanford University, Center for Research on the Context of Secondary Teaching.

Taylor, W. L. & Piche, D. M. (1991). *A report on shortchanging children: The impact of fiscal inequity on the education of students at risk* (Prepared for the Committee on Education and Labor, U.S. House of Representatives). Washington, DC: U. S. Government Printing Office.

Trimble, K., & Sinclair, R. L. (1986, April). *Ability grouping and differing conditions for learning: An analysis of content and instruction in ability-grouped classes.* Paper presented at the annual meeting of the American Educational Research Association, San Francisco.

Tyack, D. (1974). *The one best system.* Cambridge, MA: Harvard University Press.

Useem, E. L. (1990, Fall). You're good, but you're not good enough: Tracking students out of advanced mathematics. *American Educator, 14*(3), 24-27, 43-46.

Wehlage, G., Rutter, R. A., Smith, G. A., Lesko, N., & Fernandez, R. R. (1989). *Reducing the risk: Schools as communities of support.* Philadelphia: Falmer.

Wise, A. E. (1972). *Rich schools, poor schools: The promise of equal educational opportunity.* Chicago: University of Chicago Press.

# Chapter 6

Adelman, M. (1977). Sexual orientation and violations of civil liberties. *Journal of Homosexuality, 2*(4), 327-330.

Ahrons, C. R., & Rodgers, R. (1987). *Divorced families: A multidisciplinary view.* New York: Norton.

Akbar, N. (1974). Awareness: The key to black mental health. *Journal of Black Psychology, 1,* 30-37.

Akbar, N. (1981). Mental disorder among African-Americans. *Black Books Bulletin, 7*(2), 18-25.

Akbar, N. (1985). Nile valley origins of the science of the mind. In I. Van Sertima (Ed.), *Nile Valley civilizations.* New York: Journal of African Civilization.

Anderson, S., Piantanida, M., & Anderson, C. (1993). Normal processes in adoptive families. In F. Walsh (Ed.), *Normal family processes* (2nd ed., pp. 254-281). New York: Guilford.

Aponte, H. (1980). Videotape of a black family in Newark, prepared during continuing education program on structural family therapy , New Jersey Medical School, University of Medicine and Dentistry, Newark.

Aponte, H. (1994). *Bread and spirit: Therapy with the new poor.* New York: Morton.

Berlin, I. N. (1978). Anglo adoptions of Native Americans: Repercussions in adolescence. *American Academy of Child Psychiatry, 17*(2), 387-388.

Blau, M. (1994). *Families apart: Ten keys to successful co-parenting.* New York: Putnam.

Bowen, M. (1978). *Family therapy in clinical practice.* New York: Jason Aronson.

Boyd-Franklin, N. (1989). *Black families in therapy: A multisystems approach.* New York: Guilford.

Boyd-Franklin, N., Steiner, G., & Boland, M. (Eds.). (1995). *Children, families and AIDS/HIV: Psychosocial and therapeutic issues.* New York: Guilford.

Bradt, J. O. (1988). Becoming parents: Families with young children. In B. Carter & M. McGoldrick (Eds.), *The changing family life cycle* (2nd ed., pp. 235-254). New York: Gardner.

Bronfenbrenner, U. (1979). *The ecology of human development: Experiments by nature and design.* Cambridge, MA: Harvard University Press.

Burden, D. S. (1986). Single parents and the work setting: The impact of multiple job and homelike responsibilities. *Family Relations, 35,* 37-43.

Cargan, L. (1983). Singles: An examination of two stereotypes. In A. Skolnick & J. Skolnick (Eds.), *Family in transition* (pp. 546-556). Boston: Little, Brown.

Carlson, K. (1996). Gay and lesbian families. In M. Harway (Ed.), *Treating the changing family* (pp. 62-76). New York: Wiley.

Carter, R. (1995). The influence of race and racial identity in psychotherapy. New York: Wiley.

Chambers, D. E. (1970). Willingness to adopt atypical children. *Child Welfare, 69*(5), 275-279.

Cherlin, A. (1983). Remarriage as an incomplete institution. In A. Skolnick & J. Skolnick (Eds.), *Family in transition* (pp. 368-402). Boston: Little, Brown.

Comas-Diaz, L., & Griffith, E. (1988). *Clinical guidelines in cross cultural mental health.* New York: Wiley.

Comstock, G. D. (1991). *Violence against lesbians and gay men.* New York: Columbia University Press.

Cullar, I., & Glazer, J. (1996). The impact of culture on the family. In M. Harway (Ed.), *Treating the changing family* (pp. 17-38). New York: Wiley.

DeCecco, J. (1984). *Bisexual and homosexual identities: Critical theoretical issues.* New York: Haworth.

De Vine, J. L. (1984). A systemic inspection of affectional preference orientation and the family of origin. *Journal of Social Work and Human Sexuality, 2,* 9-17.

Edminster, P. (1996). Mental health approaches to working with families with disabled children. In M. Harway (Ed.), *Treating the changing family* (pp. 219-245). New York: Wiley.

Feigelman, W., & Silverman, A. R. (1977). Single parent adoptions. *Social Casework, 58*(7), 418-425.

Francke, L. B. (1983). *Growing up divorced.* New York: Simon & Schuster.

Glazer, S. (1993, November). Adoption. *CQ Researcher, 3,* 1033-1055.

Glick, P. C. (1991, October). Speech presented at the annual conference of the Stepfamily Association, Lincoln, NE.

Glick, P. C., & Lin, S. (1986). Recent changes in divorce and remarriage. *Journal of Marriage and Family, 48,* 737-747.

Goetting, A. (1983). Divorce outcome research: Issues and perspectives. In A. Skolnick & J. Skolnick (Eds.), *Family in transition* (pp. 367-382). Boston: Little, Brown.

Goldenberg, H., & Goldenberg, I. (1994). *Counseling today's families.* Pacific Grove, CA: Brooks/Cole.

Greif, G. (1988). Single fathers: Helping them cope with day-to-day problems. *Medical Aspects of Sexuality, 22,* 185-225.

Groze, V. K., & Rosenthal, J. A. (1991). Single parents and their adopted children: A psychosocial analysis. *Families in Society, 72,* 67-77.

Harway, M. (Ed.). (1996). *Treating the changing family: Handling normative and unusual events.* New York: Wiley.

Harway, M., & Wexler, K. (1996). Setting the stage for understanding and treating the changing family. In M. Harway (Ed.), *Treating the changing family* (pp. 3-16). New York: Wiley.

Henggeler, S. W., & Borduin, C. M. (1990). *Family therapy and beyond: A multisystemic approach to treating the behavior problems of children and adolescents.* Belmont, CA: Wadsworth.

Henggeler, S. W., Melton, G. B., & Smith, L. A. (1992). Family preservation using multisystemic therapy: An effective alternative to incarcerating serious juvenile offenders. *Journal of Consulting and Clinical Psychology, 60,* 953-961.

Hess, B., & Waring, J. (1983). Changing patterns of aging and family bonds in later life. In A. Skolnick & J. Skolnick (Eds.), *Family in transition* (pp. 521-537). Boston: Little, Brown.

Hetherington, F. M., Law, T., & O'Connor, T. (1993). Divorce: Challenges, changes and new chances. In F. Walsh (Ed.), *Normal family processes* (2nd ed.) (pp. 208-233). New York: Guilford.

Hines, P. (1988). The family life cycle of poor black families. In B. Carter & M. McGoldrick (Eds.), *The changing family life cycle* (2nd ed.) (pp. 513-544). New York: Gardner.

Hofferth, S. L., & Phillips, D. A. (1987). Child care in the United States, 1970 to 1975. *Journal of Marriage and the Family, 49,* 559-571.

Kadushin, A., & Martin, J. A. (1988). Substitute care: Adoption. In A. Kadushin & J. A. Martin (Eds.), *Child welfare services* (4th ed., pp. 533-668). New York: Macmillan.

Kalter, N. (1990). *Growing up with divorce: Helping your child avoid immediate and later emotional problems.* New York: Free Press.

Koh, F. M. (1988). *Oriental children in American homes* (Rev. ed.). Minneapolis: East West Press.

Ladner, J. (1977). *Mixed families: Adopting across racial boundaries.* Garden City, NY: Doubleday.

Laird, J. (1993). Lesbian and gay families. In F. Walsh (Ed.), *Normal family processes* (2nd ed.) (pp. 282-328). New York: Guilford.

Laird, J., & Green, R. J. (1996). *Gay and lesbian couples and families.* San Francisco: Jossey-Bass.

Linton, R. (1945). *The cultural background of personality.* New York: Appleton-Century-Crofts.

Lowery, C., & Settle, S. (1984). Effects of divorce on children: Differential impact of custody and visitation patterns. *Family Relations, 34,*

McGoldrick, M., & Carter, B. (1988). Forming a remarried family. In B. Carter & M. McGoldrick (Eds.), *The changing family life cycle* (2nd ed., pp. 399-432). New York: Gardner.

McGoldrick, M., Giordano, J., & Pearce, J. (1996). *Ethnicity and family therapy* (2nd ed.). New York: Guilford.

McGoldrick, M., Pearce, J., & Giordano, J. (Eds.). (1982). *Ethnicity and family therapy.* New York: Guilford Press.

McRoy, R. G., Zurcher, L. A., Lauderdale, M. L., & Anderson, R. E. (1984). The identity of transracial adoptees. *Social Casework: The Journal of Contemporary Social Work, 65*(1), 34-37.

Menning, B. (1977). *Infertility: A guide for the childless couple.* Englewood Cliffs, NJ: Prentice Hall.

Miller, N. (1992). *Single parents by choice.* New York: Insight Books.

Minuchin, S. (1974). *Families and family therapy.* Cambridge, MA: Harvard University Press.

Minuchin, S., Montalvo, B., Guerney, B. G., Jr., Rosman, B. L., & Schumer, F. (1967). *Families of the slums: An exploration of their structure and treatment.* New York: Basic Books.

Mirkin, M. (1994). *Women in context: Toward a feminist reconstruction of psychotherapy.* New York: Guilford.

Nobles, W. (1985). Africanicity and the black family: The development of a theoretical model. Oakland, CA: Black Family Institute Publishers.

Nobles, W. (1986). *African psychology: Toward its reclamation, reascension and revitalization.* Oakland, CA: Black Family Institute Publishers.

Norton, A. J., & Glick, P. G. (1986). One-parent families: A social and economic profile. *Family Relations, 35,* 9-13.

O'Rourke, L., & Hubbell, R. (1990). *Intercountry adoption.* Washington, DC: National Adoption Information Clearinghouse.

Pahz, J. A. (1988). *Adopting from Latin America: An agency perspective.*
    Springfield, IL: Charles C. Thomas.
Papernow, P. (1993). *Becoming a stepfamily: Patterns of development in
    remarried families.* San Francisco: Jossey-Bass.
Peck, J., & Manocherian, J. (1988). Divorce in the changing family life cycle. In
    B. Carter & M. McGoldrick (Eds.), *The changing family life cycle* (2nd
    ed.). New York: Gardner.
Pinderhughes, E. (1989). *Understanding race, ethnicity and power: The key to
    efficacy in clinical practice.* New York: Free Press.
Piotrowski, C., & Hughes, D. (1993). Dual-earner families in context: Managing
    family and work systems. In F. Walsh (Ed.), *Normal family processes* (2nd
    ed., pp. 185-207). New York: Guilford.
Quinn, P., & Allen, K. R. (1989). Facing challenges and making compromises:
    How single mothers endure. *Family Relations, 38,* 390-395.
Risman, B. J. (1986). Can men "mother"? Life as a single father. *Family
    Relations, 35,* 95-102.
Rolland, J. S. (1993). Mastering family challenges in serious illness and
    disability. In F. Walsh (Ed.), *Normal family processes* (2nd ed., pp.
    444-473). New York: Guilford.
Rutter, V. (1994, May/June). Lessons from stepfamilies. *Psychology Today,* pp.
    30-33, 60-67.
Salzer, L. P. (1986). *Infertility: How couples can cope.* Boston: G. K. Hall.
Schwartz, L. L. (1996). Adoptive families: Are they normative? In M. Harway
    (Ed.), *Treating the changing family* (pp. 97-113). New York: Wiley.
Seibt, T. (1996). Nontraditional families. In M. Harway (Ed.), *Treating the
    changing family* (pp. 39-61). New York: Wiley.
Skolnick, A., & Skolnick, J. (Eds.). (1983). *Family in transition.* Boston: Little,
    Brown.
Small, J. W. (1984). The crisis in adoption. *International Journal of Social
    Psychiatry, 30*(1-2), 129-142.
Sporakowski, M. J. (1988). A therapist's views on the consequences of change
    for the contemporary family. *Family Relations, 37,* 373-378.
Strozier, A. M. (1996). Families with chronic illness and disability. In M.
    Harway (Ed.), *Treating the changing family* (pp. 246-270). New York:
    Wiley.
Taeuber, C. (Ed.) (1991). *Statistical handbook on women in America.* Phoenix,
    AZ: Oryx.
Tizard, B. (1991). Intercountry adoption: A review of the evidence. *Journal of
    Child Psychology and Psychiatry, 32*(5), 743-756.
Triseliotis, J. (1991). Perception of permanence: Adoption and fostering.
    *Journal of Social Policy, 15*(4), 6-15.
Turner, P., & Smith, R. (1983). Single parents and day care. *Family Relations,
    32,* 215-226.

U.S. Bureau of Census. (1991). Households, families, marital status, and living arrangements: March, 1991. In *Current population reports* (Series No. P-20). Washington, DC: Government Printing Office.

Veevers, J. E. (1983). Voluntary childless wives: An exploratory study. In A. Skolnick & J. Skolnick (Eds.), *Family in transition* (pp. 538-545). Boston: Little, Brown.

Visher, E., & Visher, J. (1979). *Stepfamilies: A guide to working with stepparents and stepchildren.* New York: Brunner/Mazel.

Visher, E., & Visher, J. (1988). *Old loyalties, new ties: Therapeutic strategies with stepfamilies.* New York: Brunner/Mazel.

Visher, E., & Visher, J. (1993). Remarriage, families and stepparenting. In F. Walsh (Ed.), *Normal family processes* (2nd ed., pp. 235-253). New York: Guilford.

Wallerstein, J. S., & Kelly, J. B. (1980). *Surviving the breakup: How children and parents cope with divorce.* New York: Basic Books.

Walsh, F. (Ed.) (1993). *Normal family processes* (2nd ed.). New York: Guilford.

Warren, C. A. B. (1974). *Identity and community in the gay world.* New York: Wiley.

West, C. (1993). *Race matters.* Boston: Beacon.

## Chapter 7

Aaron, R., & Powell, G. (1982). Feedback practices as a function of teacher and pupil race during reading group instruction. *Journal of Negro Education, 51,* 50-59.

American Association of Colleges for Teacher Education. (1990). *Teacher education pipeline II: Schools, colleges, and departments of education enrollments by race and ethnicity.* Washington, DC: Author.

American Association of Colleges for Teacher Education, Commission on Multicultural Education. (1973). No one model American. *Journal of Teacher Education, 24*(4), 264-265.

American Council on Education and the Education Commission of the States. (1988). *One-third of a nation: A report of the commission on minority participation in education and American life.* Washington, DC: Author.

Au, K. H. (1993). *Literacy instruction in multicultural settings.* Fort Worth, TX: Harcourt Brace College Publishers.

Baker, G. C. (1974). Instructional priorities in a culturally pluralistic school. *Educational Leadership, 32*(3), 176-182.

Banks, J. A. (1988). *Multiethnic education* (2nd ed.). Newton, MA: Allyn & Bacon.

Banks, J. A. (1991). Teaching multicultural literacy to teachers. *Teaching Education, 4*(1), 135-144.

Banks, J. A. (1993). Multicultural education: Historical development, dimensions, and practice. In L. Darling-Hammond (Ed.), *Review of research in education* (Vol. 19, pp. 3-50). Washington, DC: American Educational Research Association.

Banks, J. A., Carlos, E. C., Garcia, R. L., Gay, G., & Ochoa, A. S. (1976). *Curriculum guidelines for multiethnic education.* Arlington, VA: National Council for the Social Studies.

Baptiste, H. P., Jr. (1979). *Multicultural education: A synopsis.* Lanham, MD: University Press of America.

Baptiste, H. P., Jr., & Baptiste, M. L. (1980). Competencies toward multiculturalism. In H. P. Baptiste, Jr., M. L. Baptiste, & D. M. Gollnick (Eds.), *Multicultural teacher education: Preparing educators to provide educational equity* (pp. 44-72). Washington, DC: American Association of Colleges for Teacher Education, Commission on Multicultural Education.

Baptiste, H. P., Jr., Baptiste, M. L., & Gollnick, D. M. (Eds.). (1980). *Multicultural teacher education: Preparing educators to provide educational equity.* Washington, DC: American Association of Colleges for Teacher Education, Commission on Multicultural Education.

Baratz, S. S., & Baratz, J. C. (1970). Early childhood intervention: The social science base of institutional racism. *Harvard Educational Review, 40,* 29-50.

Boyd, W. L. (1991). What makes ghetto schools succeed or fail? *Teachers College Record, 92*(3), 331-362.

Brown, C. E. (1992). Restructuring for a new America. In M. E. Dilworth (Ed.), *Diversity in teacher education* (pp. 1-22). San Francisco: Jossey-Bass.

Caliguri, J. P. (1970*). Suburban interracial education projects: A resource booklet.* Washington, DC: U.S. Office of Education.

Cardenas, J., & First, J. M. (1985). Children at risk. *Educational Leadership, 3*(1), 5-8.

Carter, R. T., & Goodwin, A. L. (1994). Racial identity and education. In L. Darling-Hammond (Ed.), *Review of research in education* (Vol. 20, pp. 291-336). Washington, DC: American Educational Research Association.

Center for Education Statistics. (1987). *The condition of education.* Washington, DC: U.S. Government Printing Office.

College Board. (1985). *Equality and excellence: The educational status of black Americans.* New York: Author.

Collins, J. (1982). Discourse style, classroom interaction and differential treatment. *Journal of Reading Behavior, 14,* 429-437.

Commission on Minority Participation in Education and American Life. (1988). *One-third of a nation: A report of the Commission on Minority Participation in Education and American Life.* Washington, DC: American Council on Education.

Cremin, L. A. (Ed.). (1957). *The republic and the school.* New York: Teachers College Press.

Cremin, L. A. (1961). *The transformation of the school.* New York: Knopf.

Cummins, J. (1986). Empowering minority students: A framework for intervention. *Harvard Educational Review, 56*(1), 18-36.

Cummins, J. (1995). Underachievement among minority students. In D. B. Durkin (Ed.), *Language issues: Readings for teachers* (pp. 130-159). White Plains, NY: Longman.

Darling-Hammond, L., & Goodwin, A. L. (1993). Progress toward professionalism in teaching. In G. Cawelti (Ed.), *Challenges and achievements of American education* (Association for Supervision and Curriculum Development Yearbook, pp. 19-52). Alexandria, VA: ASCD.

Darling-Hammond, L., Pittman, K. J., & Ottinger, C. (1987). *Career choices for minorities: Who will teach?* Washington, DC: National Education Association.

Degler, C. N. (1984). *Out of our past* (3rd ed.). New York: Harper & Row.

Delpit, L. (1995). *Other people's children.* New York: New Press.

Dilworth, M. E. (1990). *Reading between the lines; Teachers and their racial/ethnic cultures* (Teacher Education Monograph No. 11). Washington, DC: ERIC Clearinghouse on Teacher Education & American Association of Colleges for Teacher Education.

Duran, R. P. (1994). Cooperative learning for language-minority students. In R. A. DeVillar, C. J. Faltis, & J. P. Cummins (Es.), *Cultural diversity in schools* (pp. 145-160). Albany: State University of New York Press.

Espiritu, Y. L. (1992). *Asian American panethnicity: Bridging institutions and identities.* Philadelphia: Temple University Press.

Estrada, L. J., & Vasquez, M. (1981). Schooling and its social and psychological effects on minorities. In W. E. Sims & B. Bass de Martinez (Eds.), *Perspectives in multicultural education* (pp. 53-74). New York: University Press of America.

Fine, M. (1991). *Framing dropouts: Notes on the politics of an urban public school.* Albany: State University of New York Press.

Fordham, O. (1988). Racelessness as a factor in black students' school success: Pragmatic strategy or pyrrhic victory? *Harvard Educational Review, 58,* 54-84.

Fuller, M. L. (1992). Teacher education programs and increasing minority school populations: An educational mismatch? In C. A. Grant (Ed.), *Research and multicultural education* (pp. 184-202). London: Falmer.

Garcia, E. E., McLaughlin, B., Spodek, B., & Saracho, O. N. (Eds.). (1995). *Meeting the challenge of linguistic and cultural diversity in early childhood education* (Yearbook in Early Childhood Education, Vol. 6). New York: Teachers College Press.

Garcia, G., & Pearson, P. D. (1991). Modifying reading instruction to maximize its effectiveness for "all" students. In M. S. Knapp & P. M. Shields (Eds.), *Better schooling for children of poverty* (pp. 31-60). Berkeley, CA: McCutchan.

Garibaldi, A. M. (1988). *Educating black male youth: A moral and civic imperative.* New Orleans: New Orleans Public Schools.

Gay, G. (1977). Curriculum for multicultural teacher education. In F. H. Klassen & D. M. Gollnick (Eds.), *Pluralism and the American teacher* (pp. 31-62).

Washington, DC: American Association of Colleges for Teaching of Education, Ethnic Heritage Center for Teacher Education.

Gay, G. (1983). Multiethnic education: Historical developments and future prospects. *Phi Delta Kappan, 64*(8), 560-563.

Gollnick, D. M. (1977). Multicultural education: The challenge for teacher education. *ERIC Clearinghouse on Teacher Education, 28*(3), 57-59.

Gollnick, D. M. (1992). Multicultural education: Policies and practices in teacher education. In C. Grant (Ed.), *Research and multicultural education: From the margins to the mainstream* (pp. 218-239). Bristol, PA: Falmer.

Gollnick, D. M., Osayande, K. I. M., & Levy, J. (1980). *Multicultural teacher education: Case studies of thirteen programs* (Vol. 2). Washington, DC: American Association of Colleges for Teacher Education.

Gonzalez, R. D. (1990). When minority becomes majority: The changing face of English classrooms. *English Journal, 79,* 16-23.

Goodlad, J. I. (1984). *A place called school.* New York: McGraw-Hill.

Goodwin, A. L. (1991). Problems, process, and promise: Reflections on a collaborative approach to the minority teacher shortage. *Journal of Teacher Education, 42*(1), 28-36.

Goodwin, A. L. (1997). Multicultural stories: Preservice teachers' conceptions of and responses to issues of diversity. *Urban Education, 32*(1), 117-145.

Goodwin, A. L., Genishi, C., Asher, N., & Woo, K. (1997). Voices from the margins: Asian American teachers' experiences in the profession. In D. M. Byrd & D. J. McIntyre (Eds.), *Research on the education of our nation's teachers* (Teacher Education Yearbook No. 5, pp. 219-241). Thousand Oaks, CA: Corwin.

Goodwin, A. L., & Macdonald, M. (1997). Educating the rainbow: Authentic assessment and practice for diverse classrooms. In A. L. Goodwin (Ed.), *Assessment for equity and inclusion: Embracing all our children* (pp. 211-227). New York: Routledge.

Grant, C. A. (1981). Education that is multicultural and teacher preparation: An examination from the perspective of preservice students. *Journal of Educational Research, 75*(2), 95-101.

Grant, C. A., & Gomez, M. (1996). *Making schooling multicultural: Campus and classroom.* Englewood Cliffs, NJ: Prentice Hall.

Grant, C. A., & Koskela, R. A. (1986). Education that is multicultural and the relationship between preservice campus learning and field experiences. *Journal of Education Research, 79,* 197-203.

Grant, C. A., & Secada, W. G. (1990). Preparing teachers for diversity. In W. R. Houston (Ed.), *Handbook of research on teacher education* (pp. 403-422). New York: Macmillan.

Haberman, M. (1991). Can cultural awareness be taught in teacher education programs? *Teaching Education, 4,* 25-31.

Henington, M. (1981). Effect of intensive multicultural, non-sexist instruction on secondary students teachers. *Educational Research Quarterly, 6*(1), 65-75.

Hilliard, A. G. III. (1990). Misunderstanding and testing intelligence. In J. I. Goodlad & P. Keating (Eds.), *Access to knowledge* (pp. 145-158). New York: College Board.

Irvine, J. J. (1991a). *Black students and school failure.* New York: Praeger.

Irvine, J. J. (1991b, February). *Culturally responsive and responsible pedagogy: The inclusion of culture, research, and reflection in the knowledge base of teacher education.* Paper presented at the annual meeting of the American Association of Colleges for Teacher Education, Atlanta.

Irvine, J. J. (1992). Making teacher education culturally responsive. In M. E. Dilworth (Ed.), *Diversity in teacher education* (pp. 79-92). San Francisco: Jossey-Bass.

Jackson, J., & Kirkpatrick, D. (1967). *Institutes for preparation of counselors and teacher leadership in desegregated schools.* Washington, DC: U.S. Office of Education.

Jordan, C. (1985). Translating culture: From ethnographic information to educational program. *Anthropology and Education Quarterly, 16,* 105-123.

King, S. H. (1993). The limited presence of African-American teachers. *Review of Educational Research, 63*(2), 115-140.

Klassen, F. H., & Gollnick, D. M. (1977). *Pluralism and the American teacher.* Washington, DC: American Association of Colleges for Teacher Education, Ethnic Heritage Center for Teacher Education.

Klassen, F. H., Gollnick, D. M., & Osayande, K. I. M. (1980). *Multicultural teacher education: Guidelines for implementation* (Vol. 4). Washington, DC: American Association of Colleges for Teacher Education.

Ladson-Billings, G. (1994). *Dreamkeepers.* San Francisco: Jossey-Bass.

McDiarmid, G. W., & Price, J. (1990). *Prospective teachers' views of diverse learners: A study of participants in the ABCD project* (Research Report No. 90-6). East Lansing: Michigan State University, National Center for Research on Teacher Education.

Moll, L. C. (1991). Social and instructional issues in literacy instruction of "disadvantaged" students. In M. S. Knapp & P. M. Shields (Eds.), *Better schooling for children of poverty* (pp. 61-84). Berkeley, CA: McCutchan.

National Center for Education Statistics. (1991). *Projections of education statistics to 2002* (No. 91-490). Washington, DC: U.S. Department of Education, Office of Educational Research and Improvement.

National Center for Education Statistics. (1992). *Schools and staffing in the United States: A statistical profile, 1987-1988* (No. 92-120). Washington, DC: U.S. Department of Education, Office of Educational Research and Improvement.

National Commission on Excellence in Education. (1983). *A nation at risk.* Washington, DC: U.S. Government Printing Office.

Nieto, S. (1992). *Affirming diversity.* New York: Longman.

Oakes, J. (1985). *Keeping track: How schools structure inequality.* New Haven, CT: Yale University Press.

Oakes, J., & Lipton, M. (1990). Tracking and ability grouping: A structural barrier to access and achievement. In J. I. Goodlad & P. Keating (Eds.), *Access to knowledge* (pp. 187-204). New York: College Board.

Olneck, M. R. (1990). The recurring dream: Symbolism and ideology in intercultural and multicultural education. *American Journal of Education, 98*(2), 147-174.

Ornstein, A. (1982). The education of the disadvantaged: A 20-year review. *Educational Researcher, 24,* 197-211.

Passow, A. H. (1991). Urban schools a second (?) or third (?) time around: Priorities for curricular and instructional reform. *Education and Urban Society, 23*(3), 243-255.

Purkey, W. W., & Novak, J. M. (1984). *Inviting school success* (2nd ed.). Belmont, CA: Wadsworth.

Ramirez, M. III, & Castaneda, A. (1974). *Cultural democracy, bicognitive development and education.* New York: Academic Press.

Ramsey, P. G. (1987). *Teaching and learning in a diverse world.* New York: Teachers College Press.

Ramsey, P. G., Vold, E. B., & Williams, L. R. (1989). *Multicultural education: A source book.* New York: Garland.

Research About Teacher Education Project. (1990). *RATE IV--Teaching teachers: Facts and figures.* Washington, DC: American Association of Colleges for Teacher Education.

Shade, B. J. (1982). Afro-American cognitive style: A variable in school success? *Review of Educational Research, 52,* 219-244.

Simpson, A. W., & Erickson, M. T. (1983). Teachers' verbal and non-verbal communication patterns as a function of teacher race, student gender, and student race. *American Educational Research Journal, 20,* 269-288.

Sleeter, C. E. (1992). *Keepers of the American dream: A study of staff development and multicultural education.* London: Falmer.

Sleeter, C. E., & Grant, C. A. (1987). An analysis of multicultural education in the United States. *Harvard Educational Review, 57,* 421-444.

Smith, Y., & Goodwin, A. L. (1997). The democratic, child-centered classroom: Provisioning for a vision. In A. L. Goodwin (Ed.), *Assessment forequity and inclusion: Embracing all our children* (pp. 101-120). New York: Routledge.

Takaki, R. (1989). *Strangers from a different shore: A history of Asian Americans.* New York: Penguin.

Thornton, S. (1991). Teacher as curricular-instructional gatekeeper in social studies. In J. P. Shaver (Ed.), *Handbook of research on social studies teaching and learning* (pp. 237-248). New York: Macmillan.

Today's numbers, tomorrow's nation: Demographics awesome challenge for schools. (1986, May 14). *Education Week,* pp. 14-37.

Trueba, H. T. (1989). *Raising silent voices: Educating linguistic minorities for the 21st century.* New York: HarperCollins.

Tyack, D. (1974). *The one best system.* Cambridge, MA: Harvard University Press.

Walsh, C. (1987). Schooling and the civic exclusion of Latinos: Toward a discord of dissonance. *Journal of Education, 10*(11), 6.

Washington, V. (1981). Impact of antiracism/multicultural training on elementary teachers' attitudes and classroom behavior. *Elementary School Journal, 81*(3), 186-192.

Zimpher, N. L., & Ashburn, E. A. (1992). Countering parochialism in teacher candidates. In M. E. Dilworth (Ed.), *Diversity in teacher education* (pp. 40-61). San Francisco: Jossey-Bass.

## Chapter 8

Aguirre, A., Jr., Martinez, R., & Hernandez, A. (1993). Majority and minority faculty perceptions in academe. *Research in Higher Education, 34,* 371-385.

Ayvazian, A. (1996, February). *Faculty fear: Barriers to effective mentoring across racial lines.* Paper presented at the annual Teachers College Winter Roundtable on Cross-Cultural Counseling and Psychotherapy, New York.

Barr, D. J., & Strong, L. J. (1988). Embracing multiculturalism: The existing contradictions. *NASPA Journal, 26,* 85-90.

Bergquist, W. H. (1992). *The four cultures of the academy.* San Francisco: Jossey-Bass.

Birnbaum, R. (1988). *How colleges work: The cybernetics of academic organization and leadership.* San Francisco: Jossey-Bass.

Bloom, A. (1987). *The closing of the American mind.* New York: Simon & Schuster.

Boyer, E. L. (1990). *Campus life: In search of community.* Princeton, NJ: Carnegie Foundation for the Advancement of Teaching.

Butler, J. E. (1991). The difficult dialogue of curriculum transformation: Ethnic studies and women's studies. In J. E. Butler & J. C. Walter (Eds.), *Transforming the curriculum: Ethnic studies and women's studies* (pp. 1-19). Albany: State University of New York Press.

Carter, R. T., & Quereshi, A. (1995). A typology of philosophical assumptions in multicultural counseling and training. In J. G. Ponterotto, J. M. Casas, A. Suzuki, & C. M. Alexander (Eds.), *Handbook of multicultural counseling and development* (pp. 239-260). Thousand Oaks, CA: Sage.

Cheatham, H. E. (Ed.). (1991). *Cultural pluralism on campus.* Washington, DC: American College Personnel Association (ACPA) Media.

*Chronicle of Higher Education.* (1996). Almanac issue, *153.*

Fleming, J. (1984). *Blacks in college.* San Francisco: Jossey-Bass.

Freire, P. (1970). *Pedagogy of the oppressed.* New York: Continuum.

Fried, J. (1995). Believing is seeing. In J. Fried (Ed.), *Shifting paradigms in student affairs: Culture, context, teaching, and learning* (pp. 39-66). Washington, DC: ACPA Media.

Hall, R. M., & Sandler, B. R. (1984). *Out of the classroom: A chilly campus climate for women?* Washington, DC: Association of American Colleges, Project on the Status and Education of Women. (ERIC Document Reproduction Service No. ED 254 125)

hooks, b. (1994). *Teaching to transgress.* New York: Routledge.

Howard-Hamilton, D., Owens, D., & Robinson, W. (1993). Leaders for the next millenium: An African-American student leadership retreat. *Journal of College Student Development, 34,* 221-222.

Katz, J. H. (1989). The challenge of diversity. In C. Woolbright (Ed.), *Valuing diversity on campus* (pp. 1-21). Bloomington, IN: Association of College Unions International.

Kuh, G. D., & Hall, J. T. (1993). Cultural perspectives in student affairs. In G. D. Kuh (Ed.), *Cultural perspectives in student affairs work* (pp. 1-20). Washington, DC: American College Personnel Association (ACPA) Media.

Kuh, G. D., & Whitt, E. J. (1988). *The invisible tapestry: Culture in American colleges and universities.* Washington, DC: ASHE-ERIC Higher Education Reports.

Levine, A., & Cureton, J. (1992). The quiet revolution: Eleven facts about multiculturalism and the curriculum. *Change, 24,* 24-29.

Livingston, M. D., & Stewart, M. A. (1987). Minority students on a white campus: Perception is truth. *NASPA Journal, 24,* 39-49.

Manning, K., & Coleman-Boatwright, P. (1991). Student affairs initiatives toward a multicultural university. *Journal of College Student Development, 32,* 367-374.

McCormick, T. (1991, April). *An analysis of some pitfalls of traditional mentoring for minorities and women in higher education.* Paper presented at the annual meeting of the American Educational Research Association, Chicago. (ERIC Document Reproduction Service No. ED 334 905)

Milem, J. F., & Astin, H. S. (1993). The changing composition of the faculty: What does it really mean for diversity? *Change, 25,* 21-27.

Minnich, E. K. (1990). *Transforming knowledge.* Philadelphia: Temple University Press.

Mitchell, J. (1990). Reflections of a black social scientist: Some struggles, some doubts, some hopes. In N. Hidalgo, C. McDowell, & E. Siddle (Eds.), *Facing racism in education* (pp. 68-83). Cambridge, MA: Harvard Educational Review.

Moore, W. J. (1988). Black faculty in white colleges: A dream deferred. *Educational Record, 68,* 116-121.

Morgan, G. (1986). *Images of organization.* Beverly Hills, CA: Sage.

Moses, Y. T. (1989). *Black women in academe: Issues and strategies.* Washington, DC: Association of American Colleges, Project on the Status of Women. (ERIC Document Reproduction Service No. ED 311 817)

Phillip, M. C. (1994). For minority men, a pathos to tenure: Fairness of evaluations questioned at Western Connecticut State. *Black Issues in Higher Education, 11,* 12-17.

Pope. R. L. (1993). Multicultural organizational development in student affairs: An introduction. *Journal of College Student Development, 34,* 201-205.

Pope, R. L. (1995). Multicultural organization development: Implications and applications for student affairs. In J. Fried (Ed.), *Shifting paradigms in student affairs: Culture, context, teaching, and learning* (pp. 233-249). Lanham, MD: American College Personnel Association.

Pope, R. L., Ecklund, T. R., & Mueller, J. A. (1989, March). *Combating racism in higher education.* Paper presented at the American College Personnel Association Convention, Washington, DC.

Ray, M., & Rinzler, A. (1993). *The new paradigm in business: Emerging strategies for leadership and organizational change.* New York: Tarcher/Putnam.

Reyes, M., & Halcón, J. J. (1990). Racism in academia: The old wolf revisited. In 'N. Hidalgo, C. McDowell, & E. Siddle (Eds.), *Facing racism in education* (pp. 68-83). Cambridge, MA: Harvard Educational Review.

Reynolds, A. L. (1996). Using the multicultural change intervention matrix (MCIM) as a multicultural counseling training model. In D. B. Pope-Davis & H. L. K. Coleman (Eds.), *Multicultural counseling competencies assessment, education, and training and supervision* (pp. 209-226). Thousand Oaks, CA: Sage.

Rudolph, F. (1977). *Curriculum: A history of the American undergraduate course of study since 1636.* San Francisco: Jossey-Bass.

Sands, R. G. (1992). Faculty-faculty monitoring and discrimination: Perceptions among Asian, Asian-American, and Pacific Island faculty. *Equity and Excellence, 25,* 124-129.

Schein, E. H. (1985). *Organizational culture and leadership.* San Francisco: Jossey-Bass.

Schlesinger, A. M., Jr. (1992). *The disuniting of America.* New York: Norton.

Senge, P. M. (1990). *The fifth discipline: The art and practice of the learning organization.* New York: Doubleday.

Simonson, R., & Walker, S. (Eds.). (1988). *Multicultural literacy: Opening the American mind.* St. Paul, MN: Graywolf.

Smith, E. P., & Davidson, W. S. (1992). Mentoring and the development of African-American graduate students. *Journal of College Student Development, 33,* 531-539.

Stewart, J. B. (1991). Planning for cultural diversity: A case study. In H. E. Cheatham (Ed.), *Cultural pluralism on campus.* Washington, DC: American College Personnel Association (ACPA) Media.

Tinto, V. (1993). *Leaving college: Rethinking the causes and cures of student attrition.* Chicago: University of Chicago Press.

Turner, C. S. V., & Thompson, J. R. (1993). Socializing women doctoral students: Minority and majority experiences. *Review of Higher Education, 16,* 355-370.

*Webster's ninth new collegiate dictionary.* (1987). Springfield, MA: Merriam-Webster.

Woolbright, C. (Ed.). (1989). *Valuing diversity on campus: A multicultural approach.* Bloomington, IN: Association of College Unions-International (ACUI).

Wright, D. J. (Ed.). (1987). *Responding to the needs of today's minority students* (New Directions for Student Services No. 38). San Francisco: Jossey-Bass.

# Chapter 9

Arredondo, P., Toporek, R., Brown, S. P., Jones, J., Locke, D. C., Sanchez, J., & Stadler, H. (1996). Operationalization of the multicultural counseling competencies. *Journal of Multicultural Counseling and Development, 24,* 42-78.

Baker, A., & Dixon, J. (1991). Motivational interviewing for HIV risk reduction. In W. R. Miller & S. Rollnick (Eds.), *Motivational interviewing: Preparing people to change addictive behavior.* New York: Guilford.

Berg-Cross, L., & Chinen, R. T. (1995). Multicultural training models and the person-in-culture interview. In J. G. Ponterotto, J. M. Casas, L. A. Suzuki, & C. M. Alexander (Eds.), *Handbook of multicultural counseling* (pp. 333-356). Thousand Oaks, CA: Sage.

Brown, M. T., & Landrum-Brown, J. (1995). Counselor supervision: Cross-cultural perspectives. In J. G. Ponterotto, J. M. Casas, L. A. Suzuki, & C. M. Alexander (Eds.), *Handbook of multicultural counseling* (pp. 263-286). Thousand Oaks, CA: Sage.

Carter, R. T., & Qureshi, A. (1995). A typology of philosophical assumptions in multicultural counseling and training. In J. G. Ponterotto, J. M. Casas, L. A. Suzuki, & C. M. Alexander (Eds.), *Handbook of multicultural counseling* (pp. 239-262). Newbury Park, CA: Sage.

Cushman, P. (1995). Ideology obscured: Political uses of the self in Daniel Stern's infant. In N. R. Goldberger & J. B. Veroff (Eds.), *The culture and psychology reader.* New York: New York University Press.

Freire. P. (1970). *Pedagogy of the oppressed.* New York: Continuum/Seabury Press.

Freire, P. (1995). *Pedagogy of hope: Reliving pedagogy of the oppressed.* New York: Continuum.

Garland, R. J., & Dougher, M. J. (1991). Motivational intervention in the treatment of sex offenders. In W. R. Miller & S. Rollnick, (Eds.), *Motivational interviewing: Preparing people to change addictive behavior.* New York: Guilford.

Greenfield, P. M. (1994a). Preface. In P. M. Greenfield & R. R. Cocking (Eds.), *Cross-cultural roots of minority development* (pp. ix-xvii.). Hillsdale, NJ: Erlbaum.

Greenfield, P.M. (1994b). Independence and interdependence as developmental scripts: Implications for theory, research, and practice. In P. M. Greenfield & R. R. Cocking (Eds.), *Cross-cultural roots of minority development* (pp. 1-37). Hillsdale, NJ: Erlbaum.

Greenfield, P. M., & Cocking, R. R. (Eds.). (1995). *Cross-cultural roots of minority development*. Hillsdale, NJ: Erlbaum.

Heyward, C. (1993). *When boundaries betray us: Beyond illusions of what is ethical in therapy and life*. San Francisco, CA: Harper.

hooks, b. (1994). *Teaching to transgress: Education as the practice of freedom*. New York: Routledge.

Ingleby, D. (1995). Problems in the study of the interplay between science and culture. In N. R. Goldberger & J. B. Veroff (Eds.), *The culture and psychology reader*. New York: New York University Press.

Ivey, A. E. (1995). Psychotherapy as liberation: Toward specific skills and strategies in multicultural counseling and therapy. In J. G. Ponterotto, J. M., Casas, L. A. Suzuki, & C. M. Alexander (Eds.), *Handbook of multicultural counseling*. Thousand Oaks, CA: Sage.

Kitayama, S., & Markus, H. R. (1995). Culture and self: Implications for internationalizing psychology. In N. R. Goldberger & J. B. Veroff (Eds.), *The culture and psychology reader*. New York: New York University Press.

LaFromboise, T. D., Foster, S., & James, A. (1996). Ethics in multicultural counseling. In P. B. Pederson, J. G. Draguns, W. J. Lonner, & J. E. Trimble (Eds.), *Counseling across cultures* (4th ed.). Thousand Oaks, CA: Sage.

Miller, W. R. (1995). Increasing motivation for change. In R. K. Hester & W. R. Miller (Eds.), *Handbook of alcoholism treatment approaches: Effective alternatives* (2nd ed.). Boston: Allyn & Bacon.

Miller, W. R., Brown, J. M., Simpson, T. L., Handmaker, N. S., Bien, T. H., Luckie, L. F., Montgomery, H. A., Hester, R. K., & Tonigan, J. S. (1995). What works? A methodological analysis of the alcohol treatment outcome literature. In R. K. Hester & W. R. Miller (Eds.), *Handbook of alcoholism treatment approaches: Effective alternatives* (2nd ed.). Boston: Allyn & Bacon.

Miller, W. R., & Rollnick, S. (1991). *Motivational interviewing: Preparing people to change addictive behavior*. New York: Guilford.

Pedersen, P. (1994). *A handbook for developing multicultural awareness* (2nd ed.). Alexandria, VA: American Counseling Association.

Pedersen, P. B., Draguns, J. G., Lonner, W. J., & Trimble, J. E. (1996). Introduction: Priority issues of counseling across cultures. In P. B. Pederson, J. G. Draguns, W. J. Lonner, & J. E. Trimble (Eds.), *Counseling across cultures* (4th ed.). Thousand Oaks, CA: Sage.

Pinderhughes, E. (1989). *Understanding race, ethnicity, and power: The key to efficacy in clinical practice.* New York: Free Press.

Ponterotto, J. G., Casas, J. M., Suzuki, L. A., & Alexander, C. M. (Eds.). (1995). *Handbook of multicultural counseling.* Thousand Oaks, CA: Sage.

Pope-Davis, D. B., & Dings, J. G. (1995). The assessment of multicultural counseling competencies. In J. G. Ponterotto, J. M. Casas, L. A. Suzuki, & C. M. Alexander (Eds.), *Handbook of multicultural counseling* (pp. 287-311). Thousand Oaks, CA: Sage.

Reynolds, A. (1995). Challenges and strategies for teaching multicultural counseling courses. In J. G. Ponterotto, J. M. Casas, L. A. Suzuki, & C. M. Alexander (Eds.), *Handbook of multicultural counseling* (pp. 320-330). Thousand Oaks, CA: Sage.

Rollnick, S., & Bell, A. (1991). Brief motivational interviewing for use by the nonspecialist. In W. R. Miller & S. Rollnick (Eds.), *Motivational interviewing: Preparing people to change addictive behavior.* New York: Guilford.

Saunders, B., Wilkinson, C., & Allsop, S. (1991). Motivational intervention with heroin users attending a methadone clinic. In W. R. Miller & S. Rollnick (Eds.), *Motivational interviewing: Preparing people to change addictive behavior.* New York: Guilford.

Shweder, R. (1995). Cultural psychology: What is it? In N. R. Goldberger & J. B. Veroff (Eds.), *The culture and psychology reader.* New York: New York University Press.

Stern, D. (1985). *The interpersonal world of the infant: A view from psychoanalysis and developmental psychology.* New York: Basic Books.

Sue, D. W., Arredondo, P., & McDavis, R. J. (1992). Multicultural counseling competencies and standards: A call to the profession. *Journal of Counseling and Development, 70,* 477-486.

Taylor, C. (1994). The politics of recognition. In A. Gutman (Ed.), *Multiculturalism.* Princeton, NJ: Princeton University Press.

Tober, G. (1991). Motivational interviewing with young people. In W. R. Miller & S. Rollnick (Eds.), *Motivational interviewing: Preparing people to change addictive behavior.* New York: Guilford.

Wallace, B. C. (1991). *Crack cocaine: A practical treatment approach for the chemically dependent.* New York: Brunner/Mazel.

Wallace, B. C. (1993). Cross-cultural counseling with the chemically dependent: Preparing for service delivery within our culture of violence. *Journal of Psychoactive Drugs, 24*(3), 9-20.

Wallace, B. C. (1994, February 18). *How to avoid engaging in violence in psychotherapy: considerations of race and gender.* Paper presented at the 1994 annual Winter Roundtable on Cross-Cultural Counseling, Columbia University, Teachers College, New York.

Wallace, B. C. (1995). Women and minorities in treatment. In A. . Washton (Ed.), *Psychotherapy and substance abuse.* New York: Guilford.

Wallace, B. C. (1996). *Adult children of dysfunctional families: Prevention, intervention, and treatment for community mental health promotion.* Westport, CT: Praeger.

West, C. (1993). *Beyond eurocentrism and multiculturalism.* Monroe, ME: Common Courage Press.

## Chapter 10

Ahronheim, J. C., Moreno, J., & Zuckerman, C. (1994). *Ethics in clinical practice.* Boston: Little, Brown.

American Society of Human Genetics. (1996). Human diversity collection. *American Journal of Human Genetics, 59*(4), 972.

Babbie, E. R. (1970). *Science and morality in medicine.* Berkeley: University of California Press.

Boone, C. K. (1988, August/September). Bad axioms in genetic engineering. *Hastings Center Report,* pp. 9-13.

Bronfenbrenner, U. (1979). *The ecology of human development: Experiment by nature and design.* Cambridge, MA: Harvard University Press.

Bronfenbrenner, U. & Weiss, H. (1983). Beyond policies without people: An ecological perspective on child and family policy. In E. Zigler, S. L. Kagan, & E. Klugman (Eds.), *Children, families and government: Perspectives on American social policy.* Cambridge, UK: Cambridge University Press.

Burns, C., & Engelhardt, H. T. (1974). Introduction: The humanities and medicine. *Texas Reports on Biology and Medicine Special Issue, 32,* ix.

Carter, R. T., & Qureshi, A. (1995). A typology of philosophical assumptions in multicultural counseling and training. In J. G. Ponterotto, J. M. Casas, L. A. Suzuki, & C. M. Alexander (Eds.), *Handbook of multicultural counseling* (pp. 239-262). Thousand Oaks, CA: Sage.

Christakis, D. A., & Feudtner, C. (1993). Ethics in a short white coat: The ethical dilemmas that medical students confront. *Academic Medicine, 68,* 249-254.

Crane, D. (1975). *The sanctity of social life: Physicians' treatment of critically ill patients.* New York: Russell Sage.

Curzer, H. J. (1993). Is care a virtue for health care professionals? *Journal of Medicine and Philosophy, 18,* 51-69.

Edelstein, L. (1967). Hippocrates of Cos. In P. Edwards (Ed.), *The encyclopedia of philosophy* (Vol. 3). New York: Macmillan.

Epstein, C. J. (1997). 1996 ASHG presidential address: Toward the 21st century. *American Journal of Human Genetics, 60,* 1-9.

Finucane, T. E., & Carrese, J. A. (1990). Racial bias in presentation of cases. *Journal of General Internal Medicine, 5,* 120-121.

Fox, R. C. (1989). *The sociology of medicine: A participant observer's view.* Englewood Cliffs, NJ: Prentice Hall.

Freire, P. (1972). *Pedagogy of the oppressed.* UK: Sheed & Ward.

Giroux, H., & Purple, D. (1983). *The hidden curriculum and moral education: Deception or discovery?* Berkeley, CA: McCutchan.

Hafferty, F. W. (1991). *Into the valley: Death and the socialization of medical students.* New Haven, CT: Yale University Press.

Hafferty, F. W., & Franks, R. (1994). The hidden curriculum, ethics, teaching, and the structure of medical education. *Academic Medicine, 69,* 861-871.

Hickson, G. B., Clayton, E. W., Entman, S. S., Miller, C. S., Githens, P. B., Whetten-Goldstein, K., & Sloan, F. A. (1994). Obstetricians' prior malpractice experience and patients' satisfaction with care. *Journal of the American Medical Association, 272*(20), 1583-1587.

Hippocrates. (1962). The oath (W. H. S. Jones, Trans.). In W. H. S. Jones (Ed.), *Hippocrates I* (p. 299). Cambridge, MA: Harvard University Press.

Katz, J. K. (1985). The sociopolitical nature of counseling. *Counseling Psychologist, 13,* 615-624.

Kleinman, A. A. (1980). *Patients and healers in the context of culture: An exploration of the borderline between anthropology, medicine, and psychiatry.* Berkeley: University of California Press.

Kolata, G. (1996, November 4). Ban on medical experiments without consent is relaxed. *New York Times,* pp. A1, C6.

Leape, L. L. (1994). Error in medicine. *Journal of the American Medical Association, 272*(23), 1851-1857.

Leiderman, D. B. & Grisso, J. (1985). The Gomer phenomenon. *Journal of Health and Social Behavior, 26,* 222-232.

Lipkin, M. (1974). *The care of the patient.* New York: Oxford University Press.

Marsh F. H., & Yarborough, M. (1990). *Medicine and money.* Westport, CT: Greenwood.

McIntosh, P. (1992). White privilege and male privilege: A personal account of coming to see the correspondences through work in women's studies. In M. L. Andersen & P. H. Collins (Eds.), *Race, class, and gender: An anthology* (pp. 70-81). Belmont, CA: Wadsworth.

Mizrahi, T. (1986). *Getting rid of patients: Contradictions in the socialization of physicians.* New Brunswick, NJ: Rutgers University Press.

Pellegrino, E. D. (1973). Toward an expanded medical ethics: The Hippocratic ethics revisited. In R. Bulger (Ed.), *Hippocrates revisited* (pp. 133-147). New York: MEDCOM.

Pellegrino, E. D. (1993). The metamorphosis of medical ethics: A 30-year retrospective. *Journal of the American Medical Association, 269,* 1158-1162.

Pellegrino, E. D., & Thomasma, D. C. (1981). *A philosophical basis of medical practice: Toward a philosophy and ethic of the healing professions.* New York: Oxford University Press.

Pinderhughes, E. (1989). *Understanding race, ethnicity, and power in clinical practice.* Chicago: Free Press.

Richmond, J. B., & Fein, R. (1995). The healthcare mess: A bit of history. *Journal of the American Medical Association, 273*(1), 69-71.

Self, D. J., Baldwin, D. C., & Olivarez, M. (1993). Teaching medical ethics to first year students by using film discussion to develop their moral reasoning. *Academic Medicine, 68*(5), 384-385.

Shem, S. (1978). *The house of God.* New York: Dell.

Shilts, R. (1988). *And the band played on: Politics, people, and the AIDS epidemic.* New York: St. Martin's Press.

Valenstein, P. N. & Howanitz, P. J. (1995). Ordering accuracy: A College of American Pathologists Q-Probes study of 577 institutions. *Archives of Pathology and Laboratory Medicine, 119,* 117-122.

Veatch, R. (1983). The physician as stranger: The ethics of the anonymous patient-physician relationship. In E. Shelp (Ed.), *The clinical encounter: The moral fabric of the patient-physician relationship* (pp. 187-207). Dordrecht, The Netherlands: D. Reidel.

# Chapter 11

Abdullah, K. (1997, November 7). Personal communication.

Branch, C. (1997). *Clinical interventions with gang adolescents and their families.* Boulder, CO: Westview.

Branch, C., & Carter, R. (1996). *Racial identity development across the lifespan.* Unpublished manuscript.

Bronfenbrenner, U. (1979). *The ecology of human development.* Cambridge, MA: Harvard University Press.

Bronfenbrenner, U., & Crouter, A. C. (1983). The evolution of environmental models in developmental research. In P. H. Mussen (Ed.), *Handbook of child psychology: Vol. 1. History, theory, and methods* (W. Kessen, Vol. Ed.). New York: Wiley.

Carter, R. T. (1995). *The influence of race and racial identity in psychotherapy.* New York: Wiley.

Heimann, P. (1981). On countertransference. In R. Langs (Ed.), *Classics in psychoanalytic techniques.* New York: Jason Aronson. (Original work published 1950)

Hirschfeld, L. (1997, April 12). Personal communication.

Kernberg, O. (1976). *Object relations theory and clinical psychoanalysis.* New York: Jason Aronson.

Kernberg, O. (1981). Countertransference. In R. Langs (Ed.), *Classics in psychoanalytic techniques.* New York: Jason Aronson. (Original work published 1965)

Little, M. (1981). Countertransference and the patient's response to it. In R. Langs (Ed.), *Classics in psychoanalytic techniques.* New York: Jason Aronson. (Original work published 1951)

Poe-Yamagata, E. (1996). *Female offenders in the juvenile justice system* (National Center for Juvenile Justice in Brief, Vol. 1, No. 2).

Reich, A. (1981). On counter-transference. In R. Langs (Ed.). *Classics in psychoanalytic techniques.* New York: Jason Aronson. (Original work published 1951)

Tower, L. (1981). Countertransference. In R. Langs (Eds.), *Classics in psychoanalytic techniques.* New York: Jason Aronson. (Original work published 1956)

Vontress, C. (1968). *The great white father syndrome.*

## Chapter 12

Beamon, K. (1997, Spring). How Texaco's hard lessons can fuel your career. *Minority MBA*, 6-9.

Brady, T. (1996, June). The downside of diversity. *Management Review, 85*(6), 29-34.

Capowski, G. (1996, June). Managing diversity. *Management Review, 85*(6), 12-17.

Carter, R. T., & Block, C. J. (1992, August). *Applying white racial identity theory to organizations.* Paper presented at the 100th annual convention of the American Psychological Association.

Fenichel, O. (1945). *The psychoanalytic theory of neurosis.* New York: Norton.

Gordon, J. (1996, May). Different from what? Diversity as a performance issue. *Training.*

Jamieson, D., & O'Mara, J. (1991). *Managing workforce 2000: Gaining the diversity advantage.* San Francisco: Jossey-Bass.

Johnson, S. D. (1987). Knowing that versus knowing how: Toward achieving expertise through multicultural training for counseling. *Counseling Psychologist, 15*(2), 320-331.

Johnson, S. D., & McRae, M. B. (1992). Toward training for competence in multicultural counselor education. *Journal of Counseling and Development, 70*(1), 131-135.

McCune, J. (1996, June). Diversity training: A competitive weapon. *Management Review.*

McGarraghy, J., & Thompson, D. (1995). *Diversity initiatives in higher education: A view from the top.* Unpublished manuscript, Baruch College, City University of New York.

Morgan, G. (1997). *Images of organization* (2nd ed.). Thousand Oaks, CA: Sage.

Morrison, A. M. (1996). *Leadership diversity in America.* San Francisco: Jossey-Bass.

Paskoff, S. M. (1996, August). Ending the workplace diversity wars. *Training.*

Pierce, C. (1967). Violence and counterviolence: The need for a children's domestic exchange. *American Journal of Orthopsychiatry, 39*(4), 553.

Pierce, C. (1970). Offensive mechanisms: The vehicle for microaggression. In F. Barbour (Ed.), *The black seventies.* Boston: Porter Argent.

## Chapter 13

Allport, G. (1954). *The nature of prejudice.* Reading, MA: Addison-Wesley.

Altman, I., & Rogoff, B. (1987). Worldviews in psychology: Trait interactional, organismic and transactional perspectives. In D. Stokols & I. Altman (Eds.), *Handbook of environmental psychology* (pp. 7-40). New York: Wiley.

Barker, J. (1992). *Future edge.* New York: Morrow.

Birman, D. (1994). Acculturation and human diversity in a multicultural society. In E. Trickett, R. Watts, & D. Birman (Eds.), *Human diversity: Perspectives on people in context.* San Francisco: Jossey-Bass.

Campbell, J., Lawler, E., & Weick, K. (1970). *Managerial behavior, performance and effectiveness.* New York: McGraw-Hill.

Geber, B. (1990, July). Managing diversity. *Training,* pp. 23-30.

Glick, W. (1985). Conceptualizing and measuring organizational and psychological climate: Pitfalls in multilevel research. *Academy of Management Review, 13,* 133-137.

Glick, W. (1988). Response: Organizations are not central tendencies: Shadowboxing in the dark, round 2. *Academy of Management Review, 13,* 133-137.

Hanover, J. (1993). *Impact of workforce diversity training: The role of the environment in transfer of training.* Unpublished doctoral dissertation, DePaul University.

Helms, J. (1994). The conceptualization of racial identity and other "racial" constructs. . In E. Trickett, R. Watts, & D. Birman (Eds.), *Human diversity: Perspectives on people in context.* San Francisco: Jossey-Bass.

Howe, J. (1977). Group climate: An explanatory analysis of construct validity. *Organizational Behavior and Human Performance, 19,* 106-125.

Jacobson, F. M. (1988). Ethnocultural assessment. In L. Comas-Diaz & E. F. Griffith (Eds.), *Clinical guidelines in cross-cultural mental health* (pp. 135-148). New York: Wiley.

Jones, J. (1991). The politics of personality: Being black in America. In R. Jones (Ed.), *Black psychology* (3rd ed.). Berkeley, CA: Cobb & Henry.

Jones, J. (1994). Our similarities are different: Toward a psychology of affirmative diversity. In E. Trickett, R. Watts, & D. Birman (Eds.), *Human diversity: Perspectives on people in context.* San Francisco: Jossey-Bass.

Kochman, T. (1981). *Black and white styles in conflict.* Chicago: University of Chicago Press.

Kossek, E., & Zonia, S. (1993). Assessing diversity climate: A field study of reactions to employer efforts to promote diversity. *Journal of Organizational Behavior, 14,* 61-81.

Lewin, K. (1947). Group decision and social change. In *Readings in social psychology.* New York: Henry Hall.

Marshak, R. (1994). Lewin meets Confucius: A re-view of the OD model of change. *Journal of Applied Behavioral Science, 29,* 393-415.

Nobles, W. (1986). *African psychology: Towards its reclamation, reascension, & revitalization.* Oakland, CA: Black Family Institute.

Pedersen, P. (1993). Mediating multicultural conflict by separating behaviors from expectations in a cultural grid. *International Journal of Intercultural Relations, 17,* 343-353.

Perkins, U. (1975) *Home is a dirty street: The social oppression of black children.* Chicago: Third World Press.

Powell, G., & Butterfield, D. (1978). The case for subsystem climate in organizations. *Academy of Management Review, 3,* 151-157.

Ramirez, M. (1983). A psychology of the Americas. *A psychology of the Americas* (pp. 1-18). New York: Pergamon.

Stewart, E., & Bennett, M. (1991). *American cultural patterns.* Yarmouth, ME: Intercultural Press.

Sue, S., & Morishima, J. (1982). Personality, sex-role conflict, and ethnic identity. In *The mental health of Asian Americans* (pp. 93-125). San Francisco: Jossey-Bass.

Tajfel, H., & Turner, J. (1986). The social identity theory of intergroup behavior. In D. Eotvhrl & W. Austin (Eds.), *Psychology of intergroup relations.* Chicago: Nelson Hall.

Triandis, H. (1988). Collectivism v. individualism: A reconceptualisation of a basic concept in cross-cultural psychology. In G. Verma & C. Bagley (Eds.), *Cross-cultural studies of personality, attitudes and cognition.* New York: St. Martin's Press.

Walter, J., & Lonner, W. (1994). Culture and human diversity. In E. Trickett, R. Watts, & D. Birman (Eds.), *Human diversity: Perspectives on people in context.* San Francisco: Jossey-Bass.

Watts, R., & Carter, R. (1991). Psychological aspects of racism in organizations. *Group and Organization Studies, 16,* 328-344.

Werner, M. (1993). *The interrelationships between organizational climate, culture, and managerial priorities.* Unpublished doctoral dissertation, DePaul University.

## Chapter 14

Alcoff, L., & Potter, E. (Eds.). (1993). *Feminist epistemologies.* New York: Routledge.

Alderfer, C. P. (1982). Problems in changing white males' behavior and beliefs concerning race relations. In P. S. Goodman & Associates (Eds.), *Change in organizations: New perspectives on theory, research, and practice* (pp. 122-165). San Francisco: Jossey-Bass.

Anner, J. (Ed.). (1996). *Beyond identity politics: Emerging social justice movements in communities of color.* Boston: South End Press.

Arnold, R., Burke, B., James, C., D'Arcy, M., & Thomas, B. (1991). *Educating for a change.* Toronto: Between the Lines and The Doris Marshall Institute for Education and Action.

Beckhard, R. (1969). *Organization development: Strategies and models.* Reading, MA: Addison-Wesley.

Bennis, W. G., Benne, K. D., Chin, R., & Corey, K. E. (1976). *The planning of change* (3rd ed.). New York: Holt, Rinehart & Winston.

Bernstein, P. (1983). *Workplace democratization: Its internal dynamics.* New Brunswick, NJ: Transaction Books.

Bolman, L. G., & Deal, J. E. (1991). *Reframing organizations: Artistry, choice, and leadership.* San Francisco: Jossey-Bass.

Brown, L. D., & Covey, J. G. (1989). Organization development in social change organizations: Some implications for practice. In W. Sikes, A. B. Drexler, & J. Gant (Eds.), *The emerging practice of organization development* (pp. 27-37). Alexandria, VA: NTL Institute and University Associates.

Burgoyne, J. G. (1994). Stakeholder analysis. In C. Cassell & G. Symon (Eds.), *Qualitative methods in organizational research* (pp. 187-207). London: Sage.

Calvert, L. M., & Ramsey, V. J. (1996). Speaking as female and white. *Organization, 3,* 468-485.

Cooperrider, D. L., & Pasmore, W. A. (1991). The organization dimension of global change. *Human Relations, 44,* 763-787.

Cox, T. (1990). Problems with research by organizational scholars on issues of race and ethnicity. *Journal of Applied Behavioral Science, 26,* 5-23.

Cox, T. (1993). *Cultural diversity in organizations: Theory, research and practice.* San Francisco: Berrett-Koehler.

Cox, T., & Blake, S. (1991). Managing cultural diversity: Implications for organizational competitiveness. *Academy of Management Executive, 5*(3), 45-56.

Drucker, P. F. (1989). What business can learn from nonprofits. *Harvard Business Review, 67*(4), 88-93.

Drucker, P. F. (1990). *Managing the non-profit organization: Principles and practices.* New York: HarperCollins.

Freedman, A. (1996). The values and legacy of the founders of NTL: An interview with Ken Benne. *Journal of Applied Behavioral Science, 32,* 332-344.

Freeman, J. (1979). Resource mobilization and strategy: A model for analyzing social movement organization actions. In M. N. Zald & J. D. McCarthy (Eds.), *The dynamics of social movements* (pp. 167-189). Cambridge, MA: Winthrop.

French, W. L., & Bell, C. H. (1978). *Organization development* (2nd ed.). Englewood Cliffs, NJ: Prentice Hall.

Gabriel, Y. (1991). Turning facts into stories and stories into facts: A hermeneutic exploration of organization folklore. *Human Relations, 44,* 857-875.

Gordon, A. F. (1995). The work of corporate culture: Diversity management. *Social Text 44, 13*(3), 3-30.

Gordon, A. F., & Newfield, C. (Eds.). (1996). *Mapping multiculturalism.* Minneapolis: University of Minnesota Press.

Hanson, P. G., & Lubin, B. (1995). *Answers to questions most frequently asked about organization development.* Thousand Oaks, CA: Sage.

Harding, S. (1986). *The science question in feminism.* Ithaca, NY: Cornell University Press.

Harding, S. (1991). Who knows? Identities and feminist epistemology. In J. E. Hartman & E. Messer-Davidow (Eds.), *Engendering knowledge* (pp. 100-115). Knoxville: University of Tennessee Press.

Hirschhorn, L. (1988). *The workplace within: Psychodynamics of organizational life.* Cambridge, MA: MIT Press.

Holvino, E. (1993). *Organization development from the margins: Reading class, race, and gender in OD texts.* Unpublished doctoral dissertation, University of Massachusetts, Amherst.

Jackson, B., & Hardiman, R. (1994). Multicultural organization development. In E. Y. Cross, J. H. Katz, F. A. Miller, & E. W. Seashore (Eds.), *The Promise of diversity: Over 40 voices discuss strategies for eliminating discrimination in organizations* (pp. 231-239). Burr Ridge, IL: Irwin.

Jackson, B., & Holvino, E. (1988). Developing multicultural organizations. *Journal of Religion and the Applied Behavioral Sciences, 9*(2), 14-19.

Kelleher, D., McLaren, K., & Bisson, R. (1996). *Grabbing the tiger by the tail.* Ottawa: Canadian Council for International Cooperation.

Klor de Alva, J., Shorris, E., & West, C. (1996, April). Colloquy, Our next race question: The uneasiness between Blacks and Latinos. *Harper's,* pp. 55-63.

Lakey, B., Lakey, G., Napier, R., & Robinson, J. (1995). *Grassroots and nonprofit leadership: A guide for organizations in changing times.* Philadelphia: New Society.

MacDonald, H. (1993, July). The diversity industry. *New Republic,* pp. 22-25.

Miller, F. A., & Katz, J. H. (1995). Cultural diversity as a developmental process: The path from monocultural club to inclusive organization. In J. W. Pfeiffer (Ed.), *The 1995 Annual: Vol. 2. Consulting* (pp. 267-281). San Diego: Pfeiffer.

Minkoff, D. C. (1993). The organization of survival: Women's and racial-ethnic voluntarist and activist organizations, 1955-1985. *Social Forces, 71*(4), 887-908.

Mohanty, C. T., Russo, A., & Torres, L. (Eds.). (1991). *Third World women and the politics of feminism.* Bloomington: Indiana University Press.

Morrison, A. (1993). Diversity: Interview with Ann Morrison. *Training and Development Journal, 47*(4), 39-43.

Palmer, C. (1994). The equitable company: Social justice in business. In R. Boot, J. Lawrence, & J. Morris (Eds.), *Managing the unknown by creating new futures* (pp. 59-77). London: McGraw-Hill.

Palmer, J. (1994). Diversity: Three paradigms. In E. Y. Cross, J. H. Katz, F. A. Miller, & E. W. Seashore (Eds.), *The promise of diversity* (pp. 252-258). Burr Ridge, IL: Irwin.

Patton, C. (1990). *Inventing AIDS*. New York: Routledge.

Powell, W. W., & Friedkin, R. (1987). Organizational change in nonprofit organizations. In W. W. Powell (Ed.), *The nonprofit sector: A research handbook* (pp. 180-192). New Haven, CT: Yale University Press.

Prasad, P. (1991). Organization building in a Yale union. *Journal of Applied Behavioral Science, 27,* 337-355.

Rothschild, J., & Witt, J. A. (1986). *The cooperative workplace.* Cambridge, MA: Cambridge University Press.

Salamon, L. M. (1994). The rise of the nonprofit sector. *Foreign Affairs, 73*(4), 109-122.

Staggenborg, S. (1995). Can feminist organizations be effective? In M. M. Ferree & P. Y. Martin (Eds.), *Feminist organizations* (pp. 339-355). Philadelphia: Temple University Press.

Thomas, D. A., & Ely, R. J. (1996, September-October). Making differences matter: A new paradigm for managing diversity. *Harvard Business Review,* 79-90.

Thomas, R. R. (1990, March-April). From affirmative action to affirming diversity. *Harvard Business Review,* 107-117.

Trinh, T. M. H. (1989). *Woman, native, other: Writing postcoloniality and feminism.* Bloomington: Indiana University Press.

Weick, C. (1979). *The social psychology of organizing.* Reading, MA: Addison-Wesley.

Young, D. R. (1991). The structural imperatives of international advocacy associations. *Human Relations, 44,* 921-941.

Young, D. R., & Hammack, D. C. (1993). Nonprofit organizations in a market economy: Common threads and research issues. In D. C. Hammack, & D. R. Young (Eds.), *Nonprofit organizations in a market economy* (pp. 398-419). San Francisco: Jossey-Bass.

Zald, M. N., & McCarthy, J. D. (Eds.). (1979). *The dynamics of social movements.* Cambridge, MA: Winthrop.

Zald, M. N., & McCarthy, J. D. (1988). *Social movements in an organizational society.* New York: Transaction Books.

## Chapter 15

Brink, P. (1984). Value orientation as an assessment tool in cultural diversity. *Nursing Research, 33*(4),198-203.

Carter, R. (1990). Cultural value differences between African Americans and White Americans. *Journal of College Student Development, 31,*71-79.

Gallagher, T. J. (1992). Language, Native people, and land management in Alaska. *Arctic, 45*(2), 145-149.

Gamble, D. J. (1986). Crushing of cultures: Western applied science in northern societies. *Arctic, 39*(1), 20-23.

Gilligan, C. (1982). *In a different voice: Psychological theory and women's development.* Cambridge, MA: Harvard University Press.

Hall, E. T. (1959). *The silent language.* Garden City, NY: Doubleday.

Harris, P. R., & Moran, R. T. (1991). *Managing cultural differences.* Houston: Gulf.

Kluckhohn Center for the Study of Values. (1995). *User's manual for the value orientation method.* Bellingham, WA: Author.

Kluckhohn, F. R., & Strodtbeck, F. L. (1961). *Variations in value orientations.* Evanston, IL: Row, Peterson.

Likert, R. (1967). *The human organization.* New York: McGraw-Hill.

Ortuno, M. M. (1991). Cross-cultural awareness in a foreign language class: The Kluckhohn model. *Modern Language Journal, 75,* 449-459.

Osborne, D., & Gaebler, T. (1993). *Reinventing government.* Reading, MA: Addison-Wesley.

Samovar, L. A., & Porter, R. E. (1988). *Intercultural communication: A reader.* Belmont, CA: Wadsworth.

# Name Index

Alderfer, C. P., 17, 53
Allport, Gordon, 203

Aponte, H., 91
Arredondo, P., 132
Astin, J. S., 124
Atkinson, D. R., 6
Au, Katherine, 82
Ayvazian, A., 125

Babbie, E. R., 155
Baldwin, James, 85
Banks, James, 71
Baptiste, H. P., Jr., 105
Baptiste, M. L., 105
Barr, D. J., 120, 121
Beamon, K., 188
Bell, A., 143
Bennent, A., 7, 8
Berg, D., 61, 62
Bergquist, W. H., 117
Berra, Yogi, 22
Bion, Wilfred, 64
Bisson, R., 217
Blake, S., 215
Block, C. J., 187
Boone, C. K., 150
Borduin, C. M., 91

Bourdieu, Pierre, 39
Boyd-Franklin, N., 93
Boyer, E. L., 116
Bradt, J. O., 97
Branch, C., 165
Bressler, Marvin, 27-27
Bronfenbrenner, U., 91, 169-170
Brown, L. D., 213, 217
Buchanan, Patrick, 20
Buerney, B. G., 91
Burns, C., 147
Bush, George, 20

Carlson, K., 95, 96
Carnevale, A. P., 4, 13
Carter, Robert T., 11, 80, 90, 109, 129, 136, 159, 165, 187, 199, 238
Chinn, P. C., 82
Clinton, Bill, 20-21
Cocking, R. R., 138-139
Coleman-Boatwright, R., 128
Cooperrider, D. L., 213
Covey, J. G., 213, 217
Cox, T., 4, 5, 6, 7, 13, 215, 221
Crane, D., 158
Crouter, A. C., 169-170
Cureton, J., 123
Cushman, P., 137-138

285

# Subject Index

Alcoholics, treatment of, 143
Ambivalence, 185-186, 188, 189-190
Americans with Disabilities Act, 1990, 12
Assimilation, 12

Basic assumption group, 64
Behavior, 55-60
*Brown v. Board of Education, 105*

Center for Creative Leadership, 184
Child guidance, 167
The Citadel, 187-188, 190-191
Civil Rights Act, 1964, 12
Coalition of Essential Schools, 83
Comprehensive System of Mathematics
    Program (CSMP), 78
Counseling skills and techniques, 141-145
Cross-race relationships, 55-56
Cultural Environment Transitions Model, 128
Culture:
    as country of origin, 15
    in context of higher education, 116-119
    of violence in the United States, 131
    organizational, 9-10
    pedagogy responsive to, 109-110
    role in counseling, 141-143
    value orientations, 8
    white Anglo-Saxon, 7-8

*See also under* Higher education; Identity;
    Institutions; Medicine and medical
    practice; Teachers

Deculturalization, 80
Denial:
    as defense, 189
    The Citadel as example of, 187-188
    *See also under* Diversity in organizations
Denver, Col. municipal probation court,
    167-168
Diversity:
    common ground model for, 195-197
    devaluing of, 30
    in for-profit organizations, 214
    in organizations
    lack of among teachers, 108
    lack of research on, 51
    literature of, 4-5
    model for nonprofits, 193-195
    racial, 16-17
    standpoint approach in consultation,
        225-226
    traditional perspective, 15-16
    ubiquitous approach, 13-14
    universal perspective, 11-12
    *See also under* Social change organizations
Diversity in organizations:
    and affirmative action laws, 189
    climate of, 205-206

289

# About the Editor

**Robert T. Carter**, Ph.D., is Professor of Psychology and Education, Chair of the Department of Counseling and Clinical Psychology, and Director of Training of the Counseling Psychology Program at Teachers College, Columbia University. Dr. Carter is known internationally for his work on Black and White racial identity. He has published in the areas of psychotherapy process and outcome, career development, cultural values, racial identity issues, educational achievement, and equity in education through the lens of racial identity. He has been retained to consult on organizational, legal and educational issues associated with race and diversity. Dr. Carter also is the Conference Director for a national conference known as the Teachers College Winter Roundtable on Cross-Cultural Psychology and Education

Dr. Carter authored *The Influence of Race and Racial Identity in Psychotherapy: Towards a Racially Inclusive Model* (John Wiley & Sons, 1995); co-edited with Chalmer E. Thompson *Racial Identity Theory: Applications for Individuals, Groups and Organizations* (Lawrence Erlbaum, 1997); co-authored with D. Sue, J. M. Casas, M. J. Fouad, A. Ivey, M. Jensen, T. LaFromboise, J. Manese, J. Ponterotto, and J. Vazquez-Natall *Multicultural Counseling Competencies: Individual Professional and Organizational Development* (Sage Publications, 1998); and is series editor for the *Discussions from the Roundtable—The Counseling Psychologists* and *The Roundtable Book Series on Multicultural Psychology and Education* (Sage Publications). He is co-editor for the special issue of the *Teachers College Record* on Multicultural Education (Spring 2000).

Dr. Carter is also a legal consultant. He works with organizations and individuals on such issues as organizational development, teacher training, desegregation, racial discrimination, cross-racial adoption, and biracial custody. He is a Fellow in the American Psychological Association (Div. 17, Counseling Psychology, and 45, Society for the Study of Ethnic Minority Issues) and former Chair of the Fellowship Committee for Division 17. He has also served on the editorial boards of *The Counseling Psychologist, Journal of Counseling and Development, Journal of Counseling Psychology* and *Journal of Multicultural Counseling and Development.*

# About the Contributing Authors

**Clayton P. Alderfer**, Ph.D., is Professor and Director of Organizational Psychology at Rutgers Graduate School of Applied & Professional Psychology and Editor of the Journal of Behavioral Science. Author and editor of several books, he has written many articles for professional journals. He is an organizational consultant to private, public, and not-for-profit organizations on leadership, race relations, organizational change, and family firms.

**Nancy Boyd-Franklin**, Ph.D., is an African American family therapist, psychologist, and Professor at Rutgers University in the Graduate School of Applied and Professional Psychology. An internationally recognized lecturer, Dr. Boyd-Franklin has written numerous articles and is the author of *Black Families in Therapy: A Multisystems Approach* (Guilford Press, 1989) and *Boys to Men: Raising African American Male Adolescents* with A.J. Franklin and Pam Toussaint (Dutton Press, 2000), and an editor of *Children, Families and HIV/AIDS: Psychosocial and Psychotherapeutic Issues* (Guilford Press, 1995). Her latest book is *Reaching Out in Family Therapy: Home-Based School and Community Interventions* (forthcoming, Guilford Press, 2000) with Dr. Brenna Bry.

**Curtis W. Branch**, Ph.D., is Clinical Assistant Professor of Medical Psychology in Psychiatry at College of Physicians and Surgeons, Columbia University. His research interests include neuropsychological correlates of conduct disorders, adolescent gang members, and the ontogenetic course of ethnic identity development. Research studies by Dr. Branch have appeared in a variety of developmental and clinical journals.

**Linda Darling-Hammond**, Ed.D., is currently the Charles E. Ducommun Professor of Teaching and Teacher Education at Stanford University where her research, teaching and policy work focus on issues of school restructuring, teacher education, and educational equity. She is also the Executive Director of the National Commission on Teaching and America's Future whose work has already led to sweeping policy changes affecting teaching and schooling at all levels of government. Dr. Darling-Hammond is author or editor of eight books, including *The Right to Learn: A Blueprint for Creating Schools that Work*, which was awarded the Outstanding Book Award from the American Educational Research Association in 1998, and more than 200 journal articles, book chapters, and monographs on issues of education policy and practice.

**Arthur C. Evans, Jr.**, Ph.D., is a licensed clinical psychologist and Director of Managed Care for the Connecticut Department of Mental Health and Addiction Services. He is Assistant Clinical Professor in the Department of Psychiatry, Yale School of Medicine, and is on the adjunct faculty of Quinnipiac College, Hamden, Connecticut. Dr. Evans is a partner and co-founder of ACCT Associates, P.C., a multicultural, multidisciplinary, clinical and training enterprise located in New Haven, Connecticut. In addition, Dr. Evans is president of the Board of Directors of the New England Institute of Addictions Studies and Diversity Committee Chairperson of the Steering Committee of the Addiction Technology Transfer Center of New England, Brown University. He is also a board member and co-founder of the Connecticut Institute of Cultural Literacy and Wellness.

**Michele Fine**, Ph.D., is Professor of Social/Personality Psychology at the Graduate School and University Center of the City University of New York. Her most recent books include *The Unknown City* (with Lois Weis); *Off-White: Essays on Race, Power and Society* (with Lois Weis, Linda Powell and Mun Wong) and *Becoming Gentlemen* (with Lani Guinier and Jane Balin). Beyond her graduate school teaching and research, Dr. Fine is actively involved with public school reform and participatory research with and for women in prison.

**Thomas J. Gallagher**, Ph.D., is a "leadership specialist" with the Oregon State University Extension Service. Previously he was Professor of Natural Resources at the University of Alaska where he conducted research on cross-cultural aspects of management. He is a Kellogg Leadership Fellow and a scholar of the Kluckhohn Center for the Study of Values.

**A. Lin Goodwin**, Ed.D., is Associate Professor of Education and the Co-Director of the Preservice Program in Childhood Education in the Department of Curriculum and Teaching, Teachers College, Columbia University. She is the editor of *Assessment for Equity and Inclusion: Embracing All Our Children*, and the author or co-author of numerous articles and book chapters. Dr. Goodwin also serves as a consultant and staff developer to a wide variety of organizations around issues of diversity, educational equity, professional teaching standards, teacher assessment and curriculum development.

**Evangelina Holvino**, Ed.D., is President of Chaos Management Ltd., and a consultant and facilitator who has been working in the USA, Europe, Southeast

Asia, West Africa, Latin America and the Caribbean since 1979 specializing in group and organizational approaches to social change. She was Professor at the School for International Training in Vermont and is an adjunct faculty member at the American University. Dr. Holvino has served on the Board of Directors at the Boston Center of the A. K. Rice Institute and The NTL Institute for Applied Behavioral Sciences. She is a research associate with the Gastón Institute for Latino Community Development and Public Policy, and a senior research fellow with the Center for Gender in Organizations, Simmons Graduate School of Management.

**Samuel D. Johnson, Jr.**, Ph.D., is currently Vice President for Student Development and Dean of Students at Baruch College of the City University of New York, where he has served for the past thirteen years. He is also Professor and Chairman of the Department of Student Development and Counseling at Baruch College. Formerly, he taught graduate trainees in Counseling Psychology at Teachers College, Columbia University. Dr. Johnson maintains an active national consulting practice for the American Management Association, colleges, school districts, hospitals, social service agencies, and corporations.

**Vivian Ota Wang**, Ph.D., is Assistant Professor in Counselor Education/ Counseling Psychology Programs and Director of the Asian Cultural Studies Program in the Division of Psychology in Education at Arizona State University. Dr. Ota Wang is also a Board Certified Genetic Counselor at the University of Colorado. She has published and presented in areas of social justice related to multicultural counseling program development and evaluation, racial-cultural identity development, and genetics and health psychology in the United States and China. She recently served as the guest editor of *The Multicultural Genetic Counseling Special Issue* for *The Journal of Genetic Counseling*.

**Raechele L. Pope**, Ed.D., is Associate Professor of Higher Education at the State University of New York at Buffalo. She received her doctorate from the University of Massachusetts at Amherst in Organization Development with concentrations in Multicultural Organization Development and Higher Education. Her research interests and publications focus on multicultural organization development, multicultural competence, and psychosocial development of students of color.

**Karen L. Proudford**, Ph.D., is Assistant Professor of Management at the Earl G. Graves School of Business and Management, Morgan State University, where she teaches courses in organizational behavior and human resource management. She holds a bachelor's degree in accounting from Florida A&M University and a Ph.D. in management from the Wharton School, University of Pennsylvania. Her research interests include employee participation, group and intergroup dynamics, diversity and conflict, and she has published several articles on these and related topics.

**Corlisse D. Thomas** is Class Dean at Columbia University. Her career in the field of Student Affairs spans fifteen years and includes her graduate work at Teachers College, Columbia University. She is currently a doctoral candidate in Higher Education at Teachers College, Columbia University.

**David A. Thomas**, Ph.D., is Professor of Business Administration at the Harvard Business School. For fifteen years, his research, writing and consulting have focused on the role of race in the career development of executives and managers of color, and the challenges of managing a culturally diverse workforce. His articles and case studies appear in numerous journals, edited volumes and magazines. He is the 1998 recipient of the Executive Development Roundtable's Annual Award for scholarly contributions in the field of executive development.

**Barbara C. Wallace**, Ph.D., is Associate Professor in the Department of Health and Behavior Studies at Teachers College, Columbia University. She is also a clinical psychologist licensed in New York State. Dr. Wallace provides intensive training to professionals and paraprofessionals covering multicultural competency, diversity, chemical dependency, and relapse prevention. She is the author of several books which codify much of what she teaches in training seminars.

**Roderick Watts**, Ph.D., is a community and clinical psychologist currently working as Associate Professor of Psychology and Director of Clinical Psychology Training at DePaul University in Chicago. He has served as a program development and evaluation consultant to foundations, universities, and other nonprofit organizations on a variety of projects. His action and research interests include manhood development, human diversity, sociopolitical development, racial identity, and qualitative research methodology. Dr. Watts recently co-edited two books: *Human Diversity: Perspectives on People in Context* and *Manhood Development in Urban African American Communities*.